# Seed Sovereignty, Food Security

## Also by Vandana Shiva

*Making Peace with the Earth: Beyond Resource,*
*Land and Food Wars*

*Soil Not Oil: Environmental Justice in an Age of Climate Crisis*

*Globalization's New Wars: Seed, Water & Life Forms*

*Earth Democracy: Justice, Sustainability, and Peace*

*Water Wars: Privatization, Pollution and Profit*

*Stolen Harvest: The Hijacking of the Global Food Supply*

*Staying Alive: Women, Ecology, and Development*

*Biopiracy: The Plunder of Nature and Knowledge*

*Ecofeminism* (coauthored with Maria Mies)

*Monocultures of the Mind: Biodiversity,*
*Biotechnology and Agriculture*

*The Violence of the Green Revolution:*
*Ecological Degradation and Political Conflict in Punjab*

# Seed Sovereignty, Food Security

## WOMEN IN THE VANGUARD OF THE FIGHT AGAINST GMOs AND CORPORATE AGRICULTURE

## Edited by
## Vandana Shiva

North Atlantic Books
Berkeley, California

Published by
North Atlantic Books
Berkeley, California

Cover photo © iStockphoto.com/AfricaImages
Cover design by Jasmine Hromjak
Book design by Mary Ann Casler
Printed in the United States of America

*Seed Sovereignty, Food Security: Women in the Vanguard of the Fight against GMOs and Corporate Agriculture* is sponsored and published by the Society for the Study of Native Arts and Sciences (dba North Atlantic Books), an educational nonprofit based in Berkeley, California, that collaborates with partners to develop cross-cultural perspectives, nurture holistic views of art, science, the humanities, and healing, and seed personal and global transformation by publishing work on the relationship of body, spirit, and nature.

North Atlantic Books' publications are available through most bookstores. For further information, visit our website at www.northatlanticbooks.com or call 800-733-3000.

Library of Congress Cataloging-in-Publication Data
Names: Shiva, Vandana, editor.
Title: Seed sovereignty, food security : women in the vanguard of the fight against GMOs and corporate agriculture / edited by Vandana Shiva.
Description: Berkeley, California : North Atlantic Books, [2016]
Identifiers: LCCN 2015021347 | ISBN 9781623170288 (trade pbk.) | ISBN 9781623170295 (ebook)
Subjects: LCSH: Plant genetic engineering--Moral and ethical aspects. | Transgenic plants—Moral and ethical aspects. | Crops—Genetic engineering—Moral and ethical aspects. | Agricultural biotechnology—Moral and ethical aspects. | Food security—Moral and ethical aspects. | Women in agriculture.
Classification: LCC QK981.5 .S44 2016 | DDC 581.4/67—dc23
LC record available at http://lccn.loc.gov/2015021347

1 2 3 4 5 6 7 8 9 SHERIDAN 21 20 19 18 17 16

Printed on recycled paper

# Contents

## Global South

# Seed Sovereignty, Food Security

Vandana Shiva

Seed and food the world over have been shaped by millions of years of nature's contribution and centuries of women's intelligence, skills, hard work, and perseverance. Today, women are again in the vanguard of defending seed freedom and food sovereignty in the context of globalization, which—worldwide—has facilitated corporate grab, through patents on seed associated with genetic engineering. Corporations have done this via a mechanistic paradigm of biology and agriculture, and through a reductionist paradigm of the economy.

This volume demonstrates how women as activists, scientists, and scholars are at the forefront of shaping new scientific and economic paradigms to reclaim seed sovereignty and food security across the world. They are leading movements to change both practice and paradigm: how we grow and transform our food. As seed keepers and food producers, as mothers and consumers, they are engaged in renewing a food system that is better aligned with the ecological processes of the Earth's renewal, the laws of human rights and social justice, and the means through which our bodies stay well and healthy.

## The Industrial Paradigm of Agriculture

The industrial paradigm for food production is clearly no longer viable. It is unviable because it came from labs producing tools for warfare, not from farms and fields producing food and nourishment. The industrial paradigm of agriculture has its roots in war; an industry that grew by making explosives and chemicals for the war remodeled itself as the agrochemical industry when the major twentieth-century wars ended. Explosives factories started making synthetic fertilizers; war chemicals began to be used as pesticides and herbicides. Whether it is chemical fertilizers, or chemical pesticides, their roots are in war. They are designed to kill. That is why thousands were killed in India, in Bhopal on December 2, 1984, and why hundreds of thousands continue to be maimed because of leaks from a pesticide plant owned by Union Carbide (now Dow Chemical). That is also why chemicals like Roundup (glyphosate) are being implicated in new disease epidemics by scientists like Stephanie Seneff of MIT, who identify the processes through which these chemicals cause harm.

In 1984, because of the Bhopal disaster and extreme violence in Punjab—projected as the granary of India—I decided to study why agriculture had become so volatile. The aggressive introduction of chemicals in Indian agriculture was promoted as the Green Revolution. Introduced initially in Punjab, its main advocate, Norman Borlaug, was awarded the Nobel Peace Prize in 1970; but by 1984, Punjab had become a land of war, not peace, and peace had broken down because the sustainability of water, the health of soils and of people were all being undermined by the chemicals that drove the "Green Revolution." Poisons have contributed to a cancer epidemic in Punjab; a "cancer train" takes cancer victims from Bhatinda to Rajasthan for treatment.

A paradigm born of the violence of a militarized mind sows the seeds of violence in nature and society. It is ignorant of how seed and soil, how biodiversity are renewed. It is blind to the subtle balance by which insects (or "pests") are controlled through diversity and a complex web of life. For chemically driven agriculture, every insect is an "enemy" that must be exterminated by the most lethal weapons of chemical warfare. And even though poisons and pesticides are designed to kill, another paradigm war around "safety" has been initiated.

The violence of Punjab and Bhopal propelled me into dedicating my intellectual and activist energies to creating a nonviolent paradigm for food and farming; and it is why I started Navdanya—saving local seed varieties. Collectively, across the world, we have forged a new paradigm for agriculture referred to as agroecology. Agroecological systems produce more and better food, and return higher incomes to farmers.

The chemical push reoriented agriculture toward toxicity and corporate control. Instead of working with ecological processes and taking the well-being and health of the entire agroecosystem, with its diverse species, into account, agriculture was reduced to an external input system adapted to chemicals. Instead of recognizing that farmers have been breeders over millennia, giving us the rich agro-biodiversity that is the basis of food security, breeding was reduced to breeding uniform industrial varieties that respond well to chemical inputs. Instead of small farms producing diversity, agriculture became focused on large monoculture farms producing a handful of commodities. Correspondingly, the human diet shifted from having 8,500 plant species to about eight globally traded commodities available. The scientific paradigm was also transformed. Instead of encouraging a holistic approach, the practice of agriculture was compartmentalized into fragmented disciplines based on reductionism.

Just as gross domestic product (GDP) fails to measure the real economy and the health of nature and society, the category of "yield" fails to measure the real costs and real outputs of farming systems. As the United Nations observed, the so-called high yielding varieties (HYVs) of the Green Revolution should in fact be called high response varieties, as they have been bred for chemicals; they are not high yielding in and of themselves. The narrow measure of "yield" propelled agriculture into deepening monocultures, displacing diversity and eroding natural and social capital. The social and ecological impact of this broken-down model has pushed the planet and society into deep crisis.

- Industrial monoculture agriculture has pushed more than 75 percent of our agro-biodiversity to extinction.
- 75 percent of bees have been killed because of toxic pesticides. Einstein had cautioned, "When the last bee disappears, humans will disappear."
- 75 percent of the water on the planet is being depleted and polluted for chemical-intensive industrial agriculture. The nitrates in water from industrial farms are creating "dead zones" in our oceans.
- 75 percent of land and soil degradation is caused by chemical-industrial farming.
- 40 percent of all greenhouse gas emissions responsible for climate change come from a fossil fuel, chemical-intensive industrial globalized system of agriculture. Fossil fuels that are used to make fertilizers, run farm machinery, and transport food thousands of miles from where it is grown contribute to carbon dioxide emissions. Chemical nitrogen fertilizers emit nitrogen oxide, which is 300 percent more destabilizing for the climate than carbon dioxide. And factory farming is a major source of methane.

While this ecological destruction of natural capital is justified in terms of "feeding people," the problem of hunger has grown. One billion people are permanently hungry; another two billion suffer from food-related diseases. When the focus of agriculture is the production of commodities for trade, instead of food for nourishment, hunger and malnutrition are the outcome. Only 10 percent of corn and soy grown in the world are used as food; the rest goes for animal feed and biofuel. Commodities do not feed people, food does.

A high-cost external input system is artificially kept afloat with $400 billion in subsidies—that is more than $1 billion a day. So-called "cheap" commodities have a very high cost financially, ecologically, and socially. Industrial, chemical agriculture displaces productive rural families; it is also debt-creating, and debt and mortgages are the main reason for the disappearance of the family farm. In extreme cases, as in the cotton belt of India, debt created by the purchase of high-cost seed and chemical inputs has pushed more than 127,000 farmers to suicide in a little over a decade.

The false argument that genetically modified organisms (GMOs) are needed in order to increase food production to feed growing populations is a desperate attempt to extend the life of a failing paradigm. A series of myths are formulated to bolster this argument, centered around GMOs.

Living organisms, including seed, are self-organized complex systems. As Mae-Wan Ho points out in her contribution in this volume, they adapt and evolve, and are "fluid" at the level of the genome. Genes are influenced by the environment, as the new discipline of epigenetics shows. GMOs or genetically engineered seeds and food are being promoted as a technological miracle for feeding the world, and ending malnutrition and hunger. However, after twenty years of commercialization, all promises of the GMO miracle have been discredited. The following GMO myths need to be challenged and disproved.

*Myth 1: GMOs are an "invention" of corporations, and therefore can be patented and owned.* Living organisms, including seeds, thus become the "intellectual property" of the GMO industry. Using these property rights, corporations can forcibly prevent farmers from saving and sharing seeds, and can collect royalties on their patented products. A Monsanto representative is on record stating that his company wrote the intellectual property agreement of the World Trade Organization (WTO). He added that they were the "patient, diagnostician, physician"; they defined the problem—farmers save seeds—and offered a solution: seed saving should be made illegal.

The claim to invention is a myth because genetic engineering does not create a plant or an organism; it is merely a tool to transfer genes across species. Living organisms are self-organizing, self-replicating systems. They make themselves. Unlike machines, they cannot be engineered. There are only two ways of introducing genes from unrelated species: one is the use of a gene gun, the other is through plant cancer. Just as a mover of furniture is not the maker or owner of the house to which the furniture is moved, the GMO industry is merely the mover of genes from one organism to another, not the creator or inventor of the organism, including seeds and plants.

Through the false claim of "invention" and creation, the GMO industry is appropriating millions of years of nature's evolution, and thousands of years of farmers' breeding.

*Myth 2: Genetic engineering is more accurate and precise than conventional breeding.* All breeding has been based on breeding within the same species: rice is bred with rice, wheat with wheat, corn with corn.

The tools of genetic engineering allow the introduction of genes from unrelated species into a plant, and include genes from bacteria, scorpions, fish, and cows. The introduction of genes from unrelated species is a blind technology, neither accurate nor precise. When genes are introduced into the cells of a plant using a gene gun, it is not known if the cell has absorbed the gene or not. That is why every GMO also uses an antibiotic-resistance marker gene, to separate cells that have absorbed the gene from those that have not. This means that every GMO in food has antibiotic-resistance genes that can mix with bacteria in the human gut and aggravate the crisis of antibiotic resistance we are currently facing.

Further, since the introduced gene does not belong to the organism, genes from virulent viruses are added as "promoters" to express the trait for which genes have been introduced. These additional transformations are evidence of the unreliability and inaccuracy of the gene transfer technology. Moreover, nothing is known about what these genes do when they enter our body as food. In the case of herbicide-tolerant crops like Roundup Ready soy and corn, the combination that needs to be considered for its impact on the environment and on health is both Roundup (glyphosate) and the new genes in the food crop.

*Myth 3: GMOs are just like naturally occurring organisms, and are therefore safe.* Myth 3 is inconsistent with myth 1. To establish ownership, the GMO industry claims novelty. To avoid responsibility for adverse impact, it claims naturalness. I have called this "ontological schizophrenia." GMOs have an impact on the environment, on our health, and on farmers' socioeconomic status; that is why we have an international UN Biosafety Protocol.

I was appointed a member of the expert group that worked on the framework of the protocol to implement Article 19.3 of the Convention on Biological Diversity. The unscientific principle of "substantial equivalence" has been institutionalized in order to avoid research on biosafety. Substantial equivalence assumes that the GMO is substantially equivalent to the parent organism. This leads to a "don't look, don't see, don't find" policy, and not having looked for impacts, GMOs are declared "safe." Ignorance of impacts, however, is not proof of safety.

There is as yet no proof of safety.[1]


*Myth 4: GMOs are based on cutting-edge science; GMO critics are "anti-science."* Genetic engineering is based on an obsolete paradigm of genetic determinism, a linear and deterministic flow of information from genes, which are called "master molecules," to proteins. Francis Crick called this the "central dogma" of molecular biology. Genetic determinism assumes that genes are atoms of biological determinism, with one gene carrying one trait, and determining the traits in an organism. But these are assumptions that come from the idea of control and domination; this is patriarchal ideology, not science.

Cutting-edge science teaches us that these assumptions are false. Genes are fluid, not fixed.[2]

Each gene contributes to multiple traits; each trait is an expression of many genes acting in concert. As Richard Lewontin states in the doctrine of DNA:

DNA is a dead molecule, among the most non-reactive chemically inert molecules in the world. It has no power to reproduce itself. When we refer to genes as self-replicating, we endow them with a mysterious, autonomous power that seems to place them above the more ordinary materials of the body. Yet if anything in the world can be said to be self-replicating, it is not the gene, but the entire organism as a complex system.[3]

Living organisms, including seed, are self-organized, complex systems; moreover, genes are influenced by the environment, as the new discipline of epigenetics shows.[4]

On the basis of the latest and independent science, leading scientists across the world have contributed to the new science of biosafety; and corporate ideology, parading as science, has launched a brutal, violent, and unscientific attack on every scientist speaking the truth about GMOs on the basis of detailed scientific research on the impact of GMOs. This includes Dr. Arpad Pusztai, Dr. Ignacio Chapela, Dr. Eric Seralini, and me.

The GMO debate is science versus ideology, with GMOs being promoted through blind ideology—the ideology of mechanistic, reductionist, deterministic assumptions about the world, combining with the ideology of unbridled corporate greed.

*Myth 5: GMOs increase yields and are the answer to world hunger.* Genetic engineering as a tool for the transfer of genes is not a breeding technology; it does not contribute to breeding high yielding crops. Yields come from conventional breeding; all that genetic engineering does is add a Bt toxin gene or a gene for herbicide tolerance, and antibiotic-resistance marker and virus genes. These do not increase production of food, but they do contribute to the production of risks from toxins and antibiotic resistance.[5]

Even the argument that GMOs increase yield indirectly by controlling weeds and pests is incorrect because rather than controlling pests and weeds, Bt *GMOs have contributed to the emergence of new pests and superpests resistant to the Bt toxin,* and herbicide-resistant crops have led to superweeds resistant to Roundup. Hence, new GMOs have now been developed that are resistant to 2,4-D, an ingredient of Agent Orange.[6]

When one notes the fact that when Roundup is sprayed, food crops are destroyed, GMO cultivation in fact leads to a decline in food and nutrition production at the systems level. As Navdanya studies show, biodiverse organic systems can increase nutrition per acre, and have the potential to feed two Indias.[7]

*Myth 6: GMOs reduce chemical use and are therefore environmentally beneficial.* Two applications of genetic engineering account for most commercial planting, Bt crops, and HT crops. Herbicide-tolerant crops account for 63 percent of the cultivation of GM crops. Bt crops have led to an increase in pesticide use because of new pests and pest resistance in the bollworm. As the Directorate of Plant Protection shows, pesticide use has increased with the increase of Bt cotton cultivation.[8] Herbicide-tolerant crops are designed to make crops resistant to herbicide spraying.[9]

*Myth 7: GMOs promote free choice.* The myth of "free choice" begins with a "free market" and "free trade." When five transnational corporations control the seed market, it is not a free market, it is a cartel.

When corporations write the rules of "free trade," it is corporate dictatorship, not free trade.

When enforcing patents and intellectual property rights (IPR) laws written by themselves, corporations prevent farmers from saving seed; it is not "free choice," it is seed slavery.

In India, Monsanto has locked local seed companies into licensing agreements to *only sell Bt cotton.* The labels have different names, but they are all "Bollgard," Monsanto's Bt cotton. This is illusionary "free choice": the reality is seed monopoly.

When corporations spend millions to prevent the labeling of GMOs and deny citizens the *right to know* and the *right to choose,* free choice is being stifled.[10]

## "One Agriculture, One Science": Capitalist Patriarchy's Domination and Control

The paradigm of capitalist patriarchy is seeking to increase its domination over agriculture through centralization, monocultures, commodification, and corporate control. On July 22, 2014, the International Crops Research Institute for the Semi-Arid Tropics (ICRISAT) announced the formation of "One Agriculture, One Science," an international partnership across India, Africa, and the United States, launched at an expert consultation workshop jointly organized by ICRISAT, the University of Florida, Michigan State University, and Iowa State University, in Gainesville, Florida. It was attended by experts from land-grant universities in the United States, the Indian Council of Agricultural Research (ICAR), the Alliance for a Green Revolution in Africa (AGRA), the Regional Universities Forum for Capacity Building in Agriculture (RUFORUM, a consortium of forty-two universities in nineteen African countries), the United States Department of Agriculture (USDA), the US Agency for International Development (USAID), and the Consultative Group for International Agricultural Research (CGIAR) centers.

While "One Agriculture, One Science" is falsely promoted as a new and innovative project, it is in fact a repeat of how the Green Revolution was launched in the 1960s. Then, too, the US land-grant universities were involved in training our scientists in the "Monoculture of the Mind" of the chemical paradigm, displacing the diversity of agricultural systems adapted to different ecosystems. Then, too, the USDA and USAID were involved in pushing the Green Revolution. Then, too, World Bank–governed CGIAR centers played a key role in promoting it—they were in fact created to launch it. The International

Maize and Wheat Improvement Center (CIMMYT) in Mexico was created to introduce the Green Revolution in maize and wheat; the International Rice Research Institute (IRRI) in the Philippines was set up to spread the Green Revolution in rice. ICRISAT was established later and is the CGIAR center specializing in semi-arid crops.

The only difference between the 1960s and today is that Big Money and Big Ag are directly pushing a monoculture to create monopolies for profits through ownership of seeds and sales of chemicals. AGRA was launched by Bill and Melinda Gates and their foundation—the Gates Foundation owns 500,000 shares in Monsanto, indicating that philanthropy and business merge when Big Money meets Big Ag. Monsanto is not just the biggest seed corporation today; it has bought up the biggest climate data corporation, The Climate Corporation, and a soil data corporation, Solum, which it has renamed Granular.[11]

The objective is to overwhelm farmers with Big Data and make them dependent on Monsanto for every aspect of farming—seed, soil, climate data—all of which become commodities that Monsanto sells and farmers have to pay for. But Big Data is not knowledge, which comes from experience, interconnectedness, and participation. Big Data from One Corporation contributes, as written in the International Commission on the Future of Food and Agriculture's "Manifesto on the Future of Food," to "information obesity." It is also a means of control. Locking in forty-two African universities that work across diverse cultures in diverse ecosystems—deserts and rainforests, mountains and coasts—into "One Agriculture, One Science," for example, is a recipe for impoverishing and enslaving Africa, intellectually and economically.

There are three major reasons why this grand announcement will aggravate, instead of solve, problems in agriculture. The branding exercise that resulted in "One Agriculture, One Science" is a failure in itself. For "experts" to believe that different climates, different ecosystems, and different cultures can be prescribed "One" solution is laughable. Either they are not aware that the rainfall in Cherrapunji is different from the rainfall in Oaxaca, that it's hotter in Maharashtra than in Oregon, or they simply don't care whether a farmer's crop fails or succeeds as long as they have extracted every last dollar, rupee, or rand from him or her.

The "One Agriculture" push by Big Ag corporations ignores the findings of all UN agencies, including the International Assessment of Agricultural Knowledge, Science and Technology for Development (IAASTD), a team of four hundred scientists that has been working together for more than six years. The IAASTD report states:

> We must look to small holder traditional farming to deliver food security in third world countries, through agroecological systems which are sustainable. Governments must invest in these systems. This is the clear evidence.[12]

"One Agriculture, One Science" ignores evidence of the failure of Green Revolution chemical monocultures and the success of diverse agroecological systems in addressing hunger while protecting the planet. "One Agriculture, One Science" is a call against diversity, and will further erode the ecological foundations of agriculture, leaving the world's food systems at the mercy of billionaires and big corporations. It is also a recipe for undermining the seed sovereignty and food security of small-scale farmers and agrarian economies.

Agriculture varies according to water availability. The *khejri* tree in the desert of India and the baobab tree in the desert of Africa are critical to ecological and food security. In the rainforest ecosystems of the Western Ghats, the spice gardens mimic the multitiered structure of the forest. In the high altitude Himalayas we grow crops like amaranth and buckwheat that cannot grow in the hot plains.

Whereas farmers have bred hundreds of thousands of varieties, and thousands of species, the Green Revolution has reduced the agriculture and food base to a handful of globally traded commodities. Genetic engineering has further narrowed commercially planted crops to four—corn, soy, cotton, and canola—and two traits, Bt and HT. Indian farmers evolved 200,000 kinds of rice, and thousands of varieties of wheat, pulses, and oilseeds, as well as of brinjals, bananas, and mangoes.

Mega Monoculture has no place for the diverse knowledges of our diverse cultures. It is top-down, driven by "experts" who have no respect for the knowledge of farmers, the foundation of the science of agroecology.

## Women in the Vanguard

On the one hand are women scientists and activists pointing to grievous harm; on the other are corporations who sell the pesticides, while also controlling the regulatory and scientific systems that should control them. In 1987, I was at a conference on new biotechnologies called "The Laws of Life." The old agrochemical industry was present, now morphed into the biotechnology industry, in an attempt to push through ownership of seed through genetic engineering. Where national governments or local farmers were reluctant to fall in line, a combination of bribery and coercion was used to introduce laws and patents on local seed production and exchange.

In every country where GMOs and new seed laws have been pushed, women have risen in resistance—from Europe to Africa, from Bangladesh to Mexico.

Women are not just sowing the seeds of resistance against an agriculture based on monocultures and corporate monopolies; they are also sowing the seeds of alternative paradigms of science and alternative agricultural practice. A scientifically and ecologically robust paradigm of agriculture is emerging from the struggles of women, farmers, and ecological scientists, in the form of agroecology and biodiversity-intensive, organic farming as an alternative to the wrecked paradigm of industrial agriculture.

Chemical agriculture treats soil as inert and as an empty container for chemical fertilizers. The new paradigm recognizes the soil as living, in which billions of soil organisms create soil fertility. Their well-being is vital to human well-being.

Chemical agriculture destroys biodiversity. Ecological agriculture conserves and rejuvenates biodiversity.

Chemical agriculture depletes and pollutes water. Organic farming conserves water by increasing the water-holding capacity of soils through recycling organic matter.

In the five decades since the Green Revolution, ecological science has taught us the value of diversity to ensure sustainability, an increase in food production, and resilience. At the ecological level, agroecology and biodiversity-based, organic farming rejuvenate the natural capital on which sustainable food security depends—soil, biodiversity, and water.

Biodiversity and soils rich in organic matter are the best strategy for climate resilience and climate adaptation. While rejuvenating natural capital, ecological agriculture also rejuvenates social capital and increases human well-being and happiness. While reducing the ecological footprint, organic agriculture increases output when measured through multifunctional benefits, instead of through the reductionist category of "yield." Navdanya's report "Health Per Acre" shows that when measured in terms of nutrition per acre, ecological systems produce more food: food production can be doubled ecologically. Our new book, *Wealth Per Acre,* takes into account the true costs of industrial agriculture and lists the benefits of ecological and fair systems.[3]

We can conserve diversity, allow other species to flourish, defend our seed freedom and food sovereignty, while producing more and gaining real freedom.

Women are showing the way to having both bread and freedom.

## Endnotes

[1]    www.ensser.org/increasing-public-information/no-scientific-consensus
      -on-gmo-safety.
[2]    www.i-sis.org.uk/fluidGenome.php.
[3]    www.nybooks.com/articles/archives/2011/may/26/its-even-less-your
      -genes.
[4]    www.brucelipton.com/resource/article/epigenetics.

5   www.ucsusa.org/sites/default/files/legacy/assets/documents/food_and
    _agriculture/failure-to-yield.pdf; www.navdanya.org/attachments/Latest
    _Publications9.pdf.

6   http://touch.latimes.com/#section/-1/article/p2p-81540199.

7   Vandana Shiva and Vaibhav Singh, "Health Per Acre: Organic Solutions to
    Hunger and Malnutrition," Navdanya, March 26, 2011, www.navdanya.org
    /attachments/Health%20Per%20Acre.pdf.

8   http://ppqs.gov.in/IpmPesticides.htm.

9   http://news.cahnrs.wsu.edu/2012/10/01/pesticide-use-rises-as-herbicide
    -resistant-weeds-undermine-performance-of-major-ge-crops-new-wsu-study
    -shows.

10  www.mintpressnews.com/survey-overwhelming-majority-americans-say
    -want-gmo-labeling/192210; www.farms.com/ag-industry-news/efforts
    -are-being-made-to-overturn-vermont-s-gmo-labeling-law-314.aspx;
    http://commondreams.org/news/2014/10/03/here-we-go-again-monsanto
    -spends-millions-defeat-states-gmo-labeling-effort.

11  www.stltoday.com/business/local/monsanto-buys-soil-analysis-firm/article
    _7dabf164-73fa-5cf7-958e-f03de6e403c5.html.

12  International Assessment of Agricultural Knowledge, Science and Technology
    for Development (IAASTD), Agriculture at a Crossroads, http://apps.unep
    .org/publications/pmtdocuments/-Agriculture%20at%20a%20crossroads%20
    -%20Synthesis%20report-2009Agriculture_at_Crossroads_Synthesis_Report
    .pdf.

13  Vandana Shiva and Vaibhav Singh, *Wealth Per Acre* (Dehradun, India: Natraj
    Publishers, 2014).

# International

## Reflections on the Broken Paradigm

# Fields of Hope and Power

## Frances Moore Lappé and Anna Lappé

## Introduction

A light mist hangs over bright green mountains that roll south toward the northern Indian city of Dehradun. Half a dozen farmers are with us, sipping tea. A farmer and former self-described "pesticide peddler" tells us about the recent transformation in this small valley. Like many farmers in the country, they had been sold on the costly chemical-intensive agriculture path pushed by the Indian government since the 1960s. Over time, its failure became tragically evident in crushing debt, deteriorated soils, health problems, worsening pest pressures— all leading to an epidemic of farmer suicides.

Then came Navdanya, the farmer network founded in 1987 by Vandana Shiva. Promoting agroecology, Navdanya had helped the farmers we were meeting to reclaim traditional farming practices and revalue indigenous seeds, creating the "biodiversity registries" they proudly show us. As our teacups empty, the farmers describe the changes they've already seen in their community: more resilient crops, empowered community, and healthier lives.

Since our last visit in 2002, a decade ago, we've watched as the changes we witnessed in the foothills of the Himalayas have taken root—and with quickening speed. In just a decade, for example, land in organic agriculture worldwide has tripled.[1] Navdanya itself has helped half a million farmers protect thousands of varieties of rice and other crops. We've seen this pathway—variously called ecological agriculture, agroecology, and organic farming—gain recognition and validation. As we'll note in this chapter, major studies now confirm its capacity to meet food needs while maintaining healthy soils, protecting and conserving water, and sparing farmers and eaters from pesticide exposure, among other benefits. We'll share these highlights and underscore, as well, the social power of ecological farming, often expanding via the leadership of women, who are 70 percent of the farmers in the Global South.[2] We will share glimpses of communities aligning with nature—including human nature—not only to grow food healthfully but to create communities in which all can eat healthfully.

But first let us paint the big canvas of global change: the path from corporate-dependent agriculture and its frightening consequences, to ecological farming and its life-enhancing promise.

## From the Scarcity Scare to Aligning with Nature

In these still-early years of the twenty-first century, awareness is spreading that we now know how to nourish ourselves, meeting the needs of all, by aligning with nature. This pivotal moment might best be expressed as a release from the failing premise of *lack,* lack of both "goods and goodness"—the view that there's not enough food and energy, nor enough positive human capacities—to a very different starting point: an ecologically and evidence-based premise of possibility. The dominant mental map of scarcity presumes a world of separate entities, all struggling in eternal competition over scarce goods. It is a fearful mindset fixed on quantities. In the world of food, this mindset leads to a focus on producing ever more, and over the last thirty years food production has indeed kept well ahead of population growth.[3]

Yet this narrow focus—blinding us to whether people have access to what's grown, its quality and nutrition, or the ecological consequences of production—has led to a world with almost a billion hungry people, along with another two billion who suffer from the food-linked health problems of nutrient deficiencies and excessive weight.

In other words, our food supply has become a health hazard for roughly half the world's people.[4]

Within a frame of scarcity, focusing simply on *quantities*, we've been made blind to another frame, one centered in the *qualities of relationships*. Yet, it is the quality of human and ecological relationships that determines whether we experience scarcity or not, now and in the future. But before exploring the new, let's pause to ground ourselves, gaining clarity about why the frame driving the global food system—built on extractive, chemical, and corporate-dependent farming—has proved to be so destructive and therefore, ultimately, not viable.

As the experience of many countries demonstrates, corporate- and chemical-dependent agriculture has proved unable to create healthy farming communities in part because it locates control—who has a say—far from the fields and those who work them. It places control in the hands of those who sell farm inputs, operating within a global economy of increasing concentration. From seed purveyors to grain traders and processors to supermarkets, less and less competition puts farmers and consumers at increasing disadvantage. To offer just one example, worldwide, just three commercial seed and agrochemical companies—Monsanto, DuPont, and Syngenta—control nearly half the global seed market.

The World Bank in 2009 reported that purchases of just three corporate inputs—pesticides, seeds, and fertilizer—amount to almost half of the total costs of small-scale farmers using chemical methods in Andhra Pradesh, India.[5] And with farmers' dependency on global corporations comes another dependency—on local moneylenders for cash to buy their inputs. Heartbreaking indebtedness follows. Such loss of control has led to despair so deep as to contribute to more than 17,500 farmer suicides each year in India between 2002 and 2006.[6]

In a global economy with no built-in link between farmers' production and people actually eating, the recent, rapid diversion of farmland to fuel production—despite mounting hunger—should come as no surprise. Roughly 40 percent of US corn now goes to agrofuel.[7] In fact, since 2005, the annual amount of US corn going to ethanol alone has been greater than the total annual increment in all grain consumption worldwide. In 2010, it was twice as great.[8] Stunning. Now US farmers are growing the first corn genetically modified specifically for making ethanol.[9] Beyond corn and sugarcane going toward fuel, the share of vegetable oil during the last decade diverted to industrial use, especially fuel, doubled to 24 percent,[10] and the production of vegetable oil as feedstock for biofuel alone is projected to increase by 60 percent within the next eight years.[11] Eighty-five percent of palm oil is grown in Malaysia and Indonesia, where it is the largest threat to rainforests in Southeast Asia; and it is now expanding in the Amazon region.[12] Much of the oil gets diverted to the European Union and China for fuel.[13]

## Opaque, Volatile, Global Markets

### Speculation

Debate rages on the extent to which speculation has triggered food price spikes, hurting the world's poorest the most, but it is undeniable that the escalation of commodity speculation strongly correlates with unprecedented food price spikes, which first hit in 2007–2008. Assets allocated to commodity index trading—including food—rose twentyfold from 2003 to March 2008, reaching $260 billion, reported portfolio manager Michael Masters testifying before a US congressional committee in 2008.[14] Twentyfold! Unlike "traditional speculators," Masters noted, "Index Speculators ... never sell." They "buy futures and then roll their positions ..." The result is the opposite of how a market is supposed to work: instead of higher prices dampening demand, "[D]emand ... actually increases the more [that] prices increase," Masters testified.[15]

In early 2012, the Food and Agriculture Organization (FAO) Food Price Index in real terms was still well above its 2008 spike and almost at 2011's historic peak.[16] Masters estimated that commodity prices increased more in the aggregate over the five years before 2008 than at any other time in US history.[17] He concluded: "Index Speculators' trading strategies amount to virtual hoarding via the commodities futures markets, and provide no benefit."[18]

## Landgrabs

Extreme power imbalances are also enabling foreign interests, including governments, to purchase farmland in the Global South—often displacing small-scale farmers. Over the last decade alone, about 560 million acres—an area roughly equal to that of western Europe— has been affected by what many are calling a "landgrab."[19] Following the financial collapse of 2008, wealthy investors began looking for the next best place to grow their fortunes. Commodity price spikes, in 2008 and again more recently, plus growing concerns about the impact of climate change on our global food supply, encourage both foreign and private investors to see agriculture as a safe bet. Some are even calling farmland the "strategic resource that oilfields are now."[20] Some governments, too—including several Middle Eastern states, China, Japan, and South Korea—are snapping up farmland as "part of a long-term strategy for food security," reports the Oakland Institute, a leader in the global challenge to landgrabs.[21]

Investors argue that these deals bring in new resources;[22] and turn "unused" or "underutilized" land into vibrant farmland. But foreign purchases can mean even further loss of control of agricultural resources and less accountability over how the land is used. These arrangements are often "between partners with vastly unequal power," says Oxfam International's Duncan Green.[23] As a result, for example, private investors and foreign governments leased land in Ethiopia in 2008 for as little as $1 per hectare per year, according to Bloomberg Business.[24] But their detractors say ... *Unoccupied? Unused? Hardly!* Many of these deals are being forged over land that is tended in traditional patterns of common ownership without formal title. "Seventy percent of the population in sub-Saharan Africa lives on their traditional lands that, because of colonial heritage, are [now] classified as state lands. [So] governments believe that they can give away their land without consultation or legal redress," says the Oakland Institute.[25] An additional, major concern among those tracking and resisting the spike in landgrabs is the tendency of "buyers" to use these lands not to produce food for people, but for biofuels or livestock feed.

Given all these pressures, in 2011 the United Nations' High Level Panel of Experts on Food Security concluded that price increases and greater hunger are not the "inevitable consequence of world economic development...." They are "the result of a public policy implemented by the United States and European Union governments; the result of a clear—and reversible—political choice."[26] We would stress that such policies include those allowing the explosion of speculation in agricultural commodities and the takeover of land held by the world's most vulnerable people. In all these ways and more, a corporate-dependent farming and food system is failing because it ignores the relational questions of power, questions that determine who controls resources and, therefore, who can eat what is grown.

## Corporate-Chemical Agriculture: A Climate Culprit

The corporate-dependent food system is not viable for yet another reason: Humanity faces the historic challenge of climate disruption, and evidence mounts that the dominant food system is a huge reason the carbon cycle is so out of whack, as Anna Lappé's book, *Diet for a Hot Planet*, brings to light. Generally underrecognized is this extraordinary finding: If one includes all stages of food production and distribution, the global food system minimally contributes 29 percent of greenhouse gases.[27]

Fortunately, in the midst of loss and fear another path is emerging that is freeing us from the limiting frame of lack. The emergent path flows from an ecological worldview in which we humans see ourselves as any other organism in an ecosystem. And in an ecosystem, there are no "parts," as the visionary German physicist Hans-Peter Dürr once reminded us: "There are only participants." So we each count, as our every action affects the whole.

In an ecosystem, it is context—the relationships shaping participants—that is all important. How does the context—our local and global culture's rules and norms, which we are creating—either block or facilitate the flourishing of life? Shifting from a fixation on quantities to a focus on relationships, we can envision and create a food and farming system that sustains healthy relationships among flora and fauna, while enhancing the power of its human members to create healthy and fulfilling lives.

Certainly, as the concentration of economic power suggested above sinks in, it's easy to feel overwhelmed—as if the global food economy is all locked up. But no. While agribusiness dominates much of the food supply in industrialized countries, with just three companies— ADM, Bunge, and Cargill—controlling most of grain trade, globally half a billion small-scale farms still feed the world's majority, says the UN Environment Programme.[28] We can also thank pastoralists, hunters and gatherers, and let's not forget the 800 million urban and near-urban farmers and gardeners.[29]

It is also true that more than 85 percent of the world's food is consumed in the country where it is grown, according to UN agricultural data.[30] Often it is sold within the same region, much of it outside the formal market system. In Indonesia, for example, home gardens, typically the domain of women, are estimated to provide more than a fifth of household income and 40 percent of the domestic food supply.[31]

## Agri-culture Emerging

Worldwide, this new culture of agriculture is rejecting the dominant model's near fixation with the yield of a narrow range of crops grown as monocultures. Whereas the dying model isolates agriculture from its relational context—from its culture—the emergent understanding is all about agri-*culture*, beautifully articulated by Wendell Berry in his 1982 *Gift of Good Land,* and twenty years later by Jules Pretty in *Agri-culture: Reconnecting People, Land and Nature.* While this turning toward agri-culture—reembedding agriculture in relationships of mutuality—has been building for decades on indigenous knowledge and courageous farmers' movements, it gained new global attention and credibility among scholars and practitioners worldwide with the 2008 release of *Agriculture at a Crossroads: International Assessment of Agricultural Knowledge, Science and Technology for Development* (IAASTD).

The report, developed painstakingly over four years by four hundred scientists, has gained the support of fifty-nine governments, cosponsored by numerous agencies, including the World Health Organization, the World Bank, and the United Nations Food and Agriculture Organization.[32] Its repeated reference to the "multifunctionality" of agriculture may sound wonky, but it expresses much of what the global food movement has been saying: that ending hunger and meeting the global climate crisis require agriculture that simultaneously enhances producers' livelihoods, knowledge, resiliency, health, and more balanced gender relations, while enriching the natural environment and helping to balance the carbon cycle. Among its other conclusions, the assessment stressed the essential role of sustainable agriculture in enhancing biodiversity and the wise management of livestock, forests, and fisheries. The assessment urges support for "biological substitutes for industrial chemicals or fossil fuels" and "reducing the dependency of the agricultural sector on fossil fuels."[33]

A statement by civil society organizations, timed for release with the report, declared that it represents the beginning of a "new era of agriculture" and offers "a sobering account of the failure of industrial farming."[34] In other words, a core insight of a growing global food movement is that agriculture can only serve life as it is understood as a *culture of healthy relationships,* both in the field—among soil organisms, insects, animals, plants, water, sun—and in the human communities it supports.

Manifesting this understanding, farmers and citizens passionate about healthy food and farming are linking across cultures to amplify their voices. A rising international force for this new agri-*culture* of democratic and ecological relationships is Via Campesina, founded in 1993 when small-scale farmers and rural laborers gathered in Belgium from four continents.[35] Its vision is "food sovereignty," a term chosen to emphasize power: that producers and consumers must be at the center of decision making about the direction of our food system.[36] Today Via Campesina is giving voice to 150 local and national organizations and two hundred million small-scale farmers in seventy countries who believe in the power of the peasant and in the role of small-scale agriculture because they are living it.[37] They sum up their stance in one of their simple but profound mottoes: Small-scale farmers can "feed the planet and cool the world." In less than two decades, Via Campesina has gained such standing that it recently became part of the broader Civil Society Mechanism of the UN Committee on World Food Security, created in 1974 to help address the food price crisis.[38]

The theme of food sovereignty widens the lens beyond narrow calculations on which system produces greater output. "Food sovereignty" asks us to appreciate that ecological approaches, unlike corporate-input farming, build farmer and community knowledge and strengthen social and problem-solving networks. In other words, these approaches build democratic power. In a study of sustainable farming projects involving ten million farmers across the African continent, for example, researchers found that adopting sustainable practices not only increased production significantly but, more importantly, increased the overall wealth of farming communities by encouraging women's participation and education, and by building social bonds that have helped these communities strengthen their economies and continue to learn, develop, and adapt their farming practices.[39]

## Challenging the Scarcity Scare

As we counter those locked in the failing paradigm, fixed on a contest over yields, we would never downplay the need for a sufficient supply of food. So let's stay with this question for a moment: what is the evidence that ecological agriculture can produce enough?

We begin by noting that production is hardly the only factor in the "enough" equation—not when one-third of the world's food is wasted, according to the United Nations.[40] In part this waste itself is a reflection of extreme power imbalances built into the dominant system; for much of the waste happens because farmers are too poor to afford proper storage and have too weak a political voice to secure access to markets. And, often, without access to those markets, farmers make calculated decisions not to plant and harvest to their farm's full potential—an incalculable loss of the food that might have been grown. Increasingly, there's also the diminished potential of farmland to feed people as it shifts to livestock feed and to fuel production. So, serious discussion of adequacy of supply requires addressing the power relations at the root of all such food waste—and wasted potential—not just measuring yields. In addition, evidence from a range of studies by respected bodies demonstrates that ecological farming can produce enough for the current population and for the expected increase. The just-mentioned IAASTD megastudy pulls together a range of evidence to make the case that, in fact, sustainable agriculture is the only pathway capable of feeding humanity. Studies from the National Research Council[41] in the United States to the FAO[42] point in a similar direction: a consensus is forming.

A 2006 report by Dr. Jules Pretty described the results of a large study that analyzed 286 projects in fifty-seven countries, involving 12.6 million farmers on 91 million acres, who were "engaged in transitions towards agricultural sustainability." Reliable yield comparisons were made in 198 of the projects and showed a "geometric mean" yield increase of 64 percent "across the very wide variety of systems and crop types."[43] In 2007, an interdisciplinary team led by Dr. Catherine Badgley at the University of Michigan carried out a multiyear study that estimated that moving globally to organic, ecologically attuned farming practices could produce an "organic food supply [that] exceeds the current food supply in all food categories, with most estimates over 50 percent greater than the amount of food currently produced," and meet the needs of the current and anticipated world population.[44]

Then in 2009, the UN Conference on Trade and Development published a policy brief describing organic agriculture as a "good option" for creating food security in Africa, citing a 116 percent rise in productivity on 114 African farms that converted to organic or near-organic production.[45]

Ecological approaches can produce the food we need. Some call the approach "sustainable intensification," which means producing abundant food while reducing agriculture's negative impacts. We can move beyond the fear of scarcity.

## Ecological Farmers as Climate Heroes

The case for ecological farming deepens as we broaden the conversation beyond yields to consider the role that agriculture plays in contributing to the climate crisis and in potentially helping us mitigate and adapt to the crisis. New evidence shows that these farming methods can make a huge contribution to balancing the carbon cycle, as well as helping us gain resiliency to adapt to the impact of climate change. Compared to chemical farming, organic farming produces one-half to two-thirds fewer greenhouse gas emissions per acre, says an FAO overview.[46] By moving worldwide to organic practices, in two decades agriculture could be carbon neutral—releasing no more than it's absorbing—says the UN Environment Programme.[47] By focusing on creating healthy soils—better able, for example, to retain water—and by relying on a diversity of crops, ecological farming offers greater resiliency in dealing with climate extremes than does chemical-dependent farming.[48]

GRAIN, an international nongovernmental organization based in Spain, estimates that if we were to stop deforestation for farming—

and if organic, nonchemical practices were combined globally with reintegration of livestock and farming, and if all this were combined with a shift to big local markets with shorter food distribution routes— our food and farming sector could actually reduce total global greenhouse gas emissions by half in a few decades.[49]

Despite claims by the industry, genetically engineered seeds, with their risks and embedded costs, are not the way toward more drought-resilience or water-tolerant crops. The effort to develop a genetically engineered virus-resistant sweet potato in Kenya is a cautionary tale. Research failed after a decade and millions of dollars spent. Meanwhile, researchers in Uganda, working with conventional breeding techniques, developed new varieties of sweet potato that not only maintained yield levels but also exhibited virus resistance, not to mention higher levels of beta-carotene.[50] A superior approach is taking better advantage, for example, of cassava, which is one of the most widely consumed African staple crops. It also turns out to be one of the region's most robust plants. Naturally resistant to pests, disease, and droughts, cassava offers Africans a promising, native solution for adapting to climate change.[51]

## Agriculture Aligning with Nature

### Ethiopia

*Why Africa?* Because global media too often portray the continent as the world's "basket case," plagued by poor soil, economies, and people.[52] This portrayal blinds us to powerful stories from which the whole world can learn.

To set the stage, we note that, in the rest of the Global South, but particularly in Africa, women provide most of the labor to produce food for the household.[53] In much of Africa, crops like legumes and vegetables are grown primarily in home gardens, almost exclusively the domain of women. In eastern Nigeria, for example, "home gardens occupying only 2 percent of a household's farmland accounted for half the farm's total production," found the FAO.[54] Yet women are handicapped by lack of control over the land and lack of access to credit; when farming depends on purchasing inputs requiring credit, women are typically left out.[55]

To highlight Africa's promise, particularly the contribution of women, we focus first on Ethiopia, where agriculture matters a great deal. In this landlocked country, it provides 40 percent of the GDP, 90 percent of exports, and 85 percent of employment.[56] Yet most of its agriculturalists are desperately poor. Today, in the wake of unprecedented droughts, worse than the country has seen in sixty years, millions are going hungry.[57]

Our story is about one particularly drought-prone area, the northern Ethiopian region of Tigray, where farmers often struggle to feed themselves, and where women are particularly affected. As of 2004, roughly one-third of the population is estimated to be made up of de facto female-headed households because so many men have died during civil wars, and widows rarely remarry.[58] Despite their responsibilities, by tradition women have not been allowed to plow fields or work with animal herds. Women are also handicapped by lack of education: about half of Ethiopian women are married before the age of fifteen, and once married they rarely remain in school.[59]

In 1996, the Institute for Sustainable Development[60] in Addis Ababa, working with the Bureau of Agriculture and Rural Development, launched an ambitious agroecological project in Tigray.[61] Dr. Sue Edwards, British-born botanist, and her team at the institute chose to focus on this particularly hard-hit region to see whether an ecological approach could help restore soil fertility and raise crop yields.[62] The region is home to about four million people, 85 percent of whom live in rural areas.[63] Tigray's climate is harsh; it receives only 500 to 700 millimeters of rainfall a year,[64] and even this precipitation concentrates in a short rainy season, from the end of June to mid-September. The rest of the year is dry, very dry. Tigray farmers typically live without running water or electricity. Women often walk two or three hours a day, or longer, to fetch water for cooking and cleaning. Incomes average just twenty to fifty cents a day, with the poorest farmers only managing to store food reserves for four to five months, so the hungry season lasts more than half the year. Farmers "have to harvest on empty stomachs," Edwards told us.

What a testing ground this was to see the difference agroecology might make. Starting in just four farming communities, the project focused on introducing three practices: compost-making, trench-bunding (creating small earthen barriers to prevent rain runoff), and tree-planting.[65] Villagers elected leadership to govern each project, enabling the development of bylaws that cover the ways households work together. In addition to attending regular training over two years, villagers met monthly to review plans and evaluate their progress. Within just two years, the villages experienced such success that the approach spread quickly—eventually to forty-two communities within the project's first nine years.[66]

Farmers participated in field trials comparing crops grown with ecological methods like compost, crops raised with chemical fertilizer, and others grown without any inputs at all. Using crop sampling systems accepted by the FAO, the project was able to collect rigorous data on all three.[67]

The results have been striking. By 2006, researchers found significantly higher yields in the ecological test sites of every single crop compared with the chemically fertilized plots, and even more dramatic yield benefits compared with plots using no inputs. Yields of corn raised using ecological methods were 129 percent higher than those of corn in plots farmed with chemical methods. Compared to no-input fields, the ecologically farmed land produced yields more than *threefold* greater.[68] And there were other benefits as well: Compost used in the ecological systems helped maintain soil fertility year to year, so farmers could rotate compost applications, meaning they didn't have to produce enough compost for all their land every year. Farmers also discovered that they had to deal with fewer challenging weeds, and their plants were more resistant to pests, such as the teff shoot fly.[69]

Social gains have been just as evident. Improvements in crop productivity have enabled families for whom food insecurity, and real hunger, was a constant threat to produce enough food to have a full year's reserve. Some are now even producing a surplus that they sell.

"These farmers, they're getting out of grinding poverty," said Edwards.

The effect on women has been particularly profound. The Tigray Project has encouraged them to pre-germinate certain plants in nurseries and then transplant them outdoors when the rainy season begins. This expedites the growing process, gives women an agricultural role, and safeguards their agricultural livelihoods against weather fluctuations due to climate change.[70] The Tigray Project has also trained unemployed single mothers in seed-planting and growth and animal husbandry (goats, sheep, cows, and bees), so they can become self-reliant.[71] The training also educates women on how to use microcredit, helping them manage and maintain long-term economic security.[72]

Much more than a one-dimensional farming intervention, the project is about building relationships, the key to solving a host of problems. Their newfound feeling of empowerment has spurred communities to develop legally recognized policies governing land ownership and stewardship of their natural resources. As a result, many communities have discovered solutions for managing animal grazing, which had earlier been a big barrier to crop development.[73]

Today, many of the ecological practices promoted in the Tigray Project are spreading to millions more acres throughout Ethiopia, as official FAO reports laud the success. One noted that the Tigray Project "demonstrates that ecological agricultural practices such as composting, water and soil harvesting, and crop diversification ... can bring benefits to poor farmers, particularly to women-headed families. Among the benefits demonstrated are increased yields and productivity of crops ..."[74] Plus, the project's positive contribution to stabilizing climate can be measured in its decreased use of synthetic fertilizers, which means fewer greenhouse gas emissions, especially from one of the most potent: nitrous oxide. Leguminous crops, residues, cover crops, and agroforestry all increase the soil's organic matter, which improves its carbon sequestration capacity. More stable crop yields and healthier soils and forests enable the land and its people to better deal with climate stresses, including variability in rain and temperature.[75]

Agroecology has also spurred the development of agricultural cooperatives, as well as promoted the concept of gender equality— because it doesn't rely on credit, access to which women are often denied, agroecology enables women to enjoy more employment and economic and social freedom.[76]

Previously known as one of the most degraded regions in Africa, Tigray is now seen as a model for attaining food security, agricultural productivity, and land regeneration. So the Ethiopian government has taken similar projects and initiatives to other areas of the country.[77] In addition to the FAO's recognition, the African Union has cited Tigray's composting, water and soil conservation, agroforestry, and crop diversification as a framework for improving the productivity of smallholder farmers.[78]

Beyond Ethiopia, numerous similar initiatives in other regions in Africa show that it's possible to increase yields without depending on cash-costly and climate-costly inputs.[79] Better yet, these techniques can be developed and embraced by farmers themselves, without their becoming beholden to corporate executives a world away, being burdened with the high costs of commercial seeds or chemical inputs, or being at the mercy of volatile fertilizer prices.[80]

## Niger

To many, the West African country of Niger exemplifies a place where climate change and deep poverty meld into heartbreaking images of destitution on increasingly scorched earth. Indeed, three-fourths of Niger is now desert, and the news from the country from mid-2010 to the present has brought troubling images of famine.[81]

Grim ... yes?

But here, too, there's another story. Over two decades, poor farmers in the country's south have "regreened" 12.5 million desolate acres, a momentous achievement not of planting trees but of abetting their "natural regeneration" through a farmer-managed strategy reviving a centuries-old practice. Farmers leave selected tree stumps among the crops in their fields and protect their strongest stems as they grow. Part of a global shift toward agroforestry with huge positive climate dividends, the trees then help protect the soil, bring increased crop yields, and provide fruit, nutritious leaves, fodder, and firewood.

In all, Niger farmers have nurtured the growth of some 200 million trees, yet few foresaw this breakthrough. In the mid-1980s, it looked to some as though Niger would be "blown from the map," writes Chris Reij, a Dutch specialist in sustainable land management, but farmer regreening has since brought enhanced food security for 2.5 million people, or about 16 percent of the population.[82] In late 2010, even as many in Niger were facing food shortages, village chief Moussa Sambo described his village near the capital city, Niamey, as experiencing the greatest prosperity ever, with young men returning. "We stopped the desert," he said, "and everything changed."[83]

And why hadn't hungry farmers in Niger figured all this out long ago? we asked Reij.

Well, they had. But in the early twentieth century, French colonial rulers turned trees into state property and punished anyone tampering with them.[84] So farmers began to see trees as a risk to be avoided and just got rid of them. Then, in 1960, Niger gained its independence, and over time, Reij says, farmers' perceptions changed. They now feel they own the trees in their fields.[85] In 2011, Niger's drought worsened, and by early 2012, six million people were threatened with famine. Have regreening efforts lessened the drought's devastation?

While no thorough analysis has yet been possible, Niger's national committee responsible for the famine early-warning system noted a hopeful sign: In the Kantché department in southern Niger, where tree cover has been encouraged, five villages with 350,000 people have produced a cereal surplus every year since 2007, including the drought year, 2011.

Trees help farmers when drought causes low cereal yields. "The poorest households often derive significant income from their on-farm trees in the form of fodder, firewood, fruit, and leaves, some of which is sold on the market," Reij reported in early 2012.[86] Selling leaves from a single mature baobab tree can bring in as much as US$75, a lot in a country in which most live on less than US$2 a day.[87]

Reij noted in 2012 that in the Maradi region, near the town of Illéla, "water harvesting"—digging "half moons" in the soil to reduce runoff—has rehabilitated barren, degraded land. In a number of villages, farmers have begun setting "rules for the protection and management of the trees" that are now thriving because of their efforts.[88] Villagers on bicycles patrol the rehabilitated area and impose sanctions on those breaking the rules.[89] As in the Tigray story, relating to the Earth in new ways is only part of the story: essential also are new enforceable social agreements to ensure ecological restoration.

Embedding an ethic of tree protection in the young of Niger, along with skills to contribute, is part of the new agri-culture; in this area of Niger, Reij reported, schoolchildren are trained to prune trees to help restore the land. And they are teaching each other. Kids in one school "received a delegation of school children from another village and they will inform and train them in re-greening." The children's "enthusiasm" impressed Reij, as farmer-managed regreening is being introduced into the curriculum of a primary school.

Despite these extraordinary regreening achievements, these success stories are not widely known. Only in the last five years have a few stories been carried in major media. The whole of southern Niger "was assumed to be highly degraded ... Few thought to look for positive changes at a regional scale," Reij explained.[90] And "if people don't know to look for it, they don't see it."[91]

Could this be evidence of the worldview that presumes "scarcity" is working against us?

Now aware, though, we can take heart from African farmers' creativity in the face of a deteriorating environment. If proven agroforestry practices, like those in Niger, were used on the more than two billion acres worldwide where they're suitable, in thirty years agroforestry could have a striking impact—accounting for perhaps one-third of agriculture's large potential contribution to righting the carbon balance.[92]

## India

### NAVDANYA

As part of her Research Foundation for Science, Technology and Ecology, Vandana Shiva founded Navdanya in the wake of what is known as the Punjab violence and the Bhopal chemical tragedy in 1984, in order to conserve biodiversity and economically support farmers while fostering indigenous knowledge and traditions. Navdanya works in nearly half of all Indian states and, since its founding in 1987, has established more than one hundred community seed banks.

In 1995, with international collaborators, Navdanya formed Diverse Women for Diversity, a local-to-global initiative that empowers women to participate in furthering biodiversity, cultural diversity, and food and water security conversations and movements. Locally, Diverse Women for Diversity works as Mahila Anna Swaraj—meaning "women's food sovereignty groups," or self-help groups. "Swaraj" is self-government or self-rule, a pillar of Gandhian philosophy. Its goal is to expand women's biodiversity conservation and sustainable, organic agriculture knowledge and skills, free of dependence on large agricultural corporations.

Globally, Navdanya has enabled the voices of Diverse Women for Diversity to be heard at world food summits, World Bank conferences, and World Trade Organization meetings, creating a precedent for gender balance and ecological perspectives to be presented in agricultural and trade policy discussions. In villages, Navdanya's community seed banks and community biodiversity registers protect and document local plant varieties, helping to spread these non-genetically engineered seeds to more and more villages. In addition to agricultural work, Swaraj advocates for women's rights in partnership with the National Alliance of Women for Food Rights.

Today, as a result of Navdanya and the determined work of Swaraj groups, more than five thousand varieties of rice, wheat, bean, millet, vegetables, and medicinal plants have been conserved. Collectively, this movement is India's largest direct market, fair trade, organic network.

Our chapter began in the state of Uttarakhand, the east Indian Himalayas, where a decade ago we first encountered those working with Navdanya. To capture what has evolved since, we share glimpses of the lives of women villagers working with Navdanya today.[93]

Navdanya's Mahila Anna Swaraj is made up of ten to twenty women who, among their many activities, contribute equally to a common savings account to assist individual or collective enterprises. Navdanya coordinators serve as advisers to Swaraj groups, which meet monthly to share knowledge and have fun. The groups have also revitalized the tradition of working collectively in each other's fields, and once a year, Swaraj group members gather to reflect on and rejoice in their progress.

The local seed banks that Navdanya has encouraged throughout India enhance resilience and food security. Linking neighboring villages, the seed banks can assist a family or village whose seasonal crop has failed and who needs seeds for the next season. Participants in Navdanya seed banks are expected either to replace twice the amount of any seed they receive or pass twice the amount to two farmers in need, free of charge. As extreme weather becomes more common at the same time many farmers have converted to hybrid seeds, whose vitality is gone after one season, seed banks for recovering from loss are becoming increasingly critical.

Part of the Navdanya network since 2007, Pushpa Devi, thirty-four, is a farmer in Bhoniyada village. She is married with one son and three daughters, and heads her village council. Before joining Navdanya, Pushpa used chemical fertilizer, but made the change to organic methods because she saw that illness had increased and that her crops failed when rains were poor. For her, chemical farming, contrary to its promise, had increased her pest problems. Since turning to organic farming, pest problems have decreased. Pushpa has noticed the climate changing, bringing more frequent heavy rains that threaten the food supply, so she is a careful seed saver. Asked how she selects seeds, Pushpa told a Navdanya interviewer quite simply, "By seeing which are the healthier ones. Like when we sit together you can see me, I am healthy."

Renu Bhatt, forty-four, in Bhatwari village, learned from her mother-in-law to keep seeds and stores them in Garhwali baskets, which are coated with clay and cow dung. She expresses pride that she is now able to teach others and work together: "If any person has a demand, then we discuss together and try and come up with a solution ... give them what they need," explained Renu about her savings group. She herself, for instance, recently borrowed Rs. 1,500 at 2 percent interest to buy a sewing machine and wool for knitting.

Bakshni Devi, roughly sixty, in Kuran village, is also a seed keeper and her home serves as the community seed bank. Big white sacks, each with small bags and pots of seeds inside, fill her home. Villagers select which farmers can contribute to the seed banks based on the farmers' knowledge and the need of the bank for specific varieties and quantities. Seed sharing links villages with community seed banks so that everyone knows where to turn if there is a crop loss.

Shivday Devi, sixty-three, in Mani Guha village, has been a Navdanya member for a decade. She reports that she has never used chemicals on her land and, even if they were offered for free, she would refuse them. She spoke of the dignity that organic farming and seed banks offer farmers. "Here," Shivday said, "in agriculture, nobody is our boss, we are our own bosses."

ANDHRA PRADESH

From Navdanya's remarkable achievements, we venture south to Andhra Pradesh, India's fourth-largest state, which has been called the "pesticide capital of the world,"[94] and is among those states hit hardest by farmer suicides.[95]

In 2004, however, a big change got under way. The Andhra Pradesh state-sponsored Society for the Elimination of Poverty and the Ministry of Rural Development formally began to support what became known as Community Managed Sustainable Agriculture. From the beginning, many village women were leaders in a transition to ecological agriculture. During the pilot phase, 2005 and 2006, non-governmental organizations partnered with the Centre for Sustainable Agriculture and Centre for World Solidarity, based in the city of Tarnaka, to further what they called "non-pesticide farming." Village by village, farmers began to make pledges to each other to forgo pesticides and adopt ecological practices. During this initial phase, farmers in 450 villages in nine districts of the state took part.[96] But as of 2011, the movement had spread to more than eight thousand villages, covering almost three million acres.[97]

What is motivating this fast-moving shift? As elsewhere, the answer is mounting illness and health care costs from pesticide exposure, and diets impoverished by monoculture; together with the burden of paying for commercial seeds, fertilizer, and pesticides that typically account for almost half a farmer's total cultivation expenditure.[98]

Change is also spreading because farmers see their neighbors' success. In this process, Meenakshi, a nineteen-year-old landless tribal woman from Koduru village in the Srikakulam district emerged in 2004 as a local symbol of possibility. Distressed by her family's cycle of debt, and with encouragement from her women's self-help group, Meenakshi challenged her husband to a contest. They agreed that he would use his preferred chemical farming practices on half the family's quarter acre of leased land; while on her half she would use natural fertilizers like cow dung, urine, jaggery, gram flour, microbe-rich clay, as well as traditional pest control methods. In a signed contract, they vowed that the approach that reaped the largest profit at season's end would thereafter be used for their entire land share.

Meenakshi's approach won. She earned Rs. 15,000, which was Rs. 5,000 more than her husband's profit—demonstrating how sustainable ways can cut costs and increase yields. Now, as one of sixty-three state-level Community Resource Persons, Meenakshi teaches others the methods she used. "I teach from my own experience and that is why I can address the doubts and problems of the farmers," Meenakshi told a Forbes.com reporter.[99]

To protect poor farmers from risk of hunger, leaders have adopted a go-slow approach, enabling farmers to avoid any dip in yields during the transition to ecological methods. They're encouraged first to try eco-farming on one-quarter acre to determine for themselves the results. Freeing themselves from the need to purchase pesticides, farmers in the region are also identifying plants, 108 so far, suitable for preparing homemade pest control potions. With the help of extension workers, farmers are both learning and sharing knowledge about multicropping, water harvesting, preparation of natural pest controls, the art of composting, and the value of trees to good farming. "Farmers' knowledge is the basic input," says D. V. Raidu, director of the Community Managed Sustainable Agriculture (CMSA) program in the state government.[100]

As in Niger, where farmers' work to regreen their land involves making and enforcing rules together, in the CMSA approach villagers take a public "oath to follow certain rules which structure the programme, including participation in meetings, training and following certain [farming] practices," says the Centre for Sustainable Agriculture in Tarnaka.[101]

The impact of ecological farming on farm family income and food security has been stunning. Indebtedness has fallen as costs of cultivation have dropped by 30 to 40 percent.[102] Market premiums for higher quality and better tasting products, along with decreased spoilage, have boosted farmers' profits. "In fact, some of the farmer groups reported up to 100 percent higher profits through CMSA than the previous methods," noted a World Bank blog.[103] With one hectare a family can now earn a net income as high as US$2,500 to US$4,000,[104] whereas the average small ("marginal") farmer in India earns roughly US$492 a year.[105]

With the new practices spreading, many rural people report better health. Their exposure to toxic pesticides in the fields is eliminated, their food is less contaminated by pesticide residues, and as farms have revived the practice of growing a variety of crops, diets are becoming more diverse. Where these shifts are occurring, "cases of acute toxicity due to spraying of pesticides have completely gone away," reported D. V. Raidu in 2011.[106]

A leader in what is becoming a statewide effort is the Deccan Development Society (DDS), a women's movement working in more than seventy villages in the Medak district of the state. To bring attention to the importance of protecting biodiversity and to spread knowledge of seed saving and sharing, in 1999 DDS launched an annual traveling biodiversity festival. The colorful celebration involves a festive seed caravan of decorated bullock-carts. Accompanied by music and dancing, the carts carry hundreds of traditional seed varieties; in 2012, the festival reached fifty-five villages, with stops for teaching and sharing.[107]

By May 2011, the state agriculture and rural development departments of Andhra Pradesh had joined forces to further this transition to ecological farming. There are roughly 930,000 women's self-help groups; and the state agencies' goal is that by 2020 women's organizations will help to involve more than eight million farmers in spreading sustainable farming practices to 80 percent of the state's cultivable land.[108]

If their bold goal is reached, a revolutionary change will have occurred in just fifteen years.

*Brazil*

We turn next to Brazil, where agroecology is emerging within a struggle for land by the country's poorest, and often hungriest, people—rural landless workers. Hunger in many parts of Africa is often misleadingly cast as a consequence of resource scarcity, but for Brazil that rationale would be a joke: this lush and rich country boasts one of the world's highest GDPs and ranks third among agricultural exporters; it also has one of the world's most extreme concentrations of wealth. Three percent of Brazil's population controls two-thirds of the country's land, of which 42 percent is left unused.[109] At the same time, almost a quarter of Brazilians live below the poverty line,[110] and four million are homeless, landless, and jobless.[111] Many poor live in the country's urban *favelas,* but the majority of Brazil's poor people are in the countryside, working as day-laborers or farming small, rented plots with no land of their own.[112]

For thirty years the largest social movement in Brazil, and perhaps in all of Latin America, the landless workers' movement, or Movimento do Trabalhadores Rurais Sem Terra in Portuguese, known by the acronym MST, has been striving to push the country in a very different direction: toward dispersed farmland ownership, including cooperatives, managed by smallholders using ecological practices.

Soon after we arrived in Brazil a decade ago to learn more about the MST, Adelir, a young man who'd been a MST member since the age of nine, told us that "most of the people you'll meet here were called 'cold meals' before they joined the movement." When we looked really puzzled, he explained: "Because when you're landless, you have to work on somebody else's land, and you have to bring your lunch, and you work so hard you never have time to make a fire and cook hot food. By the time you get home you're so tired, you eat cold food, too. So landless workers are called 'cold meals.'" Later, Adelir's mother Irene spoke about life before the movement: "You see," she said, "before, we weren't just landless, we were everythingless."

This movement that changed life for Adelir's family arose during a dark period in Brazil's history: a long, deadly military dictatorship lasting from 1964 to 1985. In the early 1980s, landless workers in southern Brazil began to organize and devised a strategy to challenge the land injustice: Groups of landless families began nonviolently occupying land unused by the wealthy owners—acts of civil disobedience supported by the Pastoral Land Commission and similar religious groups influenced by Catholic social teachings.

These acts built toward the 1985 founding, nationally, of the MST, which now boasts 1.5 million members[113] that span all of Brazil's twenty-three states.[114] Over the decades, the movement has led more than 2,500 land occupations and settled more than 370,000 families on almost twenty million acres of land to which they have won the legal right.[115] In this long struggle, almost 1,500 MST members have been killed, mostly at the hands of angry landowners and the police force.[116]

From its birth, MST's goal has been nationwide land reform—"Brazil without *latifundios*" (large estates) is how we saw it expressed on posters during our visit there. The country's 1988 constitution has helped significantly. It states that "property shall fulfill its social function," and affirms the government's power to "expropriate ... for purposes of agrarian reform, rural property" that fails to meet this requirement. After 1988, the MST could therefore argue that its seizure of unused land is civil disobedience to compel the government to uphold the constitution.

Following the land occupations, families end up living in encampments, often protected from the elements only by shacks made of wood frames covered in black plastic, waiting for official legalization of their claims. Currently, there are about nine hundred encampments with 150,000 landless families petitioning for land ownership.[117] During a process that can take years, MST families receive training in ecological farming, for in the MST's struggle for land and dignity, agroecology is fundamental.[118] As in our previous examples from India, the movement teaches families to collect, use, and exchange their own seeds. And trainings emphasize freedom from expensive chemical fertilizers and increasing crop productivity and diversity using ecologically sound approaches.

Among the movement's larger goals are resistance to genetically engineered seeds and the promotion of organic farming. In fact, the MST established Brazil's first organic seed line, BioNatur, which offers more than ninety organic plant varieties.[119] In 2004, it built the Chico Mendes Center for Agroecology in Ponta Grossa, Paraná, ironically on land that biotech giant, Monsanto, formerly used to grow genetically engineered crops. The center produces organic seeds native to Brazil for distribution to MST farmers,[120] and it experiments with new techniques to promote reforestation and better use of native species, and to discover medicinal uses of plants.[121]

MST families have established several thousand farming communities with more than one thousand schools serving 950,000 kids and 17,000 adult students. The MST encourages members to join together in farming cooperatives; and the movement has spawned almost one hundred food processing cooperatives for fruit, vegetables, dairy products, grains, coffee, and meat, among other products that indirectly benefit about seven hundred rural towns.[122] We wanted to know *why*—why has MST taken leadership in promoting agroecological farming throughout its settlements, and even funded some members to get higher degrees in nonchemical farming techniques.

We asked Antonio Capitani, a leader in an MST encampment we visited. "It took time," he acknowledged, "for people to understand why we shouldn't use pesticides." It's tough, he lamented, convincing farmers to use an organic approach when chemicals give instant results. "I know what pesticides do," Antonio continued. "I spent four days in the hospital with lung and kidney problems because of pesticides. The doctors who work for the landowners don't want to tell you that pesticides are the problem."

"So is danger to you, we mean the farmers, the main reason you and the MST are trying to move members to organic farming?" we ask. Jacir Pagnussatti, a younger MST member of the community, jumped in to answer: "It's not just that farming without using pesticides means less hazard and lower costs for us. Why would we go to all this trouble and risk to grow food that's just going to hurt people? We are concerned about the people in the cities, too."

In the MST movement, members seemed to gain a sense of power over their lives that then enabled them to take responsibility for the impact of their choices on others—including those who eat the food they produce. We realized that within this agrarian reform movement, ecological practices are an aspect of realigning human relationships in ways benefiting the natural world and also help to elicit the best in us as we relate to one another. Beyond avoiding health risks for oneself and one's customers, motivating farmers also is the financial gain they enjoy: shifting to agroecology, MST farmers have seen their costs drop from US$500–US$700 per hectare to only US$28.[123]

This movement is succeeding because, although it confronts the government in order to gain access to land, it has also earned its respect and collaboration. For example, when the Luiz Inácio Lula da Silva administration (2003–2010) instituted the Food Acquisition Program to buy produce from small-scale farmers for use in schools and hospitals, the MST stepped up. At least 2,300 MST families across São Paulo state have participated.[124] Via the program, farm families are guaranteed an annual income of approximately US$3,480—a huge improvement, considering thirty-five million poor Brazilians make at most US$730 a year.[125] As of 2008, FAO estimates that the arrangement had relieved malnutrition and improved food security for 11.4 million people.[126] The federal government's National Education Program in Land Reform has also funded an MST educational effort in agroecology that, in 2010, graduated its first 120 students from a three-year program.[127]

So, why does the MST seem to be succeeding, when for hundreds of years all such striving for fairer access to land in Brazil had been wiped out with peasant blood? We asked this question of a movement founder, João Pedro Stédile. "My grandparents were immigrants from Austria," João Pedro began. "They and my parents worked the land in southern Brazil for more than a century but ended up with nothing to show for it. As I grew up, I was influenced by Catholic religious teachings. The church taught us it was wrong to conform to inequity."

Listening to João Pedro, it seemed clear to us that one major reason for the MST's success is the strong values captured in his comments. Then, aware of the obstacles the movement has faced—from government hostility to bad press to violent attack—we posed the most basic question: In the beginning, what made you think the MST could ever succeed? João Pedro looked surprised. "Being successful was never the motivation. We simply didn't have other options." But he quickly moved on to what he considered the basis of MST's accomplishments so far: "There are no individual solutions in this world," João Pedro said, explaining that within the MST everything is done as a group. "The conservative church always used to say, 'Get used to being poor. God will give you what you want in heaven.' But my Franciscan mentors offered me a different version of the Gospel: 'God will help those who organize.'"

The MST's ethic of democratic organizing has for some time included an emphasis on gender equity, in a country that has among the lowest proportion of women in public office in the world. In MST communities the rule is that the two elected coordinators must be one man and one woman. (We are uncertain of the extent to which such gender balance is respected in MST communities across the entire country, but it is certainly what we observed.) The MST goal is that women make up half of participants in all MST education and training courses, as well as in leadership in the organization's national bodies. The rights of MST women are also protected via joint land-use titles and the right to credit in the names of both members of a couple.

To make its commitment to gender equity vivid, the MST has strived each year to carry out direct actions involving women's leadership around March 8, International Women's Day. In 2012, for example, more than one thousand MST members occupied land owned by Suzano Papel e Celulose in the state of Bahia to denounce the company's social and environmental impact. With operations in eighty countries, Suzano is the world's second-largest producer of eucalyptus cellulose for making paper. The MST argues that its vast size and monoculture contribute to unemployment, poverty, social inequality, and displacement of peasants.[128]

Through its focus on building democratic social forms, including elected leadership from the encampment level to its top echelons, as well as cooperative forms of enterprise, the MST is building relationships of mutual accountability that have been shown to bring forth the best in human beings. And at the same time, the movement is working to remake our relationships with nature through its eco-farming and reforesting efforts, so that humans align with nature's regenerative power. All these require huge changes within. Here again we quote João Pedro Stédile:

> The first step is losing naive consciousness, no longer accepting what you see as something that cannot be changed. The second is reaching the awareness that you won't get anywhere unless you work together. This shift in consciousness, once you get it, is like riding a bike, no one can take it from you. So you forget how to say "Yes, sir" and learn to say "I think that ..." This is when the citizen is born.[129]

## Hope in Action

We've taken you far and wide to see a different world emerging.

What moves us is the contrast between what we have shared here and widespread perceptions of a corporate-controlled global food system that is entrenched and immovable—perhaps not healthy or tasty or ecologically sane, but efficient and, well, the only realistic path: it's either the centralized, corporate system, so many believe, or starvation. We now have evidence, both in lived experience and in formal research results from vastly different parts of the world, to the contrary: we know that human beings can align with nature to meet our food needs.

We can see that aligning with the laws of nature to grow food requires that we embrace more clearly our own nature as well—all of it. To bring forth the best in us, we each need to feel efficacious, connected to others, and to have meaning in our lives. We also know that, to meet these needs and manifest our best, we need rules and norms that reinforce the best in us. Thus it's clear that we must together create and enforce rules that disperse power, as they create fairness and inclusion, protecting the dignity of all and the integrity of nature at the same time. In this way, as in all our examples, we can create communities of empowered knowledge-seekers who enjoy learning and contributing. With this understanding, we can take a deep breath of relief. We can release our fear of scarcity and trust our place in the nature of things, for the stories here are but a mere taste of millions like them throughout our world.

## Endnotes

1    Economic and Social Development Department, "11.3.1: Land under Organic Management," *World Agriculture: Towards 2015/2030: An FAO Perspective* (Food and Agriculture Organization of the United Nations, 2003), www.fao.org/docrep /005/Y4252E/y4252e13.htm.

2    Zainab Salbi, "The Next Green Frontier," *World Pulse*, March 29, 2010, www.worldpulse.com/node/19106, accessed May 14, 2012.

3    http://faostat.fao.org/site/609/default.aspx#ancor.

4    Olivier De Schutter, "'Obesogenic' Food Systems Must Be Reformed: Five Ways to Tackle Disastrous Diets," March 12, 2012, www.grain.org/bulletin _board/entries/4480-obesogenic-food-systems-must-be-reformed, accessed March 22, 2012.

5    T. Vijay Kumar et al., "Ecologically Sound, Economically Viable: Community Managed Sustainable Agriculture in Andhra Pradesh, India," World Bank, 2009: 7, www.indiawaterportal.org/sites/indiawaterportal.org/files /Community_managed_sustainable_agriculture_ Andhra_Pradesh_SERP _ World_Bank_2009.pdf, accessed March 22, 2012.

6   Associated Press, "Drought, Debt Drive Indian Farmers to Suicide," August 27, 2009, www.msnbc.msn.com/id/32585162/ns/world_news-south_and _central_asia/t/drought-debt-drive-indian-farmers-suicide/#.T2tRM 9m8iWY, accessed March 22, 2012.

7   Holly Jessen, "Ethanol: One Market for a Growing Corn Supply," *Ethanol Producer Magazine,* September 12, 2011, www.ethanolproducer.com/articles /8135/ethanol-one-market-for-a-growing-corn-supply, accessed January 25, 2012.

8   United States Department of Agriculture, "FAS: PSD Online Custom Query," 2011, www.fas.usda.gov/psdonline/psdQuery.aspx, accessed December 22, 2011.

9   Suzanne Goldenberg, "GM Corn Being Developed for Fuel Instead of Food," *Guardian,* August 15, 2011, www.guardian.co.uk/environment/2011/aug/15 /gm-corn-development-food-fuel, accessed January 25, 2012.

10  Food and Agriculture Organization, "Price Volatility and Food Security," HLPE, July 2011: 33, www.fao.org/fileadmin/user_upload/hlpe/hlpe _documents/HLPE-price-volatility-and-food-security-report-July-2011.pdf, accessed December 19, 2011.

11  Peter Thoenes, "Recent Trends and Medium-Term Prospects in the Global Vegetable Oil Market," FAO, November 2011: 11, www.fao.org/fileadmin /templates/est/COMM_MARKETS_MONITORING/Oilcrops/Documents /Kiev_handout.pdf, accessed April 4, 2012.

12  United Nations Environment Programme, "Oil Palm Plantations: Threats and Opportunities for Tropical Ecosystems," UNEP Global Environmental Alert Service, December 2011: 2, www.unep.org/pdf/Dec_11_Palm_Plantations .pdf, accessed May 22, 2012.

13  Rachel Smolker et al., "Devastated Lands, Displaced Peoples, Agrofuel Costs in Indonesia, Malaysia, Papua New Guinea," *Pacific Ecologist,* Summer 2009: 36–39, www.pacificecologist.org/archive/17/pe17-biofuels-devastate-se-asia .pdf, accessed May 22, 2012.

14  Michael W. Masters, "Testimony of Michael W. Masters before the Committee on Homeland Security and Governmental Affairs," United States Senate, May 20, 2008, http://hsgac.senate.gov/public/_files/052008Masters.pdf, accessed January 25, 2012.

15  Ibid.

16  FAO, "The FAO Food Price Index Rose Further in February," March 8, 2012, www.fao.org/worldfoodsituation/wfs-home/foodpricesindex/en/, accessed March 22, 2012.

17  Frank Veneroso, "Reserve Management: The Commodity Bubble, the Metals Manipulation, the Contagion Risk to Gold and the Threat of the Great Hedge Fund Unwind to Spread Product," 2007, www.venerosoassociates.net /Reserve%20Management%20Parts%20I%20 and%20II%20WBP%20 Public%2071907.pdf, accessed January 25, 2012.

[18]  Masters, "Testimony of Michael W. Masters before the Committee on Homeland Security and Governmental Affairs."

[19]  Oxfam, "Land and Power: The Growing Scandal Surrounding the New Wave of Investments in Land," September 22, 2011, www.oxfamamerica.org/files /bp151-land-power-rights-acquisitions-220911-en.pdf, accessed March 22, 2012.

[20]  Deborah MacKenzie, "The 21st-Century Land Grab," *New Scientist*, December 6, 2008.

[21]  Daniel Shepard and Anuradha Mittal, "The Great Land Grab: Rush for World's Farmland Threatens Food Security for the Poor," http://media .oaklandinstitute.org/sites/oaklandinstitute.org/files/LandGrab_final_web .pdf, accessed May 23, 2012.

[22]  GRAIN, "Seized! GRAIN Briefing Annex," *GRAIN Briefing*, October 2008, www.iatp.org/files/451_2_104684.pdf, accessed May 17, 2012.

[23]  Duncan Green, personal communication.

[24]  William Davidson, "Ethiopia's Farm Investment Plans Falter on the Flood Plain," Bloomberg News, 2013, http://www.bloomberg.com/news/articles /2013-11-24/ethiopian-drive-to-lure-farm-investment-founders-on-flood -plain, accessed September 9, 2015.

[25]  http://www.oaklandinstitute.org/land-rights-issue.

[26]  FAO, "Price Volatility and Food Security."

[27]  Sonja J. Vermeulen, Bruce M. Campbell, and John S. I. Ingram, "Climate Change and Food Systems," *Annual Review of Environment and Resources* 37, (2012): 195, accessed December 12, 2014, doi: 10.1146/annurev-environ -020411-130608.

[28]  FAO, "Save and Grow," 2011, www.fao.org/ag/save-and-grow/en/1/Index .html, accessed May 22, 2012.

[29]  WorldWatch Institute, "State of the World 2007: Our Urban Future," 2007, www.worldwatch.org/node/4840, accessed May 21, 2012.

[30]  ETC Group, "Who Will Feed Us? Questions and Answers for Food and Climate Crises," *Communiqué*, Issue 102, November 2009: 1, www.etcgroup.org /upload/publication/pdf_file/ETC_Who_Will_Feed_Us.pdf, accessed March 22, 2012.

[31]  FAO, "Women, Agriculture, and Food Security," 2001, www.fao.org/world foodsummit/english/fsheets/women.pdf, accessed March 22, 2012.

[32]  IAASTD, *Agriculture at a Crossroads: Global Report* (Washington, DC: Island Press, 2008), www.agassessment.org/reports/IAASTD/EN/Agriculture%20 at%20a%20Crossroads_Global%20Report%20 (English).pdf, accessed March 22, 2012.

[33]  Ibid.

[34]  IAASTD, "A New Era of Agriculture Begins Today: International Agriculture Assessment Calls for Immediate Radical Changes," April 15, 2008, www.agassessment-watch.org/press.htm, accessed May 17, 2012.

35   La Via Campesina, "The International Peasant's Voice," February 9, 2011, www.viacampesina.org/en/index.php?option=com_content& view=category &layout=blog&id=27&Itemid=45, accessed March 22, 2012.

36   Forum for Food Sovereignty, "Declaration of the Forum for Food Sovereignty, Nyéléni, 2007," Sélingué, Mali, February 27, 2007, www.world -governance.org/IMG/pdf_0072_Declaration_of_Nyeleni_-_ENG.pdf, accessed March 22, 2012.

37   Food Movements Unite! "La Via Campesina," www.foodmovementsunite .org/authors/via_campesina.html.

38   La Via Campesina, "La Via Campesina Opposes Land Grabbing at the UN Committee on Food Security," 2011, www.viacampesina.org/en/index.php /main-issues-mainmenu-27/agrarian-reform-mainmenu-36/1072-la-via -campesina-opposes-land-grabbing-at-the-un-committee-on-food-security, accessed July 20, 2015.

39   United Nations Environment Programme—United Nations Conference on Trade and Development (UNEP-UNCTAD) Capacity-Building Task Force on Trade, Environment, and Development, *Organic Agriculture and Food Security in Africa* (New York: United Nations, 2008), 11–16, www.unctad.org/en /docs/ditcted200715_en.pdf, accessed March 28, 2012.

40   FAO, "Cutting Food Waste to Feed the World: Over a Billion Tonnes Squandered Each Year," 2011, www.fao.org/news/story/en/item/74192/icode/, accessed March 22, 2012.

41   Committee on Twenty-First Century Systems Agriculture; National Research Council, *Toward Sustainable Agricultural Systems in the 21st Century* (Washington, DC: National Academies Press, 2010), http://books.nap.edu/catalog .php?record_id=12832, accessed March 28, 2012.

42   Linda Collette et al., "Save and Grow: A Policymaker's Guide to the Sustainable Intensification of Smallholder Crop Production," FAO, 2011, www.fao .org/ag/save-and-grow/, accessed March 28, 2012.

43   Jules Pretty, "Agroecological Approaches to Agricultural Development: Version 1," RIMISP Background Paper for the World Development Report 2007, November 2006: 2–3, www.rimisp.org/getdoc.php?docid=6440, accessed March 28, 2012.

44   Catherine Badgley et al., "Organic Agriculture and the Global Food Supply," *Renewable Agriculture and Food Systems* 22 (2007): 86–108.

45   UNCTAD, "Sustaining African Agriculture: Organic Production," *UNCTAD Policy Briefs*, 6 (2009): 1, www.unctad.org/en/docs/presspb20086_en.pdf, accessed March 28, 2012. Based on: UNCTAD-UNEP Capacity-Building Task Force on Trade, Environment, and Development, *Organic Agriculture and Food Security in Africa* (New York: United Nations, 2008), 16, www .unctad.org/en/docs/ditcted200715_en.pdf, accessed May 22, 2012.

46   FAO, "Organic Agriculture and Climate Change," 2005, www.fao.org /DOCREP/005/Y4137E/y4137e02b.htm, accessed March 26, 2012.

47   Kate Trumper et al., *The Natural Fix? The Role of Ecosystems in Climate Mitigation* (Cambridge, UK: UN Environment Programme, 2009), 41, 55, www.unep.org/pdf/BioseqRRA_scr.pdf, accessed May 17, 2012.

48   International Federation of Organic Agriculture Movements, "The Contribution of Organic Agriculture to Climate Change Mitigation," IFOAM EU GROUP, 2009, www.ifoam.org/growing_organic/1_arguments_for_oa /environmental_benefits/pdfs/IFOAM-CC-Mitigation-Web.pdf, accessed May 22, 2012.

49   GRAIN, "Food and Climate Change."

50   Government Office for Science, "Synthesis Report C9: Sustainable Intensification in African Agriculture—Analysis of Cases and Common Lessons," in *Foresight Project on Global Food and Farming Futures* (London: Government Office for Science, 2011), 11.

51   BBC News, "Cassava 'Offers Climate Change Hope' for Africa," February 28, 2012, www.bbc.co.uk/news/world-africa-17190622, accessed April 18, 2012.

52   PRI Radio: The World, "The Neglected Positive Image of Africa," October 10, 2011, www.theworld.org/2011/10/the-neglected-positive-image-of -africa/, accessed April 18, 2012.

53   SOFA Team and Cheryl Doss, "The Role of Women in Agriculture," ESA Working Paper No. 11-02, FAO, March 2011, www.fao.org/docrep/013 /am307e/am307e00.pdf, accessed April 18, 2012.

54   FAO, "Women, Agriculture and Food Security," 2001, www.fao.org/world foodsummit/english/fsheets/women.pdf, accessed May 22, 2012.

55   UNCTAD-UNEP Capacity-Building Task Force on Trade, Environment, and Development, *Organic Agriculture and Food Security in Africa*, 13–14.

56   Technical Centre for Agricultural and Rural Cooperation (CTA), "Country Study: Ethiopia," December 2008, Assessment of Agricultural Information Needs in African, Caribbean & Pacific (ACP) States: Eastern Africa. Report prepared by Abebe Kirub. Project: 4-7-41-255-7/d.

57   Paul Vallely, "Africa's Worst Drought in 60 Years Threatens Famine for 10m," *The Independent*, July 6, 2011, www.independent.co.uk/news/world /africa/africas-worst-drought-in-60-years-threatens-famine-for-10m -2307420.html, accessed April 18, 2012.

58   Fiona Meehan, *Female Headed Households in Tigray, Ethiopia: A Study Review*, Report No. 35, Norway, Drylands Coordination Group, December 2004, www.drylands-group.org/noop/file.php?id=470, accessed March 5, 2012.

59   Jennifer Wilder et al., *Women's Empowerment in Ethiopia: New Solutions to Ancient Problems* (Watertown, MA: Pathfinder International, September 2007), www.pathfind.org/site/DocServer/PI_WE_paper_final.pdf?docID=10202, accessed March 5, 2012.

60   The Gaia Foundation, "The Institute for Sustainable Development," *Gaia Foundation Partners*, 2012, www.gaiafoundation.org/partner/institute -sustainable-development, accessed March 26, 2012.

61    Hailu Araya and Sue Edwards, "The Tigray Experience: A Success Story in Sustainable Agriculture," *Environment & Development* 4 (2006).

62    Sue Edwards et al., "The Impact of Compost Use on Crop Yields in Tigray, Ethiopia," Institute for Sustainable Development, International Conference on Organic Agriculture and Food Security, FAO, 2007, ftp://ftp.fao.org/docrep/fao/010/ai434e/ai434e00.pdf, accessed July 20, 2015.

63    Ibid.

64    Ibid.

65    Araya and Edwards, "The Tigray Experience," 5.

66    Ibid., 2–3.

67    Edwards et al., "The Impact of Compost Use on Crop Yields in Tigray, Ethiopia."

68    Sue Edwards, personal communication, February 2009, quoted in *Diet for a Hot Planet* by Anna Lappé (New York: Bloomsbury, 2010).

69    Edwards et al., "The Impact of Compost Use on Crop Yields in Tigray, Ethiopia."

70    Jakob Lundberg and Fredrik Moberg, "Ecological in Ethiopia: Farming with Nature Increases Profitability and Reduces Vulnerability" (Stockholm: Swedish Society for Nature Conservation, 2008), www.ifoam.org/about _ifoam/around_world/aosc_pages/pdf/Ecological_in_Ethiopia.pdf, accessed April 18, 2012.

71    Ibid.

72    Ibid.

73    UNCTAD-UNEP Capacity-Building Task Force on Trade, Environment, and Development, *Organic Agriculture and Food Security in Africa*, 16.

74    Sue Edwards et al., *Successes and Challenges in Ecological Agriculture: Experiences from Tigray, Ethiopia* (Rome: FAO, 2010), 237, 289, www.fao.org/docrep /014/i2230e/i2230e09.pdf, accessed March 22, 2012. See also: Lundberg and Moberg, *Ecological in Ethiopia*.

75    African Union, "Conference on Ecological Agriculture: Mitigating Climate Change, Providing Food Security and Self-Reliance for Rural Livelihoods in Africa," Addis Ababa, Ethiopia, November 26–28, 2008, www.fao.org/docrep /014/i2230e/i2230e01.pdf, accessed February 23, 2012.

76    FAO, *Rural Women and Food Security: Current Situation and Perspectives* (Rome: FAO, 1998), www.fao.org/DOCREP/003/W8376EW8376E00. HTM, accessed April 18, 2012. See also: UNCTAD-UNEP Capacity-Building Task Force on Trade, Environment, and Development, *Organic Agriculture and Food Security in Africa*, 13.

77    Araya and Edwards, "The Tigray Experience."

78    African Union, "Conference on Ecological Agriculture."

79    Pretty, "Agroecological Approaches to Agricultural Development." See also: RIMISP Background Paper for the World Development Report 2007, November 2006: 2–3, www.rimisp.org/getdoc.php?docid=6440, accessed March 28, 2012.

[80] Thomas Hargrove, "World Fertilizer Prices Soar as Food and Fuel Economies Merge," International Center for Soil Fertility and Agricultural Development, 2008.

[81] Adam Nossiter, "Famine Persists in Niger, but Denial Is Past," *New York Times,* May 3, 2012, www.nytimes.com/2010/05/04/world/africa/04niger .html, accessed April 18, 2012.

[82] Chris Reij et al., "Agroenvironmental Transformation in the Sahel," Discussion Paper 00194, International Food Policy Research Institute, November 2009: 2, 7, 19, www.ifpri.org/sites/default/files/publications/ifpridp00914 .pdf, accessed April 18, 2012.

[83] Alex Perry, "Land of Hope," December 13, 2010, www.time.com/time /magazine/article/0,9171,2034377-2,00.html, accessed April 18, 2012.

[84] Mark Hertsgaard, "Regreening Africa," *The Nation,* November 19, 2009, www.thenation.com/article/regreening-africa?page=0,0, accessed April 18, 2012.

[85] Chris Reij, personal communication with the authors, June 30, 2010.

[86] Chris Reij, "Food Security and Water in Africa's Drylands," Africa Regreening Initiatives, March 8, 2012, http://africa-regreening.blogspot.com /2012/03/food-security-and-water-in-africas.html, accessed April 18, 2012.

[87] Central Intelligence Agency, "The World Factbook: Africa: Niger," 2012, www.cia.gov/library/publications/the-world-factbook/geos/ng.html, accessed April 18, 2012.

[88] Reij, "Food Security and Water in Africa's Drylands."

[89] Ibid.

[90] Reij et al., "Agroenvironmental Transformation in the Sahel."

[91] Chris Reij, "Investing in Trees to Mitigate Climate Change," in *State of the World 2011* (New York: W. W. Norton, 2011), 88.

[92] H. Neufeldt et al., "Trees on Farms: Tackling the Triple Challenge of Mitigation, Adaptation, and Food Security," World Agroforestry Centre Policy Brief 07, World Agroforestry Centre, Nairobi, 2009: 3, http://worldagroforestry .org/downloads/publications/PDFs/mitigation-adaptation-food-security .pdf, accessed April 18, 2012.

[93] The profiles that follow are taken from interviews conducted by Navdanya.

[94] GRAIN, "Saying 'No' to Chemical Farming in India," July 12, 2008, www .grain.org/article/entries/679-saying-no-to-chemical-farming-in-india, accessed April 18, 2012.

[95] National Crime Records Bureau, "Accidental Deaths & Suicides in India. New Delhi: Ministry of Home Affairs," 2006: tables 2.10–2.11, http://ncrb.nic.in /adsi/data/ADSI2006/home.htm, accessed January 25, 2012.

[96] Centre for Sustainable Agriculture, "In the Hands of the Community: Inspiring Stories from Community Managed Sustainable Agriculture CMSA Programme," implemented under Indira Kranthi Patham, Rural Development Department, Government of Andhra Pradesh, 2008, www.scribd.com /doc/21383196/In-the-Hands-of-the-Community, accessed May 14, 2012.

97   Savvy Soumya Misra, "Community Managed Sustainable Agriculture: Interview with Raidu DV," *Indian Agrarian Crisis,* June 25, 2011, http://agrarian crisis.in/2011/06/25/1442/, accessed January 25, 2012.

98   T. Vijay Kumar et al., "Ecologically Sound, Economically Viable: Community Managed Sustainable Agriculture in Andhra Pradesh, India," World Bank, 2009, 7.

99   Udit Misra, "Back to the Roots for Andhra Pradesh Farmers," October 6, 2010, http://forbesindia.com/article/on-assignment/back-to-the-roots-for -andra-pradesh-farmers/17822/1, accessed February 16, 2012.

100   Soumya Misra, "Community Managed Sustainable Agriculture."

101   Centre for Sustainable Agriculture, "In the Hands of the Community," 29–30.

102   Udit Misra, "Back to the Roots for Andhra Pradesh Farmers."

103   Smita Jacob, "Paving the Way for a Greener Village," World Bank blog: Development in a Changing Climate, December 21, 2011, http://blogs.world bank.org/climatechange/paving-way-greener-village, accessed February 16, 2012.

104   Udit Misra, "Back to the Roots for Andhra Pradesh Farmers."

105   National Commission for Enterprises in the Unorganized Sector, "The Challenge of Employment in India," 2009, www.cdhr.org.in/Images/PDF /The_Challenge_of_Employment_in_India.pdf, accessed April 13, 2012.

106   Soumya Misra, "Community Managed Sustainable Agriculture."

107   Deccan Development Society, "Thirteenth Mobile Biodiversity Festival Is Inaugurated 14th January–13th February 2012," www.ddsindia.com/www /pdf/MBF%202012%20Inaugural.pdf, accessed February 16, 2012.

108   Smita Jacob, "Paving the Way for a Greener Village."

109   WarOnWant.Org, "Factsheet: Landless Workers' Movement," War on Want, Food Justice Information, July 13, 2010, www.waronwant.org/component /content/article/315-food-justice-inform/16978-factsheet-landless-workers -movement-mst, accessed February 27, 2012.

110   Adam Raney and Chad Heeter, "Brazil: Cutting the Wire, Witnessing a Land Occupation," *Frontline: Rough Cut,* December 13, 2005, www.pbs.org/front lineworld/rough/2005/12/brazil_cutting.html#, accessed February 27, 2012.

111   WarOnWant.Org, "Landless in Brazil," War on Want: Food Justice Programme, June 10, 2002, www.waronwant.org/overseas-work/food-sovereignty /landless-in-brazil, accessed February 27, 2012.

112   Ibid.

113   Raney and Heeter, "Brazil."

114   WarOnWant.Org., "Factsheet."

115   Eric Holt-Gimenez et al., *Food Rebellions: Crisis and the Hunger for Justice* (Oakland, CA: Food First Books, 2009), 104.

116   "We Are Millions," *New Internationalist,* December 12, 2009, www.newint .org/features/special/2009/12/01/we-are-millions/, accessed May 22, 2012.

[117] "What Is the MST?" Friends of the MST website, www.mstbrazil.org/whatismst, accessed April 18, 2012.

[118] WarOnWant.Org, "Factsheet."

[119] "MST and Agroecology: BioNatur (Organic) Seeds," www.mstbrazilorg/?q=seeds, accessed April 18, 2012.

[120] Biodiversidad en América Latina y El Caribe, "Brasil: Centro Chico Medes de Agroecologia: Terra Livre de Transgênicos e Sem Agrotócivos," June 2, 2005, www.biodiversidadla.org/content/view/full/16526, accessed March 1, 2012.

[121] Ibid.

[122] WarOnWant.Org, "Landless in Brazil."

[123] Ibid.

[124] WarOnWant.Org., "Factsheet."

[125] Ibid.

[126] Rosilene Cristina Rocha, "Experiences on the Implementation of the Right to Food—Brazil," International Right to Food Forum, FAO, October 2008, www.fao.org/righttofood/rtf_forum/files/Session02_Country%20Presentations_Brazil_Rosilene%20Rocha.ppt, accessed April 18, 2012.

[127] Sue Branford, "Food Sovereignty: Reclaiming the Global Food System," War on Want, October 2011: 33, www.waronwant.org/attachments/Food%20sovereignty%20report.pdf, accessed February 27, 2012.

[128] "MST Women Occupy Field of Forestry and Cellulose Company in Bahia," La Revolucion Vive, March 1, 2012, www.larevolucionvive.org.ve/spip.php?article1980&lang=es, accessed April 18, 2012.

[129] Frances Moore Lappé and Anna Lappé, *Hope's Edge: The Next Diet for a Small Planet* (New York: Tarcher, 2002), 80.

# The Ethics of Agricultural Biotechnology

Beth Burrows

> *In every fancied case of harm, apply the rule, "If the community is not harmed, I am not harmed either." But if the community should indeed be harmed, never rage at the culprit; rather, find out at what point his vision failed him.*
>
> —*The Meditations*, Marcus Aurelius

I grew up in the Middle West of the United States in the 1950s, strongly advised not to discuss religion or morals or ethics or sex with anyone. I was told such conversation was impolite and usually led to arguments. Later in the 1960s and 1970s, I learned that there were "different strokes for different folks" and, with that understanding, I was able to avoid serious ethical discussions for two more decades. Whenever I stumbled upon "values education" in public schools, I was told that the conversation was only intended to ensure that we had values and was not meant to interfere with the content of those values. So, the few times we did discuss "ethics" in any guided, public way, it was only to agree to disagree and then—before anyone got too upset about the disagreements—to celebrate diversity. By the end of the millennium, there hardly seemed a point in talking about "ethics" at all. In the United States, either we had "gotten" ethics privately (from home or church or elsewhere) or we hadn't (in which case, that fact was presumably noted somewhere in our records). In any case, we were not prepared to discuss ethics publicly. As a result, today I am not even sure how to talk about ethics, who is "ethical" enough to lead the discussion, and what the conversation would be like, beyond starting with, "What do you think?," listening a while, and then saying, "That's interesting."

I did not mention any of this when, a few years back, I was asked to write an article on the ethics of agriculture. Instead, I felt flattered and made the mistake of saying yes. A few days later, I panicked. Asked to consider, discover, or create a set of principles for right conduct, I panicked. With an empty bag of ethical tools, I began to imagine the public humiliation of attempting to climb a steep mountain on ethically flabby legs. A few more days passed and I realized things were worse than I had first imagined. Whose ethics was I to talk about? Whose highest expectations for whose conduct? My own, as citizen? As eater? The agricultural community's? The biotechnology industry's? That of the people of the United States? That of people generally, the whole species? What exactly was I looking for? Was I simply to judge whether agriculture or agricultural biotechnology was "ethical"—whatever "ethical" meant? Could I assume—against all earlier teaching—that everybody's ethics, all our highest expectations and aspirations for conduct, were the same, that there actually was one ethical standard for judging agriculture?

My confusion—ethical or not—was total. Not only was I not skilled in ethical discourse, I wasn't sure what I had agreed to write about.

The local library was not helpful; only one book in the ethics section of the Edmonds Public Library contained the word *agriculture*. And most of the other books didn't seem to agree on ethics at all. Apparently, there are different types of ethics.

My next research step involved a telephone call to a farmer I know, a man of great patience and kindness. "Hello, Beth," he sighed and asked, "Have you called to pick another fight about genetic engineering?"

Half wondering if he was right, I said I was trying to understand the goal of farming, what agriculture ought to be, and how it ought to behave. He sighed again and asked about my family. Eventually he said that agriculture ought to feed people, everyone, and that it ought to earn the farmer a living. He talked about "loving the life" and how people "ought to know what they're doing" and he asked me not to quote him because he didn't want to fight with anyone; he said he "ought to mind his own business." I next phoned other farmers. The ones willing to talk about ethics added to the first farmer's list some other "oughts" (and "shoulds") about "taking care of" the land and the animals and the seed. After several phone calls, I had a short list of "oughts"—all from farmers who didn't want to be quoted. Oddly, I noticed, their "oughts" about agriculture weren't much different from a list of "wants" I had made almost a decade earlier.

It was in 1992, at the end of a daylong town hall meeting sponsored by Farm Aid. Panel Two had spent hours discussing "The future of US agriculture: what do we want to eat and how do we want it grown?" The panel was taking one-minute statements from the floor and one person after another stepped up to say how wrong everything was in agriculture. The room was heavy with depression by the time my turn came. "I am an eater," I said, "and as an eater, I would like to say thanks to all the family farmers for the great job they've done in feeding us all these years." I received a round of applause and, thus encouraged, I added:

> I would also like to state for the record: I don't want pesticides in my food, I don't want rBGH in my milk, I don't want human genes in my pork, I don't want to eat the products of patented seeds, I don't want tomatoes that sit on a shelf for a year, I don't want food that's been harvested by farmers and farmworkers who can't earn a living, I don't want food that was grown at the price of the soil or the water or the farmer anywhere, and I don't want imported food that's been grown on the backs of exploited workers or in the degraded soils of any country.
>
> What do I want? I want to know what I'm eating, I want it properly grown, properly labeled, properly inspected, and properly

costed....What I want is the democracy I thought I grew up in and the food I used to find in the stores. I want healthy farmers and healthy farms everywhere. I want to eat without fear and live without fear and a hundred years from now, I want one of my relatives to stand up somewhere and once again say thanks to the family farmer ... for the superb job they've been doing all these years!

Looking at that old speech and removing the specifics, I was surprised to find that my "wants" and the farmers' "oughts" contained similar themes. Implicitly, we all held deep expectations—maybe even the skeleton of what we hold to be "self-evident"—about agriculture. In very different ways, we expressed a sense that agriculture ought to feed people—everyone (now and in the future), that the people who engaged in agriculture ought to be able to earn a living, that agriculture was an activity that ought to take place in a community and ought to be subject to community standards, and that there were extensive responsibilities connected with agriculture, including those between farmers and those whom they feed. Every "ethical" strand, including the responsibilities connected to land, seed, and water, seemed related to an understanding that agriculture was a social activity.

My next research move was to see whether these themes were unique, whether they—or other themes—appeared in other places where other people discussed their goals for agriculture. I looked at two kinds of statements within easy reach of my computer: declarations and sign-on letters that have been issued over the years by activists and current websites of agricultural biotechnology companies. Let me talk about one of each of those.

In 1998, about forty women from Asia, Africa, Europe, North and South America wrote a statement that was presented to the Plenary of the Fourth Conference of the Parties to the Convention on Biological Diversity.[1] The women were the first participants in Diverse Women for Diversity.

All activists and scholars concerned about food and agriculture issues, their joint statement was a celebration of diversity, sustainability, responsibility, community, self-determination, and the need for precaution. Although they used quite a different language than the farmers I had telephoned or my own long-ago Farm Aid statement, the words of the women's statement reflected the same broad themes. The farmers had said that agriculture ought to feed everyone; the women sought "a world of nutritious, safe, and affordable food for all." The women asserted that "communities have boundaries and rights" and "sovereignty ... with respect to their knowledge and resources" and they asserted that "... we and our communities will make the decisions that affect our lives, our livelihoods, our lands, and the community of species with which we share our space." The women did not use a language of "ought" or "want"; instead they made assertions and rejections, including the rejection of "ways of relating" and "technologies and products" ... "that roll back hard won social and environmental protections, appropriate and monopolise the living diversity of our planet, and threaten our democracies, our farms, our livelihoods, our cultures, and our communities" and "the food security, health and well-being of any living being...."

Their language was filled with the images of a community "minding" its "own business" and asserting its own standards.

Superficially, there seemed to be one assertion in the women's statement that did not quite match the farmers' words or my own at Farm Aid. The women said:

> We recognise the wisdom that joins precaution to the search for knowledge. We see that precaution is needed to prevent harm to all that we love and value and steward and seek to understand, and we know that whosoever arrogantly discards the precautionary principle puts at risk the very basis of our lives.

Certainly, the need to value and steward had been there in the farmers' concern for the land and for animals and seeds; would it be such a stretch, I wondered, to consider the call for precaution simply a differently worded response to long experience with people who "ought to know what they're doing" but do not?

Next, I turned to the website of Monsanto Corporation, the world's largest agricultural biotechnology company: www.monsanto.com, as it appeared in January 2001. From that website, I learned that the company's stated "business purpose and mission" are based on a vision of "abundant food and a healthy environment." While "abundant food" is not quite a vision of an agriculture that "ought to feed … everyone" or even a vision of "food for all"—indeed, some might argue that having a goal of "abundant food" without intending to feed everyone is the US agriculture we have today—still, that part of the Monsanto mission statement was at least close in sentiment to the statements of the farmers and myself and the women. Whether or not we all share an intention to feed everyone, I think we would all agree that there ought to be enough food to do so.

Reading on in 2001, I discovered that the company pledged to "work to achieve sustainable agriculture through new technology and new practices" and through dialogue, transparency, respect, sharing, and delivering benefits—all terms whose meaning the website carefully explained. The explanations included the company's intention to comply with regulatory systems that "are science-based … and that make timely decisions."

Despite the emphasis on "new technology and new practices," the website, like the statements of the farmers and the women, tacitly affirmed that agriculture occurs in the context of a community and ought to be subject to that community's standards. The identity of the community of reference was quite different for the company than it had been for the farmers, the women, or myself. And the willingness to comply with standards was constrained by critically different beliefs and values (e.g., science-based regulatory systems that make timely decisions versus the precautionary principle), but still, if I don't get too picky, if I resist the temptation to look for the devil in the details, it may be possible to see the very broad outlines of an already-existing shared ethic, or perhaps a shared meta-ethic, of agriculture.

That possibility in mind, I felt encouraged to hope that we may all be using the same map to climb the same ethical mountain concerning agriculture. We may not need to construct an entirely new set of ethics for agriculture or for eating. We may be able to use the ethics that we already refer to and expect others to recognize when we state where we ought to be going (or what we ought to be doing).

So what's the problem? Why do I still feel dissatisfied?

Perhaps the problem isn't ethics, per se. It may be that the "ethical" difficulties that prevent us from agreeing on the specifics—those "details" that I avoided—are not so much in the content of our ethics as in the structure of the economic and political environments that influence the order in which we place our ethical values, the choices we make about whether and when to exercise those values, and the consequences we perceive emanating from the choices we make.

Let me be honest about why I was thinking about the ethics in the first place. Isn't it because things in agriculture are not working as they "ought to be"? Isn't it because we are already measuring our agricultural failures (and our ethical violations) in terms of (1) losses of topsoil, fertility, habitat, species, varieties, yields, farmers, and rural cultures; (2) gains in pesticide use, soil salinity, soil compaction, water pollution, and concentration of ownership at every level of the food chain;[2] (3) continuing patterns of overconsumption in some communities and starvation in others; and (4) continuing patterns of farmer and farmworker oppression throughout the world?

Let's remember where we—and agriculture—were at when the last millennium ended: At the end of the twentieth century, people in a variety of communities, faced with what they perceived to be the forcible penetration of their agricultural markets and fields by the products of a new technology—genetic engineering—objected. On the brink of what they were being told was a revolution in agriculture and aquaculture, they objected. Still dealing with the unintended side effects of past well-meaning technologies (pesticides, for example), they considered that this new technology, and the political and legal arrangements created to facilitate its spread, might put their farmers at risk, their food security at risk, their food systems into the hands of others, and deny them a part in the decisions that affected their lives, including the very basic decision about what they would eat.[3] They were, to put it mildly, upset.

In 1997, Freida Morris and Martine Benjamin wrote about that upset:

> Some of the global concern stems from worry about the safety of genetically engineered food. Some of it comes from ethical and environmental objection to tampering with the natural world, and some of it is in response to the affront of having meaningful food choices co-opted by far-off corporations. Without mandatory LABELS to indicate when this food had been genetically engineered, those who wish NOT to partake of such food will be condemned to uncertainty about whether our vegetables, for example, contain DNA from bacteria, viruses, insects, animals, and even other people. Effectively, religious and ethical choices will become the domain of food manufacturers and seed companies. We oppose this new form of bondage. We object to the New Pharaohs who would force us to eat the unlabelled food of THEIR choice.[4]

That's certainly how it looked when US and Canadian representatives at the biosafety protocol negotiations refused to even consider meaningful biosafety if it meant labeling their export commodities, that's how it looked when (speaking for the United States) Rafe Pomerance ranted at the negotiations in Cartagena that he wasn't going to let anything—and he was referring to the wishes of the majority of people in the world—he wasn't going to let anything get in the way of $68 billion-a-year industry in the United States, and that's how it looked when the United States tried to throw biosafety into the WTO and make environmental and human health considerations the subject of decision making by trade experts.[5]

People protested, sometimes massively, sometimes individually.[6] Sometimes the protests were about the patent laws and treaty arrangements that facilitated the development and spread of the technology, sometimes they were about lack of labeling and the effective denial of meaningful food choices. It wasn't only farmers and environmentalists and consumer advocates who protested. Had the biotechnology industry leadership been a bit more alert, they might have remembered their own childhoods and noted that the right to control one's own food choices is one of the oldest and most cherished forms of self-determination. Remember the first George Bush, former president of the United States? That George, hardly a radical guy, once said that he didn't care what other people told him, he didn't like broccoli and he wasn't going to eat it anymore. It didn't matter to that George whether some people thought the broccoli was safe or was good for him or was the result of hard work by a lot of well-intended people. That George wasn't going to eat it and, as president of the United States, he staunchly asserted that he no longer had to eat it.

By the end of the last millennium, people around the world just wanted what George wanted, the right to eat what they wanted. And some of them didn't want genetically engineered food.

On the political plate at the end of the 1990s (and stretching into the first decade of the current millennium) were a whole host of issues about agriculture. And they were piled on top of a whole host of other unresolved issues—about how we make decisions about technology, about who is in charge of the decision making, about what is the practical meaning of democracy, about whether science alone can or should address the issues of concern, about how we make judgments in the face of scientific uncertainty, about why and how the public should be involved in decision making, about how to compare the significance of the risks and uncertainties that are attached to different technologies, and about how to create an atmosphere of trust so we can start working on these issues.[7] And while all that was on our plate, a long series of events was operating to poison the wells of our ability to have meaningful discussions with each other. To mention just a few of the highlights:

In the last General Agreement on Tariffs and Trade, the treaty that created the World Trade Organization, much of the world was forced, for the sake of desperately needed market openings, to take up an alien patent system and extend patents to living organisms. Once patentable, all living organisms and their parts, all biodiversity, became valuable commodities in the marketplace. At the same time, those whose biodiversity had already been appropriated to create most of the food we eat and much of the medicine we use were not paid back or recognized for what had been taken from them. They were also not consulted on its use or given a royalty. The fact that many were spiritually offended by what had been done was hardly even noticed. Some of those whose plants and animals and the knowledge of how to use them had been appropriated without their consent called the arrangement "biopiracy" and resisted not only the patent system that seemed to encourage biopiracy, but the entry into their markets of costly patented seeds and animals that were derived, at least in part, from germplasm that had been stolen from them.[8]

Agricultural biotechnology companies, for whatever reasons, tested genetically engineered products in countries without well-developed regulatory regimes. When the presence of these products became apparent, people worried they had been tricked into accepting something whose environmental and human health ramifications they didn't know.[9] They felt as if genetically engineered food had been dumped on them. In early 2001, one food industry consultant indicated that market flooding had been the intentional means of gaining "acceptance" of genetically engineered food in the United States.[10] That same year, one wary country, desperate for food aid, refused a gift of genetically engineered food even though it was intended for use as animal feed.[11]

Regulatory agencies in the United States, the world's foremost proponent of genetically engineered crops, did not publish all the details of environmental risk assessments because of the need to protect "confidential business information."[12] This, together with the fact that testing was not mandatory for genetically engineered food,[13] led scientists and activists in many places to suspect that the tests, if they were done at all, may not have been adequate to protect human and environmental health.

US regulatory agencies, particularly the Food and Drug Administration (FDA), allowed those they regulated to do the research about the safety of their own products.[14] This created further suspicion about the results of testing.

The vice president for food and agriculture of the Biotechnology Industry Organization, upon hearing that monarch butterflies might be put at risk by the pollen of genetically engineered Bt corn, commented by saying that "more monarchs succumb to high-velocity collisions with car windshields than ever encounter corn pollen."[15] Some people were appalled at the quality of his response and questioned the industry's commitment to biosafety. "If more children are killed by hunger than by the gun in a high school in Colorado, does that mean we should not be concerned about the gun?" I remember asking.[16]

The agricultural biotechnology industry resisted the labeling of genetically engineered food, saying (in some fora) they could not discern enough difference to label.[17] When scientific tests were devised to identify food as being genetically engineered,[18] people became suspicious of subsequent pronouncements by the industry. When the industry resisted the labeling of genetically engineered food, saying it was unnecessary and might even be misleading, the food was safe, and it was substantially equivalent to what people were already eating anyway, some people eventually figured out that lack of labeling effectively means a lack of liability for the manufacturer, and a lack of any ability to trace the long-term human health consumption effects for the consumer.

In these same years, there was greater and greater concentration in the seed industry. Only a handful of companies controlled most of the world's commercial seed and with the granting of patents on life-forms extended to new seed varieties, varieties could effectively be owned for a time and farmers could be forced to pay royalties and technology fees. And given the inevitability of pollen flow, eventually every farmer could expect to have someone's patented genes become part of his crop, whether he wanted them or not. And once they did, the farmer, even if he was angry that someone else's damned pollen had contaminated his crop, would be considered the criminal, and would eventually owe patent royalties to the owner of the genes that had trespassed on his land.

And in these same years, the farmers in the developing world would come to be encouraged to use the patented descendants of the seeds their ancestors had once had freely shared. And once they did that, once they bought the new seed and stopped saving seed as they had for centuries, they not only lost the old varieties but were trapped in a system that indentured them to the seed companies. And if they resisted buying the new seeds, even if they resisted because they were not convinced about the safety of the new seeds, they were told they were causing starvation in their countries. And if they thought to demand royalties for the germplasm their ancestors once had given freely, they were called greedy.

And in these same years, as industrialized agriculture reached its full maturity, consumers in the North learned about mad cow disease and mercury in tuna and later about avian flu and the problem of sea lice in farmed fish.

And in these same years, scientists at the highest levels publicly disparaged those who asked questions about agricultural biotechnology. One example that comes to mind occurred at a meeting of the National Academy of Science and Engineering conference on "Incorporating Science, Economics, and Sociology in Developing Sanitary and Phytosanitary Standards in International Trade," January 25–27, 1999. According to my notes of the meeting, Jean-Christophe Bureau, of Station d'Economie et Sociologie Rurales, Institut National de la Recherche Agronomique (INRA), France, began his presentation on "Accounting for Consumer Preferences in International Trade" by asking, "Who are these people who are afraid of GMOs? In my labo-ratory, we think they are little old ladies in England." (He got a big laugh from the distinguished little old men in the audience.)

And in those same years, US and other Northern diplomats, in-cluding Canadian, tried to force others to adapt their own worldview and level of risk aversion. In forum after forum, government represen-tatives from the North appeared to put trade expansion above all other goals;[19] industry tried to subvert the opposition by the use of spies;[20] the academy attempted to keep the "opposition" out of the discussion because, as the American Society of Plant Physiologists claimed, the opposition's arguments were "more confusing to the audience than ... enlightening";[21] the precautionary principle, the better-safe-than-sorry principle that most people use every day, was labeled radical and scorned by US officialdom as a basis for making decisions;[22] the US public was expected to trust its regulatory system but could plainly see a revolving employment door between industry and the regulators;[23] the law persecuted a farmer for patent infringement because geneti-cally engineered pollen had blown onto his field;[24] public money was used to invent sterile seeds and some governments acted like it was a wonderful idea;[25] academic science became indentured to industry because the public was unwilling to fund its work and the academy was unwilling to resist the temptation of being funded by industry; scientists, from Pusztai to Chapela, were persecuted for the interpreta-tion they gave to their results;[26] other scientists pretended that an ab-sence of evidence is the same as evidence of absence of effects;[27] little biosafety funding led to little biosafety research and little biosafety research led to little evidence of lack of biosafety and little evidence of lack got interpreted as "there are no problems"; biosafety was per-ceived, at least by some in the agricultural biotechnology industry, as an exercise in public relations;[28] academic scientists appeared to give no honor nor research funds nor encouragement to the students who would become regulators; many in the industrialized world still be-lieved that future generations could correct their every mistake; even though there was clear evidence that people everywhere could have been fed without a new technology, people in some places still starved; some gave higher priority to the growth of a new technology than to the exercise of individual civil rights.[29] When all of this and much, much more was on our political plates, we may not have lacked ethics so much as we lacked the political will to implement and enforce the ethics we shared and gave lip service to but rarely ever implemented.

Do I have to bring the scenario up to date, to list the latest company acquisitions by Monsanto, the latest regulatory outrages in Europe or Australia or India, the latest hateful crops, the latest infamous acts to ensure the dominance of patented seeds even in countries racked by war, do I have to make another long list before we can agree that we know what is wrong? We know we ought to be feeding everyone, we know the community to which we belong is an ecological as well as a political community, and we know the standards of basic minimal decency (and self-preservation).

Earlier, I let a corporate website off the ethical hotseat too easily. Frankly, I did it because if I were really to believe that the people in corporations do not share ethics with the rest of us, I might have to examine the possibility that a significant proportion of the world's food system is in the hands of sociopaths.

I think that we have allowed a system to flourish that creates little or no incentive for eliciting ethical behavior on anyone's part. There is ample psychological evidence to indicate that even children who know how to behave "altruistically" do not do so in the absence of all incentives and models.[30] In the existing political environment, at least wherever profit is put before "feeding people everywhere," even the reputation of "ethics" has fallen on hard times.

In 1992, I attended a conference in Seattle entitled "The Future of Intellectual Property Protection for Biotechnology in the United States, Europe, and Japan." For three days eminent speakers discussed patents. The last day of the conference, one of the panelists—I didn't record his name—bemoaned the situation in Europe where at that time it was nearly impossible to obtain a patent on any form of life. The panelist hoped his colleagues in other places would never have to face the situation he faced with "environmentalists and those who would bring ethics and other irrational considerations to the table." Those were the words I recorded that day: "ethics and other irrational considerations."

No member of the audience challenged the pairing of the words "ethics" and "other irrational considerations." Not one learned lawyer. Not one high official. Not one heavily credentialed academic. Not one expert.

A year earlier, biologist Martha Crouch had spoken to a conference of the National Agricultural Biotechnology Council in the United States. She talked of the religion and cosmology that supported indigenous systems of agriculture in Liberia and Mexico, and she noted that in those places "… people have direct incentive to use the land wisely, they have the power to do so, and they have the knowledge to be able to participate in feedback loops." She went on to ask:

> What underlying rituals and cosmologies guide technological agriculture, and who has the power to respond to feedback? In technological societies such as ours, the world revolves around global industrialism … all things are profane.…Culture has been uprooted as the sense of place has been taken out of the picture; the varieties and techniques are deemed successful to the extent they can be applied to vast areas, rather than specific locales. Less than 5 percent of the population is involved directly in growing food, so very few people have the opportunity to see what happens on the land. Thus the knowledge to respond to changes is in the hands of a small fraction of the community. The rural people who see the water, soil, and organisms on a daily basis are often not the same ones who have the power to respond, because urban generated global market forces drive the adoption of genotypes and practices.… Monocultures are a logical outcome of the business worldview.

Outlining how the transformation to monocultures takes place, Crouch said:

By turning everything it touches into commodities, biotechnology also has the effect of making products and processes that fit more easily into the global market. Seeds that used to be saved by the farmer now must be purchased every year, for example. Genotypes that used to be specific to a slope, soil type, and rainfall amount in a particular valley are replaced by a genotype that will grow in a whole region. Markets that respond to short term increases in production replace subsistence or local markets that respond to the need for a secure food supply in unpredictable conditions. Diversity is lost.[31]

We may analyze the problems that bring us to where we are today in terms of mistaken priorities or human cupidity or corporate dominance or rampant capitalism or unbridled globalization or plain old-fashioned greed. Whatever the language of the analysis, I repeat—I do not think we should attribute our problems to a lack of ethics. We have ethics. We know the broad outlines of what we should do. What we lack is the political will to implement and enforce the ethics that told us years ago that something has gone terribly wrong in agriculture and in much of the rest of our lives.

Those of us who do not go hungry have a choice at every meal, with every bite. We can let our food choices be constrained by history and international trade agreements, we can continue to swallow the repressive policies some food represents, continue to pretend that we can't afford to pay a little more for our food than we do in the North, continue to accept a patenting system that seems too difficult and complicated to change, continue to pretend we are all just "little people" who can do nothing but be cola-ed, starbucked, starlinked, big macked, and bushwhacked to death. Or we can resist by saying, "No patents on life," by making all our food choices ethical, ecological, political, and—dare I say it—sensual choices.

Many years ago, early on in the discussions about a genetically engineered food system, about the time a product came down the food pipeline called the Flavr Savr tomato—it was a tomato with a thick skin, engineered to travel well without bruising—at about the time that Flavr Savr appeared, a rural sociologist and professor at the University of Wisconsin named Jack Kloppenburg opened a conference in San Francisco by hurling a big red heritage tomato against the wall of the conference center. As the tomato's wonderful fragrance filled the room and we watched its abundant juices ooze down the wall, Jack turned to the audience and said, "Now, that's a tomato."

The food you eat or grow or purchase affects the future. Not just your future and your family's future but the future of the entire world. When people choose locally grown food and/or organic food, they are not only avoiding industrial agriculture and fast food. They are also voting for a sustainable future and against a network of supply and demand that destroys human health, local communities, traditional ways of life, and the environment.

### Statement by Diverse Women for Diversity to the Plenary of the Fourth Conference of the Parties to the Convention on Biological Diversity on May 4, 1998

We are women from diverse regions and diverse movements committed to the continuation of the rich and abundant life on Earth. We come from different backgrounds, in full recognition of our history, and we believe there are and should be limits to human use and appropriation of the Earth and its diverse living beings. We take responsibility for our use of the things of this Earth and demand that all others of our species do the same.

We are moral human beings. We know that we occupy a given time and given space and are responsible for how we live in that time and the condition in which we leave that space for the future. We do not accept distrust, greed, violence, and fear as ways of relating to each other or to other beings. We reject such ways of relating, whether they take the form of negative personal actions, unacceptable products, or structural alliances among transnational corporations and national governments that trade weapons, risk wars, and form free trade treaties and other devices that roll back hard won social and environmental protections, appropriate and monopolise the living diversity of our planet, and threaten our democracies, our farms, our livelihoods, our cultures, and our communities.

We support Article 8j of this Convention because we recognise that communities have boundaries and rights. And we insist that the sovereignty of communities with respect to their knowledge and resources take precedence over the freedom of outsiders to access and appropriate that knowledge and those resources.

We assert that we and our communities will make the decisions that affect our lives, our livelihoods, our lands, and the community of species with which we share our space.

We recognise the wisdom that joins precaution to the search for knowledge. We see that precaution is needed to prevent harm to all that we love and value and steward and seek to understand and we know that whoever arrogantly discards the precautionary principle puts at risk the very basis of our lives.

We seek a world of good health and nutritious, safe, and affordable food for all.

We reject the patenting of life in any form and we avoid those technologies and products that threaten the food security, health and well-being of any living being.

We recognise and celebrate the diversity and interrelatedness of species, cultures, and ways of knowing. We reject that which does not sustain the diversity of life and culture and so we reject the World Bank, the International Monetary Fund, the World Trade Organisation, the Multilateral Agreement on Investments, and other such agreements and collusions. And we support the Convention on Biological Diversity, this important little treaty that creates tiny spaces for people to act and beckons us all to take a small step in a new direction and move towards mutual respect and joint well-being.

## Endnotes

1. The Fourth Conference of the Parties (COP 4) to the Convention on Biological Diversity met in Bratislava, Slovakia, in May 1998. Diverse Women for Diversity, of which the author is a cofounder, held its first meeting a few days before the first plenary of the COP 4. At that first plenary, Diverse Women was invited to present its statement to the opening plenary of COP 4.

2. For more details on this, see the work and the website of the ETC Group.

3. See, for example, Vandana Shiva, *Stolen Harvest: The Hijacking of the Global Food Supply* (Cambridge, MA: South End Press, 2000).

4. Freida Morris and Martine Benjamin, "Haggadah for the Last Seder without Genetically Engineered Food," Edmonds Institute, Washington, 1997.

5. See the description in Beth Burrows, "Resurrecting the Ugly American," *Food and Water Journal,* Spring 1999: 32–35.

6. See Beth Burrows, "How Do You Spell Patents? P-I-R-A-C-Y," *Boycott Quarterly* 1, no. 3 (Winter 1994): 4–7.

7. For a discussion of many of these issues, see Economic and Global Research Council Change Program Special Briefing #5, "The Politics of GM Food: Risk, Science and the Public Trust," October 1999, www.susx.ac.uk/Units/gec/gecko/gm-brief.htm.

8. Patents on life were found repugnant for a variety of reasons. See Beth Burrows, "Where Nothing Is Sacred," in *Conserving the Sacred for Biodiversity Management,* eds. P. S. Ramakrishnan, K. G. Saxena, and U. M. Chandrashekara (New Delhi: Oxford & IBH, 1998).

9. Over the years, there have been many reports from Central and South America and central and eastern Europe of unauthorized testing and distribution of genetically engineered organisms in countries with little or no regulation of genetic engineering. See, e.g., Iza Kruszewska, "Playing God—Genetic Engineering of Food in Central and Eastern Europe," Greenpeace International, 1996; and Reuters, "Russia Denies Knowledge of GM Maize Imports," September 17, 1999.

10. Quoted in Stuart Laidlaw, "Starlink Fallout Could Cost Billions," *Toronto Star,* Edition 1, January 9, 2001.

11. See, e.g., Agence France Presse, "US Withdraws Genetically Engineered Animal Feed Donations after Bosnia's Hesitation," January 30, 2001, www.centraleurope.com/bosniatoday/news.php3?id=273802.

12. See Jane Rissler and Margaret Mellon, "Public Access to Biotechnology Applications," *Natural Resources and Environment* 4(3): 29–31, 54–58. See also: Beth Burrows, "Confidential Business Information (and the Cost of Doing Business as Usual)," Third World Network Briefing Paper, 5th Meeting of the Biosafety Working Group, August 17–19, 1998, Montreal.

13. For information on US regulatory oversight of genetic engineering, see http://aphis.usda.gov/biotech/OECD/usregs.htm.

[14] Ibid.

[15] Biotechnology Industry Organization, Press Release, "Academic Researchers and Industry Associations Agree Reports on Bt Crop Impact on Monarch Butterflies Overblown," June 21, 1999, www.bio.org/news/article.html?XP_PUB=press_release.

[16] Beth Burrows, "The Environment, Technology and Intellectual Property: The Politics of Eating" (unpublished presentation given at Wenatchee Valley College conference on Genetic Engineering and Food, November 1, 1999).

[17] This was frequently the argument of the US delegation in the early discussions of biosafety at the Convention on Biological Diversity.

[18] The first tests were devised by Dr. John Fagan, a molecular biologist who founded Genetic ID.

[19] The dominance of the trade ethic has been apparent since the days of the North American Free Trade Agreement negotiations, if not before.

[20] See John Stauber and Sheldon Rampton, *Toxic Sludge Is Good for You* (Monroe, ME: Common Courage Press, 1995), 55–59.

[21] Brian Hyps, "Note from ASPP Public Affairs Director," in Peggy G. Lemaux, "Safe in the Ivory Tower?," *ASPP News* 26, no. 6 (November/December 1999): 12, http://ucbiotech.org/resources/biotech/talks/misc/ivrytwr.html.

[22] The constant refrain of US negotiators at Convention on Biological Diversity and Biosafety negotiations was that the United States advocated a "precautionary approach" but not the precautionary principle. For discussion of the precautionary principle, see *Protecting Public Health and the Environment: Implementing the Precautionary Principle,* eds. Carolyn Raffensperger and Joel Tickner (Washington, DC: Island Press, 1999).

[23] See early publications of the Edmonds Institute on the revolving door.

[24] For the story of Percy Schmeiser, see Daniel Girard, "David and Goliath in a Food Fight: Monsanto Co. Alleges Farmer Unlawfully Used Its Genetically Modified Canola Seed," *Toronto Star,* April 15, 2000, www.thestar.com/thestar/back_issues/index.html; and David Margoshes, "Saskatchewan Farmer Battles Monsanto, Sues Them Back," *Vancouver Sun,* April 14, 1999: B1.

[25] For information about Terminator technology, see the website of the ETC Group: www.etcgroup.org. See also: Martha Crouch, "How the Terminator Terminates: An Explanation for the Non-scientist of a Remarkable Patent for Killing Second Generation Seeds of Crop Plants," Edmonds Institute, Washington, 1998.

[26] For the story of Dr. Arpad Pusztai, for example, see Peta Firth, "Leaving a Bad Taste," *Scientific American,* May 1999; Christopher Leake and Lorraine Fraser, "Scientist in Frankenstein Food Alert Is Proved Right. Accusations of Cover-up after Top Pathologist Backs the Professor Whose Tests Brought Him Humiliation," *UK Mail,* January 31, 1999; Michael Sean, Gillard Laurie Flynn, and Andy Rowell, "International Scientists Back Shock Findings of

Suppressed Research into Modified Food," *Guardian*, February 12, 1999: 6; "Research into Food Safety—Chronology," *Guardian*, February 12, 1999: 6.

[27] The gaps in our knowledge about genetic engineering and its impacts have been documented and discussed for several years. See, for example, Jack D. Doyle, Guenther Stotsky, Gwendolyn McClung, and Charles W. Hendricks, "Effects of Genetically Engineered Microorganisms on Microbial Populations and Processes in Natural Habitats," *Advances in Applied Microbiology* 40 (1995): 237ff. The oft-cited notion that there is no evidence of the negative effects of such organisms sounds hollow in the face of the realization that there has been insufficient ecological research to draw that conclusion.

[28] See Kurt Eichenwald, Gina Kolata, and Melody Petersen, "Biotechnology Food: From the Lab to a Debacle," *New York Times*, January 25, 2001: 1.

[29] *Moore v. Regents of the University of California* 793P.2d 479, 271 Cal. Rptr. 146 (1990). See also: George J. Annas, "Outrageous Fortune: Selling Other People's Cells," in *Standard of Care: The Law of American Bioethics* (New Delhi: Oxford University Press, 1993), 167–177.

[30] See, e.g., Albert Bandura and Richard H. Walters, *Social Learning and Personality Development* (New York: Holt, Rinehart, and Winston, 1963); William W. Hartup and Nancy L. Smothergill, eds., *The Young Child: Reviews of Research*, vol. 1 (Washington, DC: National Association for the Education of the Young Child, 1967).

[31] Martha Crouch, "Biotechnology and Sustainable Agriculture," in *Ethics and Patenting of Transgenic Organisms* (Ithaca, NY: National Agricultural Biotechnology Council, 1992), 94–98.

# Food Politics, the Food Movement, and Public Health

Marion Nestle

The principal theme of any discussion on food politics is that food choices are political as well as personal. That notion, perhaps surprising when my book *Food Politics* was first published in 2002, is now well recognized. Then, personal responsibility was assumed to be the primary determinant of food choice. Today, it is widely accepted that food marketing influences food choices and that our "eat more" food environment—one that promotes food that is highly varied, ubiquitous, convenient, close at hand, inexpensive, presented in large portions, and eaten frequently—encourages "mindless" consumption of more calories than are needed or noticed.[1]

Also increasingly recognized are the contradictory results of this environment. On the one hand, overweight has become *normal* among adults and children—in all but the poorest or war-torn countries of the world, increasing proportions of the population are overweight. On the other hand, we are witnessing the development of an international movement to reverse obesity trends and to promote more healthful diet and activity patterns, especially among children. This movement is expressed most forcefully in demands for restrictions on food marketing to children and for legal and legislative actions to ensure such restrictions, particularly in schools.

These restrictions are opposed even more forcefully by food companies. One example is the efforts of the sugar industry to prevent international agencies from suggesting that populations would be healthier if they ate less sugar. Because science provides circumstantial, but not definitive, evidence for an association between sugar intake, obesity, and other health problems, "science-based" standards in the United States allow up to 25 percent of daily calories from added sugars, an upper limit that sugar trade associations prefer to interpret as a recommendation. In the early 2000s, the World Health Organization (WHO) began developing a global strategy to reduce risk factors for chronic disease, obesity among them. In 2003, it published a research report that advised restricting intake of "free" (added) sugars to 10 percent or less of daily calories. Although this percentage was similar to that embedded in the United States Department of Agriculture (USDA)'s 1992 Pyramid (7–13 percent of calories depending on total intake), sugar industry groups strenuously objected, enlisted senators to pressure the Department of Health and Human Services (DHHS) secretary to withdraw funding from WHO, and induced the DHHS chief counsel to send a critique of the report to WHO that had essentially been written by industry lobbyists. When released in 2004, WHO's "Global Strategy on Diet, Physical Activity and Health" omitted any mention of the background report or the 10 percent recommendation.[2]

## The Anti-Obesity Movement

In seeking to reverse rising rates of overweight, especially among children, health advocates as well as lawyers, legislators, and investment bankers have singled out food-industry marketing as a significant influence on food choice. They have put food companies on notice that selling junk foods to children is no longer acceptable. Food companies, they say, must improve their products and marketing practices or face losses of sales, legal challenges, and regulatory restrictions.

*Food Politics* was not alone in predicting this reaction. By 2003, three British investment banking firms had warned food industry clients that obesity posed a threat to company profits. UBS Warburg, for example, advised food companies to stop hiding behind personal responsibility. With sales of organics and healthier foods growing rapidly, "The issue for food and drink companies is whether they can adapt to these changes (or even lead them) or will they be left behind promoting anachronistic processed foods and sugary drinks while their target customer has moved on."[3] Investment banks advised companies to produce healthier foods and market them more responsibly—or face lawsuits and regulations.

Investment analysts view marketing to children as the industry's Achilles' heel. As *Food Politics* explains, the personal responsibility argument does not apply to children too young to distinguish sales pitches from information. Marketing junk food to young people crosses ethical boundaries and makes companies vulnerable to advocacy challenges.

Since 2002, academic researchers, national government agencies, and international health agencies have thoroughly documented the effects of food marketing on children's food attitudes and behavior.[4] In the United States, the Institute of Medicine (IOM) summarized this research in three reports published from 2004 to 2006;[5] the second of these reports focused on food marketing. It makes chilling reading. The IOM considered 123 peer-reviewed studies examining how food marketing affects children's food preferences and requests, eating habits, and body weight. Its cautious conclusion: the idea that food marketing increases the risk of obesity "cannot be rejected." Attribute the caution to politics. In preparing this report, the IOM operated under a handicap. Because Congress requires government-sponsored committees to make public all documents used in deliberations, food companies refused to reveal proprietary information about their marketing practices. Even so, the report describes the extent of the research enterprise devoted to selling foods to children; the methods food companies use to identify the psychological underpinnings of children's food choices; the ways these methods affect children's requests for brands; and the effects of such choices on health. Selling food to children is big business and much effort goes into it.

One key observation of this and other reports is the shift in marketing methods from those that are visible to parents to those that are not. Television remains the dominant method for reaching children, but the balance is shifting to product placements in toys, games, educational materials, songs, and movies; cartoon licensing and celebrity endorsements; and stealth methods such as "advergames" and "viral" campaigns involving word of mouth, cell-phone text messages, and the internet—methods largely invisible to today's busy and sometimes electronically challenged parents.[6]

The IOM food marketing report warned companies to voluntarily regulate themselves or "Congress should enact legislation mandating the shift." It summarized the policies of at least fifty other countries that regulate television advertising aimed at children, based largely on a 2004 WHO report.[7] In the United States, decades of attempts to regulate marketing to children have been blocked by industry invocations of self-regulation and of First Amendment protections of commercial speech.

For a long time the Supreme Court has interpreted this protection as applying to "commercial" speech—advertising and marketing—as much as to political, artistic, and religious speech;[8] thus, the IOM "or else" demand that Congress regulate food marketing must be viewed as a call for reinterpreting First Amendment protections to allow policy change. In the meantime, lawyers and legal advocacy groups are exploring ways to use legal strategies to address childhood obesity.[9]

For all of the reasons why food marketers are in schools in the first place—a large, captive, impressionable audience with influence—schools are prime targets for obesity intervention. Parents, teachers, and food service directors in schools across the country have transformed meal programs to deliver healthier food along with a curriculum that teaches children about where food comes from and how it is produced.[10] As effective and important as these grassroots efforts may be, they must be instituted school by school and depend on individuals rather than policy. This makes statewide approaches seem attractive.

Although more than thirty states have considered or enacted laws related to nutrition standards, nutrition education, reporting of body weights, or physical activity,[11] intense lobbying by industry prevents the passage of most of these bills or dilutes their impact. In 2004, as part of reauthorization of the Women, Infants and Children (WIC) program, Congress required local school districts to establish wellness programs by 2006, but provided only minimal funding for this purpose; the programs remain local and voluntary.[12]

In December 2006, the New York City Board of Health ruled that fast-food restaurants and places like Starbucks, which sell uniformly sized foods *and* already provide nutrition information, must post calories on menus and menu boards.[13] This precedent-setting action occurred because New York City has exceptionally high rates of obesity and heart disease, and its health commissioner and mayor wanted to do something about them. A provision to make calorie labeling national was included in the health care reform act signed into law in 2010, despite initial opposition by the National Restaurant Associations.[14] Its provisions become effective late in 2016.

## Food-Industry Strategies

Obesity poses difficult challenges for food companies, caught as they are between the demands of advocates and those of stockholders. Pressures from advocates, regulators, lawyers, and Wall Street put food companies in an impossible dilemma. If they stop marketing junk food to children, they lose sales. Food companies first dealt with this dilemma by denying responsibility for contributing to an "eat more" food environment. Later, while they continued lobbying, attacking critics, and promoting physical activity, they also adopted additional strategies. They pressed states to pass laws protecting them from legal liability. At the same time, they reformulated products to make them appear "better-for-you," identified the "healthier" versions through self-endorsements, and pushed for use of a greater range of health and structure/function claims to market those products. To address concerns about marketing, they invoked voluntary self-regulation as the primary strategy.[15]

Virtually all major food companies have tweaked the contents of existing products or created new products to make them appear healthier. PepsiCo advertised snack foods with "0 grams trans fat." General Mills added whole grains to all of its cereals, thereby creating Whole Grain Count Chocula, increasing the fiber content from zero to one gram per serving. The company also replaced some of the sugars in Cocoa Puffs with the artificial sweetener Splenda, but these products failed to sell and were withdrawn at the end of 2006. Post/Kraft improved Fruity Pebbles by reducing sugars from twelve to nine grams per serving and adding three grams of polydextrose "fiber." Although the labels on these products are easily interpreted as advertising them as health foods, the companies make no such claim; instead, they offer the products as "better-for-you" options. This strategy assumes that making small improvements will make the products, as well as the children and adults who consume them, "healthier." It remains uncertain whether artificial sweeteners and polydextrose are better for children or whether such products produce measurable health benefits.[16]

Most major food companies have established their own criteria for nutritional evaluation of their own products. PepsiCo identifies its self-identified "better-for-you" products with green Smart Spots. General Mills cereals sport Goodness Corners. Kellogg cereals have flags, and Kraft's "healthier" products are Sensible Solutions. The companies' criteria allow many products high in sugars, fat, and calories to qualify. In 2006, Hannaford, a supermarket chain in the Northeast, recruited a group of independent nutrition scientists to develop a "Guiding Stars" program based on nutritional standards for awarding one, two, or three stars. By these independent criteria, less than 25 percent of the store's 27,000 products, and virtually none of the food companies' self-endorsed products, qualified for even one star.[17] By independent criteria, therefore, junk foods are not health foods.

Health claims sell foods and food companies care little about scientific substantiation. When the FDA denied claims on the basis of lack of scientific substantiation, companies sued—and usually won. The courts told the FDA it could not require companies to base health claims on science, on First Amendment grounds. Although FDA research demonstrates that consumers tend to interpret health claims as backed by science, the court decisions convinced it to begin allowing "qualified" health claims (those lacking in significant substantiation); the FDA began considering such claims in 2003 and has permitted them ever since.

The result of the current free-for-all in health claim regulation is most evident in supermarket cereal aisles. In 2006, you could buy Kellogg's Smart Start, "healthy heart with oat bran, potassium, and low sodium" that "contains ingredients that can help lower BOTH blood pressure & cholesterol," despite an ingredient list that includes sugars in eleven places. Post/Kraft Honey Nut Shredded Wheat was labeled "Lose 10 Lbs. The Heart Healthy Way!" Cereals from several makers say their products help "support a healthy immune system," a "structure/function" claim like the ones allowed for dietary supplements. Kellogg's sugar-sweetened cereals are advertised in India as "containing the goodness of chapattis," and appear in Panama with endorsements by the Pediatric Association of Guatemala.

In August 2006, Tim Lang and his colleagues at City University London published an evaluation of statements made by the world's twenty-five largest food companies about diet, physical activity, and obesity prevention. Their report examined the companies' published positions on twenty-eight questions such as "Is there a commitment on sugar?" "Is there a commitment on portion size?" "Is there a policy specifically focused on children and food marketing?" Because they found few companies making such commitments, they concluded that this industry is "not yet fully engaged with the seriousness and urgency" of the challenge of childhood obesity. I supervised related case studies of McDonald's and Kraft that supported this conclusion.[18]

That year, the American Academy of Pediatrics (AAP) said self-regulation wasn't working and called for federal regulation of food marketing to children. The First Amendment allows "advertisements [to] be restricted or even banned if there is a significant public health risk. Cigarette advertising and alcohol advertising would seem to fall squarely into this category, and ads for junk food could easily be restricted." The AAP told pediatricians to counsel patients to limit children to no more than two hours a day of television and to lobby for outright bans on advertising junk foods in schools and on children's television as well as for a 50 percent decrease in the time allowed for commercials during those programs.

## Looking Forward

Advocates as well as investment analysts, lawyers, and legislators have placed food companies on notice that they will have to change business practices in response to childhood obesity, but efforts to get companies to do so meet with industry lobbying efforts that appear nothing less than ferocious.[19] The ferocity, along with alliances to defend the right to market to children and lobbying to be kept free of liability, are largely invisible to the public. What the public sees is the public relations—the tinkering with product formulas and the promises about marketing practices. The "healthier" versions may be *better* choices, but they are not necessarily *good* choices. Children would be much better off eating fruits, vegetables, and whole grains, not "better-for-you" highly processed junk foods. Food companies cannot resolve the impossible dilemma on their own. For business reasons, they cannot—and will not—stop making nutritionally questionable food products and marketing them to children. Because sales of processed foods are stagnant in America, companies such as Kraft, McDonald's, Coca-Cola, and Pepsi-Cola have turned their attention to the developing world. Obesity is a global problem and its solution must also be global.

## Endnotes

[1]  B. Wansink, *Mindless Eating: Why We Eat More Than We Think* (New York: Bantam, 2006); B. Wansink and J. Sobal, "Mindless Eating: The 200 Daily Food Decisions We Overlook," *Environment and Behavior* 39 (2007): 106–123.

[2]  WHO, *Diet, Nutrition, and the Prevention of Chronic Disease*, WHO Technical Report Series 916, Geneva, 2003, http://whqlibdoc.who.int/trs /WHO_TRS_916.pdf; WHO, "Global Strategy on Diet, Physical Activity and Health," April 24, 2004, www.who.int/dietphysicalactivity/strategy /eb11344/strategy_english_web.pdf. See also: A. Waxman, "The WHO Global Strategy ... the Controversy on Sugar," *Development* 47 (2004): 75–82; and J. Zarocostas, "WHO Waters Down Draft Strategy on Diet and Health," *Lancet* 363 (2004): 1373.

[3]  J. Streets et al., "Absolute Risk of Obesity," UBS Warburg Global Equity Research, November 27, 2002, and March 4, 2003; S. Massot and R. Fujimori, "Obesity: A Lingering Concern," Morgan Stanley Global Equity Research, October 31, 2003; A. Langlois et al., "Food Manufacturing: Obesity: The Big Issue," JP Morgan European Equity Research, April 16, 2003. And see follow-up report by A. Langlois et al., "Obesity: Re-shaping the Food Industry," January 24, 2006.

[4]  S. Linn, *Consuming Kids: The Hostile Takeover of Childhood* (New York: New Press, 2004); J. B. Schor, *Born to Buy: The Commercialized Child and the New Consumer Culture* (New York: Scribner, 2004). See, for example, G. Hastings et al., "Review of Research on the Effects of Food Promotion to Children," Food Standards Agency (UK), September 2003; and World Health Organization, "Marketing of Food and Non-alcoholic Beverages to Children," report of a WHO Forum and Technical Meeting, Geneva, 2006.

[5]  Institute of Medicine, "Preventing Childhood Obesity: Health in the Balance," 2005; "Food Marketing to Children and Youth: Threat or Opportunity?," 2005; and "Progress in Preventing Childhood Obesity: How Do We Measure Up?," 2006. All from National Academies Press, Washington, DC, www.nap.org.

[6]  "Out of Balance: Marketing of Soda, Candy, Snacks and Fast Foods Drowns Out Healthful Messages," Consumers Union and California Pan-Ethnic Health Network, September 2005; E. S. Moore, "It's Child's Play: Advergaming and the Online Marketing of Food to Children," Kaiser Family Foundation, July 2006.

[7]  C. Hawkes, "Marketing Food to Children: The Global Regulatory Environment," World Health Organization, Geneva, 2004, http://whqlibdoc.who.int /publications/2004/9241591579.pdf.

[8]  W. E. Parmet and J. A. Smith, "Free Speech and Public Health: A Population-Based Approach to the First Amendment," *Loyola Law Review* 39 (2006): 363–446; M. M. Mello, D. M. Studdert, and T. A. Brennan, "Obesity—The

New Frontier of Public Health Law," *New England Journal of Medicine* 354 (2006): 2601–2610.

9   See H. K. Gordon, "Eat, Drink, and Sue: A New Mass Tort?," *New York Law Journal Corporate Update,* March 30, 2006; J. Alderman and R. A. Daynard, "Applying Lessons from Tobacco Litigation to Obesity Lawsuits," *American Journal of Preventive Medicine* 30 (2006): 82–88; and S. Gardner, "Litigation as a Tool in Food Advertising: A Consumer Advocacy Viewpoint," *Loyola Law Review* 39 (2006): 101–120. For reasons why legal strategies are worth pursuing, see E. Fried, "Obesity: The Sixth Deadly Sin," *Gastronomica,* Winter 2007: 6–10.

10   US Government Accountability Office, "School Meal Programs: Competitive Foods Are Widely Available and Generate Substantial Revenues for Schools" (GAO-05-563), August 2005, www.gao.gov/new.items/d05563.pdf. For examples of the school food movement in action, see Alice Waters, "Edible Schoolyard," www.edibleschoolyard.org/homepage.html; Center for Eco-Literacy www.ecoliteracy.org/programs/rsl.html; R. W. Surles, *Chef Bobo's Good Food Cookbook* (Des Moines, IA: Meredith Books, 2004); and A. Cooper and L. M. Holmes, *Lunch Lessons: Changing the Way We Feed Our Children* (New York: Collins, 2006).

11   Several groups track obesity legislation. See National Council of State Legislatures, Childhood Obesity—2005 Update and Overview of Policy Options, www.ncsl.org/programs/health/ChildhoodObesity-2005.htm; National Association of State Boards of Education, "Healthy Schools: State-Level School Health Policies," www.nasbe.org/HealthySchools/States/Topics .asp?Category=C&Topic=1; Health Policy Tracking Service, "State Actions to Promote Nutrition, Increase Physical Activity and Prevent Obesity: A Legislative Overview," Robert W. Johnson Foundation, July 11, 2005, http://www.rwjf.org/en/library/research/2005/07/state-actions-to -promote-nutrition--increase-physical-activity-a.html; and follow-up report in July 2006, www.rwjf.org/files/publications/other/Balance072006.pdf.

12   Child Nutrition and WIC Reauthorization Act of 2004, Public Law 108-265, § 204, 118 Stat. 729 (2004).

13   The New York City ruling of December 5, 2006, www.nyc.gov/html/doh /downloads/pdf/public/notice-adoption-hc-art81-50.pdf.

14   New York State Restaurant Association, New York City legislative update, December 7, 2006, www.nysra.org.

15   M. Simon, *Appetite for Profit: How the Food Industry Undermines Our Health and How to Fight Back* (New York: Nation Books, 2006).

16   M. Nestle, *What to Eat* (New York: North Point Press, 2006).

17   Hannaford describes and summarizes media reports about its Guiding Stars program www.hannaford.com/home.shtml.

18   T. Lang, G. Rayner, and E. Kaelin, "The Food Industry, Diet, Physical Activity and Health: A Review of Reported Commitments and Practice of 25 of the

World's Largest Food Companies," City University London, 2006, www.city.ac.uk/press/The%20Food%20Industry%20Diet%20Physical
% 20Activity%20and%20Health.pdf. See also: A. Lewin et al., "Food Industry Promises to Address Childhood Obesity: Preliminary Evaluation," *Journal of Public Health Policy* 27 (2006): 327–348.

19  D. J. Wood, "Top Legal Issues for 2007," *Advertising Age*, December 18, 2006:
8. See F. Lawrence, "Food Agency Takes on Industry over Junk Labels,"
*Guardian*, December 29, 2006, www.guardian.co.uk/frontpage
/story/0,,1979245,00.html.

# Autism and Glyphosate: Connecting the Dots

Stephanie Seneff

## Introduction

Autism, and, more generally, autism spectrum disorder, is a complex disorder characterized by impaired brain development. The syndrome manifests as awkward social interaction along with delayed verbal and nonverbal communication and repetitive behaviors. The extreme cases can never achieve independent living. The incidence of autism has risen alarmingly over the past two decades in the United States, exactly in step with the increased usage of Roundup as an herbicide on corn and soy crops. While the autism rate was estimated to be 1 in 10,000 in 1970, the most recent number from the Centers for Disease Control and Prevention (CDC) is 1 in 68 for twelve-year-olds in 2014. This number reflects the age group who were born in 2002—the number would surely be much worse for children born today.

While correlation does not necessarily mean causation, the correlation between Roundup usage on corn and soy in the previous four years and the rate of autism in first grade in the US public school system is 0.997, looking at trends from 1995 to 2010. This is almost a perfect match, as shown in Figure 1. At the very least, awareness of such strong correlation ought to inspire research to see if there are good reasons, biologically, why Roundup might cause autism.

I have long suspected that the autism epidemic we are witnessing today is due to exposure to environmental toxicants, and I have been frustrated by the fact that most of the research dollars are going

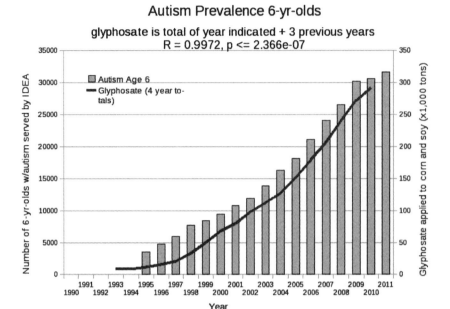

FIGURE 1

toward looking for genetic causes. While some children are more susceptible to the toxic chemicals due to their genetic predisposition, it is clear that the rapid rise in autism cannot be explained by genetics alone, since evolution is by nature a slow process.

The active ingredient in Roundup is glyphosate, a deceptively innocent-looking molecule consisting of the amino acid glycine with a phosphonomethyl group attached to it. Glyphosate is the most widely used herbicide on the planet, in part because of its perceived nontoxicity to humans. It is a general-purpose herbicide: it kills essentially all plants except for the genetically modified (GM) Roundup Ready (RR) corn, soy, sugar beets, canola, alfalfa, cotton, and tobacco plants that have been genetically augmented with a special bacterial gene. These plants don't die following glyphosate exposure, but they also don't necessarily degrade the glyphosate that they readily take up, so it is inevitable that glyphosate residue ends up in the derived foods and other products. While it was promised that the genetic modification would lead to reduced use of herbicides, the exact opposite has happened, as more and more weeds growing among the RR crops are developing resistance to glyphosate over time. The US government is doing very little to monitor the levels of glyphosate in foods, mainly because it is widely believed that glyphosate is nearly harmless to humans. A recent study found alarming levels of glyphosate in GM RR soy, where none was detected in either the organic or the conventionally grown soy that were analyzed for comparison purposes.[1] Glyphosate was used to control weeds for the conventional soy, but the farmer had to be careful not to expose the plant because it too would die from glyphosate toxicity.

The animal studies conducted by the agrochemical industry are flawed in at least two ways: they are too short, and they only test the active ingredient (glyphosate) in isolation. While the industry studies on rats typically last for only three months, the insidious effects of glyphosate don't become obvious in such a short time. A recent study involving rats exposed to Roundup and GM foods over their entire lifespan found considerable toxicity, including liver and kidney disease as well as large mammary tumors and a substantially shortened lifespan.[2] Recent in vitro studies of human cell lines involved comparisons among several herbicides and insecticides.[3] Mesnage and colleagues wrote in the abstract: "Despite its relatively benign reputation, Roundup was by far the most toxic among the herbicides and insecticides tested." They also showed that the adjuvants in Roundup lead to more than a hundredfold increase in toxicity compared to glyphosate alone.

Figure 2 shows a list of some of the comorbidities associated with autism and a list of some of the known biological effects of glyphosate. If we can show that there are links between these two lists, then the remarkable correlation between glyphosate usage on corn and soy and the autism rate in the school system can be justified directly through a causal effect. In the remainder of this essay, I will first describe the importance of gut bacteria to brain health and the role of impaired aromatic amino acid synthesis in the pathology of autism. Then I focus on the mineral manganese, showing how its deficiency can explain several features of autism and is anticipated as a consequence of glyphosate exposure. I also describe the many roles of cytochrome p450 (CYP) enzymes in biology, and how their impaired function contributes to autism. In addition to addressing the essential roles of sulfate in the body, especially the brain, and explaining how it is likely negatively impacted by glyphosate, I link autism to anemia and to preeclampsia, a serious illness that appears during the third trimester of pregnancy. I identify a likely role for aluminum in autism, particularly through its effects on the brain stem nuclei, especially the pineal gland—how glyphosate works synergistically with aluminum to increase its toxicity. I review the evidence, explicitly connecting the dots between glyphosate's effects and autism's pathologies. Following a section that suggests specific nutritional treatment and prevention programs, I conclude with a plea to reconsider whether chemical-based agriculture is worth the price in terms of human health.

| (A) | (B) |
|---|---|
| Overgrowth of gut pathogens | Chelation of manganese |
| Low aconitase | |
| Mitochondrial damage | |
| Excess glutamate in brain | Chelation of cobalt |
| Encephalopathy | Chelation of aluminum |
| Hypersensitivity to vaccines | Chelation of iron |
| Anemia | Disruption of |
| Cobalamin deficiency | heme synthesis |
| Low serum sulfate | Inactivation of |
| Low vitamin D | CYP enzymes |
| Low serotonin | Suppression of |
| Sleep disorder | shikimate pathway |
| Hypothyroidism | |
| Low folate | |

Figure 2

## Gut Bacteria and the Shikimate Pathway

Monsanto, glyphosate's inventor, claims that glyphosate is harmless to human cells because our cells don't possess the biological pathway that glyphosate disrupts in plants, namely, the shikimate pathway. However, the way in which glyphosate disrupts this pathway is through disruption of a manganese-dependent enzyme. Glyphosate has a remarkable ability to chelate the mineral manganese (form a cage around it and make it unavailable). Glyphosate also chelates many other minerals, including iron, zinc, cobalt, and magnesium, making them unavailable to the plants, and therefore making the plants deficient in these minerals. People who eat the plants would also become deficient, even if their foods did not contain the glyphosate residue. I believe that mineral deficiencies are the key source of many of the ailments facing humans in the modern world.

A huge flaw in Monsanto's argument is that our gut bacteria do possess the shikimate pathway, and they depend upon it to produce a set of three aromatic amino acids, tryptophan, tyrosine, and phenylalanine.[4] Since our cells don't have this pathway, they themselves are unable to make these very important nutrients, so we depend upon our gut bacteria to supply these nutrients for us, if they are deficient in our food. These essential amino acids are precursors to the neurotransmitters dopamine, serotonin, melatonin, and adrenaline, as well as thyroid hormone, folate, and vitamin E. Many of these important biological molecules have been shown to be deficient in association with autism. Impaired serotonin processing in the brain is associated with autism.[5] Maternal low thyroid hormone is associated with nearly a fourfold increase in the risk of autism in the child.[6] Sleep depends on melatonin produced by the pineal gland. Disrupted sleep is a common feature of autism, and is associated with seizure disorders.[7] Impairments in folate-related genes lead to reduced DNA methylation capacity in women that can increase risk of autism in their offspring.[8]

There is an explosion of recent literature on the importance of the gut bacteria to human health, and the links between gut health and brain health mediated by the "gut–brain axis."[9] Essentially, our gut bacteria communicate with our brain, revealing their state of health, and when they are sick our brain responds in kind. Furthermore, much research has shown that autism is linked to disturbances in the digestive system: "leaky gut syndrome," gluten intolerance, and overgrowth of pathogens like *Clostridium difficile* (C. diff) are common features of children with autism.[10] Autistic children often have food allergies such as gluten intolerance, chronic constipation and/or diabetes, cramping, bloating, undigested food in the stool, issues with absorption of vitamins and minerals, and leaky gut issues. In fact, the severity of gastrointestinal problems is directly linked to the severity of autism.[11] Toxic phenolic compounds like *p*-Cresol are released into the bloodstream by the gut pathogens, and they can harm the neurons in the brain. High urinary *p*-Cresol is also linked to autism.

Many autistic children are placed on a gluten-free diet, and mothers believe this has improved their symptoms. According to Samsel and Seneff,[12] the recent explosion in the number of people suffering from gluten intolerance in the American population is directly linked to glyphosate application to wheat. While GM RR wheat has not been released into the market, the practice of desiccation of wheat just before the harvest with Roundup has grown in popularity in recent years, and this has almost surely led to a substantial increase in the glyphosate residues found in wheat. This is the simplest explanation for the gluten intolerance epidemic, and the number of plausible links between glyphosate's known mechanisms and the pathologies associated with celiac disease are stunning.[13]

Recent literature has shown that GMO foods cause inflammation in the gut and/or an imbalance between beneficial and pathogenic bacteria in the gut in chickens, cows, and pigs.[14] Glyphosate impairs the growth of lactobacillus, a beneficial bacterium that grows well on milk (lactose). Lactobacillus is uniquely dependent on high concentrations of manganese for protection from oxidative damage. Glyphosate's chelation of manganese may well explain glyphosate's negative effect on lactobacillus growth. Lactobacillus has been successfully used as a probiotic to treat anxiety, a common comorbidity of autism.

## Manganese

Manganese deficiency due to glyphosate's chelation effects is a strong candidate to explain several other known features of autism. Recent studies on dairy cows in Denmark investigated the effects of GM RR corn and soy feed on mineral content in the blood. Sampling cows from eight different farms, Krüger and colleagues found severe deficiency in manganese and cobalt in the cows on all the farms, along with detectable levels of glyphosate in the urine.[15] Cobalamin (vitamin B$_{12}$) depends on cobalt as a catalyst, and cobalamin deficiency, along with folate deficiency, has been implicated in autism.[16]

I had been only vaguely aware of the roles of manganese in the body when I came upon this article on Danish cows, but a systematic search of the literature on manganese was richly rewarding, giving me the sudden realization that manganese deficiency explained several phenomena associated with autism that I was already aware of. Prior to recognizing glyphosate's potential role in autism, I had written a paper together with colleagues characterizing autism as a kind of low-grade chronic encephalopathy.[17] We identified two metabolites that are overrepresented in the autism brain and that can potentially cause harm to neurons: glutamate and ammonia. It turns out that the enzyme that combines glutamate with ammonia to produce glutamine depends on manganese as a cofactor. So, manganese deficiency is a logical explanation for the excess glutamate and ammonia in the brain. Glutamate is a known excitotoxin that could damage the neurons and impair brain function. A study of the concentrations of the various amino acids in the blood, comparing autistic children with controls, revealed only glutamate and glutamine as being statistically significantly different between the two groups—with far too much glutamate and far too little glutamine in the blood from the children with autism.[18]

Autism is also associated with mitochondrial impairment. The mitochondria are the energy powerhouses of the cell—they process sugar through aerobic metabolism to produce carbon dioxide and water, along with adenosine triphosphate (ATP), the energy currency of the cell. Mitochondria necessarily release "reactive oxygen species" (ROS) as they work. These are dangerous small molecules containing highly reactive oxygen that can damage the proteins, fats, and genetic material in the cell. One of the very important mechanisms to protect the cell from damage is through the enzymatic action of manganese superoxide dismutase (MnSOD), which converts the highly reactive superoxide molecule into hydrogen peroxide. While mutated forms of certain genes involved in mitochondrial function are implicated in autism, manganese deficiency in the brain could still easily account for the mitochondrial impairment associated with autism. Children with the mutated genes would be more susceptible to manganese deficiency.

Aconitase is an essential enzyme in the mitochondria that performs a critical step in the citric acid cycle to break down glucose and produce usable energy. The iron-sulfur complex in aconitase is known to be especially susceptible to disruption by exposure to superoxide, the quintessential ROS. Thus, a deficiency in manganese in the mitochondria would lead to an impaired ability to detoxify superoxide through MnSOD, which would then be expected to reduce the amount of active aconitase in the mitochondria of affected cells. A study on children with autism showed significantly reduced aconitase levels in mitochondria taken from frozen samples from the cerebellum.[19]

## CYP Enzymes

CYP enzymes are an important class of enzymes that have many essential functions in the liver and elsewhere in the body. Several CYP enzymes are involved in producing bile acids, which are essential for digesting fats. Bile acids also carry liver-processed forms of multiple environmental toxicants, which are exported back to the gut for excretion. Thus, CYP enzymes are essential for detoxifying environmental chemicals. In fact, Samsel and Seneff proposed that impaired CYP enzyme function in the liver may account for much of the toxicity of glyphosate.[20] One way that glyphosate disrupts CYP enzymes is by nitrogen binding to proteins in the active site, but another way that it can disrupt them is through interfering with heme synthesis, since heme is an important component of these enzymes.

CYP enzymes are essential for activating vitamin D, both in the liver and in the kidneys. The United States is currently in the middle of an epidemic in vitamin D deficiency. I believe glyphosate is a key factor in this epidemic. Vitamin D goes through complex steps before it acquires its active form. Following its synthesis in the skin, it is transported to the liver, where it is oxidized by a CYP enzyme to 25(OH) vitamin D. Subsequently, in the kidneys, it is further oxidized to 1,25(OH) vitamin D. What is usually measured is the 25(OH) form produced by CYP enzymes in the liver. These are in fact exactly the same enzymes that oxidize bile acids. So, when vitamin D activation in the liver doesn't happen, it's an indicator of impaired bile acid formation, which will make it difficult to digest fats, and also lead to gallbladder issues like gall stones. Glyphosate's suppression of CYP enzymes in the liver is an easy explanation for the vitamin $D_3$ deficiency epidemic we are currently experiencing.

CYP enzymes in the liver also break down retinoic acid, so their impairment leads to excess retinoic acid in the blood. This can cause impaired fetal development and birth defects in the offspring. Aromatase, an enzyme that converts testosterone to estrogen, is also a CYP enzyme. Impaired aromatase activity has been implicated in autism, producing a "supermale" phenotype with too much testosterone and not enough estrogen.

## Sulfate Deficiency in the Brain

Thus far, we have discussed how glyphosate likely disrupts gut bacteria leading to gut dysbiosis connected with autism, how glyphosate chelates rare minerals, particularly manganese, which links to both glutamate excess and mitochondrial dysfunction in the brain, and how glyphosate's suppression of CYP enzymes leads to vitamin D deficiency and other disruptions associated with autism. In this section, I will describe the evidence linking autism to impaired supply of sulfur metabolites, particularly sulfate, to the body, and discuss how glyphosate likely interferes with sulfate supplies.

First, it is important to recognize the importance of sulfate to the body, particularly the molecule heparan sulfate that is present in the surrounding milieu of most cells in the body and that plays an important role in regulating what gets into the cell. Heparan sulfate is a complex molecule consisting of many sugar molecules linked together and slightly modified.

Sulfate is attached to the sugar molecules at random locations, and the total amount of sulfate in any given heparan sulfate molecule is highly variable. It is beyond the scope of this essay to describe all the roles of heparan sulfate, but it is notable that mice engineered to have an impaired ability to add sulfate to heparan sulfate in the brain exhibit all the features of "mouse autism."[21]

It was Rosemary Waring who conducted pioneering work on autistic children that led her to recognize the importance of impaired sulfate metabolism in autism as early as the early 1990s.[22] She and others have found that sulfate levels are unusually low in the blood of children with autism, who tend to push excess sulfate through the urine (sulfate wasting). It is a little-known fact that vitamin D protects from sulfate wasting through the urine (prevents the kidneys from exporting sulfate). It is only the doubly oxidized form of vitamin D produced by CYP enzymes in the kidneys that is able to suppress sulfate wasting. Children with autism often suffer from vitamin D deficiency.

A hypothesis that I have developed, together with colleagues, is that sulfate synthesis in the skin depends on sunlight exposure. We proposed that a well-known enzyme, endothelial nitric oxide synthase (eNOS) oxidizes sulfur to produce sulfate, and that it responds to sunlight as a catalyst for this reaction.[23] Thus, eNOS is a "moonlighting" dual-purpose enzyme that can oxidize both nitrogen and sulfur. The evidence in support of the hypothesis is strong, and it explains the role of superoxide production by eNOS, which most researchers view as a pathology. What this means, most importantly, is that sunlight exposure is important not just for the synthesis of vitamin D, but also for sulfate synthesis. We have been encouraged to stay out of the sun and to generously apply sunscreen if we go outside on a sunny day, and I think this has contributed to our deficiency problems in both vitamin D and sulfate.

It is well established that the skin produces abundant amounts of cholesterol sulfate, which protects from bacterial entry and provides a watertight barrier. Red blood cells also produce cholesterol sulfate, which they accumulate in their membranes, and, when they have too little, they are susceptible to breaking apart and dying. Cholesterol sulfate piles up in the microvilli in the placenta during the third trimester of pregnancy. This suggests that cholesterol sulfate is a crucial molecule for delivering both cholesterol and sulfate to the fetus.[24]

## Autism, Anemia, and Preeclampsia

The Vaccine Adverse Event Reporting System (VAERS), made freely available on the web by the CDC and the US Food and Drug Administration (FDA), is a valuable resource for probing different factors associated with various diseases and conditions. Children with autism or a tendency toward autism are more vulnerable to vaccine adverse reactions, and it is possible to tease out exactly which symptoms show up in association with autism. Whether the vaccine is causal in the autism or the predisposition toward autism increases sensitivity to the vaccine is a moot point. Both factors are surely in place.

I have conducted many statistical studies of VAERS. While this database of course directly yields association between certain vaccines or classes of vaccines (e.g., those that contain aluminum) and specific symptoms, it can also indirectly reveal subtle links among diseases and conditions, which can then be confirmed through a literature search. A good example of this kind of research is a study we conducted that found associations between pernicious anemia and autism.[25] Events that included symptoms that are known to be characteristic of pernicious anemia—diarrhea, constipation, fatigue, light-headedness, appetite loss, pallor, dyspnea, swollen tongue, depression, loss of balance, and numbness—predicted other pathologies that are known to be associated with autism—anxiety, eczema, asthma, prematurity, and impaired immune function—as well as predicting autism itself with high statistical significance ($p = 0.0007$). Furthermore, the unusual vaccine adverse reaction, visual disturbances, which is predicted as well, is also an unusual symptom of preeclampsia, a condition of late-stage pregnancy that greatly increases the risk of autism in the fetus. The original symptoms we selected for characterizing pernicious anemia are also common symptoms of preeclampsia.

What can we learn from all of this? It is well established that pernicious anemia is caused by cobalamin (vitamin $B_{12}$) deficiency. Might it then be that cobalamin deficiency also plays a crucial role in autism, in preeclampsia, and in a sensitivity toward vaccines? These ideas have many ramifications, and immediately invite a slew of questions. What causes the cobalamin deficiency? How does cobalamin deficiency lead to preeclampsia? To autism? Why does cobalamin deficiency make you more sensitive to vaccines? Which components of the vaccines are the main cause of the reaction? How can the problem be fixed? Prevented? These are some of the questions that have haunted me as I continue my search for answers to explain the autism epidemic in America.

My sleuthing has led me back to glyphosate, and my suspicion is that a key factor that has been heretofore overlooked is that glyphosate disrupts the first step in the synthesis of pyrrole in plants,[26] which leads to impaired chlorophyll synthesis. Pyrrole is a relatively simple but ancient biological molecule, as shown in Figure 3, but it plays a huge role in both chlorophyll in plants and corrin and porphyrin rings in animals. Pyrrole is assembled into corrin rings to make cobalamin, so impaired pyrrole synthesis leads directly to impaired cobalamin synthesis. Four pyrrole rings are assembled to make heme (see Figure 4), which is the basic unit of hemoglobin, the molecule in red blood cells that transports oxygen. Also, heme is essential in the important class of enzymes called cytochromes, which are essential for energy production in the form of ATP in the mitochondria. This of course can contribute to the mitochondrial impairment observed in autism, enhancing the damaging effects of manganese insufficiency. Heme is also a component of the CYP enzymes, discussed previously, and of eNOS, the enzyme that synthesizes sulfate in red blood cells and other cell types in response to sunlight.

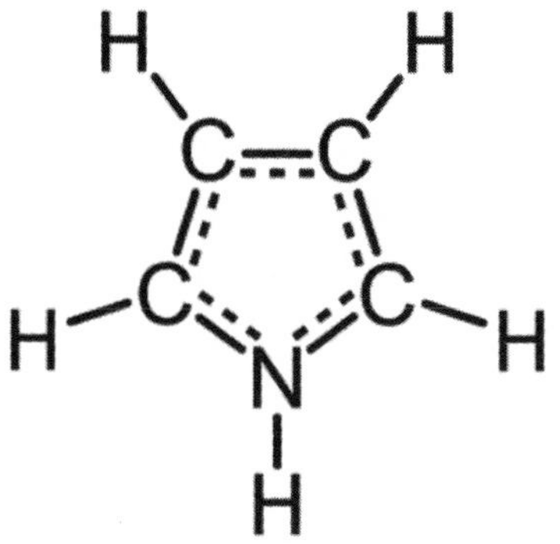

FIGURE 3 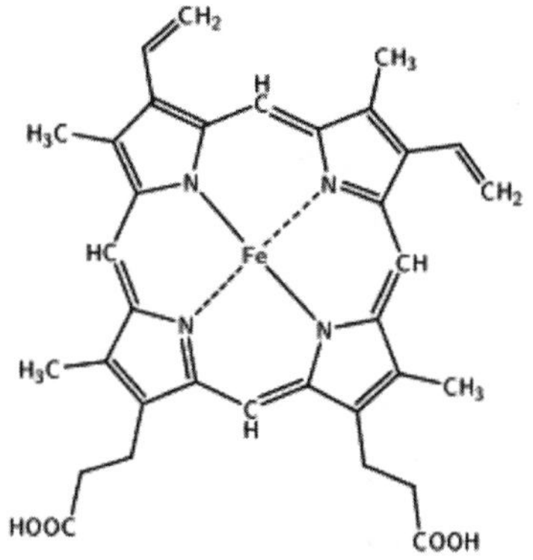                          FIGURE 4

The role of the pyrrole ring is to bind metals. In chlorophyll it binds magnesium, in cobalamin it binds cobalt, and in heme it binds iron. Porphyrin rings housing manganese also exist in biology and play an important role in microbial activities. All of these biologically important molecules can be expected to be disrupted by glyphosate. Cobalamin is a complex molecule that human cells are unable to synthesize. Cobalamin synthesized by the gut bacteria of animals becomes available in the meats derived from those animals.

If the animals are eating a diet of GM RR corn and soy (most likely in the modern agricultural practices), they are exposed to high levels of glyphosate in their feed, which then interferes with their microbes' ability to synthesize cobalamin. This can explain the extremely low levels of manganese and cobalt found in the Danish dairy cows. The switch from manure to chemical-based fertilizers has greatly decreased the bioavailability of cobalamin in plant-based foods, further compounding the problem.

So, glyphosate is a strong candidate as a toxic chemical that is disrupting the supply of cobalamin to our bodies. But how does cobalamin deficiency lead to anemia? A simple answer is that it's indirectly connected to heme deficiency because the process that disrupts cobalamin also disrupts heme. And heme deficiency is almost a definition of anemia. Anemia is a consequence of defective red blood cells. My colleagues and I identified cobalamin as plausibly playing an essential role in anchoring the sulfur atom that gets oxidized to produce sulfate in red blood cells.[27] Cobalamin fits snugly into the NOS molecule and inhibits its production of nitric oxide, which is its alternate function.[28] Without cobalamin, the red blood cells cannot produce cholesterol sulfate, and without cholesterol sulfate they fall apart! This will lead to bilirubinemia and jaundice, a common problem in newborns today that carries with it a fourfold increased risk of autism.[29]

As mentioned previously, cholesterol sulfate accumulates at a high concentration in the placental villi during the third trimester of pregnancy, the same time that preeclampsia develops. I believe that this enrichment in cholesterol sulfate is essential for delivery of cholesterol and sulfate to the fetal brain. Although sulfate deficiency has to my knowledge never been identified as a risk factor of preeclampsia, two very common treatments are heparan sulfate and magnesium sulfate. Furthermore, the impaired kidney function that often accompanies preeclampsia can be explained by insufficient heparan sulfate in the kidneys.[30]

If red blood cells are dying in large numbers due to insufficient cholesterol sulfate in their membranes, then new red blood cells will need to be produced to replace them. This will require the synthesis of massive amounts of heme to be inserted into the newly minted molecules of hemoglobin. This leads us back to the porphyrin ring problem, because porphyrin is the core constituent of heme. The pyrrole rings in porphyrin are synthesized from two amino acids: glycine and glutamate. Glycine and glutamate are two of the three amino acids that make up the glutathione molecule. Glutathione plays an incredibly important role in the liver as an antioxidant, and it is known to be depleted in association with autism. Furthermore, animal studies have shown that liver glutathione is depleted by glyphosate.[31] I propose that the liver is forced to break apart its glutathione molecules in order to retrieve an excess of these two amino acids, in order to supply the enzyme with substrate so that, even in its weakened state, it can still produce enough pyrrole rings. Conveniently, or perhaps by design, the third amino acid in glutathione is cysteine. Cysteine is an essential sulfur-containing amino acid that can be oxidized to produce sulfate. Therefore, oxidation of cysteine can help to alleviate the sulfate deficiency problem brought on by impaired eNOS function. However, this oxidation process requires that the cells put themselves at risk to oxidative damage, which can further impair mitochondrial function. Thus, I predict that glyphosate's interference with pyrrole synthesis in the liver has widespread consequences, one of which is the depletion of the antioxidant glutathione, alongside increased exposure to oxidizing agents.

A huge negative consequence of all this is based on the fact that many other important molecules in the liver and in the red blood cells also depend on heme, and impaired heme synthesis is going to impact them as well. One of these is eNOS, the enzyme that synthesizes sulfate in red blood cells. So we have come full circle—red blood cells die because they can't produce enough cholesterol sulfate using eNOS, and they can't be adequately replenished because new heme can't be synthesized fast enough due to glyphosate's interference with heme synthesis.

The liver depends on at least two other enzyme classes that need heme iron—cytochrome c enzymes in the mitochondria and the CYP enzymes, previously discussed. Insufficient supplies of cytochrome c will lead to an impaired ability to convert glucose into energy, and impaired CYP enzymes will lead to an impaired ability to detoxify many environmental toxins, making them much more dangerous than they would otherwise be. One of these is acetaminophen (Tylenol), which is often given to children to tame the fever following vaccination. Tylenol has been identified as a potential factor in autism, as well as attention-deficit/hyperactivity disorder (ADHD) and asthma.[32]

Iron deficiency is the most common nutritional deficiency in the world. Studies have shown that iron deficiency leads to reduced attention span and reduced emotional responsiveness, as well as lower scores on IQ tests.[33] Anemia leads to insufficient oxygen supply to the tissues, and this has huge consequences to the brain, which needs lots of oxygen to metabolize sugar and satisfy its very high energy demands. Iron deficiency is especially critical during the first two years of life, as infants often have an impaired ability to absorb iron from food sources. In fact, it is crucial not to clamp the cord prematurely at birth, as cord blood can be a significant source of iron for the infant. Iron deficiency is common in autistic children.[34] My colleagues and I proposed that autism can be characterized as a chronic low-grade encephalopathy—an inflammatory condition that is often triggered by low oxygen supply.[35] A similar idea had previously been proposed by Wakefield and colleagues more than a decade earlier,[36] but it got little attention at the time from the research community.

Inadequate iron impacts mainly neurons and red blood cells, both of which require high levels of iron to function. Inadequate iron leads to neuronal apoptosis (cell death). Neurons require iron in their mitochondria to produce energy for the cell. However, free iron is highly reactive and can damage the neuron. An informative review paper describes multiple forms of hereditary microcytic anemia due to defects in either iron acquisition or heme synthesis.[37] The most common genetic form of congenital sideroblastic anemia is one in which the genetic defect involves the enzyme responsible for the first step in the synthesis of pyrrole, called 5-aminolevulinate synthase 2 (ALAS2)[38] (this is the step that is disrupted by glyphosate in plants[39]). In 40 percent of the cases, however, the defect has not been traced to any genetic mutation. Might it be that glyphosate is responsible for the impaired function in these cases?

ALAS2 is unique to the erythroid cells, the cells in the bone marrow that are destined to become new red blood cells to replace the ones that have died. Thus, a defect leads to anemia because these cells cannot properly mature. Curiously, this gene is located on the X chromosome, which means that boys would be more vulnerable to a genetic defect because they only have one copy of the gene. Boys are also about four to five times more likely to have autism.

## Aluminum and Glyphosate

One very intriguing aspect of VAERS is that the total number of adverse event reports has been going up dramatically in recent years. An even more surprising observation is that the curve closely tracks the amount of glyphosate being applied to corn and soy crops, as shown in Figure 5. The autism spectrum diagnosis in the US school system over all grades is also well aligned with the other two plots. While it may be unimaginable that the correlation between glyphosate and vaccine reports could be causal, I have come up with a very plausible explanation that could account for this effect. The simple explanation is that glyphosate enhances the toxicity of aluminum.

Why is there aluminum in vaccines? It turns out that aluminum is very effective as an adjuvant, an additive that enhances the immune response to the antigen in the vaccine. In other words, the vaccine is more likely to "take" if there is aluminum. Many of the vaccines administered to young children contain aluminum, including DTaP, Hepatitis A and B, Gardasil (HPV), Hib (Haemophilus influenzae), and PCV (pneumococcal). Aluminum was long ago approved as an adjuvant, which makes it the adjuvant of choice in the design of new

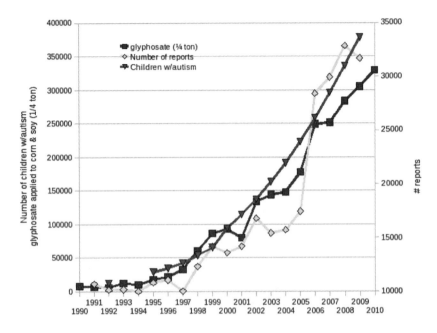

FIGURE 5

vaccines. It is very difficult to "retract" an approval by the FDA once it has been issued, even though there is now an extensive literature confirming aluminum's toxicity to the brain.[40]

Long before I was aware of the connection to glyphosate, I published, together with colleagues, a paper where we analyzed VAERS by separately examining events before and after the year 2000.[41] This study was inspired by the observation that there were many more events after 2000, and our interest was in characterizing which symptoms were more prevalent in the after-2000 pool. What we found, which was quite alarming to us, is that the symptoms that occur much more frequently after 2000 than before 2000 are the very same symptoms that occur much more frequently in the aluminum-containing vaccines over the entire time spectrum. In other words, it appears that aluminum becomes more toxic after 2000.

Some of the symptoms that occur more frequently in both aluminum-containing vaccines and after 2000 are seizures, infection, cellulitis, depression, insomnia, and death. Insomnia is of particular interest, in part because it is a feature of autism, but also because it has become a serious problem throughout the US population in recent years. Insomnia was more than three times as common in the reports for aluminum-containing vaccines as in those without aluminum, and the likelihood that this distribution could have occurred by chance was very small (0.0025). I believe this is caused by aluminum's effects on the pineal gland.[42]

The pineal gland is a tiny gland that is situated in the middle of the brain directly behind the eyes. Mystically, it is known as "the third eye" and "the seat of the soul." One of its crucial functions is to produce melatonin, the hormone that controls the wake-sleep cycle. It has been shown that aluminum accumulates preferentially in the pineal gland compared to other parts of the brain (more than twofold higher than any other region measured). Aluminum is toxic to neurons both because it displaces iron in heme and because it acts as a calcium mimetic. The pineal gland produces heparan sulfate by day, in response to sunlight, using both its eNOS and neuronal NOS (nNOS) to catalyze the reaction. By night, it produces massive amounts of melatonin, which it distributes as melatonin sulfate to all the regions of the brain via the cerebrospinal fluid.

The melatonin thus delivers sulfate to the brain tissues, and the sulfate (which it has synthesized by day) is extremely important for its role in recycling garbage. That is to say, during the day the neurons (and all other cells) build up debris, such as damaged proteins, damaged mitochondria, and damaged fatty acids, that needs to be broken down so that the raw materials can be reassembled into something useful. The sulfate that melatonin delivers is essential for this process, because it induces the highly acidic environment (think of sulfuric acid) in the lysosomes that will promote the breakdown of the damaged molecules.

Glyphosate enhances aluminum's effects in several ways. First and perhaps foremost, glyphosate interferes with the synthesis of new heme to replace the heme that is no longer functional because aluminum has displaced iron in the core of the heme molecule (see Figure 4). Second, glyphosate interferes with the supply of melatonin, because melatonin's precursor is tryptophan, a product of the shikimate pathway that glyphosate disrupts. This works synergistically with aluminum toxicity to the pineal gland. Third, glyphosate disrupts the cells' ability to make sulfate (both the red blood cells and the neurons in the pineal gland), because it interferes with eNOS activity via its effect on CYP enzymes. eNOS itself of course also contains heme, so glyphosate interferes with its resynthesis after it has been destroyed by aluminum. Aluminum, acting as a calcium mimetic, coerces eNOS into switching from sulfate synthesis to nitric oxide synthesis.[43] p-Cresol enhances aluminum uptake by cells, and p-Cresol is produced by the pathogens that glyphosate allows to overgrow in the gut due to the fact that the beneficial bacteria are more susceptible to glyphosate. Finally, glyphosate cages aluminum, just as it cages other metals, and glyphosate releases the aluminum only when it reaches an acidic environment, which is induced by sulfate anions. Upon their separation, both aluminum and glyphosate immediately become toxic to the cells. Thus, through their synergistic action, aluminum and glyphosate can easily explain the sulfate deficiency in the brain that is a key feature of autism.

## Connecting the Dots

Armed with the evidence, we are now prepared to connect the dots between symptoms of autism and biological effects of glyphosate, as illustrated in Figure 6. Glyphosate stresses the child's brain through insidious effects that involve mainly impaired antioxidant capacity combined with insufficient oxygen supply, a corrosive combination. Furthermore, the debris from oxidative damage cannot be cleared due to impaired sulfate supplies. These stresses are due in part to inadequate supply of important neurotransmitters, hormones, and vitamins like

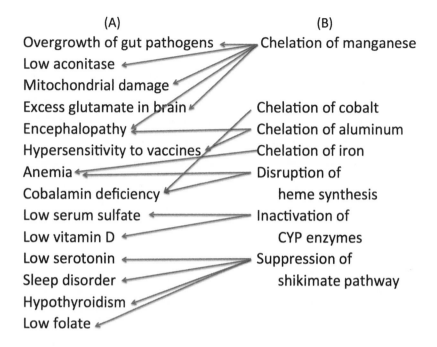

Figure 6

serotonin, melatonin, vitamin D, cobalamin, folate, and thyroid hormone. Manganese deficiency due to glyphosate's chelating effects leads to both an inability to detoxify glutamate, a well-established neurotoxin, and an inability to protect the mitochondria from oxidative damage. Glutamate is overexpressed in the brain due to oxygen deprivation, which in turn is due to impaired ability to regenerate hemoglobin that is being destroyed by aluminum, which is delivered to the red blood cells by glyphosate. The red blood cells are also destroyed due to their inability to produce enough cholesterol sulfate to protect their membranes from hemolysis. The heme synthesis to restore the red blood cell supply is impaired by glyphosate's disruption of the synthesis of its crucial component, pyrrole, and this also disrupts cobalamin synthesis and manganese homeostasis. CYP enzymes in the liver are also deficient, due both to the impaired heme synthesis and direct interference with their activity by glyphosate. This impacts the brain indirectly through several factors, including failed vitamin D activation, failed retinoic acid metabolism, failed bile acid flow, and impaired ability to detoxify other pervasive environmental chemicals. Glyphosate's negative effects on beneficial gut bacteria lead to an overgrowth of pathogens that release neurotoxic chemicals. Meanwhile, aluminum and glyphosate disrupt the pineal gland's ability to synthesize sulfate, which impairs sulfate delivery to the brain, leading to impaired sleep along with a buildup of cellular debris in the neurons.

## How to Prevent/Cure(?) Autism

Anecdotally, mothers have said that their children's autism symptoms were greatly alleviated once they put the children on a strict organic diet. These stories give me great hope to believe that the impairment in brain function in autism is reversible, especially if intervention is early. I believe that adopting a strict organic diet is the most important step in prevention of autism, both for the mother before she becomes pregnant and for the child after it is born.

The observation of a possible connection between pesticides and health issues was the momentum behind the formation of the organization Moms Across America (www.momsacrossamerica.com). Studies conducted by Moms Across America on glyphosate contamination in breast milk found alarming levels in some of the samples.[44] This suggests that, contrary to Monsanto's claims, glyphosate can bioaccumulate. It is unclear if there are effective methods to remove glyphosate from the body, but activated charcoal (in the form of biochar) and humus (organic matter in soil) have been used to treat farm animals with gut disorders.[45]

It is also imperative to minimize aluminum exposure and optimize vitamin D levels. Low vitamin D is clearly implicated in autism, and the best way to increase vitamin D levels is to get adequate sunlight exposure to the skin. Sunscreen not only blocks the rays needed to synthesize vitamin D but also interferes with the synthesis of sulfate by eNOS, as the high-SPF (sun protection factor) versions often contain both retinoic acid and aluminum, both of which suppress cholesterol sulfate synthesis. More generally, aluminum exposure should be minimized by avoiding other sources of aluminum, such as aluminum-containing antiperspirants, aluminum-containing antacids, or aluminum pots and cans. Aluminum in vaccines is extremely problematic—hepatitis B vaccine at birth (currently a requirement in the United States) is a known strong risk factor for autism,[46] and I believe that the US government needs to seriously reexamine the policy that led to the implementation of this requirement. Delaying the vaccination schedule or waiving the aluminum-containing vaccines altogether in the case of an autistic child is warranted.

A diet rich in manganese, iron, and sulfur is clearly needed to restore optimal levels of heme, cobalamin, manganese-catalyzed enzymes, and sulfur-containing metabolites. This generally means abundant cruciferous vegetables, garlic, onions, eggs, cheese, nuts, and seafood. Fermented foods, particularly with live cultures, are especially good, both for the lactate to nurture lactobacillus and for restoration of gut bacteria. Such a dietary protocol has been well promoted by Natasha Campbell-McBride as an effective treatment for autism and other diseases related to disturbances of the gut–brain axis.[47]

Several sulfur-containing supplements are available at natural foods stores, including alpha lipoic acid, chondroitin sulfate, glucosamine sulfate, *N*-acetylcysteine, taurine, and methylsulfonylmethane (MSM), although I recommend meeting nutritional needs by eating whole organic foods instead if possible. To maximize heme bioavailability to the infant, the cord should not be clamped at birth until after blood flow has stopped. One practice I enthusiastically endorse is to soak in Epsom salt baths, preferably a natural sulfur hot spring if one is available. Epsom salts are magnesium sulfate, and this is a good way to acquire sulfate while bypassing possible gut absorption issues.

## Conclusion

In this essay, I have proposed that glyphosate, the active ingredient in the most widely used herbicide in the world, may be the most important factor in the autism epidemic in the United States and elsewhere. By considering how glyphosate kills plants and by examining the research literature on autism and on glyphosate's biological effects in plant and animal models, I have reached the conclusion that the remarkable correlation between the rate of glyphosate usage on corn and soy crops in the United States and the rate of autism in the school system is indeed a reflection of a causal relationship. I have shown how glyphosate's chelation of metals such as iron and manganese, its interference with the shikimate pathway, its disruption of CYP enzyme activity in the liver, its disruption of sulfate synthesis in red blood cells and bile acid transport in the liver, its suppression of vitamin D activation, aromatase activity and retinoic acid metabolism, and its interference with the synthesis of the pyrrole ring are directly linked to pathologies in autism such as low vitamin D, impaired serotonin, impaired sleep, low serum sulfate and low brain heparan sulfate, mitochondrial oxidative damage, glutamate and ammonia toxicity in the brain, disrupted gut bacteria, and urinary p-Cresol. If I am right, then switching to an organic diet is a simple step to reverse the autism epidemic and give the children of the world a much greater opportunity for a productive life. I highly recommend to governmental bodies that they fund independent research to seriously examine a possible connection between glyphosate and autism, and that, if this hypothesis is confirmed, then glyphosate should be banned from agricultural use.

## Endnotes

[1]    T. Bøhn et al., "Compositional Differences in Soybeans on the Market: Glyphosate Accumulates in Roundup-Ready GM Soybeans," *Food Chemistry* 153, no. 15 (2014): 207–215.

[2]    G. E. Séralini et al., "Long-Term Toxicity of a Roundup Herbicide and a Roundup-Tolerant Genetically Modified Maize," republished study, *Environmental Sciences Europe* 26, no. 14 (2014).

3   R. Mesnage et al., "Major Pesticides Are More Toxic to Human Cells Than Their Declared Active Principles," *BioMed Research International* 2014 (2014): 179691.

4   A. Samsel and S. Seneff, "Glyphosate's Suppression of Cytochrome P450 Enzymes and Amino Acid Biosynthesis by the Gut Microbiome: Pathways to Modern Diseases," *Entropy* 15 (2013): 1416–1463.

5   I. Makkonen et al., "Serotonin and Dopamine Transporter Binding in Children with Autism Determined by SPECT," *Developmental Medicine & Child Neurology* 50, no. 8 (August 2008): 593–597.

6   G. C. Román et al., "Association of Gestational Maternal Hypothyroxinemia and Increased Autism Risk," *Annals of Neurology* 74, no. 5 (2013): 733–742.

7   B. A. Malow, "Sleep Disorders, Epilepsy, and Autism," *Mental Retardation and Developmental Disabilities Research Reviews* 10, no. 2 (2004): 122–125.

8   S. J. James et al., "A Functional Polymorphism in the Reduced Folate Carrier Gene and DNA Hypomethylation in Mothers of Children with Autism," *American Journal of Medical Genetics Part B: Neuropsychiatric Genetics* 153B, no. 6 (2010): 1209–1220.

9   P. Bercik, S. M. Collins, and E. F. Verdu, "Microbes and the Gut-Brain Axis," *Neurogastroenterology & Motility* 24, no. 5 (2012): 405–413.

10  J. G. Mulle, W. G. Sharp, and J. F. Cubells, "The Gut Microbiome: A New Frontier in Autism Research," *Current Psychiatry Reports* 15, no. 2 (2013): 337.

11  J. B. Adams et al., "Gastrointestinal Flora and Gastrointestinal Status in Children with Autism—Comparisons to Typical Children and Correlation with Autism Severity," *BMC Gastroenterology* 11 (2011): 22.

12  A. Samsel and S. Seneff, "Glyphosate, Pathways to Modern Diseases II: Celiac Sprue and Gluten Intolerance," *Interdisciplinary Toxicology* 6, no. 4 (2013): 159–184.

13  Ibid.

14  Samsel and Seneff, "Glyphosate's Suppression of Cytochrome P450 Enzymes and Amino Acid Biosynthesis by the Gut Microbiome."

15  M. Krüger et al., "Field Investigations of Glyphosate in Urine of Danish Dairy Cows," *Journal of Environmental & Analytical Toxicology* 3 (2013): 5.

16  Y. M. Al-Farsi et al., "Low Folate and Vitamin B12 Nourishment Is Common in Omani Children with Newly Diagnosed Autism," *Nutrition* 29, no. 3 (2013): 537–541.

17  S. Seneff et al., "Is Encephalopathy a Mechanism to Renew Sulfate in Autism?," *Entropy* 15 (2013): 372–406.

18  C. Shimmura et al., "Alteration of Plasma Glutamate and Glutamine Levels in Children with High-Functioning Autism," *PLoS ONE* 6, no. 10 (2011): e25340.

19  S. Rose et al., "Evidence of Oxidative Damage and Inflammation Associated with Low Glutathione Redox Status in the Autism Brain," *Translational Psychiatry* 2 (July 10, 2012): e134.

[20]  Samsel and Seneff, "Glyphosate's Suppression of Cytochrome P450 Enzymes and Amino Acid Biosynthesis by the Gut Microbiome."

[21]  Irie Fumitoshi, Badie-Mahdavi Hedieh, and Yamaguchi Yu, "Autism-like Socio-communicative Deficits and Stereotypies in Mice Lacking Heparan Sulfate," *OBAS* 109, no. 31 (2012): 5052–5056.

[22]  R. H. Waring and L. V. Klovrza, "Sulphur Metabolism in Autism," *Journal of Nutritional and Environmental Medicine* 10, no. 1 (2000): 25–32.

[23]  S. Seneff et al., "Is Endothelial Nitric Oxide Synthase a Moonlighting Protein Whose Day Job Is Cholesterol Sulfate Synthesis? Implications for Cholesterol Transport, Diabetes and Cardiovascular Disease," *Entropy* 14 (2012): 2492–2530.

[24]  S. Hartzell and S. Seneff, "Impaired Sulfate Metabolism and Epigenetics: Is There a Link in Autism?" *Entropy* 14 (2012): 1953–1977.

[25]  S. Seneff, R. M. Davidson, and J. J. Liu, "Is Cholesterol Sulfate Deficiency a Common Factor in Preeclampsia, Autism, and Pernicious Anemia?," *Entropy* 14 (2012): 2265–2290.

[26]  D. J. Cole, "Mode of Action of Glyphosate—A Literature Analysis," in *The Herbicide Glyphosate,* eds. E. Grossbard and D. Atkinson (London: Butterworths, 1985), 48–74; P. C. Kearney and D. D. Kaufman, eds., *Herbicides Chemistry: Degradation and Mode of Action* (Boca Raton, FL: CRC Press, 1988); O. Cebeci and H. Budak, "Global Expression Patterns of Three Festuca Species Exposed to Different Doses of Glyphosate Using the Affymetrix GeneChip Wheat Genome Array," *Comparative and Functional Genomics* 2009, Article ID 505701; A. Zaidi, M. S. Khan, and P. Q. Rizvi, "Effect of Herbicides on Growth, Nodulation and Nitrogen Content of Greengram," *Agronomy for Sustainable Development* 25 (2005): 497–504.

[27]  Seneff et al., "Is Endothelial Nitric Oxide Synthase a Moonlighting Protein Whose Day Job Is Cholesterol Sulfate Synthesis?"

[28]  J. B. Weinberg et al., "Inhibition of Nitric Oxide Synthase by Cobalamins and Cobinamides," *Free Radical Biology & Medicine* 46 (2009): 1626–1632.

[29]  R. D. Maimburg et al., "Neonatal Jaundice: A Risk Factor for Infantile Autism?" *Paediatric and Perinatal Epidemiology* 22, no. 6 (2008): 562–568.

[30]  Seneff, Davidson, and Liu, "Is Cholesterol Sulfate Deficiency a Common Factor in Preeclampsia, Autism, and Pernicious Anemia?"

[31]  N. S. El-Shenawy, "Oxidative Stress Responses of Rats Exposed to Roundup and Its Active Ingredient Glyphosate," *Environmental Toxicology and Pharmacology* 28, no. 3 (2009): 379–385.

[32]  W. Shaw, "Evidence That Increased Acetaminophen Use in Genetically Vulnerable Children Appears to be a Major Cause of the Epidemics of Autism, Attention Deficit with Hyperactivity, and Asthma," *Journal of Restorative Medicine* 2013: 2.

[33]  L. Hulthén, "Iron Deficiency and Cognition," *Scandinavian Journal of Nutrition* 47, no. 3 (2003): 152–156.

[34]   A. Latif, P. Heinz, and R. Cook, "Iron Deficiency in Autism and Asperger Syndrome," *Autism* 6, no. 1 (March 2002): 103–114.

[35]   Seneff et al., "Is Encephalopathy a Mechanism to Renew Sulfate in Autism?"

[36]   A. J. Wakefield et al., "The Concept of Entero-Colonic Encephalopathy, Autism and Opioid Receptor Ligands," *Alimentary Pharmacology & Therapeutics* 16, no. 4 (2002): 663–674.

[37]   A. Iolascon, L. De Falco, and C. Beaumont, "Molecular Basis of Inherited Microcytic Anemia Due to Defects in Iron Acquisition or Heme Synthesis," *Haematologica* 94, no. 3 (2009): 395–408.

[38]   K. Kaneko et al., "Identification of a Novel Erythroid-Specific Enhancer for the ALAS2 Gene and Its Loss-of-Function Mutation Which Is Associated with Congenital Sideroblastic Anemia," *Haematologica* 99, no. 2 (2014): 252–261.

[39]   Cole, "Mode of Action of Glyphosate"; Kearney and Kaufman, eds., *Herbicides Chemistry;* Cebeci and Budak, "Global Expression Patterns of Three Festuca Species Exposed to Different Doses of Glyphosate Using the Affymetrix GeneChip Wheat Genome Array"; Zaidi, Khan, and Rizvi, "Effect of Herbicides on Growth, Nodulation and Nitrogen Content of Greengram."

[40]   C. A. Shaw et al., "Aluminum's Role in CNS-Immune System Interactions Leading to Neurological Disorders," *Immunome Research* 9 (2013): 069.

[41]   S. Seneff, J. Liu, and R. Davidson, "Empirical Data Confirm Autism Symptoms Related to Aluminum and Acetaminophen Exposure," *Entropy* 14 (2012): 2227–2253.

[42]   W. A. Morley and S. Seneff, "Diminished Brain Resilience Syndrome: A Modern Day Neurological Pathology of Increased Susceptibility to Mild Brain Trauma, Concussion, and Downstream Neurodegeneration," *Surgical Neurology International* 5 (2014): 97. C. I. Viadro, "Sulfate, Sleep and Sunlight: The Disruptive and Destructive Effects of Heavy Metals and Glyphosate," May 8, 2014, www.articles.mercola.com/sites/articles/archive/2014/05/08/heavy-metals-glyphosate-healthe effects.aspx; accessed August 21, 2014.

[43]   Hartzell and Seneff, "Impaired Sulfate Metabolism and Epigenetics."

[44]   Z. Honeycutt and H. Rowlands, "Glyphosate Testing Full Report: Findings in American Mothers' Breast Milk, Urine and Water," April 7, 2014, www.momsacrossamerica.com/glyphosate_testing_results; accessed August 23, 2014.

[45]   A. Gerlach and H.-P. Schmidt, "The Use of Biochar in Cattle Farming," *Journal for Ecology, Wine Growing and Climate Farming*, www.ithaka-journal.net/panzenkohle-in-derrinderhaltung?lang=en; accessed August 22, 2014.

[46]   C. M. Gallagher and M. S. Goodman, "Hepatitis B vaccination of male neonates and autism diagnosis, NHIS 1997–2002," *Journal of Toxicology and Environmental Health. Part A* 73, no. 24 (2010): 1665–1677.

[47]   N. Campbell-McBride, *Gut and Psychology Syndrome: Natural Treatment for Autism, Dyspraxia, A.D.D., Dyslexia, A.D.H.D., Depression, Schizophrenia* (Cambridge, UK: Medinform, 2010).

# The New Genetics and Dangers of GMOs

Mae-Wan Ho

The original rationale and impetus for genetic modification was the "central dogma" of molecular biology that assumed DNA (deoxyribonucleic acid) carries all the instructions for making an organism, which are transmitted via RNA (ribonucleic acid) to protein to biological function in linear causal chains. This is contrary to the reality of the "fluid genome" that has emerged since the mid-1970s. In order to survive, the organism needs to engage in natural genetic modification in real time, an exquisitely precise molecular dance of life with RNA and DNA responding to and participating fully in "downstream" biological functions. That is why organisms and ecosystems are particularly vulnerable to the crude, artificial genetically modified RNA and DNA created by human genetic engineers and why genetic modification can probably never be safe.

## What's a GMO?

A genetically modified organism (GMO) is an organism with synthetic genetic material inserted into its genome. It is made in the laboratory with sterile techniques, which also means without sex. The genome is practically all of the genetic material of an organism, a copy of which is present (with few exceptions) in every cell of its body.

Every organism, for example, a plant, is made of tissues, tissues of cells, and as you go down the scale with an increasingly powerful microscope, you can see that each cell has a nucleus containing a copy of all its genetic material—the genome—packaged in structures called chromosomes. Each chromosome, when unwound, is a very long thread, called chromatin, and when you strip away the special proteins from the chromatin, you end up with the double helix DNA, the genetic material (Figure 1). The DNA is what gets chopped and changed in genetic engineering and genetic modification.

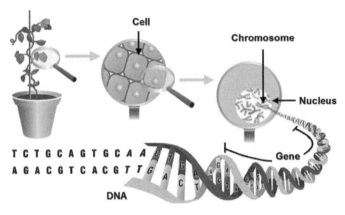

FIGURE 1

In genetic modification, foreign DNA is introduced into the genome of plant cells maintained in culture using a *vector*, a piece of DNA carrying the foreign DNA and designed to jump into the host cell genome. The foreign DNA—*transgenic DNA* or *GM construct*—typically contains more than one *gene*, a sequence of DNA that expresses a protein. Each transferred gene—a *transgene*—consists of a *coding sequence* that specifies the distinctive amino acid sequence of a protein, with a *promoter*, the signal for starting in front of it and a *terminator*, the signal for stopping behind it (see Figure 2). In addition, the GM construct usually includes one or more *marker genes* that enable the *transformed* cells (cells that have taken up and integrated the transgenic DNA) to be identified and selected. Antibiotic-resistance marker genes express antibiotic resistance, so transformed cells can be selected with antibiotics, which kill untransformed cells. Each transformed cell is then induced to grow into a plantlet that develops into a distinct transgenic plant. Because there is no control over where and in what form the transgenic DNA lands in the host genome, each resulting transgenic plant is essentially a different transgenic line.[1]

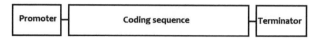

| Promoter | Coding sequence | Terminator |

FIGURE 2

The rationale and impetus for genetic engineering and genetic modification is the "central dogma" of molecular biology due to Francis Crick,[2] who shared the Nobel Prize with James Watson for the DNA double helix structure.[3] In its original form, the central dogma supposed that DNA carries all the instructions for making an organism. Individual "genetic messages" in DNA are faithfully copied or transcribed into RNA, which are then translated into proteins via a genetic code; each protein supposedly determines a particular trait such as herbicide tolerance or insect resistance—one gene, one character (Figure 3). If it were really as simple as that, genetic modification would work perfectly every time. Unfortunately, things are vastly more complicated.

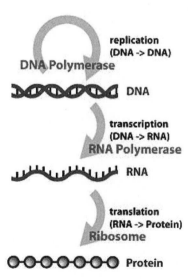

FIGURE 3

## The Fluid Genome and Natural Genetic Engineering

I first warned of the hazards of genetic modification nearly twenty years ago. In *Genetic Engineering: Dream or Nightmare?*[4] I described the new genetics of the "fluid genome"—a term coined by molecular geneticists in the early 1980s—and said that the greatest danger of genetic modification is that it is misguided by the ideology of genetic determinism (the "central dogma" of the old genetics). Genetic determinism made genetic engineering seem compelling, but was totally contrary to reality.

Instead of the linear, one-way information flow envisaged in the central dogma from DNA to RNA to protein and "downstream" biological function, there is intricate cross-talk between an organism and its environment at all levels, with feed-forward and feed-back cycles swirling through the epigenetic and metabolic networks of molecular interactions that mark and change genes as the organism goes about its business of living, their effects reverberating down the generations.

The organism is doing its own natural genetic modification with great finesse, a molecular dance of life that's necessary for survival. Unfortunately, genetic engineers don't know the dance; they are only now tracing its footprints in the genome. It is clearly impossible to modify one gene or one function at a time without affecting other functions, ultimately the entire organism. It is also this molecular dance of life that makes organisms and ecosystems so vulnerable to the unintended effects of genetic modification. Furthermore, the insults and injuries to organisms and ecosystems exposed to the GMOs can be passed on to future generations to influence the course of evolution. The human organism too shapes its own development and evolutionary future; that is why it is so important for us to take responsible action.

Indeed, new findings on the fluidity and responsiveness of the genome have made the hazards of genetically modified DNA and RNA even greater than I had envisaged, and I have updated the details in the following sections.

## GM Inherently Hazardous

Reliable evidence obtained by scientists independent of the biotech industry going back to the 1990s and by farmers in the field both show that GM feed invariably causes harm, regardless of the animal species or the food crops that were genetically modified or the genes and constructs inserted into the genome. The list below presents a consistent picture of GM-linked deaths and illnesses, with scientists confirming what farmers have experienced for years. This is particularly significant as independent scientific studies are rather meagerly supported, and scientists find it very difficult to obtain the GM material from the companies for their research. Nevertheless, the inevitable conclusion one comes to is that GM is inherently hazardous.[5]

### Accumulated Evidence on the Health Hazards of GM Food and Feed

1.  A two-year lab feeding trial, reported in 2012, found that rats of both sexes exposed to Roundup and/or Roundup-tolerant maize *not* sprayed with herbicide were two to three times as likely as controls to die and to develop large mammary glands tumors in females and kidney and skin tumors in males.[6] In other words, the GMO without the herbicide was also harmful in every respect. Pituitary disease was up more than twofold in females and liver and kidney diseases were one and a half to two times more in males on GM maize alone.

2.  A Danish farmer found excessive illnesses (including chronic diarrhea, birth defects, reproductive problems, bloating, stomach ulcers, weak and smaller piglets, and reduced litter size) and death in his pigs fed on GM soymeal. These conditions were entirely reversed when he put them on a GM-free diet.[7]

3.  A meta-analysis pooling all available data on 19 feeding trials carried out for ninety days on GM soybean and maize, both glyphosate-tolerant and Bt crops representing 83 percent of commercialized GMOs, found significant disruption of liver and kidney functions.[8]

4.  Professor emeritus Don Huber at Purdue University warned of a "pathogen new to science," associated with glyphosate-tolerant GM crops and livestock fed on them, causing unprecedented death and infertility.[9]

5.  Between 2005 and 2006, senior scientist Irina Ermakova at the Russian Academy of Sciences reported that female rats fed on glyphosate-tolerant GM soybeans produced an excessive number of severely stunted pups with more than half of the litter dying within three weeks, while the surviving pups were completely sterile.[10]

6.  Between 2004 and 2005, hundreds of farmworkers and cotton handlers in Madhya Pradesh, India, reported allergy symptoms from exposure to Bt cotton containing Cry1Ac or both Cry1Ac and Cry1Ab proteins.[11]

7.  Between 2005 and 2006, thousands of sheep died after grazing on Bt cotton crop residues in four villages in the Warangal district of Andhra Pradesh in India.[12]

8.  In 2005, scientists at the Commonwealth Scientific and Industrial Research Organisation in Canberra, Australia, tested a transgenic pea containing a normally harmless protein in beans (alpha-amylase inhibitor 1), and found that it caused inflammation in the lungs of mice and provoked sensitivities to other proteins in the diet.[13]

9.  From 2002 to 2005, scientists at the Universities of Urbino, Perugia, and Pavia in Italy published reports indicating that GM soy fed to young mice affected cells in the pancreas, liver, and testes.[14]

10. In 2003, villagers in the south of the Philippines suffered mysterious illnesses when a Monsanto Bt maize hybrid containing Cry1Ab protein came into flower; antibodies to the Cry1Ab protein were found in the villagers, there have been at least five unexplained deaths, and some remain ill to this day.[15]

11. In 2004, Monsanto's secret research dossier showed that rats fed on MON863 GM maize containing Cry3Bb protein developed serious kidney and blood abnormalities.[16]

12. Between 2001 and 2002, a dozen cows died in Hesse, Germany, after eating Syngenta GM maize Bt176 containing Cry1Ab/Cry1Ac plus glufosinate-tolerance; more in the herd had to be slaughtered on account of illnesses.[17] In 2012, biotech giant Syngenta was criminally charged in a civil court suit brought by a farmer, which ended in 2007, that its GM maize kills livestock.[18]

13. In 1998, senior scientist Arpad Pusztai and colleagues formerly of the Rowett Institute in Scotland reported damage in every organ system of young rats fed on GM potatoes containing snowdrop lectin, including a stomach lining twice as thick as controls.[19]

14. Also in 1998, scientists in Egypt found similar effects in the gut of mice fed on Bt potato containing a Cry1A protein.[20]

15. In 2002, Aventis (later Bayer CropScience) submitted data to the UK regulators showing that chickens fed on glufosinate-tolerant GM maize Chardon LL were twice as likely to die compared with controls.[21]

## What Are the Hazards of GMOs?

There are many possible hazards of GMOs associated with the fluid and responsive genome; I have put them into four categories:[22]

*Hazards of GMOs*

1. Uncontrollable, unpredictable impact on safety due to the genetic modification process*
   Scrambling the host genome*
   Widespread mutations*
   Inactivating genes*
   Activating genes*
   Creating new transcripts (RNAs), including those with regulatory functions*
   Creating new proteins

Creating new metabolites or increasing metabolite to toxic levels*

Activating dormant viruses*

Creating new viruses by recombination of viral genes in the GM insert with those in the host genome*

2. Toxicity of transgene protein(s) introduced (intentionally or otherwise)

Transgene protein toxic*

Transgene protein allergenic or immunogenic*

Transgenic protein becoming allergenic or immunogenic due to processing*

Unintended protein created by sequence inserted may be toxic or immunogenic

3. Effects due to the GM insert and its instability*

Genetic rearrangement with further unpredictable effects*

Horizontal gene transfer and recombination*

Spreading antibiotic and drug resistance*

Creating new viruses and bacteria that cause diseases

Creating mutations in genomes of cells to which the GM insert integrate, including those associated with cancer*

4. Toxicity of herbicides used with herbicide-tolerant GM crops*

Despite the lack of dedicated research, there is now a wealth of evidence that GM food and feed are unsafe, both from lab studies by independent scientists and from farmers' experiences in the field all over the world. The list of health impacts from GM feed includes birth defects, miscarriages, infertility, cancers, and mysterious new pathogens. There is also evidence that GM crops yield less, poison crops and soil, and cause the emergence and reemergence of many crop diseases.

Although the weight of evidence against the safety of GMOs is overwhelming, we are still largely in the dark as to the precise nature of

---

\*    Documented in scientific literature

the hazard(s) associated with different GMOs. Toxicity has been found for transgene products such as the Bt proteins from different strains of the soil bacteria *Bacillus thuringiensis*, expressed in many GM crops, while the multiple toxicities and carcinogenicity of glyphosate herbicides, heavily used with glyphosate-tolerant GM crops, are no longer in doubt. There remains a range of hazards that are not so easily identified, even though evidence exists for most, if not all of them, in the scientific literature. The difficulty arises due to the unpredictable and uncontrollable nature of the genetic modification process itself (category 1), which can activate or inactivate genes, scramble genomes, create new proteins, new nucleic acids, and new metabolites, and the transgenic DNA and its instability (category 3), in particular the instability of horizontal gene transfer—the direct transfer of DNA into the genomes of cells—from the GMO to all other species interacting with the GMO.

## To Conclude

The rationale and impetus for genetic engineering and genetic modification was the "central dogma" of molecular biology that assumed DNA carries all the instructions for making an organism. The mechanistic fallacy is inherent in the very term "genetic *engineering*," for it goes against the grain of the fluid and responsive genome that already emerged since the early 1980s.

Instead of linear causal chains leading from DNA to RNA to protein and downstream biological functions, complex feed-forward and feed-back cycles interconnect organism and environment at all levels, marking and changing RNA and DNA down the generations.

In order to survive, the organism needs to engage in natural genetic modification in real time, an exquisitely precise molecular dance of life with RNA and DNA responding to and participating fully in "downstream" biological functions. That is why organisms and ecosystems are particularly vulnerable to the crude, artificial genetically modified RNA and DNA created by human genetic engineers.

It is the fluid and adaptable genome that defeats all mechanistic attempts at genetic modification, which is why genetic modification can almost never be safe. It is a clash of ideology with reality.

## Endnotes

1    M.-W. Ho, "FAQ on Genetic Engineering," Institute of Science in Society Tutorial, www.i-sis.org.uk/FAQ.php.

2    F. H. C. Crick, "On Protein Synthesis," *Symposia of the Society for Experimental Biology* 12 (1958): 139–163; F. Crick, "Central Dogma of Molecular Biology," *Nature* 227 (1970): 561–563.

3    J. D. Watson and F. H. C. Crick, "A Structure for Deoxyribose Nucleic Acid," *Nature* 171 (1953): 737–738.

4    M.-W. Ho, *Genetic Engineering: Dream or Nightmare? The Brave New World of Bad Science and Big Business* (Penang, Malaysia: Third World Network, 1998), www.i-sis.org.uk/genet.php.

5    The full list presented in "Accumulated Evidence on the Health Hazards of GM Food and Feed" is drawn from M.-W. Ho, J. Cummins, and P. T. Saunders, "GM Food Nightmare Unfolding in the Regulatory Sham," *Microbial Ecology in Health and Disease* 19 (2007): 66–77, at www.i-sis.org.uk/pdf/GM_Food_Nightmare_Unfolding.pdf and from various updated studies and uncovered cases.

6    G. E. Séralini et al., "Long Term Toxicity of a Roundup Herbicide and a Roundup-Tolerant Genetically Modified Maize," *Food and Chemical Toxicology*, September 2012, http://dx.doi.org/10.1016/j.fct.2012.08.005; P. T. Saunders and M.-W. Ho, "GM Cancer Warning Can No Longer Be Ignored," *Science in Society* 56 (2012): 2–4; and P. T. Saunders, "Excess Cancers and Deaths with GM Feed: The Stats Stand Up," *Science in Society* 56 (2012): 4–5.

7    E. Sirinathsinghji, "GM Soy Linked to Illnesses in Farm Pigs," *Science in Society* 55 (2012): 8–9.

8    G. E. Séralini et al., "Genetically Modified Crops Safety Assessment: Present Limits and Possible Improvements," *Environmental Sciences Europe* 23 (2011): 10, www.enveurope.com/content/23/1/10; E. Sirinathsinghji, "GM Feed Toxic, Meta-Analysis Reveals," *Science in Society* 52 (2011): 30–32.

9    M.-W. Ho, "Emergency! Pathogen New to Science Found in Roundup Ready GM Crops," *Science in Society* 50 (2011): 10–11; M.-W. Ho, "Scientist Defends Claim of New Pathogen Linked to GM Crops," *Science in Society* 50 (2011): 12–13.

10   I. V. Ermakova, "Genetically Modified Soy Leads to the Decrease of Weight and High Mortality of Rat Pups of the First Generation: Preliminary Studies," *EcosInform* 1 (2006): 4–9 (in Russian); M.-W. Ho, "GM Soya-Fed Rats: Stunted, Dead, or Sterile," *Science in Society* 33 (2007): 4–6.

[11]  M.-W. Ho, "More Illnesses Linked to Bt Crops," *Science in Society* 30 (2006): 8–10.

[12]  M.-W. Ho, "Mass Deaths in Sheep Grazing on Bt Cotton," *Science in Society* 30 (2006): 12–13.

[13]  V. E. Prescott et al., "Transgenic Expression of Bean Alpha-Amylase Inhibitor in Peas Results in Altered Structure and Immunogenicity," *Journal of Agricultural and Food Chemistry* 53 (2005): 9023–9030; M. Malatesta et al., "Ultrastructural Analysis of Pancreatic Acinar Cells from Mice Fed on Genetically Modified Soybean," *Journal of Anatomy* 201 (2002): 409–415.

[14]  M. Malatesta et al., "Fine Structural Analyses of Pancreatic Acinar Cell Nuclei from Mice Fed on Genetically Modified Soybean," *European Journal of Histochemistry* 47 (2003): 385–388; M. Malatesta et al., "Ultrastructural Morphometrical and Immunocytochemical Analysis of Hepatocyte Nuclei from Mice Fed on Genetically Modified Soybean," *Cell Structure and Function* 27 (2002): 175–180; M. Malatesta et al., "Reversibility of Hepatocyte Nuclear Modifications in Mice Fed on Genetically Modified Soybean," *European Journal of Histochemistry* 49 (2005): 237–242; L. Vecchio et al., "Ultrastructural Analysis of Testes from Mice Fed on Genetically Modified Soybean," *European Journal of Histochemistry* 48 (2004): 449–454; M.-W. Ho, "GM Ban Long Overdue. Dozens Ill & Five Deaths in the Philippines," *Science in Society* 29 (2006): 26–27.

[15]  Ho, "GM Ban Long Overdue."

[16]  "French Experts Very Disturbed by Health Effects of Monsanto GM Corn," *GM Watch,* April 23, 2004, www.gmwatch.org.

[17]  M.-W. Ho and S. Burcher, "Cows Ate GM Maize and Died," *Science in Society* 21 (2004): 4–6.

[18]  E. Sirinathsinghji, "Syngenta Charged for Covering Up Livestock Deaths from GM Corn," *Science in Society* 55 (2012): 4–5.

[19]  A. Pusztai et al., "Genetically Modified Foods: Potential Human Health Effects," in *Food Safety: Contaminants and Toxins,* ed. J. P. F. D'Mello (Edinburgh: CAB International, 2003).

[20]  N. H. Fares and A. K. El-Sayed, "Fine Structural Changes in the Ileum of Mice Fed on Endotoxin-Treated Potatoes and Transgenic Potatoes," *Natural Toxins* 6 (1998): 219–233.

[21]  E. Novotny, "Animals Avoid GM Food, for Good Reasons," *Science in Society* 21 (2004): 9–11.

[22]  M.-W. Ho, *Genetic Engineering;* M.-W. Ho and Lim Li Ching, *The Case for a GM-Free Sustainable World* (London: Independent Science Panel Report, Institute of Science in Society and Third World Network, 2003); republished as *GM-Free: Exposing the Hazards of Biotechnology to Ensure the Integrity of Our Food Supply* (Ridgefield, CT: Vital Health, 2004), www.i-sis.org.uk /onlinestore/books.php#1.

# Global North

# Seed Emergency: Germany

Susanne Gura

## Legal Restrictions to Seed Diversity

The seed market in Europe is highly regulated. Seed varieties that are not admitted to the EU Common Catalogue administered by the EU's Community Plant Variety Office (CPVO, based in Angers, France) are banned from sale in the market. Approximately 2,500 varieties are admitted annually, half of which are ornamentals. The International Union for the Protection of New Varieties of Plants (UPOV) criteria of distinctness, uniformity, and stability (DUS) are stringently applied and extensive DUS testing is conducted. In addition, field crops must show a "value for cultivation and use." Of particular concern here is the emphasis on uniformity as uniformity has detrimental impacts on biodiversity. Industrial varieties are required to have very little internal genetic variation; this is why they cannot easily adapt to changing environmental conditions. Under difficult conditions, such as the dry and hot European summer of 2003, yields are much lower. Traditional varieties, on the other hand, contain large internal variation, enabling them to adapt to various challenges and changes in their environment.

More than a decade ago, the EU Council recognized the loss of biodiversity and asked the EU Commission to act with regard to seed legislation. In 2009, the Conservation Variety Directive was formulated, but seed savers throughout Europe did not make use of the new directive. In Germany, after its implementation in 2010, not even a dozen "conservation varieties" were registered. What went wrong?

Seed savers continued to swap their varieties or give them away in exchange for a donation, since the sale of unregistered varieties was illegal. The new directive is no better—it merely sets different conditions for the admission (called "registration") of conservation varieties. The admission fee is much lower than for industrial varieties, and DUS testing is not compulsory, but conditions are placed in order to limit the quantities reaching the market—as if there were already too many rare varieties being bought and sold!

Official set prices for rare varieties are admittedly not very low, but in order to sell them, seed savers must not only apply to register them, but also agree with others to keep total amounts within the limit, and must report on every gram of seed sold. According to the authorities, administrative work for the seed saver in Germany amounts to between 5.5 and 11 hours per variety each season. For example, the association Freie Saaten ("Free Seeds"), a regional initiative in southwest Germany, would have to hire more than three full-time staff only to fulfill these requirements in order to sell its 1,200 varieties, in addition to the admission fees. Such costs would not nearly be covered by the small amounts of seed that the association could sell.

All over Europe there are legal risks for seed savers. Only in February 2012, the owners of the Latvian farm Neslinko were persecuted by the authorities for selling tomato seeds at a garden club event.

## EU Seed Legislation Reform

The EU Commission has formulated a new seed legislation draft, as part of the Commission's "Better Regulation" initiative. An evaluation resulted largely in a very positive assessment of the existing legislation; unsurprisingly the assessment was carried out by a company that has served the agro-industry on several occasions. The "small" changes that the seed industry wants concern privatizing large parts of the DUS testing; streamlining the two different testing procedures for registration and variety protection; and extending variety protection to products so that royalties have to be paid not only for seeds, but also for products such as bread or jam. In addition, according to the European seed industry association ESA, and its international counterpart, CIOPORA, identification of varieties must be done using biotechnology methods.

Variety protection is for protecting property rights, not for varieties.

In addition to registration, European seed legislation has a second important component, the so-called seed variety protection. Breeders apply for protection of their varieties at the already-mentioned CPVO; currently, a total of nineteen thousand varieties are protected. The protection lasts for twenty-five or thirty years and allows the charging of royalties to farmers. The objective is to finance breeding work. According to German cereal breeders, the development of a single wheat variety costs about 2 million, and farmers pay between 5.95 and 10.75 royalty per metric ton of seed, equal to 2 percent of production costs. Cereal breeders claim that they invest 16 percent of their turnover in research; their argument is that they have to convince farmers to declare that they have used farm-saved seeds of a protected variety, and pay half the royalty.

But this information is not verifiable as the evaluation report simply states that the EU variety protection legislation "encourages breeders to invest in research and develop new plant varieties that meet sustainability objectives." It also reports that, on average, the market lifespan of a protected variety "is much shorter than the protection period provided under existing legislation. Nonetheless many breeders would still like to see the duration of protection extended to thirty years for all plant varieties." The positive result of the evaluation of the variety protection rights is based not on data, but on interviews with seed industry representatives who want to extend options to cash in royalties. There was no discussion of the fact that the seed industry has been using varieties bred by farmers for millennia, without any declaration of origin.

While farmers are not allowed to save seeds without royalty payment, breeders allow each other the free use of their protected varieties for further breeding purposes. Such a "breeders' exemption" does not exist in patent legislation. Breeders have to check the varieties they are using for patents on their genetic components and negotiate rights to use them, a costly procedure. There are attempts by European breeders to add the "breeders' exemption" to the EU patent legislation.

In an evaluation of the EU seed legislation, it has been noted that the distance between plant varieties has decreased in recent years, indicating a decrease of biodiversity. Many new varieties, though distinct from existing ones, are built on preexisting varieties in order to preserve the breeding progress made earlier. Genetic diversity in the market is therefore very narrow. For example, all European apple varieties in the market have at least one of three varieties—Golden Delicious, Cox Orange, or Jonathan—in their parentage.

Seed savers all over Europe have been discussing their views and experiences and have presented them to the EU Commission on various occasions, including via an open letter to several commissioners in the hope of addressing these potentially future-altering, detrimental policies and practices.

## Open-Pollinated Varieties Are Fast Disappearing

Hybridization was first applied in the 1940s by Henry Wallace, the 33rd vice president of the United States (1941–1945), who developed Pioneer Hi-Bred corn as well as hybrid chicken. When two different breeding lines are crossbred, productivity of the offspring can increase substantially. This hybrid vigor, or "heterosis effect," depletes in the next generation, so that farmers have to buy new seeds or breeding stock in order to keep up with market economics. Hybridization allows not only higher productivity, but also more market control if the original lines are kept exclusively in the breeding company. The breeding industry has developed hybrids for an increasing number of species and, as a result, open-pollinated varieties are disappearing from the market. Their numbers are decreasing in the catalogs of the seed industry with every new growing season.

Furthermore, much of the claimed breeding progress does not deliver on its promise. For example, the most important apple disease is scab, and a gene was found in a wild apple variety that is claimed to be resistant to the disease. It was bred into many apple varieties, such as Topaz; after only ten to fifteen years, the fungus causing scab was found in a number of apple varieties, indicating that the disease had broken through the "resistant" properties. Meanwhile, the oldest known German apple variety, Edelborsdorfer, is resistant to scab and has been so for approximately eight hundred years. Not just one gene is responsible for this, but a multitude of genetic factors, which continue to remain outside the control of biotechnology-based breeding.

Even organic farmers are now relying on hybrid seeds and breeds in order to reduce prices that are already high. (Interestingly, in Germany, it was found that organic methods are not more costly than conventional agricultural methods, but the distribution system is less efficient due to the smaller market.) Open-pollinated varieties could be brought back into the market and biodiversity restored if consumers made it a point to buy open-pollinated varieties by knowing how to identify them. Hybrid varieties in Europe have to be labeled "F1"; vegetables can also be labeled differently, e.g., "Trademark." But this is not widely known. In addition, garden seeds are offered at price thresholds labeled in capital letters, for example A to G, creating additional confusion for the consumer.

Around half the wheat grown in Germany is from farmer-saved seed. Wheat is self-pollinating, and hybrids of self-pollinating plants are difficult to breed. The wheat seed industry, however, still tries to earn a profit from the entire wheat area sown, including from farmer-saved seeds, and does so through unjust legislation. Since 1998, farmers in Germany have to pay royalties in the event that they sow seeds from their own harvest, but a considerable number of farmers are resisting this legislation—they are collaborating within the

Arbeitsgemeinschaft Bäuerliche Landwirtschaft (ABL) to fight these unjust, profit-driven laws.

The German cereal seed industry claims that 150 varieties of wheat are registered in the catalog of varieties admitted for sale in the European Union, which would be a large diversity and choice for farmers. But the German cereal industry should visit the exhibition of one hundred cereal varieties, "Korn," collected by four seed savers that has been attracting thousands of visitors on various occasions in Germany. Many were impressed by the powerful aspect of traditional varieties, a very rare sight nowadays, made possible by seed savers. Another exhibition on maize diversity attracted the attention of the German branch of the global maize seed market leader, Pioneer.

## The All-Powerful and Consolidated Seed Industry

Five corporations that originated in Europe are among the ten largest seed suppliers in the world: Syngenta, Groupe Limagrain, KWS, Bayer, and DLF-Trifolium. Consolidation in the vegetable seed market is notable. Bayer bought the vegetable seed companies Nunhems (in 2002), Hild (in 2010), and Abbott & Cobb (in 2012). Monsanto bought the market leader, Seminis, in 2005. According to a study commissioned by Swiss NGOs, vegetable seed markets in Europe are dominated by the two chemical corporations Syngenta and Monsanto: peppers 56 percent, tomato 62 percent, cauliflower 71 percent. The carrot seed market is dominated by Bejo Zaden and Vilmorin, seed companies based in the Netherlands and France.

The seed markets of France and Germany are valued at 3.15 billion, and account for nearly 50 percent of the EU market (about 6.4 billion); these two countries also account for 56 percent of all protected varieties. And it is primarily these two who are shaping EU seed legislation. The CPVO is located in France and its board president is German. In France all seed-related interest groups are jointly represented by the GNIS (National Interprofessional Association for Seeds and Plants) and are dominated by large seed corporations. The

EU Commission has hired a GNIS staff member to administer the seed legislation reform. The heads of both the European Seed Association and its horticultural sister organization, CIOPORA, are both Germans.

Syngenta, Bayer, and of course the global market leader, Monsanto, are chemical corporations primarily. The business model of seeds that they have developed is dependent on agrochemicals. Monsanto became known for its Roundup Ready GMO technology: genetically modified plants that resist Monsanto's own herbicide, glyphosate, with the trademark Roundup. If this devastating weed killer is sprayed, nothing survives except the GMO crop (mostly maize, rapeseed, and cotton). Bayer offers LibertyLink, a gene resistant to its glufosinate, trademarked as Basta.

Another large chemical corporation, BASF, has become notorious for its influence on the German government. The then coalition of Christian Democrats (Angela Merkel) and Liberals (Guido Westerwelle) agreed in their coalition treaty to foster BASF's genetically modified potato, Amflora—the first industry product ever to be mentioned in such an agreement. In the meantime, however, attempts to get Amflora approved for the market were withdrawn. BASF decided to also withdraw its biotech research unit from Germany and relocate it to the United States.

## A Front against GMOs

GMOs are facing rejection by the German public. Monsanto's maize MON810 is now banned, and a demonstration plot where GMOs were grown solely for public-relations purposes remains closed. But the approval procedures at the EU Commission continue. BASF has applied for approval of a disease-resistant GMO potato variety; the European Food Safety Authority (EFSA) endorsed the cultivation of Monsanto's herbicide-resistant soy. If EU Member States can't agree on a decision, the EU Commission will decide, likely in favor of the GMO. A commission proposal to allow national GMO bans got stalled.

Several organizations are campaigning and lobbying against GMOs. At the European level, the EU Group of the International Federation of Organic Agriculture Movements (IFOAM) has a focus on GM-free seeds. The Interessengemeinschaft für Gentechnikfreie Saatgutarbeit (IG Saatgut) was set up in 2005 by seed savers and organic breeders in German-speaking countries. The Bantam campaign spread seed of an open-pollinated maize variety and asked growers to register a map indicating where GMO maize is grown, since GMO cultivation has to stay within a minimum distance from conventional crops.

## Patents on Seeds in Europe

The EU Bio-patent Directive 98/44/EC stipulates that genetically modified plants and animals are patentable. With regard to conventionally bred plants and animals, the directive has been interpreted by the European Patent Office in such a way that an increasing number of patents have been granted in recent years. Stipulations that varieties and breeds, and essentially biological breeding processes, are not patentable in fact have not hindered their patenting.

On February 9, 2012, the German parliament unanimously adopted a resolution insisting that no patents be granted on conventional breeding methods, livestock and plants derived by such methods, as well as their offspring, and that the scope of product-by-process patents, which cover livestock and plants, be limited to the process described in the patent. Similarly, the EU Parliament on May 10, 2012, adopted a resolution calling on the European Patent Office "to exclude from patenting products derived from conventional breeding and all conventional breeding methods."

The No Patents on Seeds initiative engages in campaigns for clear EU patent regulations to exclude from patentability plants and animals, genetic material and processes for breeding of plants and animals, and food derived thereof. The coalition is initiated by large environmental and development organizations and is supported globally by more than three hundred NGOs and farmers' organizations. The coalition assesses that patents on seeds are used not to protect inventions, but to control the basis of global food supply. In times of steeply rising food prices, royalties are out of place.

## Hope for Organic Breeding

Organic farming associations and breeders have become alert to the disappearance of open-pollinated varieties—which is related to corporate consolidation—and have begun working actively on the issue. In Germany in the 1980s, an initiative for vegetable seeds from Demeter organic agriculture started producing open-pollinated varieties, and in 2001, the breeding company Bingenheimer Saatgut AG was founded. Today it is Europe's largest producer of organic seeds. A nonprofit breeding association, Kultursaat, was established in 1994; it has since registered forty-three newly bred vegetable varieties. Variety-specific information is given to professional gardeners so that it can be passed on to consumers and is called "Vegetables with Character." Another project entitled "Fair Breeding" is supported by several organic shops. A new association, Saat:gut, began breeding cauliflower and broccoli, two vegetables where open-pollinated varieties had been almost completely removed from the market. The foundation Zukunftsstiftung Landwirtschaft (ZSL) has been funding such breeding initiatives for a decade. At the European level, organic breeders cooperate under the association ECO-PB. Their demands for EU seed legislation reform include a new window for officially tested varieties for special breeding programs (for organic and low-input cultivation; for on-farm breeding; and for increasing biodiversity); reducing the restrictions of the Conservation Varieties Directive; and removing the sales ban for the informal biodiverse seed sector.

During the 1980s, the massive loss of agricultural plant varieties became apparent, and a few concerned people started collecting what remained and set up associations to provide protection. In Switzerland, the foundation ProSpecieRara was established; in Austria the association Arche Noah; and in Germany two associations, the Verein zur Erhaltung der Nutzpflanzenvielfalt (VEN) and the Pomologenverein. Dreschflegel, a group of around a dozen professional seed producers, was set up. Other organizations were founded to look after livestock breeds, such as the Gesellschaft zur Erhaltung der Haustierrassenvielfalt (GEH), in addition to many other regional initiatives such as Freie Saaten in the Palatinate; LebensGut-Cobstädt in Thüringen; VERN in Brandenburg; and individual collectors such as Lila Tomate and Samenfest. An umbrella association for German-speaking countries was founded in 2009 to link advocacy, education, and public relations efforts as well as to cooperate in other important areas such as compiling databases and conducting workshops. At the European level, seed savers have set up "Let's Liberate Diversity"; since 2005 annual meetings have been held to swap seeds, and discuss seed industry and policy developments. A European Coordination, supported by EU-funded projects, has been established where position details are developed and concrete activities during the EU seed legislation reform are organized. The Seed Campaign thus unites European seed savers for specific actions, such as demonstrations and seed swaps.

# GM Soy as Feed for Animals Affects Posterity

Irina Ermakova and Alexander Baranov

A Russian study sponsored by the National Association of Genetic Safety (Moscow), and jointly conducted by Dr. Alexey Surov, Institute of Ecology and Evolution, Russian Academy of Sciences (Moscow), and Dr. Alexander Baranov, Institute of Developmental Biology, Russian Academy of Sciences (Moscow), was undertaken from August 2008 to May 2010, to determine the effects of GM soy (Roundup Ready, line 40.3.2) as feed for farm animals.

The experiment was carried out on Campbell's hamsters (*Phodopus campbelli*) over a period of two years and three generations. For the group of animals that were fed GM soy, the results indicated:

- slower growth and development
- disturbance of the reproductive system in both male and female animals
- sterility in a number of third-generation animals (the first generation is the parents)
- a reduced number of offspring
- an increased number of female offspring
- the formation of "hair brush" in the oral cavity of some animals

The experiment concluded that the feed containing GM soy (line 40.3.2) had a significant adverse effect on the reproduction, ontogenesis, and common biological parameters of mammals. The results underlined the imperative for additional independent studies to be carried out on the effects of GM soy in our food.

On October 10, 2010, at the symposium on genetic modification organized by the Russian National Association for Genetic Security (NAGS), Dr. Irina Ermakova made public the results of the research led by her at the Institute of Higher Nervous Activity and Neurophysiology of the Russian Academy of Sciences (RAS) in 2005–2010. The research established a clear dependence between eating genetically modified soy and the posterity of living creatures.

Investigation of the influence of genetically modified (GM) soy (Roundup Ready, line 40.3.2) on the birthrate and survival of adult Wistar rats and their offspring was performed in two series of experiments. In the first series the group of female rats received, in addition to the stock laboratory chow, 6–7 g/rat/day soy flour prepared from certified Roundup Ready GM soy for two weeks before mating, during mating, during pregnancy, and an increased daily amount for every pup during lactation. The second and the third groups were fed in addition to the rat chow in the same way and the same amount of traditional (Trad.) soy and Protein-isolate GM soy. The fourth group of rats received only the chow, and was considered to be a positive control group. The physiological state, the weight, and the mortality rate of the pups from the first mating were analyzed. A high level of mortality (approximately 51.6 percent) was observed with pups whose mothers received the GM soy supplemented diets, and 33.3 percent of these pups weighed less than 20 g by the end of two weeks after the birth, in comparison with the Trad. soy supplemented group and with the positive control group (12.9 percent and 12.2 percent, respectively). Survived pups in the reproductive period didn't give birth to offspring. In the second series both females and males received, in addition to the stock laboratory chow, 6–7 g/rat/day of traditional or GM soy granules (without oil) for two weeks before mating and during mating. Only 30 percent of females from the GM soy group gave birth to offspring. In the control groups about 83 percent of females given traditional soy and 100 percent of females in the group without soy additives gave birth. Morphological analysis showed the pathological changes in the testes (cell degeneration, disturbance of blood outflow) and liver (vacuolization) of males fed GM soy.

TABLE 1. MORTALITY OF RAT PUPS IN THREE WEEKS AFTER BIRTH

| Groups | Number of Newborn Pups | Number of Pups That Died | Dead Pups/Total Born (%) |
|---|---|---|---|
| Control | 74 | 6 $p<0.001$* | 8.1% |
| GM soy | 64 | 33 | 51.6% |
| Protein-isolate GM soy | 33 | 5 $p<0.01$* | 15% |
| Traditional soy | 50 | 5 $p<0.001$* | 10% |

* in comparison with GM soy group

TABLE 2. MATING OF FIRST-GENERATION (F1) OFFSPRING RECEIVING GM SOY

| Females (number) | Males (number) | GM Soy Feeding Scheme | Mating Scheme | Number of Rat Pups F2 |
|---|---|---|---|---|
| 12 F1 | 12 F1 | Continuation of GM soy additives for females and males | 3 females × 3 males (in turn) $n = 36$ | 0 |
| 12 F1 | 12 F1 | Feeding by GM soy was stopped before mating for females and males | 3 females × 3 males (in turn) $n = 36$ | 0 |
| 12 F1 | 12 controls (from mothers that didn't receive any soy additives) | Stopping of GM soy additives before mating for females | 3 females × 3 males (in turn) $n = 36$ | 72 |

It was revealed that Roundup Ready soy could have a negative influence on the adult animals and their offspring, causing disturbance of reproductive functions in adult animals and a high level of mortality, decreased weight gain, and infertility of pups. The morphology and biochemical structures of rats are very similar to those of humans, and this makes the results very disturbing.

## Publications

I. V. Ermakova, "GM Soybeans Revisiting a Controversial Format," *Nature Biotechnology* 25, no. 12 (2007): 1351–1354.

I. V. Ermakova, "Influence of Soy with EPSPS CP4 Gene on Physiological State and Reproductive Functions of Rats during First Two Generations," *Modern Problems of Science and Education: Biological Sciences,* no. 5 (2009), 15–21.

I. V. Ermakova, "Genetically Modified Organisms and Biological Risks," *Proceedings "Disaster Reduction,"* 2006: 168–171.

I. V. Ermakova, "Influence of Genetically Modified Soya on the Birth-Weight and Survival of Rat Pups," *Proceedings "Epigenetics, Transgenic Plants and Risk Assessment,"* 2006: 41–48, 8.

# Seeds in France

## Tiphaine Burban

On first consideration, the seed sector in France seems to be healthy; with seventy-four selection firms, 241 production firms, and 18,800 multiplication farmers, it leads the European market for seeds and plants. For some plants like wheat and sunflowers, France is an international leader—it is the second-largest international exporter of seeds in general, and the first in exporting maize seeds. The turnover of the whole seed sector has been increasing steadily. However, at closer viewing, the situation is not so rosy; for biodiversity and small-scale farmers, the evolution of agriculture over the last century has been quite painful.

The erosion of crop biodiversity has been considerable. Numerous varieties have disappeared at an alarming rate. Thus, 80 percent of the vegetable varieties cultivated in France during the 1950s are not cultivated anymore.[1] Only three or four varieties now cover 60 percent of wheat fields in France; they are commercial varieties, with a very weak genetic patrimony, and low capacity for adaptation to climatic change.[2]

The situation of French farmers is also very critical. The weight of farmers' debt has become heavier in the last few years, reaching around 147,500 per farm in 2009,[3] a figure that has been increasing continuously since 1990,[4] principally for major crops, polycultures, and above all cattle farms. Sometimes, debts become so onerous that farms are liquidated, and farmers' suicides are a reality in France. Agriculture is the one occupational category that shows the highest suicide rate in France; it is said that two farmers end their lives every day.

The situation for seed users is not much better as they have become dependent on seed and other agricultural inputs companies. Yet, only sixty years ago, farmers were autonomous. Seed breeding was a farmer's activity and varieties were adapted to different soils. French crop diversity was very rich. How did we get to the point that big companies and small-scale farmers are in conflict, hurting the environment?

The evolution of seeds in France is a fascinating and worrying story. It is a story of giving up, giving up our farmers' autonomy and our crop patrimony. With the commercial development of the seed sector, peasants progressively lost control of their seeds, essential for the survival of their activity.

## A Story of Giving Up

Up until the nineteenth century, every peasant in France selected and produced his own seeds. During the nineteenth and twentieth centuries, and primarily after 1945, the seed sector shifted to laboratories and fields dedicated to seed multiplication. It meant a complete overhaul for peasants, who, in this race for technology, lost their seeds and their autonomy. The very nature of their activity changed. From peasants they became farmers, agricultural exploiters, and now agri-managers. In the process, they also became simple seed users.

Two main strategies, promoted by the state and the private sector, encouraged the monopolization of the seed in France: the technological strategy and the regulation strategy.

### The Technological Strategy

The Second World War created the need for reconstruction and national recovery: planning and modernization were the two principles responsible for orienting the building of the seed sector during the second half of the twentieth century. The varieties promoted needed to be efficient on every soil. Seed, this grain of life, staple of human food, became a machine capable of producing in any standard environment.

Seeds, therefore, had to become a controllable item. This is why the French National Institute for Agricultural Research (INRA), created in 1946, began the creation and propagation of "stable" varieties. Pure lines were designed so that the crop yield could be precisely estimated beforehand, as long as farmers used the same variety. Maximization of the yield was the objective; and, in fact, the numbers proved that the pure lines were efficient in achieving this goal. For example, tender wheat was developed with better baking strength, and so French wheat baking strength has been multiplied by two within the second half of the twentieth century. With pure lines began the expected "genetic progress."

However, it was the introduction of hybrids in agriculture that really consolidated the technological strategy of private and public seed research. Contrary to the United States, this happened much later in France and was tougher. In fact, F1 hybrids invaded French fields after the Second World War, when they had already spread throughout the United States some years previously. This offered the opportunity to France to assess these new modern "seeds," which had high production costs and obliged farmers year after year to buy new seeds from the market. Nothing then indicated that hybrids would benefit French agriculture; on the contrary, they were considered the "Trojan horses" of a merchant economy in a peasant economy that until then had been autonomous.[5] However, it was not the American giants who invaded the French seed market and our farmers' fields; it was French public research itself that did so. With the INRA, it undertook hybrid promotion during its period of modernization; and the maize hybrids, F1, became models of this modernity, intended to help and prove the successful recovery of French agriculture. In 1949, a propaganda campaign was launched by the French government to strongly encourage farmers to adopt the hybrid maize: "Increase your maize crops! Sow hybrids! Your interest depends on it.…" Farmers ended up accepting these "modern seeds," and by the end of the 1950s, F1 hybrids were well settled in France.

Orienting its research toward the creation of stable, pure, and almost sterile varieties, the French government industrialized agriculture. Farmers became simple producers, sowing seeds stemming from the market. Seed companies developed and progressively monopolized seed breeding, with the support of a new regulation system.

*The Regulation Strategy*

The development of strict regulations progressively sectorialized French farms to their simple function of agricultural production. In fact, in order to be able to commercialize a seed, it is necessary to get it registered and certified. A subscribed seed is a seed registered in the Official Catalogue either from France or from the European Union. To obtain the subscription, the seed variety must meet the specific criteria of distinctness, uniformity, and stability (DUS). Distinctness refers to the unique characteristic of the variety, compared to others; uniformity requires a strong similarity among plants of the same variety; stability demands that the plant's characteristics stay the same crop after crop. This subscription is granted by the Permanent Technical Committee for the Selection of Seeds and Plants (CTPS) created in 1942. Through its control of these three criteria, this public organization ensures the fixing paradigm of the variety.

Seeds must also meet the Agronomic and Technological Value (VAT) criterion. This is used to assess the "genetic progress" of the variety compared to other varieties famous for their high performance, and is based on criteria such as yields, use value, or yields regularity factors. Progressively, new varieties replace previously created varieties, according to technical progress. A decree passed in 1960 imposed the radiation of varieties from the Official Catalogue that were "outmoded." Even though private breeders opposed this law, saying it imposed a very sustained pace for seed improvement, the Ministry of Agriculture and the National Institute for Agricultural Research managed to have the law passed. Requirements concerning seed breeding are strict, and costs are heavy. In order for a selected variety to be registered and sold, the breeder must pay a large amount of money: 15,000 for ten years for big crops and 10,000 for vegetable species. This requires producing seeds in very high quantities, so as to absorb subscription costs. As a consequence, the investment needed for plant breeding and production has become very onerous.

Not only is breeding controlled, so is production. Commercialized seeds must be certified by the Official Service for Control and Certification (SOC). It checks the quality of products in seed production companies and with seed multiplier farmers, in accordance with the rules of the Ministry of Agriculture.

INTELLECTUAL PROPERTY RIGHTS

In order to protect varietal innovations and to recognize breeders' work, a system of intellectual protection was created by the International Union for the Protection of New Varieties of Plants (UPOV), founded in 1961, called the Plant Variety Rights (PVR). Delivered by the Group for the Study and Control of Varieties and Seeds (GEVES), a branch of the Permanent Technical Committee for the Selection of Seeds and Plants, the PVR is an alternative to a patent since it protects the product of the research and not the *process or genes* included in the variety. It thus has the advantage of preventing firms from monopolizing genetic resources discovered in nature, or in farming communities' stocks. However, it does not oblige the breeder to communicate details of the breeding.

In the early 1960s, while the PVR was being created, farmers could still preserve their right to sow seeds stemming from their own crops, or farm-saved seeds. A few years later, however, in 1970, a new UPOV convention considered the use of farm seeds as forgery. In theory, it became illegal to save and resow your own seeds. Fortunately, good sense prevailed and farm-saved seeds remained "farmer privilege." In 1991, the third UPOV convention tried to forbid this; France, faced with an amazing mobilization of organizations defending farmers' rights to sow their seeds, sought to authorize farm-saved seeds, on condition of paying a tax. Finally, the French government decided to retain the law of PVR 1970. Subsequently the European Economic Commission itself adopted the law, with all the French provisions. Since 1994, according to European legislation, farm-saved seeds are authorized for twenty-one varieties under the European PVR on payment of a tax. For remaining species, every farmer who planted seeds stemming from past crops could be accused of forgery. In France, two systems are in force: the French PVR of 1970 (reformed recently in 2011) and the European PVR. Seed breeding was intrinsic to farmers' activity; it then became a privilege, and was finally considered forgery—a progressive privation of farmers' rights.

REGULATED ACCESS

For seed-breeding companies there are many advantages to specializing in vegetable innovation, since the created seed is protected. To have a monopoly on a seed delivered in a market where every farmer goes to get his seeds is a great benefit. Access to breeding, however, was becoming more and more difficult; the CTPS introduced a card that was delivered to peasants who applied to be professional breeders in 1955. They had to conform to some very demanding criteria: reserving five hectares to seed production; not being millers or bakers; and having sufficient tools. Many peasants who couldn't qualify were refused breeder cards. The method was too direct and tough for most farmers, and subsequently, conditions for seed-selling were formulated to indirectly regulate access to seed and plant breeding. The decree of June 11, 1949, made registration with the catalogue a condition for selling seeds; but, as mentioned earlier, DUS and VAT criteria were very demanding and made a very important distinction between seeds. As a result, between 1950 and 1960, half the demands for subscription of a variety to the catalogue were refused.[6] Many peasants were forced to delegate seed breeding and seed production to private firms; a legal regime designed to counter monopolization was thus made to appear as a compromise with farmers.

## Unfair System

The result of the regulation and technological strategies has been the promotion of a strong private seed sector. Private seed companies captured the market and managed to defend their interest with the support of the public sector. The CTPS selects potential varieties for the Official Catalogue and in this way controls French agriculture. Since it is composed of private and public researchers, it should demonstrate public and private "partnership" in the orientation given to the seed sector. However, the private sector took the lead on it. What matters are not farmers' rights or healthy food, but private companies' interests and profits. Even though Jean-Pierre Despeghel, research leader for oleaginous plants in Monsanto Europe, explains that what motivates him in his vocation is "among many things, freedom to create. The breeder is free of his choices,"[7] farmers, as far as they are concerned, have lost their capacity to choose. There is no freedom for them.

The private sector creates what it calls "biodiversity," simply another way to monopolize French fields, French food, and the French environment. On the contrary, farmers, descendants of generations of autonomous peasants, are simple producers, users of seeds that they don't control anymore. Seed savoir faire is no longer transmitted from one generation to another, and propaganda discredits farmers' competencies. All this contributes to discouraging them from getting involved in breeding activities and in defending peasants' practices and knowledge. During a colloquium organized in February 2012 on the anniversary of the creation of the PVR, one of the participants asked what farmers could really bring to research in vegetable breeding. The National Interprofessional Association for Seeds and Plants (GNIS) declared on its website: "The conservation of genetic resources requires technical competencies that exceed a farmer's job."[8]

This presentation, partly historical, of the seed sector underlines the complexity of a system that has progressively escaped the control of peasants,. Of course one could say that demand determines supply. In that case, peasants should stop buying market seeds if they don't suit their needs. However, distinctness, uniformity, and stability criteria have created clone seeds, and the seeds and plants market is dominated by a few multinational companies. Limagrain, the first French seed company, is ranked fourth internationally after Monsanto, Pioneer, and Syngenta. It bought up the big vegetable seed companies Vilmorin, Clause, and Tézier, and became the second leader internationally in vegetable seeds, proving the positive effect of concentration. Plus, it focuses on wheat, hoping to control the sector, from seed to consumer's plate. This is why it is a shareholder in huge companies specializing in baked goods. Last but not least, it is starting GMO testing in France, and also in the United States and India. The financial weight Limagrain gained through its domination of the market makes for a political advantage too; it is now developing partnerships with the public sector to lead research on bio-technologies and promote GMOs in France, as well as around the world. French government policies no longer represent citizens' choices but the interest of a few big companies interested in gaining an advantage over their American competitors.

## A Worrying Present

Despite the strict regulation of the seed sector, which is worrying, a certain freedom has been left to farmers. The state tolerated peasants' practices, even as it was developing seed regulation. Farmers could continue sowing their own seeds, illegally, but without state repres-sion. Tolerance preserved peasant autonomy. But the situation threat-ens to get worse. Nowadays, farmers must face many new challenges that put their remaining freedom at stake.

## The GMO Threat

France was well known for its resistance to GMO crops in its fields, despite the European welcome for transgenic crops. MON810 is in-dicative of the French attitude of precaution concerning GMOs. In 1998, the European Union accepted the culture of GMO maize seeds

MON810. France decided on a moratorium to suspend this authorization, until there is conclusive proof that these GMOs are harmless. However, resistance to GMOs in France was at issue again in the winter of 2011. The Conseil d'État (the highest administrative jurisdiction in France, advising the government as well as Parliament on bills and laws) assessed that there was not enough proof of the *risks* of the GMO MON810, and decided to repeal the moratorium of 2008. This was a first success for big seed companies—the GMO threat was coming back. The same day, on the afternoon of November 28, 2011, a bill on Plant Variety Rights was passed in the National Assembly. The French seed companies' union (with Bayer, Limagrain, Monsanto, Pioneer, Vilmorin, and Syngenta) had managed to defend their claim for more financial resources for their research through a "fair" return on their creation: the compulsory voluntary contribution. The companies promoting GMOs and those defending the PVR were the same. Farmers were supposed to participate "compulsorily voluntarily" to the promotion of GMOs in French fields. Fortunately, the opposition of civil society and the precautionary French politics enabled the reinstatement of the moratorium. However, a moratorium is only a suspension of a right—the complete freedom to cultivate the genetically modified crop MON810 is still likely.

Even though GMO crops in France are not yet cultivated, their consumption is authorized. The problem lies in the definition of genetically modified crops in order to determine what can be sold and what cannot. This regulation needs to be improved, and the law widened so that full information is given to consumers; for example, since July 1, 2012, meat from animals fed without GMO grains now gets the "without GMO" label.

## Organic Farmers: Victims of the Regulation System

Yet another problem, a more permanent one, is the legislation regarding organic farmers. The regulation of organic agriculture, especially concerning the use of seeds, is draconian. Indeed, organic farmers would be the first to use traditional seeds, adapted to local environments as they require strong plants that can resist adverse climatic conditions and predators. Peasant seeds, cultivated for many years on particular soils, develop resilience and meet the criteria of organic agriculture. Commercial seeds, on the other hand, are engineered to be cultivated in any environment, and are homogenized with chemical inputs. They are unsuitable for organic agriculture. Organic farmers are also the ones who face the strictest control. In fact, to obtain recognition of their organic practices (with the label AB, Organic Agriculture, for example), they have to prove the organic origin of the inputs (such as seeds) that they are using. Since 1995, seeds destined for organic agriculture must be produced without GMOs and within organic agriculture conditions. This means that organic farmers cannot benefit from laws allowing the use of farm-saved seeds. This is a very important issue in the debate about the regulation of the seed sector, as a growing number of farmers are reverting to organic agriculture in France.

It is when the situation worsens progressively that people start worrying. Over the last few years, farmers and citizens have begun challenging the threat to biodiversity and to farmers' rights. Protesting and creating alternatives, they bring some optimism to the future of the seed in France.

## Let's Sow Our Freedom!

The reinforcement of the European regulation concerning organic seeds in 2002 led to the creation of a massive protest movement in France on the issue of free seeds. Meetings were organized in February 2003 between peasants, researchers, sociologists, and others to defend farmers' seed-breeding activity. The event gave birth to the idea of "semences paysannes" or "peasant seeds." The Peasant Seeds Network, le Réseau Semences Paysannes, was also formed with the objective of bringing together organizations working for the promotion of "free seeds."

The Peasant Seeds Network today is composed of more than sixty organizations and individual farmers. It helps members to present their points of view and their experiences, share seeds, and organize common trainings. These activities provide the movement with a platform that enables the question of peasant seeds to be taken seriously. Organizations divide themselves into working groups according to geographic areas, species, and everyone's needs. They then work on bringing specific species back into cultivation, or simply on promoting traditional varieties that could interest local farmers.

## Public Seed Banks

Farmers can obtain traditional varieties from old peasants' granaries, or from public seed banks. Indeed, public research has acknowledged the importance of biodiversity conservation as genetic patrimony. Some initiatives to preserve this vegetable richness have been implemented since the 1960s; for example, the most important French seed bank was created within the National Institute for Agricultural Research of Clermont-Ferrand. More than ten thousand different varieties of wheat, of which four thousand are from France, are preserved in it. However, the lack of financial resources and of a real political will to preserve seed biodiversity means these initiatives are inadequate. To stock seeds and to ensure seed quality are expensive; this is why a selection is made between traditional varieties; recently, about seven hundred oat varieties were discarded, having been judged as being without interest. Moreover, even though public seed banks do send seeds to gardeners who ask for them, they do not participate in the promotion of a dynamic management of varieties. Their aim is to preserve varieties in the form in which they have been discovered, storing them in freezers, and conserving their fertility.

Fortunately, the public sector also helps in the preservation of traditional seeds through the regions. Regional nature parks launch local biodiversity research and promotion programs. For example, the regional nature park of Queyras in southeast France is famous for its involvement in the Peasant Seeds Network. In the northern region of Nord-Pas-de-Calais, the Regional Genetic Resources Center (CRRG) works on finding ancient local varieties, often after having been contacted by farmers. This center leads bibliographic research and field tests to define the characteristics of particular varieties. When the CRRG assesses that a variety is of interest with regard to yields, quality, and market demand, it can help farmers financially and legally to get their varieties registered and have legal access to the market. These public organizations work on the construction of a seed bank and on the promotion of local varieties.

All these public initiatives are essential, but French farmers' autonomy remains limited within this framework.

## Our Peasant Seed Banks

It is for this reason that the "maisons de la semence," seed houses, have emerged over the last few years. These are seed banks managed by farmers themselves, in partnership with researchers, and with the support of citizens who are sensitive to this new peasant dynamic. Till now, farm-saved seeds and traditional seeds were exchanged informally between neighbors, or even between farmers from different regions of France. However, they lacked a real space in which to gather, stockpile, and test the varieties bred, cultivated, and improved by farmers themselves. More than providing a space, however, these "maisons de la semence" are a concept—they represent all the human interactions involved in seed conservation. They create social links, nourish everybody's motivation, and support exchanges and the enrichment of the savoir faire.

## Participative Seed Breeding in France

Many foundations in France are developing more participative research and more democratic science. One of the issues they focus on is peasant seeds. The Citizen Sciences Foundation, for example, works at enlarging access to science and defends farmers' participation in seed and plant breeding. The idea is to think of farmers as scientists who can participate in research programs because they have a special and beneficial knowledge about farming. Moreover, public research is evolving toward widening its experimentation field and its contributors. A number of researchers in the National Institute for Agricultural Research are now working on a peasant seed-breeding project, in partnership with farmers, sociologists, economists, and citizens. This is participative breeding, and a few programs have been implemented within this new framework. For example, INRA and the members of Triptolème, an organization of the Peasant Seeds Network, came together on the PaysBlé project. The aim of this project is to "experiment, maintain, and promote the diversity of wheat varieties cultivated on the soils of Bretagne with organic agriculture." With public financing, farmers and bakers work together with scientists, and integrate science and seed breeding. They bring back local varieties, cultivate them in small quantities in order to multiply them, and then adapt them to the environment. Finally, they define precisely the characteristics of the varieties. In the Pays de Redon, in south Bretagne, a collection of 330 wheat varieties is conserved in a dynamic way in the baker-farmers' fields of the area. Contrary to the simple use and reproduction of peasant seeds, the PaysBlé project involves peasants in real research activity, successfully. It is very clear proof that more democratic research is possible!

## Demonstrations and Petitions

In parallel, many demonstrations and petitions have taken place in the 2000s in support of peasant seeds. In 2004, a petition campaign launched by the Peasant Seeds Network demanded that the state facilitate the commercialization of organic and conserved seeds. A new campaign, "Let's Sow Biodiversity," has recently begun for the signing of a petition concerning the law on PVR of December 2011. This cyber-action collected about twenty thousand signatures, demonstrating citizen response to the issue. Even though the bill was voted in, the strong mobilization of farmers and civil society seems to be delaying its application. Seeds are a public interest issue; they are political issues that must enter the public sphere of mobilization and debate. We hope this new awareness and the alternatives it encourages will spread in the next few years.

Although these initiatives are creating a positive dynamic among farmers and citizens, their expansion remains limited by the legal framework that does not recognize the extraordinary value of peasant seeds. The regulatory system needs urgently to be reformed. Indeed, the actual evolution of the law to meet alternative peasant practices is unsatisfactory, as it does not support farmers' autonomy as it should.

The reform of French law regarding seeds may prevent varieties from disappearing, but it does not support farmers' rights. In 1997, the Official Catalogue opened a register for "ancient varieties for amateur gardeners." An order of 1997 authorized famous varieties to be commercialized to amateurs who would cultivate them for their own consumption only. But have we forgotten what "amateur" really means? It is "the one who loves," and farmers love their plants, as much as gardeners.

A decade later, in 2008, the European directive that established a register for conservation varieties was transposed into French legislation. Disappearing varieties could now be registered in the catalogue for a much lower cost than conventional varieties, and with less strict criteria, but their diffusion remained limited to the original region of the variety. In 2010, the French register for conservation varieties was further improved and it is now divided into two: a list of conservation varieties and a list of varieties without intrinsic value. The subscription criteria are widened and adapted to new agricultural practices, including organic agriculture. But many problems remain. The diffusion of conservation varieties is still very limited; it sets out the conditions only for commercialization of one variety, whereas farmers exchange a lot of their seeds among themselves. Finally, it is limited to vegetable varieties, since the National Interprofessional Association for Seeds and Plants claims that the demand for ancient and/or local varieties is not important enough to begin reforming cereal seeds' regulation. Yet some associations such as Triptolème work on preserving, cultivating, and adapting peasant wheat varieties to their needs and to their soils, sometimes breaching law barriers.

The few reforms undertaken by the government are indicative of the possibility of changing laws and regulations when citizens and organizations demand it. However, the measures mentioned above cannot give peasants much satisfaction, as the catalogue is not adapted to peasant seeds, based on their continuous evolution (rather than their stability) with rich interactions among famers. What is required is a new conception of the catalogue that excludes peasant seeds—free seeds need their own regulation that protects and promotes their development.

## Conclusion

There was a time in France when farmers sowed their own seeds, adapting them to their environment and enriching local biodiversity. There was a time when farmers were autonomous and controlled their agricultural activity.

Then there came a time when farmers lost their seeds and the knowledge for saving, breeding, and producing their seeds. They lost their autonomy, to the advantage of big private companies.

It is time now for farmers, researchers, and citizens to create alternatives to recover their autonomy and to preserve seed biodiversity and seed freedom. The seed issue concerns us all. It is about our food sovereignty, about our environment, about our freedom. Guy Kastler, seeds spokesperson of Confédération Paysanne, says, "If today we are prevented from re-sowing our own seeds, tomorrow we will be prevented from giving birth." The seed issue is a social debate, a debate that is deeply political, and must involve us all.

## Endnotes

[1]   R. A. Brac de la Perrière et al., avec la Contribution d'Elise Demeulenaere et François Delmond, Visions Paysannes de la Recherche, Fondation Sciences Citoyennes, Réseau Semences Paysannes, BEDE, 2011: 60.

[2]   Fondation Nicolas Hulot, "La Maison de la Semence," www.fnh-tv.org.

[3]   http://agreste.agriculture.gouv.fr/IMG/pdf_Gaf11p057-060.pdf.

[4]   www.agreste.agriculture.gouv.fr.

[5]   C. Bonneuil and F. Thomas, *Gènes, Pouvoirs et Profits: Recherche Publique et Régimes de Production des Savoirs de Mendel aux OGM* (Versailles: Editions Quae, 2009), 619.

[6]   Ibid.

[7]   www.gnis-pedagogie.org/pages/vocation/temoignages.htm.

[8]   www.gnis.org.

# Kokopelli v. Graines Baumaux

## Blanche Magarinos-Rey

The association Kokopelli, named after the Native American deity of farming fertility, is a nonprofit organization based in the South of France. Founded in 1999, it has been involved in the preservation and distribution of organic, open-pollinated, and free-of-rights seeds of heirloom varieties. Although this activity may appear as extremely important and valuable in the context of widespread erosion of our phytogenetic resources, Kokopelli has been sued by the state of France and held guilty by the French Supreme Court for not distributing modern, homogeneous, and proprietary varieties of seeds, and thus not complying with the applicable European legislation on the marketing of seeds. However, this harsh judicial decision was followed by such a wave of indignation from civil society, media, and politicians that it was never enforced. Nonetheless, Kokopelli's activities still face serious threats as the seed industry feels it is the watchdog for this legislation.

One of its members, the company Graines Baumaux, took the initiative in December 2005 to sue Kokopelli before civil jurisdictions, on the grounds of "unfair competition." Since then, Graines Baumaux has been claiming that it sells only registered and authorized varieties of seeds, after incurring great administrative and financial costs, and that Kokopelli, by not going through the mandatory prior authorization procedure set by the European Directives and by offering a larger collection of seed varieties for sale, is disrupting the seed market and creating conditions of unfair competition.

Graines Baumaux had an annual turnover of 14 million and annual assets worth 2 million (2011 figures). Although the company is growing steadily and has had trouble demonstrating any actual financial prejudice, it has requested compensation of 100,000 and the end of Kokopelli's activities.

In the first instance, the tribunal in Nancy partially agreed to Graines Baumaux's request and sentenced Kokopelli to pay up to 10,000 in reparations to this company. The tribunal, in its judgment dated January 14, 2008, held that Kokopelli, by selling nonregistered varieties, was responsible for acts of unfair competition leading to a "market disruption" in the seed sector.

As this judgment was questionable for a range of reasons, Kokopelli decided to appeal against it. Before the Court of Appeal, the association first decided to present a defense aiming at disputing the validity of the European Directives hampering the right to put seeds of heirloom varieties on the market. The Court of Appeal, in February 2011, accepted to suspend the course of the trial and to refer the following question, suggested by Kokopelli, to the European Court of Justice for a preliminary ruling:

> Are Council Directives 98/95/EC, 2002/53/EC and 2002/55/EC and Commission Directive 2009/145 valid in the light of the following fundamental rights and principles of the European Union, namely, freedom to pursue an economic activity, proportionality, equal treatment or non-discrimination and the free movement of goods, and also in the light of the commitments arising from the International Treaty on Plant Genetic Resources for Food and Agriculture, particularly in so far as they impose restrictions on the production and marketing of old seed and plants?

National courts in each EU country are responsible for ensuring that EU law is properly applied. But there is a risk that courts in different countries might interpret it in different ways. To prevent this happening, there is a "preliminary ruling procedure." If a national court is in doubt about the interpretation of EU law, it may ask the Court of Justice for advice. This advice is called a "preliminary ruling." The national court *must* have recourse to the European Court of Justice when the question at stake concerns the *validity* of EU law. The European Court of Justice is indeed the only judicial institution with competence for invalidating texts of European law. Its rulings have authority upon all tribunals and courts of the Member States of the European Union.

Before that European Supreme Court, Kokopelli argued that Directives 2002/53 and 2002/55, on the marketing of seeds of agricultural and vegetable species, respectively, were violating the principle of freedom to pursue an economic activity and the principle of proportionality.

The freedom to pursue an economic activity forms part of the general principles of EU law. Those principles are, however, not absolute, but must be viewed in relation to their social function. Consequently, the exercise of the freedom to pursue an economic activity may be restricted, provided that any restrictions in fact correspond to objectives of general interest pursued by the European Union and do not constitute in relation to the aim pursued a disproportionate and intolerable interference, impairing the very substance of the rights guaranteed.

We argued that, given the range of criteria set for the registration of seed varieties in the Official Catalogue and the harsh restrictions placed on the marketing of "conservation varieties," the European legislation actually ruled out heirloom varieties from the market and, by doing so, impaired the very substance of the right to pursue an economic activity.

Further, the principle of proportionality, which is one of the general principles of EU law, requires that measures implemented through provisions of EU law be appropriate for attaining the legitimate objectives pursued by the legislation at issue, but must not go beyond what is strictly necessary to achieve them.

In our case, we submitted that the prior authorization procedure set for the authorization of seeds by the two Directives—similar to the procedure set for pesticides or medical treatments, as if they represented a sanitary or an environmental threat—was the most restrictive means of regulating the conduct of an economic activity, and that a prior declaration procedure, or a simple repressive regime sanctioning frauds to regulations laying down basic requirements for seeds, or even mere labeling requirements, would guarantee good quality of seeds in the market and fair and loyal trade in the EU economic space.

Regarding the Directive of the Commission 2009/145 on the marketing of "conservation varieties," Kokopelli put forward the violation, by several of its restrictive provisions, of the fundamental principle of equal treatment or nondiscrimination, of the principle of free movement of goods within the European Union, and of the commitments entered into by the latter under the terms of the International Treaty on Plant Genetic Resources for Food and Agriculture (ITPGRFA), in particular its Article 9.

The principle of equal treatment, or of nondiscrimination, requires that comparable situations must not be treated differently and that different situations must not be treated in the same way unless such treatment is objectively justified. On that basis, we argued that heirloom varieties were in a different situation than modern widespread varieties, namely a situation of particular biological and economic precariousness or vulnerability, given their disappearance from the market and farms since the 1960s. For that reason, their marketing and distribution should be incentivized by EU law, and not deterred. Contrary to that, Directive 2009/145 placed such burdens and restrictions on the production and marketing of "conservation varieties" that it violated the correct understanding of how the principle of nondiscrimination should be applied.

Concerning the free movement of goods, we questioned the obligation to produce and sell "conservation varieties" only in their "region of origin," as required by Directive 2009/145. That geographic restriction goes against the European single market that guarantees the free movement and marketing of all goods in all Member States.

Moreover, to our knowledge, no other goods are burdened by such restrictions. Some agricultural goods, with denomination of origin, must be produced in certain regions of Europe, but they can be sold anywhere in Europe afterward. These restrictions, intended to conserve certain phenotypic characteristics of old varieties, should be faced by Member States and their botanical conservatories, not by economic operators, especially when they're small.

Finally, we hoped that the Court would interpret the International Treaty on Plant Genetic Resources for Food and Agriculture and its famous Article 9 on farmers' rights—in spite of its very poor and "soft" drafting—in a teleological way. In this sense, we have stressed that the European Union, by signing this international commitment, expressed its intention to not "limit any rights that farmers have to save, use, exchange and sell farm-saved seed/propagating material." However, we did not ignore that Article 9 leaves its application to the discretion of its underwriters by using the very insidious expression "subject to national law and as appropriate."

On January 19, 2012, Advocate General of the European Court of Justice, Mrs. Juliane Kokott, published her opinion on the case.[1] To our great satisfaction, it validated almost all our arguments. It therefore seemed quite probable that Kokopelli would win the case.

Indeed, the Court is helped by nine "advocates general," fully members of the Court, whose job is to present opinions on the cases brought before the Court. They must do so publicly and impartially. Their role is similar to that of a public prosecutor in a national legal system. They are responsible for collating evidence and representing the EU interest in cases before the European Court of Justice. As of 2003, advocates general are only required to give an opinion if the Court considers the case raises a new point of law. Although the written opinions of the advocates general are advisory and do not bind the Court, they are nonetheless very influential, and it is rare that the Court does not follow the opinion of the advocate general to whom the case was assigned.

In our case, the Advocate General proposed that the Court should rule as follows:

> The prohibition against the sale of seed of varieties that are not demonstrably distinct, stable and sufficiently uniform and, where appropriate, of satisfactory value for cultivation and use, established in Article 3(1) of Council Directive 2002/55/EC of 13 June 2002 on the marketing of vegetable seed, is invalid as it breaches the principle of proportionality, the freedom to conduct a business within the meaning of Article 16 of the Charter of Fundamental Rights of the European Union, the free movement of goods established in Article 34 TFEU and the principle of equal treatment within the meaning of Article 20 of the Charter of Fundamental Rights.

This opinion is focused on Article 3(1) of Directive 2002/55 because this provision is absolutely key in the whole European legal corpus on the marketing of seeds, particularly as it requires that varieties shall be either accepted prior to their marketing or simply prohibited—the criteria for their acceptance being that of distinctness, uniformity, and stability, as well as satisfactory value for cultivation and use for agricultural species.

Considering this article invalid brought into question the very foundation of what constitutes the legislation on seeds, and modern breeding in general. According to the opinion of the Advocate General, accepted and nonaccepted varieties should coexist in the market for the greatest benefit of farmers, consumers, seed economic operators, and biodiversity in general.

That is exactly what Kokopelli had said from the beginning....

Although well reasoned, with courageous references and interpretation of the applicable legal basis, the opinion of the Advocate General[2] was not followed by the Court.

With the July 12, 2012, ruling, the Court surprisingly decided that:

> Consideration of the question raised has disclosed no factor of such a kind as to affect the validity of Council Directive 2002/55/EC

of June 13, 2002 on the marketing of vegetable seed, and of Commission Directive 2009/145/EC of November 26, 2009 providing for certain derogations, for acceptance of vegetable landraces and varieties which have been traditionally grown in particular localities and regions and are threatened by genetic erosion and of vegetable varieties with no intrinsic value for commercial crop production but developed for growing under particular conditions and for marketing of seed of those landraces and varieties.[3]

Unfortunately, the Court ignored our arguments or got several of them mixed up, making obvious in many parts of its decision that it hadn't carefully read our submission. The arguments we had made concerning Directive 2009/145, for example, have often been taken as critiques of Directive 2002/55. The Court also ignored the fact that Kokopelli not only trades seeds of vegetable species, but also agricultural crops like cereals or maize. Its ruling appeared to be rather superficial and drafted more like a press release than a legal verdict. The interpretation of EU law by the judges, mostly taken up from the Commission's simplistic submission, took the texts literally and remained superficial, without going into the details of what they really mean when looking at implementing measures and regulations and without assessing their true implications and consequences in real life.

It is true that the seed legislation is rather complex, and requires, for its understanding, the mastery of several agronomic notions. However, it is within the reach of anyone truly willing to investigate the issue, and we expected the Court to have this will, as we have been used to its rather refined legal and practical analysis on other topics in the past.

One must also note that the Court was under pressure from the seed industry, as we were confidentially informed that the European Seed Association (ESA), based in Brussels, had sent a long letter disputing the opinion of the Advocate General to the Court, and that this letter remained in the Court during several months before being sent back. Indeed, the ESA had no legitimacy to intervene in this trial whatsoever, as it was not a party to the proceedings. We are not aware whether this letter had any impact on the Court's opinion, but we surely regret that such an incident troubled the course of theoretically impartial proceedings.

Nevertheless, the Court ruling gave rise to much indignation across Europe, and the file was sent back to the French Court of Appeal, in Nancy, for that jurisdiction to decide upon the particular litigation between Kokopelli and Graines Baumaux, in light of what had just been decided at the European Supreme Court level.

Back in Nancy, we decided to change our defense strategy and be more aggressive on the legal terrain chosen by our opponent, namely the unfair competition argument, forwarded by Graines Baumaux itself. We thoroughly investigated what Graines Baumaux, as well as many other major operators on the French seed market, were doing commercially and found that the vast majority of them were either discreetly or blatantly selling varieties not registered in any Official Catalogue! We strongly demanded that this commercial context be considered when evaluating Kokopelli's supposed "misconduct."

Graines Baumaux, in particular, had nearly fifty nonregistered varieties in its 2012 and 2014 commercial catalogues, and we were able to prove it by having a bailiff's report prepared and notified to the Court.

Graines Baumaux argued that these varieties were mere mistakes or spelling errors committed by official authorities, but it could not provide evidence to support this argument.

Therefore, Kokopelli contended that Graines Baumaux, by committing exactly the same acts it accused its competitor of, lacked interest to act and that its action should be dismissed altogether.

Alternatively, we also demanded the strict interpretation of EU and French law on the marketing of seeds, by putting forward the exact definition of the term "marketing," that is, "the sale, holding with a view to sale, offer for sale and any disposal, supply or transfer *aimed at commercial exploitation*." That definition allowed us to argue that seeds traded to home gardeners, who have no intention of commercially exploiting their private harvest, were not concerned by the legal obligations set by the legislation, and that the corresponding varieties were then not to be submitted to the mandatory registration process.

Apart from these defense arguments, we also counterattacked Graines Baumaux by making well-documented counterclaims. In particular, we put forward that Graines Baumaux had published many disparaging documents and manuscripts on Kokopelli, calling it, for example, "a collector of Aztec antiques" or an "intellectual crook."

Finally, we argued that Graines Baumaux had committed parasitism—which is merely one of the illustrations of unfair competition—by buying all "adwords" relating to Kokopelli on several search engines on the internet.

On September 9, 2014, the Court of Appeal made its deliberation public. To our great satisfaction, it rejected most of Graines Baumaux's demands, in particular the ones based on an alleged unfair competition related to the lack of registration of the seed varieties distributed by Kokopelli. The first-instance judgment was therefore reversed, making Kokopelli the final winner of this long judicial battle.

In substance, the Nancy Court of Appeal stated that Kokopelli could not be accused of unfair competition as long as the association markets public-domain varieties that could be registered in the Official Catalogue by Graines Baumaux itself if this company truly wished to expand its commercial catalogue in the same proportion as Kokopelli. Graines Baumaux was thus trapped in its own declarations that registering varieties in the Official Catalogue was very simple and cheap.

That doesn't mean, however, that Kokopelli's activities were officially endorsed by the Court of Appeal. On the contrary, the argument that the sale of seeds not "aimed at commercial exploitation," namely to home gardeners, would not be subject to registration requirements in the Official Catalogue was rejected by the Court. Indeed, the Court found, after a particularly Byzantine grammar lesson, that "the wording of Article 2 of the Directive can be interpreted as meaning that its provisions apply to the sale, or offering for sale or other forms of transfer of seeds made in the course of commercial operations, which excludes seed sales to third parties for any other purpose, such as to conduct experiments, and allows to remove from the scope of the text exchanges of seeds between home gardeners who do not trade their vegetable seeds." The Court therefore only excluded seed exchanges among home gardeners from the scope of the legislation. Any seed transfer, either against payment or free of charge, not "aimed at commercial exploitation," as formulated by the law, but "in the course of a commercial operation," as stated by the Court, falls under the scope of the legislation and its registration requirements.

This interpretation is, to say the least, questionable. However, it is likely to have repercussions throughout Europe, and we hope the European legislator will correct it in the context of the current legislation reform project.

Anyway, in the particular dispute between Kokopelli and Graines Baumaux, the decision of the Court of Appeal of Nancy means that while it is true that Kokopelli commits illegal acts through the sale of unregistered seed varieties, these acts do not generate an unfair competition vis-à-vis Graines Baumaux and generally "do not have the effect of distorting competition." These considerations bring Kokopelli to safety vis-à-vis Graines Baumaux and the seed industry in general, and it is obviously essential.

As for mutual accusations of defamation, the Court pit the parties against each other and sentenced them to pay each other 5,000. If by this part of its decision the Court seems to show a will to reconcile the parties and decide fairly, we should not forget that it is Graines Baumaux that had been filing charges against Kokopelli for almost ten years and wanted to see its activities purely and simply ceased. We can therefore say that Graines Baumaux's initiative has simply failed and that Kokopelli comes out a winner of this long judicial battle.

Moreover, we should also insist that this long saga, although time, money, and energy consuming, has been a great opportunity to raise consciousness about Kokopelli's work, in particular, and the threats hanging over seed and biodiversity, in general. That is one of the reasons why these issues are today undoubtedly much more popular in the French and European population than they were ten years ago.

That which doesn't kill us surely makes us stronger.

## Endnotes

[1]   For relevant excerpts from the opinion of the Advocate General, see "Excerpts from the Opinion of Advocate General Kokott Delivered on January 19, 2012." For more details, see http://curia.europa.eu/—Case C-59/11: "Opinion," ECLI:EU:C:2012:28. http://curia.europa.eu/juris/document/document.jsf?text=&docid=118143&pageIndex=0&doclang=EN&mode = req&dir=&occ=first&part=1&cid=13345.

[2]   Ibid.

[3]   For relevant excerpts from the ruling of the European Court of Justice, see "Excerpts from the Ruling of the European Court of Justice: An 'Ode to Productivity.'" For more details, see http://curia.europa.eu/—Case C-59/11: "Judgment," ECLI:EU:C:2012:447. http://curia.europa.eu/juris/document/document.jsf?text=&docid=125002&pageIndex=0&doclang = EN&mode=lst&dir=&occ=first&part=1&cid=238051.

## Excerpts from the Opinion of Advocate General Kokott Delivered on January 19, 2012

### Introduction

1.  It is well known that the number of plant varieties grown in European agriculture is on the decrease. Many traditional varieties are disappearing or are simply preserved in seed banks for future generations. Instead, the fields are dominated by a handful of varieties individual specimens of which, moreover, seem very similar to each other.

2.  For that reason, biodiversity in agriculture is in significant decline. It is possible that, as a result, certain varieties which could, for example, adapt more successfully to climate change or to new diseases than the varieties that currently predominate will, in the future, no longer exist. Today, the end-consumer's choice of agricultural products is already restricted.

3.  One would imagine that this development is primarily driven by the economic interests of farmers who, where possible, grow the most productive varieties.

4.  However, the present case demonstrates that the restriction of biodiversity in European agriculture results, at least in part, from rules of European Union ("EU") law. In fact, seed for most of the plant varieties used in agriculture may only be marketed if the variety is officially accepted. Acceptance presupposes that the variety is distinct, stable and sufficiently uniform. In certain cases, productivity, that is that the variety is of "satisfactory value for cultivation and use," must also be proved. Such proof cannot be adduced in relation to many "old varieties." Consequently, the question arises whether this restriction on trade in seed is justified.

### Concerning the Principle of Proportionality

*i) The legislature's efforts to balance the interests concerned*

80.  According to the recitals in the preamble to the directive under review and the arguments advanced in most of the submissions made

in the present proceedings, the prohibition against the marketing of seed of varieties that are not accepted is based on the notion that the objectives pursued are in the interests of economic operators. High levels of productivity and protection against seed of varieties not satisfying the criteria for acceptance are matters that correspond to the economic interests of many farmers.

81. However, the rules also concern the interests of economic operators and consumers who are not primarily interested in high productivity levels and standard products. In addition, they also touch upon the public interest in the genetic diversity of agricultural varieties.

82. Economic operators whose interests are not primarily focused on productivity are considerably restricted as a result of the existing system. Seed producers, seed merchants, farmers and consumers of agricultural products cannot use varieties with characteristics which differ from those of accepted varieties. If, for example, a variety that is not accepted has a different taste to that of accepted varieties or produces a better yield under certain growing conditions, it may—all the same—not be marketed. In addition, efforts to develop varieties that are not accepted into varieties satisfying the acceptance criteria are rendered more difficult.

83. At the same time, consumer choice is restricted. Consumers do not have access to food or other products made from varieties not satisfying the acceptance criteria, nor may they grow those varieties themselves, for example in their own gardens.

84. Restricting farmers to the use of accepted varieties ultimately reduces genetic diversity on European farmland as fewer varieties are grown and there is less genetic variation between the various individual plants of those varieties. [ ... ]

86. Although seed banks and cultivation in limited areas can contribute to the conservation of varieties that are not accepted, such measures typically depend on public funding. By contrast, commercial use of varieties that are not accepted would be a much more robust means of ensuring their conservation and, in practical terms also, would result in greater biodiversity.

87. In the light of the recitals and the arguments advanced in the observations submitted to the Court, in particular, by the Council and the Commission, it is not evident that the legislature took account of those interests prior to the adoption of Directive 2009/145. For that reason alone, the provision at issue appears manifestly disproportionate.

## ii) Balancing the disadvantages and aims

88. If, nonetheless, the legislature engaged in an (undocumented) exercise to weigh up those interests, it clearly failed to achieve the objective of securing an appropriate balance between disadvantages and aims.

89. The advantages of a sales prohibition over less onerous measures, such as labelling requirements, are—as set out above—in essence limited to preventing the mistaken use of seed that has not been accepted. However, that risk would be minimal, if sufficiently clear warnings were prescribed.

90. By contrast, there is no reason to fear that European farmers will lose access to high-quality seed. Even in the absence of a prohibition against the marketing of varieties that are not accepted, farmers can make use of varieties that are listed in the catalogue of varieties and thus satisfy the acceptance criteria. In the light of the yield qualities of accepted varieties, there is also no reason to anticipate any appreciable predatory competition from varieties that are not accepted. [ ... ]

92. According to the Council, a further advantage of the marketing prohibition is the fact that this prevents even the use of seed that is not accepted. Such seed may be harmful or incapable of ensuring optimal agricultural production. I understand this argument to mean that farmers—if necessary, even against their will—are, in practice, to be compelled to use productive varieties. However, that constitutes only a very limited advantage as, in principle, it is for farmers to decide which varieties to grow. They could also choose not to cultivate their fields at all.

93. By contrast, the disadvantages of the prohibition against the marketing of seed of varieties that are not accepted are considerable. They impact—as I set out above—on the freedom to conduct a business, on consumers of agricultural products and on biodiversity in agriculture.

94. Consequently, it must be concluded that the disadvantages of the prohibition against the marketing of seed of varieties that are not accepted manifestly outweigh its advantages.

## Concerning Directive 2009/145

99. Pursuant to Article 4(2) of Directive 2009/145, the acceptance of conservation varieties nevertheless presupposes proof of a certain minimum quality as regards distinctness, stability and uniformity. In addition, there are considerable restrictions on the use of those varieties. Pursuant to Articles 13 and 14, seed may only be grown and marketed in its region of origin or similar regions. In conjunction with Annex I, Articles 15 and 16 also place restrictions on seed quantities. For each variety, depending on the species concerned, seed may be marketed per year only for crop production on 10 to 40 hectares of land.

101. [ ... ] having regard to the limitations inherent in those rules, it is not the objective of those rules to allow for the commercial use of the varieties involved. Consequently, insufficient consideration is given to the interests of economic operators and consumers. [ ... ]

103. In summary, it must be stated that even following the adoption of Directive 2009/145 on derogations for vegetables, disadvantages remain for economic operators and consumers whose access to old varieties that are not accepted is impeded. Those disadvantages—irrespective of any disadvantages for biodiversity—are manifestly disproportionate to the advantages of the prohibition, without any attempt having been made by the legislature to attain a balance.

## Concerning the Principle of Freedom to Pursue an Economic Activity

107. It is clear that the rules on the marketing of seed restrict that freedom. Unless a variety has been accepted, its seed may not be marketed, nor can it be purchased for growing.

108. According to Article 52 of the Charter of Fundamental Rights, any limitation on the exercise of the rights and freedoms recognised by that charter must be provided for by law and respect the essence of those rights and freedoms. Subject to the principle of proportionality, limitations may be made only if they are necessary and genuinely meet objectives of general interest recognised by the European Union or the need to protect the rights and freedoms of others.

109. Consequently, justification for interference with the freedom to conduct a business must satisfy the requirements of the principle of proportionality. As it has already been established that the sales prohibition is disproportionate, in principle, it also infringes the fundamental right to pursue an economic activity.

## Concerning the Principle of Free Movement of Goods

114. The prohibition at issue necessarily results in a restriction of trade. As that restriction, too, is justified only if it satisfies the principle of proportionality, to that extent, my reasoning above also applies here.

## Concerning the Principle of Equal Treatment or Non-discrimination

116. The difference in treatment in the present case arises from the circumstance that seed of accepted varieties may be sold, whereas seed of varieties that are not accepted may not. The sales prohibition is based on the fact that the criteria for acceptance have not been established. The absence of such proof constitutes a

difference between the varieties which, in principle, would also justify a difference in treatment; for example, a special labelling requirement for the seed of varieties that are not accepted.

117. However, as I have already set out, the disadvantages of a sales prohibition are disproportionate to the aims of the scheme. Consequently, the difference in treatment is not justified and the prohibition at issue must be regarded as invalid also on the ground of breach of the principle of equal treatment.

## Concerning the International Treaty on Plant Genetic Resources for Food and Agriculture

53. Whether the European Union is bound by the International Treaty is not at issue, as it is a Contracting Party. The question whether its nature and broad logic preclude a review of secondary law does not need to be determined by the Court in the present case. That is because the Treaty does not include any provisions which, as regards their content, are unconditional and sufficiently precise as to challenge the validity of EU legislation on the marketing of seed.

54. Article 5 of the International Treaty provides that measures should be taken "subject to national legislation" and "as appropriate." Pursuant to Article 6, "appropriate measures" are to be developed and maintained. This is followed by an illustrative list of such measures. Consequently, both provisions leave it to the discretion of States to determine the measures to be adopted. Therefore, the freedom of the European Union to regulate the marketing of seeds is not restricted as a result.

55. Article 9 of the International Treaty concerns farmers' rights. In accordance with their needs and priorities, each Contracting Party should adopt measures as appropriate and subject to its national legislation. This also does not constitute a sufficiently unconditional and precise obligation.

Source: http://curia.europa.eu/—Case C-59/11.

## Excerpts from the Ruling of the European Court of Justice: An "Ode to Productivity"

## Concerning the Principle of Proportionality

42. Kokopelli submits that it is impossible for it to market seed of "old" vegetable varieties, given that, in view of its particular characteristics, such seed cannot satisfy the criteria of distinctness, stability and uniformity, and is thus unjustifiably excluded from the official catalogues.

43. In that regard, it follows from recitals 2 to 4 in the preamble to Directive 2002/55 that the primary objective of the rules relating to the acceptance of seed of vegetable varieties is to improve productivity in vegetable cultivation in the European Union. That objective explicitly forms part of the objectives of the common agricultural policy, as laid down in Article 39(1)(a) TFEU.

44. As a means of guaranteeing increased productivity in vegetable cultivation, the establishment—under uniform rules which are as strict as possible as regards the choice of varieties accepted for marketing—of a common catalogue of varieties of vegetable species on the basis of national catalogues is capable of ensuring that that objective is attained.

45. Such an acceptance regime, which requires the seed of vegetable varieties to be distinct, stable and uniform, allows appropriate seed to be used and, consequently, agricultural productivity to be increased, on the basis of the reliability of the characteristics of the seed. [ … ]

54. In that context, it must be held that the EU legislature was entitled to take the view that the acceptance regime laid down by Directive 2002/55 was necessary in order for agricultural producers to achieve productivity which is reliable and of good quality in terms of yield.

## Concerning the Principle of Freedom to Pursue an Economic Activity

78. In the present case, it is true that the acceptance regime for vegetable seed laid down by Directives 2002/55 and 2009/145 is capable of restricting the freedom of traders in old seed, such as Kokopelli, to pursue their professional activity.

79. However, the rules set out in Articles 3 to 5 of Directive 2002/55 are intended to secure improved productivity in vegetable cultivation in the European Union, the establishment of the internal market for vegetable seed by ensuring its free movement within the European Union, and the conservation of plant genetic resources, which are objectives of general interest. As is apparent from the grounds of the present judgment relating to the alleged breach of the principle of proportionality, those rules and the measures laid down by them are not inappropriate to the attainment of those objectives, and the obstacle to the freedom to pursue an economic activity which such measures represent cannot, in the light of the aims pursued, be regarded as disproportionately impairing the right to exercise that freedom.

## Concerning Directive 2009/145

64. Directives 2002/55 and 2009/145 take into account the economic interests of traders such as Kokopelli, in that they do not rule out the marketing of "old varieties." Admittedly, Directive 2009/145 imposes geographical, quantitative and packaging restrictions in respect of seed of conservation varieties and of varieties developed for growing under particular conditions, but those restrictions fall within the scope of the conservation of plant genetic resources.

65. Furthermore, as the institutions which lodged written observations contend, the EU legislature was not pursuing the liberalisation of the market for seed of conservation varieties and of varieties developed for growing under particular conditions, but was seeking

to ease the rules of acceptance while preventing the emergence of a parallel market for such seed, which was likely to constitute an impediment to the internal market for seed of vegetable varieties.

## Concerning the Principle of Equal Treatment and Directive 2009/145

73. By taking account of the particular characteristics of the different varieties of seed, the acceptance regime established by Directives 2002/55 and 2009/145 lays down, on the one hand, general rules with regard to the marketing of standard seed and, on the other, specific cultivation and marketing conditions for seed of conservation varieties.

74. Those specific conditions fall within the scope of conservation in situ and the sustainable use of plant genetic resources.

75. In that regard, recitals 2 and 3 to Directive 2009/145 state that, in addition to the general aim of protecting plant genetic resources, the particular interest of preserving conservation varieties lies in the fact that they are especially well adapted to particular local conditions and that they are apt to be grown under particular climatic conditions.

76. It follows from this that, in laying down, by Directive 2002/55 as well as by the directive adopted to implement it—Directive 2009/145—particular cultivation and marketing conditions with regard to seed of conservation varieties, the EU legislature treated different situations differently. Consequently, those directives do not breach the principle of equal treatment.

## Concerning the International Treaty on Plant Genetic Resources for Food and Agriculture

85. The validity of the act of the European Union concerned in the light of the rules of international law may be assessed where the European Union is bound by those rules and where the nature and the

broad logic of the international treaty at issue do not preclude this and its provisions appear, as regards their content, to be unconditional and sufficiently precise.

86. In that regard, it must be noted that, as a Contracting Party, the European Union is bound by the ITPGRFA. However, as the Advocate General noted at point 53 of her Opinion, that treaty does not include any provision which, as regards its content, is unconditional and sufficiently precise to challenge the validity of Directives 2002/55 and 2009/145.

87. Paragraph 5.1 of Article 5 of the ITPGRFA, in particular, provides that each Contracting Party is, subject to national legislation, and in cooperation with other Contracting Parties where appropriate, to promote an integrated approach to the exploration, conservation and sustainable use of plant genetic resources for food and agriculture and is in particular, as appropriate, to adopt a certain number of measures. [ ... ]

89. Thus, under those provisions, the measures to be adopted in any given case are left to the discretion of the Member States.

90. Furthermore, Article 9 of the ITPGRFA, on which Kokopelli relies, states that the Contracting Parties recognise the enormous contribution that the local and indigenous communities and farmers of all regions of the world, particularly those in the centres of origin and crop diversity, have made and will continue to make for the conservation and development of plant genetic resources which constitute the basis of food and agriculture production throughout the world.

91. Paragraph 9.3 of Article 9 of the ITPGRFA provides that nothing in that article is to be interpreted to limit any rights that farmers have to save, use, exchange and sell farm-saved seed/propagating material, subject to national law and as appropriate.

92. Accordingly, that article does not contain an obligation that is sufficiently unconditional and precise to challenge the validity of Directives 2002/55 and 2009/145 either.

Source: http://curia.europa.eu/—Case C-59/11.

# If People Are Asked, They Say NO to GMOs

Florianne Koechlin

November 27, 2005, was a special day for Switzerland: all Swiss people, eighteen years and above, were asked to vote on whether they wanted a five-year moratorium on commercial releases of GM crops in Switzerland: Yes or No. Every single district, all twenty-six of them, said Yes to the moratorium; the moratorium is now part of the Swiss Constitution.

For this initiative we collected 110,000 signatures—which turned out to be quite easy—but even so the positive result was a real surprise. The Swiss government, the national parliament, all middle and right-wing parties, as well as mainstream science, had opposed the initiative. Their campaign contained all the known arguments: damage to Switzerland as a research location, loss of jobs, economic disadvantages, and so on.

A historian said that this was the first time ever in Swiss history that an initiative was successful in all districts, against the opposition of government and parliament. So when people are asked about whether they want GMOs or not, they say No. The amazing support for the moratorium came from all the "usual suspects" as well as many supporters of conservative, pro-GMO parties who voted against their own party's doctrine, and also from people who normally do not bother to vote. People say No to GM food even in the home country of Syngenta, Nestlé, and Novartis & Co. Interestingly, these companies did not feature in the campaign against the referendum; it was scientists and politicians who spoke on their behalf.

An important factor for the success of the initiative was the extremely broad coalition that supported it. You might say that a five-year moratorium is not much, and some of the more radical NGOs (Greenpeace among them) did not support us in the beginning. But this modest request made it possible to build a coalition ranging from right to left. The conservative Swiss farmers' union was on board, as well as Countrywomen Switzerland, all organic farmers' associations, all consumers, environment NGOs from the Global South, and many more. The driving force was Schweizerische Arbeitsgruppe Gentechnologie (SAG), an umbrella organization of all GMO-critical NGOs in Switzerland. It was the first time that such a broad (and fragile) coalition took shape.

The ban on GM crops—and mainly the nationwide and intensive discussion of the moratorium before the vote—had a domino effect. The Swiss Constitution contains two avenues for people's participation other than via elections: with an initiative you can initiate a vote for a new provision in the Swiss Constitution, for which you need to collect at least one hundred thousand signatures in less than eighteen months. Most initiatives are declined by voters. With a referendum you can seek a vote if you oppose a new law, for which you need to collect at least fifty thousand signatures in less than six months. Changes in the constitution are automatically put up for a vote authorized in Switzerland. Today, there is no GM food on offer in the market, and according to the statistics of the agriculture department, 99.9 percent of feed imports are GMO-free. We are proud to say that Switzerland is GMO-free: no commercial releases, no transgenic food on the shelves, no transgenic feed in the market.

A few years later, in 2009, the fifth conference of GMO-free regions in Europe was hosted in Lucerne. Switzerland, it seemed, offered the possibility of more democracy and a means to establish a moratorium for the commercial release of GMOs. I'm not very proud of being Swiss in many respects, but the legal possibility of an initiative and a referendum seems to me to be a valuable model for involving people in the democratic process. Again, in 2009, a year before the moratorium ended, there was a national discussion on how we should proceed. Government and parliament decided to prolong the moratorium for another three years, till 2013, when it was again prolonged till 2017. What had changed their minds? The government and parliament were still (nearly) the same, and a majority of them GMO-supporters. But it had become clear that the moratorium (which does not include the experimental release of GMOs) had in no way had a negative impact. (Also, of course, everybody knew that if they did not agree to a prolongation we would start another initiative.)

To quote from the recommendation of the government to parliament:

> The Government's opinion is that neither in agriculture nor for consumers is there an urgent need for GMOs in food.
>
> According to consumer opinion there is not only no need for GMO products, but the rejection of them is even perceived as an advantage. What consumers want are high-quality, natural foods which have not been genetically modified.
>
> In the long run the three year extension of the moratorium has no effect on the economy as a whole. No consequences are to be expected for the job market or for the attractiveness of Switzerland as a location for business.

The moratorium turned out to be a good selling argument too: Swissness includes gentech-free food, a competitive advantage on the European and international market for an agriculture that, in small and hilly Switzerland, consists of many small-scale farmers who would find it difficult to compete with huge monocultures.

# The Italian Context

## Maria Grazia Mammucini

In recent decades, and in the Italian context too, the advent of a model of "industrial" agriculture characterized by hyperproductivity has resulted in the loss of biodiversity and native seeds. Seed legislation has greatly facilitated this process. In Italy, and in the European Union, seeds are in fact subject to a special system that in Italy is dictated by the so-called "seed law" (L. November 25, 1971, n. 1096, and subsequent amendments). The act establishes, among other things, a National Register of Varieties that, at the community level, flows into the Community Catalogue of Vegetable Varieties. The basic mechanism for seed activity in the European Community is homogeneous in all member countries, that is to say, that seed of any variety may not be commercialized if the same variety has not been registered in the National Register or in the Community Catalogue of Vegetable Varieties.

The varieties for which registration is sought must have some very specific characteristics: they must be distinct, stable, and sufficiently homogeneous, and must have a satisfactory agronomic value or use. The local varieties cannot have, by their nature, all these characteristics simultaneously. In fact, a definition of local varieties states that they have "... a large genetic basis, are difficult to improve, in terms of agronomic value, in the respective zones of adaptation, as they are the result of a sort of recurrent simple selection, implemented by the farmers for a long period of time." Thus it is mainly because of the regulations in force that local varieties are likely to disappear and be completely supplanted by commercial varieties.

With this regulatory framework, small seed companies as well as whole national seed collections and institutions of the sector have been purchased at comparatively modest prices by large agrochemical corporations. For these corporations seeds are just one item in their sales package of materials for agriculture and chemistry, and are another strategy for vertical integration of the global market, for agricultural goods of mass consumption, for food or other uses.

Public funding for the development and conservation of seeds has steadily declined and has now reached levels so low that even the largest collections of seeds are in danger and are increasingly dependent on the so-called public-private partnerships. These partnerships allow private companies that sell seeds to further expand their control of world seed stock on the basis of their patents. While public seed collecting institutions are compelled to put their seeds for disposal for free, private companies are free to choose not to participate in this free trade system and abuse it for their own interests. In addition, each new step taken toward the concentration of seed stocks in the hands of private firms leads to a reduction of seed varieties, and to a reduction in the number of breeders and scientists who maintain these stocks.

As this strategy on seeds to support a model of industrial agriculture was gaining momentum in Italy, strong countertendencies have simultaneously developed in the agricultural and food sector. In fact, the characteristics of the Italian territory, which is mainly hilly and mountainous, and especially the choice of enhancing local agroalimentary products and their bond with the territory, have favored the development of diverse farming models at the regional level since the late '90s, based on the protection of biodiversity. Local varieties and seeds are not only a collective heritage, but also a real point of reference for the cultural, social, and agricultural identity of the country; they have an economic value and are fundamental to safe and healthy food. For this reason Italy led the way in establishing regulations based on the Convention on Biodiversity after it was ratified in 1992 and the International Treaty on Plant Genetic Resources for Food and

Agriculture in 2001. Tuscany was the first region to legislate in this area, in 1997, enacting a law to protect indigenous genetic resources (LR n. 50/97), and was also the first region in Italy that, based on the precautionary principle, legislated in 2000 to ban the cultivation of GM crops in its territory, contributing substantially to the foundation of the European Network of GMO-Free Regions.

In 2003, in line with its commitment to sustainable food and agriculture issues, the region of Tuscany, at the initiative of Governor Claudio Martini, hosted the constitutive meeting of the "International Commission on the Future of Food and Agriculture" in Florence, which was chaired by Vandana Shiva and composed of some of the leading experts in the world of alternative food systems. The commission, with support from the region of Tuscany, elaborated on and disseminated proposals for an alternative to the current food system based on diversity, locality, and sustainability, which first resulted in the "Florence Declaration on Global Food Rights," and subsequently was the basis of the commission's first "Manifesto on the Future of Food," followed by the "Manifesto on the Future of Seeds."

The region of Tuscany committed to fulfilling the principles contained in these two documents, and among the first initiatives, approved Regional Law LR n. 64/2004, which allows the circulation of seeds at the local level and identifies even more effective tools for the conservation and enhancement of local varieties. This law has a symbolic economic value well beyond the regional level. Indeed, it may be the first brick of a system of rules that, while accepting the principle of the European single market and free trade, introduces mechanisms to protect rural communities and their intellectual property against the aggression of large companies, which today are widely favored by the mechanisms of standardization at the national and supranational level, and by the current regimes of intellectual property protection.

Based on its experience of the previous regional law (1977) and on principles contained in the most important international documents, the Regional Law LR n. 64/2004 has as its main objectives:

- *The protection of its heritage of landraces and local varieties* not only from an economic and scientific perspective, but also a cultural one. The extinction of a part of indigenous genetic resources would mean the loss not only of a unique and unrepeatable heritage, but would undoubtedly affect the culture and traditions of a population, linked also to its rural and agricultural traditions. In addition, the conservation of biodiversity in the agricultural and zootechnical fields is strictly linked to policies to enhance the quality and typicality of agro-food productions.
- *The landraces and local varieties belong to the natural heritage of farming, zootechnical, and forestry interest of Tuscany,* being part of the natural elements that characterize its territory and certainly constitute an asset. The landraces and local varieties are therefore a natural heritage of Tuscany and as such the region guarantees the collective use through the tools provided. Thus this system basically has a two-pronged approach, one of which addresses the protection and the other the enhancement of the local genetic heritage.

This same regional law contains other closely linked tools for the protection and defense of landraces and local varieties. These are:

- *The Regional Directories (Repertori Regionali),* consisting of a database of local Tuscan varieties and landraces, listed and described in the directories. They have been entered by universities, research institutes, farmers' associations, and individual citizens. Currently the number of local varieties registered is about 750, of which more than 600 are at risk of extinction. The inclusion of a local variety or landrace in the directory is subordinate to the presence of the characterization of the same, both from a morphological point of view (sometimes genetic), and from the point of view of the link with the rural culture and with the agricultural and zootechnical local tradition.
- *The regional germplasm bank,* for the *ex situ* conservation of local varieties at risk of extinction of the regional directory.

- *Custodian farmers*, farmers implementing *in situ* conservation in the areas of origin of the varieties listed in the directories.

- *The conservation and security network*, created to include in the network the regional germplasm bank, the custodian farmers, and other entities who may be interested for various reasons in the conservation of a particular local variety threatened with extinction. The other entities in the network can have motives other than purely scientific ones, such as cultural, gastronomic, or linked to the boosting of tourism for the development of a depressed area. The network is, above all, a *place* where one can try to implement all the actions aimed at ensuring sustainable use of agricultural, zootechnical, and forestry resources. The participants in the network—custodian farmers' sections of banks, and others—undertake activities of conservation, both *in situ* and *ex situ*, of local endangered varieties and put them back in *circulation* within the network itself. The importance of *circulation and exchange of seeds* among farmers is essential for the conservation of biodiversity and the preservation of local varieties from extinction. In this regard, in accordance with the law on seeds, nonprofit *circulation and exchange of seeds* are allowed inside the network, in "small amounts," and in well-defined geographic areas in order to maintain and reproduce.

- The tag that stipulates "*Made from local variety/landrace—Tuscan Regional Law 64/2004*," which can be affixed to the label of a product as is or transformed, is actually obtained from local varieties or landraces at risk of extinction. Its purpose is the protection of the right to information and consumer choice whereby the consumer knows that purchasing the product contributes to the protection of biodiversity values.

This is how Tuscany has protected local varieties from the patents of multinational corporations and has sanctioned, for the first time on a legal level, collective ownership of local varieties—and, in fact, also the principle of seeds as a common good.

This major work of recovery has also provided an innovative path for scientific research methods through a participatory approach to open collaboration among farmers, local communities, and researchers, and is fertile ground for practicing a new system of knowledge for addressing the ongoing environmental and climate crisis, based on integration between scientific and traditional knowledge and investment of public resources to support a new research system capable of producing innovation for the common good.

The conservation of local varieties has also offered a real opportunity for small-scale farmers to boost local circuits of production and consumption through direct sales, even with innovative organizational forms of short chain, such as markets, shops, and purchasing groups in solidarity, supported at the regional level and by local institutions. These initiatives provide both sources of income for small-scale farmers and opportunities for citizen-consumers to rediscover local traditions and knowledge. But above all this innovative ruling has reaffirmed mass selection conducted over the centuries by farmers and the value of the work of those (old and new farmers) who have not surrendered to industrial agriculture; who with their passion and dedication, have maintained, especially in mountainous and disadvantaged areas where intensive agriculture was almost impossible, to set a reservoir of biodiversity that is now the heritage of the whole community.

Other Italian regions have followed the example of Tuscany's experience with the LR n. 64/2004, pending national legislation that would give full effect to the principles of the FAO's Convention on Biodiversity and International Treaty on Plant Genetic Resources for Food and Agriculture. Six other regions besides Tuscany have legislated on agro-biodiversity: Lazio in 2000, Umbria in 2001, Friuli-Venezia Giulia in 2002, Marche in 2003, Emilia-Romagna and Basilicata in 2008. Many regions that had not yet passed laws, however, work with specific programs and projects on agro-biodiversity. Almost all regional laws provide tools such as: directories/regional registers of local landraces and varieties; regional germplasm banks;

growers/custodian farmers; the storage and security network (germ-plasm banks, custodian farmers); the enhancement of local landraces and varieties (seeds, products).

There are many bodies, including research institutions, working on agro-biodiversity and on preserving a priceless heritage of varieties and local seeds. In particular: the network of research facilities of the Council for Agricultural Research and Economics (CRA) under the Ministry of Agriculture (from the data presented to the National Conference on Biodiversity in Florence in 2010, there are numerous accessions: 8,380 varieties of fruit; 5,202 of vineyards; 15,970 of forest species; 16,410 of cereals; 110 of vegetables; etc.); the network of facilities of the National Research Council (Consiglio Nazionale delle Ricerche, CNR) headed by the Ministry of University and Scientific Research (data indicates 80,000 varieties in the seed bank; 1,860 varieties of fruit; 2,500 olive trees; etc.); finally, the many universities and other research institutions, at the national and local levels, that work on varieties and local seeds in association with the regions and local authorities. Unfortunately most of these research institutions suffer from a chronic lack of public funding, which is seriously putting at risk a priceless heritage of local seed varieties, as well as the work of many researchers over the years who have ensured the recovery and maintenance of such assets.

In the wake of the legislation in the regions, there have been novel changes at both the national and community level regarding the marketing of seeds of conservation varieties. In 2007 the Italian seed law was modified with the introduction of innovative concepts and tools to enable the marketing of conservation varieties in Italy, in the absence of clearer rules at the community level. Subsequently, the European Commission, after years of intense debate, finally pronounced on the marketing of the seeds of conservation varieties of agricultural species (or open field) and of the tuber potato seed (blocked since 1995), and further regulatory changes are under consideration. It is clear that the regulation of conservation varieties calls into question the entire regulation of the production and distribution of seeds, with the aim of strengthening the rights of farmers, preventing the formation of monopolies, and enhancing the capacity of local communities to conserve and increase biodiversity through social interaction.

Of recent note at the national level was the bill for the protection and enhancement of agricultural and natural biodiversity, which brings to the national level the labor and strategies implemented by the regions in recent years. It provides, among other things, for the protection of intellectual property of local varieties and the possibility for the movement and exchange of seeds. The law was approved unanimously by the European Parliament's Agriculture Committee in May 2012.

One of the most valuable outcomes, partly as a consequence of these innovative regulatory instruments, is that, beginning with Tuscany, the experiences of custodian farmers spread like wildfire. The "Fierucola" of the seeds and the Association of Custodian Farmers (Associazione Agricoltori Custodi) were the very first networks of local seeds and custodian farmers; today they are flourishing, even at a national level, with important experiments and experiences in this direction such as, among others, the Network of Rural Seeds (Rete dei Semi Rurali) and the Women in the Field Association (Associazione Donne in Campo).

In all these years an enormous heritage of varieties and local seeds has thus been accumulated in our country, thanks, largely, to the commitment of the custodian farmers, who, together with researchers, technicians, and local communities, found in local authorities, and in regions in particular, the basic support to implement activities and tools that are now available to all farmers and to society as a whole.

This heritage is now a fundamental value for the future of agriculture and food. The current crisis is making unequivocally clear the failure of the industrial model of agriculture pursued for all these years by multinational agribusiness. Indeed, today the companies most affected by the crisis are the monocultural industrial companies, while those more resilient are the diversified and multifunctional organic farms based on biodiversity and local markets, for which varieties and local seeds are the basis for their work and for producing safe and healthy food for all. It is therefore essential that all those who have worked in recent years to preserve and maintain local seeds are able to form an alliance to integrate their work, making it known to all citizens, and to find innovative and creative solutions to make local seeds available for everybody. For all the farmers who want to plant them, for the many urban and peri-urban gardens that are spreading in many cities, for school gardens, for family gardens, and for everyone who, even simply with a jar, wants to contribute toward saving native seeds.

# The Untold American Revolution: Seed in the United States

Debbie Barker

An exhibition at the National Archives in Washington, DC, *What's Cooking, Uncle Sam?* traces the history of US agriculture from the horse and plow to today's mechanized farm. While the exhibition contains humorous elements, including a corporate campaign to win the War Food Administration's endorsement of its Vitamin Donuts—"For pep and vigor ... Vitamin Donuts!"—it also chronicles a sobering story of American farming and how the effects of US food and agricultural policies reach far beyond the range of Uncle Sam. Throughout, it is clear that the path of agriculture begins with the seed.

Over the past forty years, the United States has led a radical shift toward the commercialization, consolidation, and control of seeds. Prior to the advent of industrial agriculture, there were thousands of seed companies and public breeding institutions in the world; at present, the top ten seed and chemical companies, with the majority stake owned by US corporations, control 73 percent of the global market.[1] Today, fewer than 2 percent of Americans are farmers,[2] whereas in 1810, 90 percent of our citizens lived on farms.[3] This probably represents a more transformative revolution than even the Revolutionary War recorded in our history books.

This essay will provide a summary of US seed policy history in order to establish the trajectory to present-day policies that threaten seed sovereignty for farmers and citizens, as well as for natural resources, wildlife, and food safety. As an early adopter of industrial seed development, including genetically engineered (GE) seed, and a forerunner in developing intellectual property rights (IPRs) for seed ownership, the historical narrative of the United States may serve as a resource for other countries to investigate.

Following the short historical narrative, the main topics discussed will include existing legal challenges pertaining to seeds; the economic realities for farmers; effects of climate change, especially as manifested in the current drought; the current draft of the US Farm Bill; and "seed piracy" lawsuits initiated by Monsanto against US farmers. The essay concludes by discussing the renaissance of small, independent seed companies.

## The Untold American Revolution

Soon after reaching the New World, European settlers realized that the seed they had brought from Europe was unsuited to growing conditions in America. A vibrant trade of seed and agricultural commodities was quickly established with Native Americans, and this exchange established an important agricultural germplasm base. Early founding fathers, notably Thomas Jefferson and George Washington, were as passionate about agriculture (and both were ardent plant breeders) as they were about governing the country. Their aspirations for the nation centered on agrarianism. "Cultivators of the earth are the most valuable citizens. They are the most vigorous, the most independent, the most virtuous, and they are tied to their country, wedded to its liberty and interests by the most lasting bonds," Jefferson espoused.[4] George Washington concurred: "I know of no pursuit in which more real and important services can be rendered to any country than by improving its agriculture."[5]

In the colonial era, the landed gentry formed "agricultural societies" that saved, cultivated, and exchanged seeds, though these were not widely distributed to the general populace. In the early 1800s, the secretary of the Treasury initiated a program requesting US ambassadors and military officers to gather seeds and seed data from their posts around the globe. In 1839, this program became more methodical when the US Patent Office established an agricultural division, which began collecting seeds and launching free seed distributions.

The US Department of Agriculture (USDA), established in 1862, devoted at least one-third of its budget to collecting and distributing seeds to farmers across the country; by the turn of the century, the USDA had sent out more than one billion packages of seeds. The seed distribution program was enormously popular with farmers as public seed was free and of good quality. It also enabled them to conduct extensive seed breeding and provide the genetic foundations for American agriculture. Farmers enabled steady genetic improvement mainly through a simple process known as phenotypic selection, in which seeds from the healthiest and most productive plants are saved and replanted the following season. Some of the most well-known farmer-bred seed varieties developed include Red Fyfe wheat, Grimm alfalfa, and Rough Purple Chili potato.

However, the nascent seed industry saw the federal programs as a barrier to potential profit, and formed the American Seed Trade Association (ASTA) in 1883 to advocate for the end of government seed distribution. After forty years of intense lobbying by the association, Congress eliminated the USDA seed distribution program in 1924.

## Land-Grant Colleges and Extension Services

Concurrent with government seed programs, legislation was passed to provide publicly funded resources to institutions of higher learning devoted to agriculture as well as to experimental and research services for rural communities. The Morrill Land-Grant College Act of 1862, established by President Lincoln, provided public lands to US states and territories to create colleges specializing in agricultural research and instruction. Some of today's top universities, such as Michigan State and Cornell, originated because of this act. The Hatch Act of 1887 supplemented the land-grant system by funding experimental stations. The Hatch Act stipulated that all research be freely shared among the institutions and also be made available to farmers. The Smith-Lever Act of 1914 established cooperative extension services to provide "useful and practical information on subjects relating to agriculture...."

Together, these acts were intended to foster universities and institutions to improve agriculture, in part by breeding new, regionally adapted plant varieties. Publicly funded plant breeders at the USDA and land-grant universities pioneered breakthrough technologies in plant improvement, including backcrossing and hybridization. Throughout most of the twentieth century, publicly funded breeding programs provided farmers with steadily improving, high-quality seed; for example, in 1980 70 percent of soybeans and 72–85 percent of wheat by crop acreage was planted with public sector seed.[6]

## The Role of the Private Seed Sector

Until recently, private seed firms acted mainly as distributors of publicly developed seed varieties. Most distribution firms were family-owned, small or regional businesses scattered throughout the country. The private sector played a more active breeding role only in developing hybridized crops such as corn, sorghum, and sunflower. Private firms concentrated on hybrid seed because selected traits do not breed true with each successive planting, resulting in weakened traits. With the advent of hybrid seed, farmers were required, *for the first time,* to purchase seed annually to ensure effective desirable traits.

The development of hybrid crops, such as varieties of corn introduced in the 1930s, was instrumental to the growth of a private, commercial seed industry. Hybrid seeds were a biological strategy for seed companies to expand their market influence. Instead of on-farm seed saving, farmer seed breeding, and public research and distribution, hybrid seeds gave seed companies new opportunities to explore—and, too often, exploit—farmer dependency on purchased seed. As these companies expanded and gained more relevance in a shifting agricultural landscape, a new era of consolidation in the seed industry began.

The emergence of agricultural biotechnology, specifically GE seeds, in the 1990s intensified consolidation and solidified an increasing trend of seed and chemical company mergers. Thus, commercial agriculture today is often referred to as the agrochemical-seed industry. For example, nearly all GE seeds today are sold by Monsanto and are resistant to a single herbicide, glyphosate. These herbicide-resistant seeds and glyphosate—marketed as Roundup Ready by Monsanto—are sold together as a highly profitable, packaged system.

The advent of GE seeds has also led to increased pressure by agrochemical-seed companies to establish legal and policy mechanisms to further strengthen seed patents and IPR schemes. Thus, the emergence of two trends developed symbiotically: the advent of GE seeds and the dramatic rise in seed and plant patents leading to the consolidation of seed ownership. Genetically engineered seed patents are now a central mechanism by which to gain control and ownership of the genetic material of seeds.

## Legal Origins of the Right to Own Seed

Legal and policy strategies establishing IPRs and patent regimes of exclusivity also provided for market dominance by a handful of seed and chemical companies. The legal origins of private seed patents began with the Plant Patent Act (PPA) of 1930; this act allowed patents for unique plant varieties of only nonsexually reproduced plants. It is significant that when Congress passed the PPA, it explicitly did not allow a patent right to plants propagated by seeds (that is, by sexual reproduction). The law stated, "To these ends the bill provides that any person who invents or discovers a new and distinct variety of plant shall be given by patent an exclusive right to propagate that plant by asexual reproduction; that is, by grafting, budding, cuttings, layering, division, and the like, but not by seeds."[7]

Over the following decades, Congress consistently denied the right to grant patents for plants reproduced by seeds—in 1968, a proposed amendment to the PPA that would have extended patents to include sexually reproduced plants was defeated in Congress. During this period, the USDA also opposed granting patents for sexually reproducing plants, arguing that patents would threaten the development and introduction of new seed varieties. The USDA's concern was prescient of the grave loss of crop diversity that exists today. Promoting homogeneous seed stocks via seed patenting and industrial agriculture has resulted in a dramatic loss of plant biodiversity. A 1983 study by the Rural Advancement Foundation International (RAFI) revealed that over the course of eighty years, the United States lost 93 percent of its agricultural genetic diversity.[8] RAFI's report concludes that 75 percent of today's food calories, worldwide, are derived from just nine plants.[9]

Under increasing pressure from commercial seed and chemical companies, including the ASTA, Congress passed the Plant Variety Protection Act (PVPA) in 1970. The act authorized the USDA to issue Certificates of Protection for novel, sexually reproducing plant varieties. The certificates granted exclusive rights to multiply and market these seed varieties for an eighteen-year term. However, two important exemptions were established: (1) researchers must be allowed to use the PVPA-protected varieties to breed still better varieties; and (2) farmers must be allowed to save patented seed for replanting.

*Diamond v. Chakrabarty*, a landmark Supreme Court case in 1980, granted the first patent on life, a decision that galvanized a great leap forward toward establishing full patent protection for sexually reproduced seed varieties. In a 5–4 decision, the Supreme Court ruled that living organisms—in this case, a bacterium—could be patented. Shortly after this ruling, seed corporations stampeded the US Patent and Trademark Office (PTO) with more than 1,800 patent submissions for genetic material of seeds and plants. Subsequently, the US PTO began approving patent applications for sexually reproduced plants. These were classified and granted as utility patents, which, unlike the PVPA certificate, allow patent holders to exclude others from using the variety for research and agricultural purposes.

In 2001, in *J.E.M. Ag Supply v. Pioneer Hi-Bred International,* the Supreme Court upheld the US PTO's practice of seed patenting, by ruling that plants could be granted utility patents rather than the more limited patents, or certificates, under the PVPA.[10] The industry consolidation that followed such policy changes has also led to a drastic depletion of plant genetic resources as companies restructure and cut operating costs. As one example, Seminis Seeds, a leader in specialty crops and now a subsidiary of Monsanto, announced plans in 2000 to cut its seed stock by two thousand varieties, or 25 percent.[11]

In sum, a single century's shortsighted industry consolidation and business practices have nearly eliminated thousands of years of selective and attentive seed saving for regional resilience.

## Consolidation, Rising Costs, Compromised Science

Utility patents spurred a trend of seed and chemical company mergers and acquisitions in the 1980s that continues to the present. Monsanto, DuPont, Syngenta, and Bayer controlled 49 percent of the world's proprietary seed supply as of 2007.[12] As a direct consequence, the existence of small, independent seed companies rapidly declined—in 1996, there were three hundred independent seed companies in the United States; by 2009, there were fewer than one hundred.[13] Beyond the loss of small distributors, increased market concentration has also resulted in a dramatic increase in seed prices. Since the advent of GE seed, per-acre soybean seed costs have risen an astounding 325 percent.[14] In addition, the "technology fee" that companies now routinely charge has soared—the price of a bag of soybean seed increased from $4.50 in 1996 to an estimated $17.50 by 2008, due to Monsanto's Roundup Ready trait technology fee.[15]

Restricting and influencing independent scientific research is yet another result of the consolidation of the seed and chemical industry.

Many believe that the legacy of the land-grant universities and research institutes initiated during America's development has now become tainted, as these institutions too often function as handmaidens of agribusinesses. Seed and chemical companies now partner with these institutions by providing funding and, sometimes, even personnel. The seed industry represents this as a win-win situation—it provides additional resources to institutions and, in turn, the research benefits the public. Yet, the companies seem to derive the largest slice of the proverbial American pie as they use the technology and research, much of it paid for by US citizen tax dollars, to generate private profit.

Perhaps a more subtle yet profound consequence of these public-private "partnerships" is that the scope of science and research can be altered. An increasing trend in universities is to focus on devising new technologies that are then appropriated by private companies for profit. In other words, the direction of research and science in public educational bodies is more and more determined by private company agendas. Corporations provide funds mainly for quick results from technological research—such as biotechnology or nanotechnology—while long-term studies in disciplines such as biology receive little funding by comparison. It is unsurprising then that often the biological consequences of technologies developed—such as weed resistance and adverse effects on endangered species—are insufficiently addressed.

In addition to influencing the direction of science and research, public-private collaborations potentially threaten the independence, objectivity, and credibility of educational institutions. For example, Pioneer Hi-Bred prohibited university researchers from publishing their data on the mortality rates of ladybugs that had fed on an experimental variety of Pioneer GE corn (a nearly 100 percent mortality was found). Subsequently, Pioneer hired other researchers to produce more acceptable data.[16]

In sum, as noted by Bill Freese, science adviser to the Center for Food Safety, "The ability to obtain utility patents on plants has been a major factor in: consolidation of the seed industry; rising seed prices; a decline in seed saving; reduced innovation; a narrowing of seed choices for farmers; and restrictions on independent scientific research."[17]

## Current Situation

US civil society has initiated its own legal challenges in response to seed industry practices. Most of such challenges are focused on GE seeds, given that patents for this technology serve as the primary gateway to seed ownership and monopolies. During the last five to ten years, litigation challenging the commercial approval of GE crops has been somewhat successful. Much of it has centered on the USDA's lack of meaningful analysis of the adverse environmental and economic impacts of GE crops in determining approval of crops for either testing or commercialization. As a result of civil society's successful legal challenges, US courts now must recognize as "legal harms" the numerous adverse impacts of GE crops, such as the transgenic contamination of natural crops and wild plants. Thus, legal challenges by farmer, consumer, and public interest environmental advocacy groups on GE biopharmaceutical crops, GE bentgrass, GE alfalfa, and GE sugar beets have successfully established that the USDA must undertake meaningful, rigorous risk analyses regarding the risk of contamination when considering approvals or testing of GE organisms. These lawsuits established *locus standi* for farmers and environmental advocates to seek compensation or relief in US courts for the harms of GE crops, as well as be granted various forms of equitable relief (e.g., compensation) based on violations of the law.

In response, agribusiness has pumped up its volume of legal and political engagement. Millions of dollars spent in lobbying and the now well-entrenched "revolving door" syndrome seems to be paying off in terms of ensuring seed monopolies. Government agencies hire industry representatives from agribusiness and biotech firms and, in turn, these corporations recruit staff from government agencies.

Numerous scientists, lawyers, and other professionals move seamlessly between employment at agribusiness/biotech companies and government agencies, compromising the regulatory system and undermining the efforts of civil society groups.

On the direct lobbying front, food and agricultural biotechnology firms spent more than $547 million lobbying Congress between 1999 and 2009, rising from $35 million in 1999 to $71 million in 2009—an increase of 102.8 percent. In 2010 alone, ag-biotech companies contracted more than one hundred lobbying firms, in addition to employing in-house lobbyists. Additionally, millions have been spent to fund political campaigns; in 1999, more than $22 million was contributed by biotechnology corporations via political action committees (PACs).[18]

Such influence seems to have swayed recent policy decisions within the US government, often circumventing or contravening prior court decisions. For example, in early 2011, the USDA approved unrestricted, nationwide commercial planting of Monsanto's GE alfalfa, even though its own analyses and conclusions demonstrated that the approval would cause significant harm to organic and conventional alfalfa farmers and dairies, as well as to exporters. This decision is now under court challenge by civil society groups.

## Major Legal Challenges by Civil Society

In the last half-dozen years, the Center for Food Safety (CFS) and represented interested parties have initiated a string of lawsuits, successfully challenging USDA actions related to GE crops. One case regarding the USDA's first approval of GE alfalfa went all the way to the US Supreme Court in 2010; this was the first time that the highest US court had ever heard a case regarding GE crops. To date, CFS's legal successes have established that proper GE crop reviews must consider the risk of transgenic contamination through cross-pollination and other means; increased herbicide use and herbicide-resistant weeds; the economic impacts of adoption on non-GE, organic farmers and businesses; and the potential loss of choice for farmers and consumers wishing to purchase non-GE foods. As noted above, the cases also established that farmers and consumers could seek recourse in US courts for these harms; CFS litigation continues regarding numerous GE crops and is in various stages of litigation.

## OSGATA et al. v. Monsanto Co.

This US legal challenge involved a patent challenge filed by seventy-five family farmers, seed businesses, and agricultural organizations representing more than three hundred thousand individuals and 4,500 farms, seeking a court decision to bar Monsanto from suing them for patent infringement if their seeds became contaminated by Monsanto's GE Roundup Ready seed. In the face of the established historical record of more than one hundred lawsuits brought against farmers, the plaintiffs sought to protect organic farmers and other growers of non-transgenic crops from liability should unwanted transgenic contamination occur in their fields. After a district court granted Monsanto's motion to dismiss the case, the US Court of Appeals for the Federal Circuit denied *certiorari*. This means that the case will no longer be considered by the US courts.

## Bowman v. Monsanto Co.

In May 2013, the US Supreme Court ruled in the patent case *Bowman v. Monsanto* in favor of the giant seed and chemical company.

The case involved Monsanto's prosecution of a seventy-five-year-old Indiana farmer, Vernon Hugh Bowman, for alleged patent infringement because he saved and replanted soybean seeds purchased from a third party rather than purchasing new seeds from the agrochemical giant each time. Bowman contended that the patents on the seeds expired upon sale of the second-generation seeds, which he purchased from the grain elevator, and invoked the doctrine of patent exhaustion. Under this doctrine, once an unrestricted, authorized sale of a patented article occurs, the patent holder's exclusive rights to control the use and sale of that article are exhausted, and the purchaser is free to resell that article without further restraint from patent law. However, the Supreme Court did not agree with this interpretation of patent law and ruled in favor of Monsanto. CFS released a report in 2013, *Seed Giants v. U.S. Farmers,* detailing the seed industry's prosecution of farmers over alleged patent violations. The report examines the broader socioeconomic consequences of the present patent system, including links to loss of seed innovation, rising seed prices, reduction of independent scientific inquiry, and environmental issues.

Among the report's discoveries are several alarming statistics:

- As of January 2013, Monsanto, alleging seed patent infringement, had filed 144 lawsuits involving 410 farmers and 56 small farm businesses in at least twenty-seven different states.
- Today, three corporations control 53 percent of the global commercial seed market.
- Seed consolidation has led to market control resulting in dramatic increases in the price of seeds.
- From 1995 to 2011, the average cost to plant one acre of soybeans rose 325 percent, cotton prices spiked 516 percent, and corn seed prices were up by 259 percent.

### Association for Molecular Pathology v. Myriad Genetics

The lawsuit, commonly termed *Myriad,* charged that patents on genes violate the First Amendment of the US Constitution and patent law because genes are "products of nature" and, therefore, cannot be patented.

The US Supreme Court ruled that Myriad Genetics's patenting of DNA violates the US Constitution's prohibition against patents on laws of nature and natural phenomena because gene sequences, DNA, and cDNA are products of nature. The Court found that Myriad neither invented the patented DNA nor its useful characteristics or functions, and that Myriad's extraction of the patented genes from the body did not alter that conclusion. The Court decision positively impacts tens of thousands of people. Although the Supreme Court ruling still allows patents on copies of DNA called "cDNA," synthesized and edited copies of DNA, it found that even these synthetic copies of DNA may not be patentable if they are an "obvious" way to make the copy. This ruling, however, unlikely applies to transgenic seeds, which are not classified as "products of nature."

## The Farm Bill

The US Farm Bill is the most important food policy legislation that Congress considers. Every five to seven years, agricultural policies are evaluated and reauthorized through the US federal Farm Bill. On the whole, it encompasses nearly all aspects of the food system and will shape farm and food policies for a five-year period. Unfortunately, the 2014 Farm Bill fails as a vehicle to capture the needs of the food movement. The few successes of movements in the United States were largely wins to keep harmful language out of the bill, not the reforms necessary to make our model of agriculture more sustainable in the long term.

While the 2014 Farm Bill is laden with disappointing and short-sighted policies, it does include some bright spots. The Farm Bill excludes the intensely controversial amendment that would have nullified a wide swath of state food safety, animal welfare, and worker protection laws. It also excludes language that was being pushed for by the powerful meat and poultry lobby, which sought to cripple the current Country of Origin Labeling (COOL) requirement for meat, a widely popular program among consumer groups and small producers. Additionally, the Farm Bill provides fully funded vital organic farm programs, including a number of programs that seek to ensure we are expanding the number of organic farms in the United States in order to meet the surging consumer demand, and it includes language to encourage that conservation programs are resulting in sufficient high-quality pollinator habitat and local and regional food networks.

Of the disappointments, the bill cut nearly $9 billion from the Supplemental Nutrition Assistance Program (commonly referred to as food stamps), threatening the food security of Americans across the country.

The bill also decimated a critical pollinator protection provision that was passed with overwhelming bipartisan support by the House. Another shortcoming is the language that makes it extremely difficult for the Environmental Protection Agency (EPA) to track the importation of genetically engineered and pesticide-coated seeds and monitor their use.

Overall, the bill fails to include any substantial reforms to crop insurance or our subsidy limits, further benefiting the wealthiest and large-scale farms while leaving other programs and populations underfunded. The greatest disappointment is the failure of this Farm Bill to address the immediate and long-term sustainability of the US agricultural system.

*Monsanto Rider*

The "Monsanto Protection Act," also known as the "Monsanto Rider," was removed from the US Farm Bill due to diligent, consistent pressure from civil society groups. The act represented a serious assault on the fundamental safeguards of the judicial system and would have negatively impacted farmers, the environment, and public health across America. The legislation would have stripped federal courts of their authority to halt the sale and planting of an illegal, potentially hazardous GE crop and would have compelled the USDA to allow continued planting of that same crop upon request.

## Monsanto versus America's Farmers

Better Seed for a Brighter Future. *If there were one word to explain what Monsanto is about, it would have to be farmers. We create the seeds, traits, and crop protection chemicals that help farmers produce more food using fewer resources.*

—Monsanto advertisement

In sharp contrast to the claims of this advertisement, battling Monsanto has almost become a way of life for many US farmers, who are now presented with contractually binding technology agreements upon purchasing patented, mainly GE, seeds. These agreements allow Monsanto to conduct property investigations, expose the farmer to huge financial liability, bind the farmer to Monsanto's oversight for multiple years, and include a variety of other conditions that have effectively defined what rights a farmer does and does not have in planting, harvesting, and selling GE seed.

Monsanto's treatment of farmers is an assault on the foundations of farming practices and traditions that have endured for centuries in the United States and for millennia around the world, including one of the oldest traditions: the right to save and replant the seeds of one's crops. Indeed, George Washington cautioned against such behavior when he wrote, "Bad seed is a robbery of the worst kind: for your pocket-book not only suffers by it, but your preparations are lost and a season passes away unimproved." Through contracts, engineering, and patents, Monsanto has eliminated farmers' right to save seed, an inalienable right since time immemorial.

As of January 13, 2010, Monsanto had filed 136 lawsuits against farmers for alleged violations of its Technology Agreement and/or its patents on GE seeds. The majority of these cases ended in recorded damages awarded to Monsanto totaling around $23 million.[19] But the lawsuits do not record the whole story. The Center for Food Safety compiled information that was formerly available on Monsanto's website and arrived at estimates of sums paid to Monsanto by farmers in what the company labels "seed piracy matters." Such cases are often settled out of court when farmers cannot afford to pay legal fees and associated expenses. The investigation found that:

- As of June 2006, Monsanto had instituted "seed piracy matters" investigations against an estimated 2,391 to 4,531 farmers in nineteen states.
- Farmers have paid Monsanto an estimated $85.7 million to $160.6 million in settlements.

- The number of seed piracy matters reported by Monsanto is twenty to forty times the number of lawsuits found in public court records.[20]

Besides the harassment and persecution that many farmers have faced from Monsanto, other issues are turning the American dream into a nightmare for our farmers. The state of seed and concentrated seed ownership largely parallels the plight of many US farmers who are struggling to make a living as the costs of farm inputs such as seeds, fertilizers, fuel, and pesticides steadily rise.

Headlines early in 2012 touted happy days for US farmers due to increased trade and high prices paid for agricultural commodities, yet most family farmers have not benefited, as potential profits dissolve due to rising on-farm expenses and fewer or lower government payments. In addition, because of the economic recession, off-farm income has fallen; in 2009, real household income for family and small farms fell by 28 percent compared to 2007 levels, according to Timothy Wise, director of the Research and Policy Program at the Global Development and Environment Institute at Tufts University.[21]

Total farm expenditures in 2011 were $318.7 billion—averaging 11.3 percent greater than in 2010;[22] in particular, the price of seeds has contributed to rising costs. From 2001 to 2010, USDA's data reveal that corn seed and soybean seed prices rose 135 percent and 108 percent, respectively.[23] While many farmers struggled to keep going, Monsanto's net income increased 77 percent in 2011, coinciding with a sharp spike in seed prices—GE corn seed increased by 32 percent and GE soybean seed rose by 24 percent.[24]

This generated an antitrust investigation of the seed industry by the Department of Justice in 2009, with a focus on Monsanto because it controls most of the market. According to the Rodale Institute, at least one of Monsanto's patented genes exists in 90 percent of soy and 80 percent of corn planted in the United States.[25]

Not having conventional, non-GE seed available appears to be part of the strategy to boost sales of higher-cost GE seeds. As Indiana soybean farmer Troy Roush noted, "You can't even purchase them in this market. They're not available." A farmer from Arkansas concurs: "It's getting harder and harder to find conventional [soybean] seed." A Texas cotton farmer similarly reports: "Just about the only cotton-seed you can get these days is [genetically engineered]. Same thing with the corn varieties. There's not too many seeds available that are not genetically altered in some way."[26]

Another strategy to boost sales of GE seed involves promotion of a seed's chemical partner. In July 2011, the *Wall Street Journal* reported that the US Securities and Exchange Commission issued a subpoena to Monsanto to provide documents related to its customer incentive programs for Roundup in fiscal years 2009 and 2010.[27] The investigation is ongoing at the time of this writing, but could reveal that Monsanto engaged in illegal practices aimed to squeeze out competitors and manipulate the market.[28]

In the face of rising costs, many farmers have looked to obtain farm credit, long the backbone of American agriculture. However, a national survey conducted by farm advocacy organizations reveals that since 2009, farmers have increasingly been denied loans due to the recent contraction of credit markets, particularly financial stress on agricultural banks and an upturn in farmer loan defaults.[29] The difficulty of getting loans and farm credit is also affecting the future of farming in America. The price of land, water, and ever-increasing agricultural inputs puts farming out of reach for many farmers, notably those of the younger generation. For example, there were nearly 180,000 farmers below the age of thirty-five in 1997; by 2007, there were only 120,000—a decrease of one-third. The high cost of farming was the major reason credited for this decline.[30]

## Superweeds, Super Problems

High-priced seeds are creating high-stakes problems. Agronomists around the world are alarmed by the growing epidemic of weeds, or "superweeds," that have evolved a resistance to glyphosate as a result of its intensive use on GE crops[31]—as of June 2012, more than 16.7 million acres have been infested across the country.[32] Some estimate that this figure could more accurately be 30–40 million acres if all of the infestations were reported.[33]

Eliminating superweeds is an additional cost for farmers who resort to more soil-eroding tillage operations to combat these weeds, and also turn to increasingly toxic herbicide cocktails. As a result, pesticide use has increased massively in the United States ever since the adoption of GE seeds. The most comprehensive independent study to date, based on USDA data, found that GE crops used upward of 26 percent more pesticides per acre than non-GE, conventional crops.[34]

In response to increasing weed resistance to glyphosate, seed and chemical companies are developing new GE crops resistant to more toxic herbicides. Dow AgroSciences is awaiting USDA approval of corn and soybeans resistant to 2,4-D, an active ingredient in Agent Orange, which is often highly contaminated with carcinogenic dioxins. Likewise, Monsanto is planning to introduce dicamba-resistant soybeans, corn, and cotton. Dicamba has been linked to increased rates of non-Hodgkin's lymphoma[35] as well as colon and lung cancer.[36]

## Crisis in America's Heartland

More than two-thirds of the contiguous United States was under some level of drought as of July 31, 2012; more than one-quarter of affected regions are classified as being in extreme drought or worse, according to the *Drought Monitor*, a weekly report compiled by US climate experts. Some degree of dryness affects over 79 percent of the contiguous forty-eight states;[37] government records show that 2012 was the hottest year on record in the lower forty-eight states.[38] Nearly forty million out of ninety-six million planted US acres of corn are in drought conditions.[39] The primary corn and soybean agricultural areas in the United States had their sixth-driest April–July growing season since 1895, according to the National Oceanic and Atmospheric Administration.[40]

In addition, 37 percent of the main livestock-producing area in the United States experienced severe drought levels in 2012. Farmers and ranchers found it difficult to get feed for their livestock. According to Mark Svoboda of the National Drought Mitigation Center in Lincoln, Nebraska, "This is something that we hadn't seen, save for a couple of times, in the last hundred years."[41]

Texas A&M's AgriLife Extension Service reported that agriculture suffered an unprecedented $5.2 billion loss from the drought, $2.06 billion attributed to livestock alone. Once associated industries are accounted for, such as grain elevators and processing plants, losses approximated up to $8.7 billion.

Analysts also predicted that low yields of corn and soy would increase food prices not only across the nation, but worldwide. Weather and drought were a partial factor in the 2007/2008 food crisis that sparked riots in Egypt, Cameroon, Haiti, and several other countries. The Food and Agriculture Organization (FAO) recently released figures showing that the Food Price Index has increased 6 percent.[42] "There is potential for a situation to develop like we had back in 2007/08," noted FAO's senior economist and grain analyst, Abdolreza Abbassian.[43]

## Climate Change: A Permanent Trend?

While most experts agree that La Niña was a major factor behind the 2012 US drought, scientists also note that droughts may increase in frequency and intensity as anthropomorphic activities cause global temperatures to rise. Climate models tend to concur that the intensity and frequency of droughts will increase in central North America, though there is uncertainty about which specific regions will be most affected. A 2011 report by the National Center for Atmospheric Research establishes that if the world keeps heating up, regions in North

America will experience warmer air, leading to increased evaporation that will dry out soils, and persistent droughts will be more likely in the next twenty to fifty years,[44] possibly leading to Dust Bowl conditions, or worse.[45]

In times of ever-increasing extreme weather associated with global warming, seed diversity is critical for agricultural production, and indeed for global food security. Building and maintaining seed diversity provides the very resilience and adaptation needed in times of climate chaos. Instead of continuing current policies that encourage consolidation of seed ownership and uniformity of seed, societies should be shifting toward building dynamic farming systems and diverse seed repositories.

Given that the majority of Americans no longer have any connection to farming, the numerous difficulties faced by farmers—notably smaller, family farms—and economic hardships of many rural communities, it appears that the United States has faltered in fulfilling the aspirations of our founding fathers and our agrarian inheritance. It may be time to go back to the future so there can *be* a future for farming in the United States. The ideals of agrarian potential are astutely described by Thomas Jefferson in a letter to George Washington (1787): "Agriculture is our wisest pursuit, because it will in the end contribute most to real wealth, good morals, and happiness."

## Endnotes

1    ETC Group, *Who Will Control the Green Economy?* (Ottowa: ETC Group, December 2011).
2    National Institute of Food and Agriculture, USDA, "Extension," April 19, 2011, www.csrees.usda.gov/qlinks/extension.html.
3    John Opie, *Early America: 1630–1812* (Washington, DC: Environmental Literacy Council, September 2006).
4    Thomas Jefferson, *Notes on the State of Virginia* (Paris, 1785).
5    George Washington, letter dated July 20, 1794.
6    Jorge Fernandez-Cornejo, "The Seed Industry in U.S. Agriculture," *USDA Economic Research Service, Agriculture Information Bulletin* 786 (2004): Tables 17, 21, 36, 40.

[7]  Joseph Mendelson III and Andrew C. Kimbrell, *Brief Amici Curiae of American Corn Growers Association and National Farmers Union in Support of the Petitioners* (Washington, DC: Center for Food Safety, May 2001).

[8]  Gwen Sharp, "Loss of Genetic Diversity in U.S. Food Crops," *The Society Pages,* July 19, 2011, http://thesocietypages. org/socimages/2011/07/19 /loss-of-genetic-diversity-in-u-s-food-crops; accessed August 7, 2012.

[9]  Cary Fowler and Pat Mooney, *Shattering: Food, Politics, and the Loss of Genetic Diversity* (Tucson: University of Arizona Press, 1990).

[10]  *J. E. M. Ag Supply, Inc. v. Pioneer Hi-Bred International, Inc.,* 122 S. Ct. 593, 596 (2001).

[11]  Helena Paul et al., "Chapter 4: Consolidation, Contamination and Loss of Diversity: The Biotech Dream Takes Hold," in *Hungry Corporations: Transnational Biotech Companies Colonise the Food Chain* (London: Zed Books, 2003), www.econexus.info/sites/econexus/files/ ENx-HC-Ch4.pdf.

[12]  ETC Group, *Who Will Control the Green Economy?*

[13]  Matthew Wilde, "Independent Seed Companies a Dying Breed," *WCF Courier,* August 22, 2012, http://wcfcourier.com/business/local article_7cef1 ffc-b0bb-56a8-8d83-faf894bf76ad.html.

[14]  Derived from figures published by USDA Economic Research Service, *Commodity Costs and Returns,* July 5, 2012, www.ers.usda.gov/data-products /commodity-costs-and-returns.aspx.

[15]  Kristina Hubbard, *Out of Hand: Farmers Face the Consequences of a Consolidated Seed Industry* (Washington, DC: National Family Farm Coalition, December 2009).

[16]  Emily Waltz, "Under Wraps," *Nature Biotechnology* 27, no. 10 (2009): 880–882.

[17]  Bill Freese, "Letter to David B. Verrilli, Jr. re: *Bowman v. Monsanto Co.*," *U.S. Supreme Court Case No. 11-796* (Washington, DC: Center for Food Safety, August 17, 2012).

[18]  Food & Water Watch, *Food and Agriculture Biotechnology Industry Spends More Than Half a Billion Dollars to Influence Congress* (Washington, DC: Food & Water Watch, November 2010).

[19]  Center for Food Safety, *Monsanto vs. U.S. Farmers 2010 Update* (Washington, DC: Center for Food Safety, 2010), www.centerforfoodsafety.org/wp-content /uploads/2012/03/Monsanto-v-US-Farmer-2010-Update-v.-2.pdf.

[20]  Ibid.

[21]  Timothy A. Wise, "Still Waiting for the Farm Boom: Family Farmers Worse Off Despite High Prices," *GDAE Policy Brief 11-01,* Global Development and Environment Institute, Tufts University, March 2011. Farm Aid provided research assistance for this report.

[22]  US Department of Agriculture, National Agricultural Statistics Service, *Farm Production Expenditures 2011 Summary* (Washington, DC: USDA, August

2012), http://usda01.library.cornell.edu/usda/current/FarmProdEx
/FarmProdEx-08-02-2012.pdf.

23  William Neuman, "Rapid Rise in Seed Prices Draws US Scrutiny," *New York Times*, March 11, 2010, www.nytimes.com/2010/03/12/business/12seed
.html?pagewanted=all.

24  SafeLawns.org, "Monsanto's Shady Dealings under Investigation by the Securities Exchange Commission," July 16, 2011, www.safelawns.org/blog
/index.php/2011/07/monsantos-shady-dealings-under-investigation-by-the
-securities-exchange-commision.

25  Emily Main, "SEC Investigates Monsanto's Shady Dealings," Rodale 2011,
www.rodale.com/monsanto-seeds.

26  Center for Food Safety, *Monsanto vs. U.S. Farmers* (Washington, DC: Center for Food Safety, 2005), www.centerforfoodsafety.org/pubs/CFSMOnsantovs
FarmerReport1.13.05.pdf.

27  Tom Philpott, "SEC Investigates Monsanto's Roundup Biz," *Mother Jones*,
July 19, 2011, www.motherjones.com/tom-philpott/2011/07/roundup
-sec-investigates-monsanto; accessed August 23, 2012.

28  There is no update on the Monsanto subpoena issue—we cannot find out what has happened, if anything, since it was issued.

29  "Don't Bank on It: Farmers Face Significant Barriers to Credit Access During Economic Downturn," Farm Aid Food & Water Watch, National Family Farm Coalition, and RAFI-USA, March 2011, www.nffc.net/Issues
/Credit%20and%20Disaster%20Work/FARMER_CREDIT_REPORT
-MARCH_2011.pdf.

30  Clay Masters, "High Costs Make It Harder to Grow Young Farmers," National Public Radio, September 23, 2011, www.npr.
org/2011/09/23/140631752/high-costs-make-it-harder-to-grow-young
-farmers%20.

31  Stephen B. Powles, "Gene Amplification Delivers Glyphosate-Resistant Weed Evolution," *Proceedings of the National Academy of Science* 107 (2010):
955–956.

32  Bill Freese, *Comments to USDA APHIS on Environmental Assessment for the Determination of Nonregulated Status of Herbicide-Tolerant DAS- 40278-9 Corn, Zea Mays, Event DAS-40278-9* (Washington, DC: Center for Food Safety,
2012), www.centerforfoodsafety.org/wp-content/uploads/2012/04
/CFS-Science-Comments-I.pdf.

33  Ian Heap, email from Dr. Ian Heap to Charles Benbrook, August 2, 2012.

34  Charles Benbrook, *Impacts of Genetically Engineered Crops on Pesticide Use in the United States: The First Thirteen Years* (Washington, DC: The Organic Center, November 2009): 47 and Supplemental Table 7.

35  Kenneth P. Cantor et al., "Pesticides and Other Agricultural Risk Factors for Non-Hodgkin's Lymphoma among Men in Iowa and Minnesota," *Cancer Research* 55 (1992): 2447–2455.

36  Claudine Samanic et al., "Cancer Incidence among Pesticide Applicators Exposed to Dicamba in the Agricultural Health Study," *Environmental Health Perspectives* 114 (2006): 1521–1526.

37  *Drought Monitor,* National Drought Mitigation Center, July 31, 2012, http://droughtmonitor.unl.edu/archive.html.

38  National Climatic Data Center, *State of the Climate* (National Oceanic and Atmospheric Administration, July 2012), www.ncdc.noaa.gov/sotc.

39  Bonnie Berkowitz, "Drought Intensifies in Most-Parched Areas of U.S.," *Washington Post,* August 3, 2012, www.washingtonpost.com/national /health-science/drought-intensifies-in-most-parched-areas-of-us/2012 /08/02/gJQAc334RX_story.html.

40  National Climatic Data Center, *State of the Climate.*

41  Brian K. Sullivan, "Worst Drought Covers Nearly One-Fourth of Contiguous U.S.," Bloomberg, August 9, 2012, www.bloomberg.com/news/2012-08-09 /worst-drought-covers-nearly-one-fourth-of-contiguous-u-s-.html.

42  Food and Agriculture Organization, "FAO Food Price Index up 6 Percent," August 9, 2012, www.fao.org/news/story/en/item/154266/icode/.

43  Catherine Hornby and Karl Plume, "US Drought, Food Prices Fan Fears of New Crisis," Reuters, August 9, 2012, www.reuters.com/article /2012/08/09/drought-idUSL2E8J9C7X20120809.

44  Aiguo Dai, "Drought under Global Warming: A Review," *WIREs Climate Change* 2 (2011): 45–65, www.cgd.ucar.edu/cas/adai/papers/Dai-drought _WIRES2010.pdf.

45  Brad Plumer, "What We Know about Climate Change and Drought," *Washington Post,* July 24, 2012, www.washingtonpost.com/blogs/ezra-klein /wp/2012/07/24/what-we-know-about-climate-change-and-drought/.

# Reviving Native Sioux Agricultural Systems

Suzanne Foote

Years ago, Sam Moves Camp, a Sioux medicine man, told the Lakota Nation that they must return to their traditional core diet of native corn, beans, and squash as well as wild-crafted foods indigenous to the Lakota people. Sam gave very specific directions and delivered a compelling message to his people, stating:

> We must get back to the land—this is a priority. We must acknowledge the spiritually based, ecologically sound relationships and traditions of the Lakota and the plant species that we have evolved with and depended on. Together we must preserve our ancient food crops for our future survival as a people. If these traditional food crops become extinct, our culture and our spirit also will become extinct.

Sam's message correlates with several prophecies, such as those of Padmasambhava, or Guru Rinpoche as he is also known. In eighth-century Tibet, he warned that certain conditions would come to pass in our time because of humanity's behavioral patterns. People will die of starvation even as there is food to eat because the food itself will become lifeless.

In direct response to these kinds of messages, a Native American nonprofit organization—Ta S'ina Tokaheya Foundation—was established in 1989 on the Pine Ridge Indian Reservation. Ta S'ina Tokaheya, meaning First Robe, is the Lakota name of the founder: Michael Burns Prairie Sierra, a member of the Oglala Sioux Tribe. Michael had been searching for many years to find a way to address the third world living conditions present on the Pine Ridge Reservation.

Ta S'ina Tokaheya Foundation promotes economic self-sufficiency through sustainable/organic farming, seed banking based on traditional farming practices, and Ti O'spaye development (sustainable community development based on traditional Lakota models). Green building and wind energy enterprises also were incorporated. By utilizing affordable and sustainable lifestyle alternatives and reviving and incorporating traditional Lakota principles, this model has served as an example and opportunity to improve the quality of life for other reservations and nonreservation communities.

A key component of Ta S'ina's work has been the creation of a Native American seed bank to preserve ancient seed species. Traditionally, the Lakota were nomads who obtained their food primarily by hunting buffalo and harvesting wild-crafted foods. Eventually they adopted native farming practices from surrounding Plains tribes. On reservations today, however, the Sioux diet, like that of most tribes throughout North America, is heavily reliant on federal food commodities. Every registered member of the Sioux Tribe receives white sugar, white flour, powdered milk, eggs, lard, coffee, and canned meat.

As cultural traditions eroded on reservations and government food subsidies replaced the incentive for practicing sustainable food production, traditional diets based on hunting/gathering and agriculture vanished. As a direct result, death rates from diabetes, obesity, heart disease, and cancer have soared among Native Americans. However, preliminary studies have indicated that this trend can be reversed by a return to the Native American, Paleolithic diet of protein and fiber found in corn, beans, squash, grains, greens, deer, bison, and other wild-crafted food.

The traditional diet, high in fiber and protein, normalizes blood sugar levels, suppresses cravings for processed foods, and significantly reduces the occurrence of diet-related diseases.

Over the past two decades, Ta S'ina Tokaheya Foundation has focused its activities on the collection and cultivation of endangered seed
species to preserve crops that have evolved in Native American cultures. The ultimate value of seed-banking native seeds is to preserve
the inherent genetic memory they possess. This genetic memory contains a natural resistance to harsh climate conditions and an inherent
resistance to pests and disease. These seeds are extremely hardy and
reliable and are naturally acclimatized to particular bioregions; they
are also high in nutritional value. Since these seeds were the source of
survival foods for the Plains tribes, their cultivation and perpetuation
are essential not only for their nutritional value but for future food
security. These efforts have provided ways to simultaneously reclaim
Native heritage and improve health. In addition, the sale of surplus
crops and related value-added products has contributed to a growing
local economy by creating sources of income for participating members of the Lakota community.

The endangered Native American Seed Preservation Project, a
program under Ta S'ina Tokaheya Foundation, researched traditional
scientific planting methods used by the Plains tribes hundreds of years
ago. These methods included techniques to prevent cross-pollination,
such as utilizing various plant barriers to separate agricultural plots.
Companion planting also was used; as an example, pole beans would
be planted with corn for fixing nitrogen levels in the soil. Floodplains
and bottomlands were typically selected for garden plots.

The seed project primarily implemented Hidatsa farming techniques as the Hidatsa women were among the most advanced farmers
and ecologists of the Plains tribes. The Hidatsa and Mandan knew the
importance of keeping strains of corn and squash pure, because each
variety had a special use. There are nine principal varieties of corn
that were cultivated by the Plains tribes: Ata'ki tso'ki—hard white
corn; Ata'ki—soft white corn; Tsi'di tso'ki—hard yellow corn; Tsi'di
tapa—soft yellow corn; Ma'ikadicake—gummy corn; Do'ohi—blue
corn; Hi'ci ce'pi—dark red corn; Hi'tsiica—light red corn; and Ata'ki

aku' hi'tsiica—pink top corn. The Hidatsa would refer to the cross-pollination of corn as the "traveling corn." To maintain the integrity of the various strains, they configured their fields to prevent cross-pollination by creating barriers of sunflowers and separating the corn-fields by variety.

The Ta S'ina Tokaheya Foundation began the seed project by selecting a five-acre bottomland parcel outside Oglala, a site that had the richest soil on the reservation. The parcel was hand dug by members of the Lakota tribe, ranging from children to elders from the community. The gardens have brought community members together and have fostered a sense of pride. A half-acre mandala garden was designed in the shape of the morning star, and a medicine wheel garden was designed and planted with medicinal herbs. The mandala garden represents the Lakota belief that all Lakota life originates from the morning star.

We, the cofounders of the foundation [the author, her husband at the time, Michael Sierra, and sister Kristina Mayo], engaged in a vigorous seed collection and location campaign in 1992 and began with a letter to Seed Savers Exchange, requesting heirloom Native American seed species. The request for heirloom seeds was later published in the Seed Savers Exchange 1993 *Harvest Edition*. The response was overwhelming. Rare seeds were donated from individuals, seed banks, and universities throughout the United States, Canada, South America, and Africa. We received many native varieties of corn, beans, and squash that date back as early as the sixteenth century from Fort Berthoud. These particular seeds originated from peoples of the Hidatsa, Mandan, Arikara, and Sioux Nations. Other seeds were located and collected from USDA seed storage facilities.

We were able to acquire and grow all nine corn varieties mentioned earlier. Gummy corn seed was the most difficult to obtain, perhaps because it was one of the least favorite varieties used by the Plains tribes. Throughout the Ti O'spaye cornfields, companion planting was used by growing multiple varieties of dry climbing beans. One of the most prolific and flavorsome varieties is the shield figure bean, which was grown by the Hidatsa 150 years ago. Dry pole beans climb the cornstalks while fixing nitrogen levels in the soil.

Pests such as grasshoppers have been a big problem in the plains and have wiped out entire crops throughout Nebraska and South Dakota. To remedy this, turkeys, guinea hens, and chickens roam free throughout the gardens eliminating grasshoppers and depositing manure. They also provide eggs and meat for consumption within the Ti O'spaye while excess is sold to the local community.

The Lakota view food as very sacred. The "three sister" groups—corn, beans, and squash—are used for ceremonial purposes. During harvest season, a "giving thanks" ceremony is performed. Women prepare a large feast using all the crops from the garden, while ceremonial foods are placed in nature to show gratitude for the abundance of food and seed. Everyone from the Ti O'spaye (community) gathers together for this celebration. Children and elders are invariably the most enthusiastic participants. Both men and women go to the sweat lodge to pray and give thanks. For several weeks after the last harvest, seeds are collected, dried, and stored. Pumpkins and squash are sliced and dried to prepare soups during the winter months.

Ta S'ina's garden is augmented by a 30 foot × 36 foot greenhouse to propagate seedlings and extend the growing season. Crop pollination is enhanced by two adjacent bee colonies that produce several pounds of honey annually, in addition to by-products such as propolis, the glue that holds beehives together, and beeswax. Many more salable and value-added products are produced from the garden, and a proposed line of cosmetics is in the offing.

Ta S'ina also initiated an alternative housing project. Within close proximity to the garden, two model homes—one adobe and one strawbale—were constructed from local materials, both utilizing solar energy. These models are very important because, shockingly, over 80 percent of the existing homes on the reservation are without heating, lack sufficient insulation, and were built with toxic materials.

Ta S'ina Tokaheya's programs have established a working sustainable community model, an "ecovillage" if you will, through integrating traditional values and knowledge and by renewing a sense of cultural identity. Currently, the primary focus is on sustainable energy systems and production. The foundation is working very closely with the tribe in these areas, the result being the creation of a whole new economy on the reservation.

As a closing, I would like to share Michael Sierra's message to Ta S'ina Tokaheya's Ti O'spaye:

> When we first began to come together as young men and women, we started a process of restoring our customs and traditions. As a result we became healthier and also restored our own pride and dignity because of the completeness and beauty intrinsic in our way of life.
>
> Because of our culture we learned to work towards building a better future for the next seven generations. However, we could see the reality of the conditions our people have been subjected to in America. We realized it would require our full commitment and began with accepting the responsibility ourselves to change our environment.
>
> Ta S'ina Tokaheya became the focus of our efforts for modeling a way of life that incorporates a foundation based upon continuing the restorative efforts and practices of our spirituality, that encompasses our role as "Caretakers of Mother Earth," that utilizes sustainable and renewable concepts and technologies, and permits us to endeavor to achieve economic self-sufficiency.

# In Praise of the Leadership of Indigenous Women

Winona LaDuke

*A nation is not conquered until the hearts of its women are on the ground. Then it is finished no matter how brave its warriors or how strong their weapons.*

—Cheyenne proverb

*There is a powerful metaphor between the economic policies of this country, Canada, and the USA and their treatment of our Indigenous women and girls. When you look at the extreme violence taking place against the sacredness of Mother Earth, in the tar sands, for example, and the fact that this represents the greatest driver of both Canadian and US economies, then you look at the lack of action being taken for thousands of First Nations women and girls who have been murdered or just disappeared, it all begins to make sense. It's also why our women have been rising up and taking power back from the smothering forces of patriarchy dominating our economic, political and social, and I would say spiritual institutions. When we turn things around as a people, it will be women who will lead us, and it will be the creative feminine principle they carry that will give us the tools we need to build another world. Indigenous peoples have been keeping a tab on what has been stolen from our lands, and there is a day coming soon where we will collect. Until then, we will keep our eyes on the prize, organize and live our lives in a good way and we welcome you to join us on this journey.*

—Clayton Thomas-Muller, 2013

## Resistance Emerges in the North

In the winter of 2012, Chief Theresa Spence of the Attawapiskat First Nation in northern Ontario drew the world's attention when she went on a hunger strike in front of the Canadian capital in Ottawa. Spence, a modest woman, helped inspire an international movement called Idle No More, which drew attention to Canada's hyperaggressive resource extraction era, the Harper administration's equally aggressive violation of the human rights of indigenous peoples, and the destruction of the Earth.

Chief Theresa Spence is the leader of Attawapiskat First Nation—a very remote Cree community from James Bay, Ontario, at the southern end of Hudson Bay. The communities on the reserve, 1,549 residents (a third of whom are under nineteen), have weathered quite a bit: the fur trade, residential schools, a status as non-treaty Indians, and limited access to modern conveniences like a toilet, or even electricity. This is quite common in the North, but it has been exacerbated in the past five years, with the advent of a huge diamond mine in the area.

Enter De Beers, the largest diamond mining enterprise in the world. The company moved into northern Ontario in 2006, where the Victor Mine reached commercial production in 2008 and was voted "Mine of the Year" by the readers of the international trade publication *Mining Magazine*. The company states that it is "committed to sustainable development in local communities." This is good to know, because, as the Canadian MP Bob Rae discovered in 2012 on his tour of the rather destitute conditions of the village, this is also the place where the first world meets the third world in the North.

Infrastructure in the subarctic is in short supply. There is no road into the village for eight months of the year. For four months, during a freeze-up, there's an ice road. A diamond mine needs a lot of infrastructure, and all of this has to be shipped in, so the trucks launch out from Moosonee (another rather remote outpost), connected to the south by a railroad. Then, they build a better road. The problem is that the road won't work when the climate changes, and already-stretched infrastructure gets tapped out.

There is some money flowing in, that's for sure. A 2010 report from De Beers states that payments to eight communities associated with its two mines in Canada totaled $5,231,000 that year. *Forbes* magazine reports record diamond sales by the world's largest diamond company:

> ... increased 33 percent, year-over-year, to $3.5 billion.... The mining giant, which produces more than a third of the world's rough diamonds, also reported record EBITDA of almost $1.2 billion, a 55 percent increase over the first half of 2010.

As the Canadian MiningWatch group notes:

> Whatever Attawapiskat's share of that $5-million is, given the chronic under-funding of the community, the need for expensive responses to deal with recurring crises, including one that DeBeers themselves may have precipitated by overloading the community's sewage system, it's not surprising that the community hasn't been able to translate its ... income into improvements in physical infrastructure.

Attawapiskat gained international attention in 2012 when many families in the Cree community were living in tents in the dead of winter. The neighboring Kashechewan village was in similar disarray. They were boiling and importing drinking water. The village almost had a complete evacuation due to deteriorating health conditions—scabies and impetigo epidemics. And, on top of all of this, "... fuel shortages are becoming more common among remote northern Ontario communities right now," as Alvin Fiddler, deputy grand chief of the Nishnawbe Aski Nation (a regional advocacy network), explained to a reporter. That's because the ice road used to truck in a year's supply of diesel the previous winter did not last as long as usual. "Everybody is running out now. We're looking at a two-month gap until this winter's ice road is solid enough to truck in fresh supplies," said Mr. Fiddler.

Kashechewan's chief and council were poised to shut down the band office, two schools, the power-generation center, the health clinic, and the fire hall because the buildings were not heated and could no longer operate safely. According to Chief Derek Stephen, "In addition, some 21 homes had become uninhabitable due to flooding." Just as a side note, in 2007, some twenty-one Cree youth from Kashechewan attempted suicide, and the Canadian aboriginal youth suicide rate is five times the national average. Both communities are beneficiaries of an agreement with De Beers. Sort of a third world situation ... eh? In one of the richest countries in the world.

Now that story could be a story from India, Pakistan, Papua New Guinea, or the Congo, but it's a story of the North. It is a story of the indigenous communities of the North, and a story of the reality of a resource extraction state that is cannibalizing the land from which it sprang legislatively, economically, and with a new onslaught of militarization.

With our communities living in these conditions, how can there be consent given to fossil fuel extraction and mineral mining contracts? Indigenous women have resisted the dominating and coercive spirit of the predator economy that devastates the land, and our bodies, since our land was first colonized. That colonialism continues.

## The Colonization Model and the Manufacturing of Consent

The model is well known. As indigenous scholar Russ Diabo explains,

> The intent is hyper-acceleration of resource extraction and development, and these are on indigenous territories, and the way to accelerate that process is to create legislation, and to have that legislation part of the instrument through which poverty is utilized. This is the old colonial model, which is having the veneer of consent. It is to manufacture it. To manufacture poverty and then manufacture consent.

The Stephen Harper government, the present government of the settler of Canada, did what all Canadian governments have done, and has done it more aggressively. It deprives people of the basics of a dignified life: running water, infrastructure, stable health, and security. Canada, like its American counterpart, does this by systemically appropriating the resources of indigenous communities, militarizing those communities, bringing in new paramilitaries to the borders of those communities, ensuring long-term health instability in those communities, draining intellectual capital from those communities (through educational and financial institutions), and never investing in infrastructure. Then, they offer only one choice.

That choice is a series of laws and gun-barrel diplomacy that supports the intensification of resource extraction. And it turns out that what Canada does in Canada to Native people is what Canadian corporations do around the world—perhaps having learned well from their neighbor to the south. It's an important point in history because 75 percent of the world's mining companies today are Canada-based. In the present era we've seen the inefficient and extravagant consumption of the North American first world (especially the United States and Canada) drive a level of resource extraction that will not only require additional planets to continue, but will ultimately destroy the land and water with which we live.

One more time: Canada is the home to 75 percent of the world's mining corporations, and they have tended to have relative impunity in Canadian courts. Canadian corporations and their international subsidiaries are being protected by military forces elsewhere, and this concerns many. According to a UK *Guardian* story, a Quebec court of appeal rejected a suit by citizens of the Democratic Republic of the Congo against Montreal-based Anvil Mining Limited for allegedly providing logistical support to the DRC army as it carried out a massacre, killing as many as one hundred people in the town of Kilwa near the company's silver and copper mine.[1] The Supreme Court of Canada later confirmed that Canadian courts had no jurisdiction over the company's actions in the DRC. KAIROS Canada, a faith-based organization, concluded that the Supreme Court's ruling would "have broader implications for other victims of human rights abuses committed by Canadian companies and their chances of bringing similar cases to our courts."[2]

The North American economy consumes a third of the world's resources, with perhaps one-tenth of the world's population. That level of consumption requires constant interventions into other countries, and constant violations of human rights. Canadian companies will necessarily need impunity, as there is no way to extract the remaining fossil fuels without drastically accelerating the damage that's already been caused; and there is no compensation for what has been done already.

Consider that we've consumed one-half of the world's known fossil fuels, so what remains is largely difficult to extract—requiring extreme measures, and with very little return in terms of energy. Copper is close to the most inefficient product to mine from a big dig; you need to remove one billion tons of material to recover 1.6 tons of copper. The only substance with a lower recovery rate is gold. Mining projects in northern Anishinaabe territory will now mine copper, creating vast rivers of sulfuric acid. The Ramu Nickel Mine proposal in Papua New Guinea will dump raw waste into the depths of the ocean, destroying an ocean's worth of life. Both projects, one in Anishinaabe Akiing and the other in the PNG mine, are for the Chinese market, illustrating how global markets and inefficiencies impact us all. Whether the companies are Canadian or Australian, the markets today are often Chinese. In turn, much of what will be produced may end up coming back to North American markets in the form of the multitude of trade goods North America continues to purchase from China.

The rate of extraction is not only unsustainable, it is ecologically and economically disastrous. "When indigenous peoples oppose the destruction of our ecosystems we get challenged as people who are saying, 'Let's go back to the Stone Age ...,'" Caleen Sisk, Winnemem Wintu chief tells me. "The fact is that these guys with their extraction and pollution will take us back to before the Stone Age. We won't even be able to eat...." There is a monetary economy, and then there is an economy based on clean air, clean water, and food—or quality of life.

Fossil fuels are even worse. The North American economy has moved to blowing the tops off five hundred mountains in Appalachia (known as mountaintop removal) to benefit markets as far away as India. Deep-water extraction is being pushed into the most pristine and untouched regions of the ocean, and with climate change accelerating, the retreat of ice has left more ocean accessible to extraction. An example of one experiment gone awry is British Petroleum's *Deepwater Horizon* fiasco in the Gulf of Mexico. The extraction of oil and gas through fracking methods threatens groundwater and the aquifers we rely on the world over. And, finally, the aggressive push into the tar sands of the Athabasca River basin destroys an ecosystem, sickening all who live there, for the benefit of international oil interests. It is in this context that the resistance of indigenous women is essential and it is found wherever our people are.

Pamela Paimeta, a spokesperson for the Idle No More movement in Canada, talks about the movement that sprang from Canada's violations of basic human rights, in which the Harper government gutted laws that would protect communities. The administration launched an economic war against these same communities if they refused to sign mining agreements, by holding out basic transfer benefits for food, education, housing, and health, and then dismantling the environmental laws of that country, in a bill called C-45.

C-45 was passed at the end of 2012. That bill, and a series of other bills, removed roadblocks in the legislative and regulatory arena within a first world country for the benefit of mining corporations. Paimeta, a legal scholar, points out that treaty rights and the rights of indigenous nations are essential for all Canadians to support (despite all that they have been taught in schools, and despite the teaching and implementation of the construct of white privilege) and urges the larger community to see what is occurring across the country as a reality check.

The first Nations are the last best hope that Canadians have for protecting land for food and clean water for the future—not just for our people, but for Canadians as well. So this country falls or survives on whether they acknowledge, or recognize and implement, those aboriginal and treaty rights. So they need to stand with us and protect what is essential.

In some ways, the Idle No More movement's emergence, and the increasing visibility of indigenous women, is an essential step in educating a larger nonindigenous community. Native women have historically been marginalized, and have definitely been marginalized in the media, as dramatic pictures of Native people on horseback, or Native men in occupations, have captured the media more than pictures of Native women have. That is changing as they become more militant, and it is changing because there is a more enlightened North American feminist community. Native feminism does not exist in the same paradigm as non-Native feminism. *At the basics, we would say that we are not fighting for a bigger slice of the pie; we want a different pie. We want the world we were instructed to carry on by our ancestors, and our traditions. In that world, we have a good and respectful life, and with the adaptation of those values into a set of appropriate technology, we are clear on our path and what we will accept and want.*

## The Chief Occupies

Back to Chief Theresa Spence and the implication of her hunger strike in the capital, Ottawa. She hoped to meet with Prime Minister Stephen Harper, urging him to "open his heart" and meet with Native leaders angered by his policies. "He's a person with a heart but he needs to open his heart. I'm sure he has faith in the Creator himself and for him to delay this, it's very disrespectful, I feel, to not even meet with us," she said. Her actions encouraged a movement, Idle No More, which emerged in Canada and quickly spread to the United States and the rest of the world.

Idle No More consisted of protests, marches, direct action, and often, traditional round dances that would appear at the spur of the moment, as "flash mobs," at places like the Mall of America, the state capitol of Colorado, or other public spaces and city centers. The movement has captured the attention and imagination of many of the youth in indigenous communities, and it has been propelled into the media, using social media well to document stories that otherwise would never appear in mainstream media. Frankly, Natives have historically, been marginalized in the media so effectively that the only stories about the Native community that appear are of arrests (a survey of northern US Native papers will find that is the majority of coverage), or of Native poverty. That, however, is a trend that may be changing with an increasing number of Native writers, radio stations in more reservations and reserves, and the increasing presence of social media in remote communities.

## Different from Occupy

Some have likened the Idle No More movement to the Occupy movement. There is some shared terrain, particularly in terms of the significance and power of social media, and the access the information age promises to historically marginalized communities. They now control their own media. There is in the youthfulness of the indigenous movement (most of the Native community is under twenty-five years of age) a similarity to the youthfulness of the Occupy movement. The Idle No More movement itself, however, is old, mature, and evolving with technology, as is the larger movement of indigenous peoples. I do believe that the Idle No More movement resembles more the Zapatistas and the ongoing indigenization of Western Hemisphere politics, but with the added advent of instant media and cell phones, something there was little or no access to in Chiapas. We have seen our youth break open spaces in which their voices and stories have been heard, and where they have a chance to influence policy and public opinion, and to support one another and connect over shared experiences between remote communities.

Kristin Moe writes, in *YES! Magazine,* "Idle No More is one of what Subcomandante Marcos, the masked prophet of the Mexican Zapatistas, called 'pockets of resistance,' which are 'as numerous as the forms of resistance themselves.'" The Zapatistas are a part of the movement of indigenous resistance (which is five hundred years old), which crested in the early 1990s. It has continued to grow, change, and adapt in many South American countries. In Bolivia, this resulted in the election of an indigenous president and the enshrining of the Rights of Mother Earth in the Bolivian constitution. We share common histories of colonialism, and today, with a continued globalized presence, where Spain and England have been replaced by Suncor, BHP Billiton, De Beers, Conoco, and TransCanada, we understand that our resistance is still essential to survival.

Indigenous resistance is, in many cases, the strongest front, and has the capacity to protect the land, a semblance of a land-based economy for all. Native women do not by any means have a monopoly on creative resistance to colonialism, but Native women have played a significant role in that resistance. There may be some historical reasons.

## Indigenous Women Resist the Intersection of Sexism and Colonialism

There is something about never having been enfranchised or privileged by industrial society, which means that indigenous women are less colonized, even than some of their male counterparts. It's an armchair sociologist's observation. American, British, and its descendant, Canadian, colonialism liked treating with men, dealing with men, and naming men. After all, that is what the European monarchy and feudal system was accustomed to. It did not notice the clan mothers of the Iroquois Confederacy. Nor did it recognize the place of women in Anishinaabe or other indigenous societies. Hence, when decision making was put in that realm and favoring and privileging resulted, it focused not on the status of women, but on the status of men. That is how a clientele class is created in the process of colonization. In that process, the colonizer has at some point so infiltrated the world of the object of his desire that we become the colonizer ourselves.

We are "digested" (the root of "colonization" is the same as the root of "colon"), and in that digestion we begin to emulate the colonizer. There is a good argument to be made, however, that the status of Native men also diminishes with colonization, particularly as we are denied access to our lands, our waters, our food, and our ceremonies. It is a process of colonization, and it is, therefore, also a process of decolonization.

What I know is that the hierarchy of colonization finds it easiest to deal with a few appointed leaders, or those who meet with the approval of the federal or Canadian governments. A lot of decisions are made by those individuals—often after a good deal of indoctrination, force, and gun-barrel diplomacy with the Native community. Some of this is reflected in the militarization of the Indian country, which, it turns out, is heavily militarized, as old cavalry bases are turned into new weapons training centers, and more and more of our people are pulled into the US military, until we have the highest rate of enlistment of any population in North America. They still test weapons on our lands, and take over our lands for more military actions.

Gun-barrel diplomacy is Canadian Premier Stephen Harper's full-scale assault on Native resources, by starving communities. Gun-barrel diplomacy is when your land is occupied by multinational corporations that want to frack your territory for oil to export to, well, the United States or China, and the Canadian government sends paramilitary riot police into a small community, or stands by and watches as supermilitarized security forces protect multinational energy corporations.

Gun-barrel diplomacy leaves little room for talking. And so we find that often the front lines of indigenous struggles to protect our land are made up of women. That is because we have never had access to the privilege of big expense accounts of the federal government and corporations, and because, by and large, someone is still needed to look after our families and children—in the face of heartbreak, and in the face of colonization, the face of an all-out war that destabilizes our Native men. Now, this is a story about some of that process, but it is also a story of why our resistance as Native women is so strong.

## The Economics of Colonialism

*Canada has demonised us. We "lost" our land, we "lost" our language, we "lost" our heritage. We are these rambunctious, crazy people who just "lose" stuff ... that is not what happened, and that is not what is happening ...*

—Frank Molley, Mi'kmaq First Nation

*In the colonial to neocolonial alchemy, gold changes to scrap metal, and food to poison. We have become painfully aware of the mortality of wealth which nature bestows and imperialism appropriates ...*

—Eduardo Galeano, Open Veins of Latin America, 1973

This is how it works. The verb is "underdeveloping." That is what is happening to indigenous territories on an ongoing basis in North America. Tribal lands, resources, and people are being mined and destabilized, as water is contaminated, territories are impacted by mega projects, and wealth is appropriated.

The military takes indigenous lands and has taken them historically in the United States, the largest military power in the world, from Alaska to Hawaii—where a full third of the state is held by the US military, and more expansions for the so-called "Pacific Theater" are under way. Alaska alone has seven hundred used military defense sites, toxic sites that tell a story of the Cold War, and every other war since. The levels of radioactive and persistent organic pollutants in the environment impact people who are dependent on the land for their subsistence way of life.

Elsewhere, the Barrière Lake Algonquins see an estimated $100 million in revenues extracted every year from their territory in the form of logging, hydroelectric dams, and recreational hunting and fishing. The First Nation itself lives in seemingly third world conditions. A diesel generator provides power, very few jobs are available, and families live in dilapidated bungalows. These are not the lifestyles of a community with a $100 million economy in its backyard.

The six hundred Canadian First Nations have provided a lion's share of those resources. From oil and gas in Alberta to uranium in Saskatchewan, mega dam projects in Quebec, Labrador, and Manitoba, and old and new mines in Ontario. Not to mention the trees— there used to be a lot more in Canada, but now there are more stumps, fewer trees, and the money has not gone to Native communities.

The same thing has been happening in the United States.

One-third of all uranium, two-thirds of all western coal, four of the ten largest coal strip mines in the country, vast dam projects, and land seizure: all of this means a transfer of wealth and a destabilizing of traditional economics and communities. In turn, we are the poorest postal codes in both countries and lack basic infrastructure. About 14 percent of reservation households are without electricity, ten times the national rate.

Energy distribution systems on rural reservations are extremely vulnerable to extended power outages during winter storms, threatening the lives of reservation residents. Reservation communities are at a statistically greater risk from extreme-weather-related mortality nationwide, especially from cold, heat, and drought associated with a rapidly changing climate. For instance, Debbie Dogskin, a Lakota woman on the Standing Rock Reservation, froze to death in February 2014 because she couldn't pay her skyrocketing propane bills. Her propane ran out.

Ironically, she lived about a hundred miles from the Bakken oil fields, where they flare off so much gas that they light up the night sky. They have so much. Reservations need more than two hundred thousand new houses, and there is no money for them. And then there is the special case of Pine Ridge, the largest Lakota reservation, and the poster child of those who want to talk about how horrible the conditions of Native people are.

At Pine Ridge, 97 percent of the people live below the federal poverty line. The unemployment rate vacillates from 85 to 95 percent on the reservation. At least 60 percent of the homes are severely substandard, without water, electricity, adequate insulation, or sewage systems. It is hard to manage in these conditions in a first world country. And it causes stress to people.

Add to this the proposition of man camps and the degradation and victimization of Native women with the energy boom. That is why we resist them. They have no consent, either for our bodies or for our ecosystems. It is no stretch to say that this predator economics targets our lands, and our very bodies.

There is the physical destruction of peoples. In the United States, an epidemic of diabetes wreaks havoc on most tribal communities, with up to one-third of the population afflicted with the disease. Translate that into immense health costs and overall destabilization as people in the prime of their lives increasingly become impacted by a crippling disease. The physical destruction of the peoples as either a systematic or a secondary impact of an economics that views Native lives as external to their cost-benefit equations doesn't stop there.

## The Lost Boys of Aamjiwnaang

There are some communities, in fact, where the environment has become so polluted that women will be the future leaders of those communities simply because there will no longer be enough men born. One such community is Aamjiwnaang, an Anishinaabe community on the north shore of the Great Lakes. This community has chemical plants on its land. In the spring of 2013, at Aamjiwnaang, the Ojibwe blockaded the tracks of that plant. These are tracks that are full of chemical trains from some of the sixty-two industrial plants in what the Canadian government calls Chemical Valley. The Aamjiwnaang people would like to call it home, but they have a few quarrels with toxic levels of pollution in their houses. "If the Prime Minister will not listen to our words, perhaps he'll pay attention to our actions," Chief Chris Plain explained to the media at the takeover. A 2009 *Men's Health* magazine article is entitled "The Lost Boys of Aamjiwnaang" because the Ojibwe Reserve of Aamjiwnaang has few boys. Put it this way: in a normal society, there are about 105 boys born for every 100 girls; that has been the ratio for a thousand years or so. However, at Aamjiwnaang, things are different: between 1993 and 2003, there were two girls born for every boy to the tribal community, one of the steepest declines ever recorded in birth-gender ratio. As one reporter notes,

> These tribal lands have become a kind of petri dish for industrial pollutants. And in this vast, real-time experiment, the children of Aamjiwnaang (AHM-ju-nun) are the lab rats. I might have written "boys of Aamjiwnaang," but actually, there are a lot fewer of them around to experiment on ...

This trend is international, particularly in more industrialized countries, and the odd statistics at Aamjiwnaang are indicative of larger trends. The rail line, known as the St. Clair spur, carries CN (Canadian National Railway Company) and CSX trains to several large industries in Sarnia's Chemical Valley. Usually four or five trains a day move through, all of them full of chemicals. The Ojibwe have endured a constant dose of chemicals for twenty-five years, and are concerned about its health impact. They are also concerned about proposals to move tar sands oil through their community in a preexisting pipeline, known as Enbridge Line Nine.

There are places that are still beautiful, and these places deserve to live. There are many of them, as indigenous territories have largely been remote. An overlay, for instance, of biodiversity and cultural diversity means that there is a map that illustrates that indigenous territories are ecologically diverse and teeming with life—our human lives, and the lives of our relatives (whether they have wings, fins, roots, or paws). That is the balance that has been preserved by careful and mindful living.

That is not the balance of the predator economics of industrial society.

## Of Athabasca River Basin Defenders and Tar Sands Destruction

"When you destroy the earth, you destroy yourself," Melina Laboucan-Massimo explained to a reporter. "This is the common thread in indigenous thinking all over the world." Melina is from a village that has been inundated with oil spill, and is one of many young women who have voiced opposition to the destruction of the land and water for the benefit of profiting corporations.

The Cree call the vast, pine-covered region *niyanan askiy,* "our land." The Lubicon Cree, and the lands they represent, were left out of the treaty agreements made more than two hundred years ago when white settlers first carved and divided the land. Their rights to their traditional lands are still unrecognized, which means that they don't have the right to protect their lands from the tar sands extraction that has devastated their territory over the past four decades.

In her 2012 testimony before the US Congress, Laboucan-Massimo described the devastation to her family's land, which now is dotted with more than 2,600 oil and gas wells.

> What I saw was a landscape forever changed by oil that had consumed a vast stretch of the traditional territory where my family had hunted, trapped, and picked berries and medicines for generations.

The Cree and Déné people, who have lived with their traditional territories for millennium, have had over 80 percent of it made inaccessible due to tar sands expansion. Although billions of dollars of investment and resources have passed through their lands, what trickles down has been overall devastation, while corporations like Suncor and others have been emboldened in their unaccountability by the Harper government, which has, like previous governments, sanctioned a full assault on the Athabasca River system.

Researchers have found that high levels of toxic pollutants in Alberta's Athabasca River system are linked to oil sands mining and a drastically increased cancer incidence in Fort Chipewyan. Then there's what happens at the other end. The most notorious of pipeline proposals from the tar sands is the Keystone XL. "It poses a threat to our sacred water, and the product is coming from the tar sands, and our tribes oppose tar sands mining," Debra White Plume, an Oglala leader, told the press. White Plume's family, and many others, have opposed the Keystone XL pipeline, along with a myriad of uranium mining projects proposed for the Paha Sapa, the Black Hills.

> All of our tribes have taken action to oppose the Keystone XL pipeline. Members from the seven tribes of the Lakota Nation, along with tribal members and tribes in Idaho, Oklahoma, Montana, Nebraska and Oregon, are prepared to stop construction of the pipeline.

In October 2013, the Lakota rode some of the proposed pipeline route in a set of three spiritual rides organized by grassroots and national organizations, including Honor the Earth, Owe Aku, and 350.org. The routes covered territory between Wanblee on the Pine Ridge Reservation and Takini on the Cheyenne River Reservation, in a spiritual ride to honor the water and counter the oil. This ride was one of three rides (the other two were Minnesota-based pipeline rides on the Alberta Clipper and proposed Sandpiper route for fracked oil). The Lakota will ride again, and the Anishinaabe will stand with them, and with our Déné and Cree relatives.

## Lakota Oyate, and the Treaties to Protect All

The 1868 Fort Laramie Treaty is the treaty between the United States and the Lakota Nation. Oceti Sakowin treaty territory is overlapped by Montana, North Dakota, South Dakota, and Nebraska. These lands and that treaty are sacred to the Lakota; across Indian country, tribal leaders and non-Indians are demanding that those treaties be recognized as the law of the land, since they are affirmed in the US Constitution. At one of several summits of the Lakota and their allies, they reaffirmed their opposition to the black snake, the fat-taker's pipeline—also known as the Keystone XL pipeline, a project intended to benefit oil companies, not people or the planet.

Gary Dorr, from the Nez Perce Tribe in Idaho, talked about opposition to the pipeline and his tribe's legal position on the tar sands. The Nez Perce Tribe has already used its treaty rights to block the transport of so-called megaloads of mining equipment headed to Alberta's tar sands through its territory. The tribe launched blockades and won a court battle to prevent shipments from traversing its lands. At the nearby Umatilla Reservation, people have also been arrested for blocking these loads.

That battle, about whether the megaloads can go north to feed the tar sands industrial complex, or the oil can come south, is raging in the northern plains. White Plume stated,

> This whole area of the Great Plains was retained by the Lakota in the Ft. Laramie Treaty with the United States. As far as our people are concerned, that treaty is still the law. We look at this area as ancestral, as sacred, and as ours to defend. The KXL skirts actual, federally recognized reservation boundaries, but it is in our treaty territory and it is crossing our surface water and the Ogallala Aquifer.

What has been revealed recently is that TransCanada needs to build part of its infrastructure, which means a transmission line and power station through the lands of the Kul Wicasa, Lower Brulé, South

Dakota, and the Sicangu at Rosebud, South Dakota. Those power lines are part of its infrastructure, and these two bands of the Lakota Nation oppose tar sands, oppose the Keystone XL, and are refusing to comply with the development of the Keystone XL infrastructure. So that's about the latest thing that's happening right now with our people.

> Someone needs to explain to me why wanting clean drinking water makes you an activist, and why proposing to destroy water with chemical warfare doesn't make a corporation a terrorist.

Opposition to the Keystone XL pipeline has many faces, from ranchers in Nebraska and Texas who reject eminent domain takings of their land for a pipeline right-of-way, to the Lakota Nation, which walked out of State Department meetings in a show of firm opposition to the pipeline. All of them are facing a pipeline owned by TransCanada, a Canadian corporation.

In this part of the land it's just recently been spoken about in different reports from the federal government, and one report talks about parts of Mother Earth that America and other capitalist thinkers refer to as resources. They look at Mother Earth as a warehouse of resources for them to extract—gas, oil, and uranium. This federal government report was published recently and says $1 trillion worth of extractable resources are in Red Nations lands. So in looking at the long run, there will come a time when fat-taker will be knocking at your door, wanting your gas, oil, or uranium. Without skills to defend yourself, that's going to be hard times. We've seen hard times come like that to many Red Nations.

Our land base is very large here, and from here to our nearest Lakota relative is an hour and a half, and that's the Sicangu on the Rosebud Reservation. It's about four hours to the four bands on the Cheyenne River Reservation. So the distances between our homelands are great—hours and hours of travel. To protect ourselves, every community needs this training just because of the distance involved between us. Debra White Plume says:

As a Lakota woman, I do not see a division between myself and the environment. That's a concept I can't even comprehend, and that's how I feel toward the land and the water. In this area, the whooping crane, the fox, and many relatives where they live, their communities of free range, are going to be affected by this pipeline. We speak for them and for the Standing Silent Nation—the plants.

We know that on five hundred feet on each side of the pipeline, no trees are going to be allowed to grow. They're going to cut every tree in their path for all of those thousands of miles. They won't be allowed to grow back to protect the pipeline. That's part of their security, and that's criminal.

It's criminal to impact an ecosystem, not only by the possibility of contaminating water, but by what's actually in the Keystone XL— tar sands. The water wastage has damaged, maybe beyond repair, the ecosystem of the northern Athabasca River basin, as well as the boreal forest. As you look at the destruction already caused by the tar sands oil mine and now by this Keystone XL pipeline, we also have to look at it in terms of how it impacts all of life. To us it's an attack against life. That's how I see it.

We are here. And we're not going anywhere. That's what I will say about indigenous women. We are also connected to the Earth in a way that the fat-taker, the Wasichu, the corporate, predator economy is not, and will never be. That is because we understand our relationship and honor our mother. We understand that what corporations would do to the Earth is what corporations and armies have done to our women, and we give no consent. At the same time, we are visioning and creating the world we wish to live in, and we will live in. We are in the midst of work to restore local food systems, and restore and strengthen health, housing, and energy systems in our indigenous communities. And we are working at the level of policy for the creation of laws that protect water, seeds, and indeed, the rights of Mother Earth. That is what we will need—not only our strong and entrenched resistance, but the creative power of humans, of unfettered and unencumbered women, children, and men. That is how we will survive.

## Endnotes

1    Canadian Press, "Supreme Court Won't Hear Appeal in Congo Massacre Case," CBC News, November 1, 2012, www.cbc.ca/news/canada/montreal/supreme-court-won-t-hear-appeal-in-congo-massacre-case-1.1297191.

2    KAIROS, "Congolese Massacre Victims Denied Justice in Anvil Mining Lawsuit," KAIROS: Canadian Ecumenical Justice Initiatives, January 16, 2013, www.kairoscanada.org/sustainability/congolese-massacre-victims-denied-justice-in-anvil-mining-lawsuit/.

# Celebrating the Chile Nativo

Isaura Andaluz

It is August. As I drive along the banks of the Rio Grande, a smoky aroma, tinged with the scents of the rich soil, accompanies me. My mouth waters in anticipation of tasting this year's first crop of Chile Nativo, the native chile of New Mexico. Freshly picked green chiles are fire roasted, then carefully peeled and layered onto a flour tortilla, a traditional thin flatbread of New Mexico. The tortilla has been prepared with a generous dollop of sour cream, a bit of salt, and fresh crushed garlic. The coolness of the cream, the warmth of the chile, and its spiciness unfold into a subtle explosion of flavors on one's tongue. Later in the fall, the green chiles are left to ripen on the plants, where they will turn a deep red color. The red roasted chiles have a spicy, caramel flavor that is truly indescribable.

"Chile" is the Spanish word derived from *chil*, the Nahuatl (Aztecan dialect) name for capsicum plants. Its arrival in the 1500s to New Mexico has defined who we are as a people, while shaping our culture and diet. Chile is a constant reminder of how intricately we are entwined with the seasons, the land, the river, and our communities. The seeds tether us to the land in an annual ritual of planting, harvesting, saving, and sharing, and for some, to ceremonial dances. Passed down for centuries among the Native American and Hispanic people, the seeds are carefully returned to the soil, accompanied with a quiet blessing.

## Chile Nativo

Through traditional practices, landrace varieties of chile have been developed and adapted to local microclimates. They are resistant to disease, and are identified by their specific pod shape, size, and taste. They go by many names, usually in reference to the locality where they were cultivated. A partial list includes: Alcalde, Chimayo, Cochiti, Dixon, Escondida, Española, Isleta, Jarales, Jemez, Nambe, San Felipe, San Juan (Ohkay Owingeh), Santo Domingo (Kewa), Velarde, and Zia.

New Mexico's unique bioregions create prime conditions for diversity. Chile Nativo must endure high solar radiation, arid and windy conditions, and a broad range of temperatures from highs of 95°F/35°C, to nighttime lows of 65°F/18°C. The chiles range in length from two to seven inches; some are long and smooth, others curled and crinkly. The shoulders, the widest part below the stem, vary in width from ¾ to 1¾ inches (1.9–2.54 cm). The thin to medium skins make Nativo varieties excellent for drying, as they will not lose weight or flavor, due to excess water in the cell walls.

## The Mysteries of Chile

Where do chiles originate? Chile is a *Capsicum annuum,* one of five domesticated capsicums originating in Mesoamerica. As one of the earliest domesticated plants (7500 BC), its specific area of origination and domestication has evaded researchers.[1] Chile belongs to the *Solanaceae* family, which includes tobacco, potato, tomato, and petunia. Some consider chile a self-pollinating plant, but with simple observation, insect pollinators can be seen flying from flower to flower ensuring cross-pollination. Domesticated crop plants generally retain approximately 66 percent of the diversity present from the wild source,[2] but chile appears to be different. In a 2009 study conducted in Mexico, researchers took eighty samples of chile from ten states—fifty-eight semi-wild and twenty-two domesticated. The domesticated chiles were found to retain 91 percent of the level of diversity found in the semi-wild samples.[3] This finding is significant, as domesticated chiles like the Nativo may be invaluable in retaining diversity. For example, commercial chile growers in New Mexico have been experiencing severe problems with phytophthora, which causes chile wilt, for more than twenty years. Farming practices such as monoculture or failure to rotate crops may be contributing factors, but phytophthora is uncommon among Nativo farmers. Does this mean the Nativo gene pool has a resistance that modern or hybrid chiles do not?

Chile has another equally significant aspect. Genetic engineering uses a technique called "protoplast fusion," wherein a plant's cell wall has been partially or completely removed. This allows protoplast from different species to be introduced. The cell is then regenerated, creating a genetically engineered cell. Although other *Solanaceae* such as tobacco are commonly used in genetic engineering, researchers have been unable to regenerate chile from protoplasts. The chile will just not cooperate.

In 1888, Dr. Fabián Garcia, a horticulturist at New Mexico State University (NMSU), began the university's chile improvement program. His goal was to produce a stable canning chile that would have less heat, and be larger, fleshier, smoother, tapered, and shoulderless. The breeding lines he used included the *chile pasilla* (long and dark brown) and *colorado* (a red chile). Over a span of thirteen years, Dr. Garcia selectively bred the New Mexico No. 9, released in 1913. This was the first standardized variety of a new pod type called the New Mexican. It launched New Mexico as a leader in the United States for industrialized chile farming, processing, and canning. In 1958, a milder chile called New Mexico 6-4 was released, which became and remains the industry standard. NMSU continued to develop a total of twenty-one modern chile cultivars through proven classical breeding techniques. These include: Sandia (1956), NuMex Big Jim (1975), and Española Improved (1984). The last variety officially released was the NuMex Mirasol in 1993, the first year that research commenced for a genetically engineered chile resistant to phytophthora.

## Money, Power, and GE Chile

In 2008, New Mexicans were in for a shock. A bill was introduced in the New Mexico state legislature requesting $250,000 to develop a genetically engineered (GE) chile. This was the first time the general public had heard about this. An appropriation using taxpayers' funds to develop a patented GE seed? Who is behind this? Who will own the patent? The taxpayers? No. This was a coup for biotech companies.

### Contamination

In New Mexico, many farmers irrigate their crops through the use of *acequias*—irrigation ditches. As land has been passed down through generations, it is often divided into long, narrow tracts to ensure access to the *acequias*. These drain into the Rio Grande, which divides the state as it runs from the north to the south into Texas. Both waterways serve as venues for seeds to travel for miles, sprouting hidden volunteer plants the length of the state. In the fall, dried red chiles are hung into *ristras* and transported in open trucks. If a chile pod shatters, seeds can be strewn along the road and be carried by the wind.

Farmers may unknowingly come into possession of patented traits in the seeds they save because of these volunteer plants or due to cross-pollination with the GE chile, as test-site locations are undisclosed to the public. This could result in farmers being sued for patent infringement and, worse, almost certain loss of the invaluable and unique traits of their own seed, developed through years of breeding. Farmers have a right to save their own seed for future planting; this right is now at risk.

In 2008, the community sought to confront this threat through a united effort called the "Save NM Seeds Coalition."[4] Its first action was to introduce a bill aimed at protecting farmers from being sued if their seeds were to unknowingly become contaminated. The Farmer Liability Bill was introduced three times through bipartisan sponsorship (2009, 2010, and 2011). Although it has failed to pass, huge progress was made in 2011 when the bill made it to the House floor in record time, ending with a tied vote. Heavy lobbying by the GE chile players contributed to it failing upon being reheard a second time. But New Mexicans have not given up, nor have the GE chile players.

## The Players

Development of a GE crop usually includes three primary players: a biotech company, a university, and the promoter. In this case the players are Monsanto and Syngenta, New Mexico State University, and the New Mexico Chile Association. In the United States, the other players include BIO (the biotechnology trade association), the Farm Bureau, and money.

The New Mexico Chile Association (NMCA), formerly called the NM Chile Task Force, was created in partnership with New Mexico State University (NMSU). In 2006 it changed its name and became a nonprofit membership organization that lobbies for government and public funds. The NMCA is primarily composed of chile processors and businesses; it works closely with NMSU and its Agricultural Experiment Station (AES), and with biotech companies. The NMCA directs NMSU in the use of some of the funds received from the New Mexico state legislature.

Until 2012, the board of directors was composed of the owners of three of the largest food processors in New Mexico—Bueno Foods (a.k.a. El Encanto, Inc.), Rezolex, Inc., and Cervantes Enterprises. Bueno Foods is one of the oldest chile processors in the state. Rezolex is one of two companies in the United States that extracts oleoresin from paprika and operates farms in New Mexico, Texas, and Arizona. Cervantes Enterprises, with a farm operation in southern New Mexico, is primarily a processor producing approximately 80 percent of all the cayenne pepper mash used in tabasco sauces in the United States.[5] All three companies import chile from outside the United States, and Cervantes Enterprises has more acreage planted in Mexico than in New Mexico.[6] Dino Cervantes, of Cervantes Enterprises, the current board president, has close ties to the New Mexico state legislature. His aunt,

Senator Mary Jane Garcia, introduced and supported bills funding the GE chile. In 2013, his brother, Senator Joseph Cervantes, usurped the legislative process to get a bill passed that prohibits farmers from calling chiles by their geographic names unless they register with the New Mexico Department of Agriculture.[7]

The alleged need for the development of a GE chile is the unsurprising inability of our local chile industry to compete with countries like Mexico, Peru, and China. Labor costs, problems with disease, and cheap imports necessitate a GE chile that can be mechanically harvested in order to make New Mexico competitive again. The NMCA began exploring ways to market a GE chile to the public as far back as 2002. The result was a campaign promoting GE chile as "environmentally friendly agriculture," which included a GE market-friendly packaging strategy, as the solution to the industry's woes.[8]

Many of the issues facing the New Mexico chile industry have been of their own making. Most commercial chile is planted in only three southern counties—Hidalgo, Doña Ana, and Luna. Lack of ecologically sound agricultural practices such as crop rotation and the overuse of fungicides, pesticides, and herbicides have all contributed to eroding the health of the soil. For more than twenty years, phytophthora and beet curly top virus have plagued the fields. Palmer amaranth (*Amaranthus palmeri*) is a common New Mexico pigweed that is edible; it is now a superweed resistant to glyphosate as a result of other glyphosate-resistant GE crops grown in the state.

Palmer amaranth can harbor the insects that carry phytophthora and curly top virus, both of which have mutated into varieties unknown in chile fields. The amaranth can grow to heights of 6.5 feet and produce up to 460,000 seeds per plant.

Although the total acreage planted has dropped from its peak in 1992, the amount of chile harvested per acre rose from 3.37 tons in 1992, to 7.25 in 2011. These statistics only include farmers participating in USDA surveys; the produce of all others, especially smaller and Native American farmers, is not counted. Many commercial chile farmers have switched to more profitable crops. Farmers growing chile under contract for large processors make 50 to 75 cents a pound, versus $2.50 to $4.00 if sold at a local farmers' market.

New Mexico does not have the capacity—land or water—to meet the chile demand for the mass-produced salsas and chile products manufactured by the chile industry, thus the continual need for imported chiles. The majority of chile products are exported from the state, and do not necessarily contain New Mexico chile—the mild cultivar preferred by industry. Once a GE chile seed is developed, what is to prevent the NMCA from selling the GE seed to Mexico, China, or some other country?

*Funding*

So, how much money has the chile industry received? And why is there such a lack of knowledge about the research taking place? It is murky to say the least. This is partly due to the fact that the NMCA and NMSU determine how the funds are spent.

In 1992, phytophthora became a major concern of the chile industry. This prompted NMSU to secure $250,000 of recurring research funds from the New Mexico state legislature for the NMSU Agricultural Experiment Station. Funds were allocated for research on phytophthora control, development of resistant varieties, a glyphosate-resistant GE chile, and mechanical harvesting.[9] Initial funding for GE chile research was only 8 percent of the total. In 2010, NMSU's Professor Steve Hanson stated that the university would own the patent on virus-resistant crops, since the GE chile is being developed through cisgenics, a form of genetic engineering.[10] Total recurring funds from 1993 through 2011 total $4.8 million. In 2006, the NMCA lobbied for an additional $7 million in funding; and from 2006 to 2010, an additional estimated $3.5 million was secured through various bills, all for the GE chile.

The reason the public was unaware of GE chile research is because the bills introduced in the New Mexico state legislature have had innocuous names like NMSU Chile Industry Research, Chile Task Force, and Economic Sustainability of Chile Industry. Bills were sent to committees not normally designated to hear such bills, such as committees on corporations and transportation, and education. The net result: a lack of transparency and appalling evidence that tobacco settlement funds have been used for the development of this GE chile.

## GE Response: New Mexico Grown

After the introduction of the Farmer Liability Bill in January 2009, the GE players' first response was to conduct a survey showing public support for a GE chile. The New Mexico Chile Association's survey of consumers (C) and restaurant owners (RO) found:

- (C): 74 percent support genetic modification of chile plants in certain cases, mainly because they feel it will help prevent disease and save chile farms.
- (RO): 58 percent support taking a gene from one kind of plant and introducing it into another because they feel it will help prevent disease and farmers can grow more.

Interestingly, consumers were asked about "genetic modification" and restaurant owners were asked about "cisgenics"—where a gene from the same plant or related species is used to genetically engineer a seed. It is still "genetic modification," but the intention was to see how consumers and restaurant owners responded. What is even more interesting is that two years later, in 2011, local television station KOAT conducted a survey and 84 percent of respondents were against development of GE chile.

In July 2009, the NMCA copied the Save NM Seeds website (www .savenmseeds.org), inserting the word "chile" instead of "seeds": www.savenmchile.org. A billboard was posted to "Save NM Chile" and "Demand New Mexico Grown." Ultimately this action backfired for the NMCA, because once consumers discovered who was behind the GE chile they were infuriated.

"Demand New Mexico Grown" is the NMCA's emerging theme, and has been in use for years on Bueno Foods' packaging. This is the fourth "player" required for a new GE crop—an emotional appeal to rally people's support. The GE players are working to convince New Mexicans that their beloved New Mexico chile, especially green chile, is in peril—although fresh green chile constitutes only 5 percent of the New Mexico chile industry.

In 2011, the NMCA successfully lobbied to pass the New Mexico Chile Advertising Act. The NMSU Board of Regents will enforce and administer this law, whose rules are promulgated in consultation with the "chile industry." So, now, the same entities that are developing the GE chile, and will own the patent, will also decide what constitutes "New Mexico Chile." The New Mexico Department of Agriculture, which is under the NMSU Board of Regents, will enforce it. The law went into effect in July 2012. It requires the compulsory registration of all farmers and chile processors who sell a chile or chile product that bears the name "New Mexico Chile."

In 2013, the NMCA and NMSU returned to the New Mexico legislature to pass an amendment to the Chile Act called "Expanding Violations of the New Mexico Chile Advertising Act." This bill now criminalizes any grower who uses the name of any city, town, county, village, pueblo, mountain, river, or other geographic feature or features located in New Mexico, unless the grower is registered with the New Mexico Department of Agriculture. This is an attempt to take control of our local identity and our Chile Nativo by blurring history and commodifying a staple food crop.

There are also different requirements for selling fresh or processed chile. Fresh chile requires the registration of all farmers and the location of their farms; processed chile requires only a copy of the label of the product.

Why do farmers selling "fresh" have to provide the location of their farms? This puts farmers at risk of their seeds being contaminated. NMSU and NMDA, who work with the biotech companies, will now know where the chile fields are located. If farmers' seeds become contaminated, they will have to turn over their crop to the patent holder. *This bill threatens seed sovereignty—the rights of New Mexico farmers to plant their own seeds, save and exchange seed with neighbors, and pass them down to future generations.*

Over the past few years, a proliferation of seed laws have been passed in other countries that prohibit seed saving. Mexico passed one in 2007, after heavy lobbying by biotech seed companies—now it is against the law for farmers to exchange seeds unless the seeds are certified or registered with the proper entity. What does this mean for New Mexico farmers? Will we have to register our farms, certify our seeds, or be in databases to exchange our seeds with our neighbors? Will farmers be forced to only purchase seed certified by NMSU in order to call it New Mexico chile? Bueno Foods already requires this, as evidenced on their website (www.buenofoods.com): "Bueno Foods requires its farmers to use certified chile seed to maintain integrity of the genetic strain."

So who really owns the GE chile patent? NMSU has stated it will. Syngenta has been working with NMSU on a GE chile for years. Monsanto announced in January 2012 that their *phytophthora resistant chile* is in the "Advanced: Phase 3" of four phases. It includes Anaheim (from the New Mexico long mild), cayenne, jalapeño, and pasilla, from which the modern New Mexico cultivars were derived. Will all three own the patent?

No one knows what the true impact of a GE chile will be on traditional seed keepers, biodiversity, or the wild species still remaining. The 2009 study on Mexican chiles cited earlier, coauthored by a Monsanto researcher, acknowledges this at the end of the article:[11]

> Knowledge of gene flow (i.e., extent and directions) in chiles will be important to evaluate the potential effects of transgene release into the environment and the role of wild progenitor genetic diversity in conservation and breeding. Last, the impact of traditional farmer management in structuring genetic diversity and population dynamics of chile landraces should be investigated.

How can companies create and release a GE chile without understanding how it works? This arrogance may be the downfall of the agricultural system, leaving starvation, crop failure, superweeds and pests, and destruction of germplasm and diversity in its wake. This is why farmers and consumers are uniting to sound the alarm about the potential destruction of our chile, our culture, and our freedom to farm.

As the seasons end, some chiles will be left to dry on the plant for seed. They will have endured the year's extreme heat, dry conditions, pests, and other fungi or bacteria that we cannot see. For now, the seeds will prevail as they have done for centuries. For seeds are sacred; they are the memory of life.

## Update

We are now not only not able to call our chile "New Mexico," but in 2013 they amended the law to include in the name any geographic area in New Mexico, which now criminalizes us for calling our native chile by its appropriate name unless we register. Expansion of the New Mexico Chile Advertising Act makes it illegal for us to "knowingly advertise, describe, label or offer for sale chile peppers, or a product containing chile peppers, using the name of any city, town, county, village, pueblo, mountain, river or other geographic feature or features located in New Mexico."[12]

## Endnotes

[1]  E. S. Buckler, J. M. Thornsberry, and S. Kresovich, "Molecular Diversity, Structure and Domestication of Grasses," *Genetical Research* 77 (2001): 213–218.

[2]  Araceli Aguilar-Melendez et al., "Genetic Diversity and Structure in Semi-wild and Domesticated Chiles (*Capsicum annuum;* Solanaceae) from Mexico," *American Journal of Botany* 96, no. 6 (2009): 1190–1202.

[3]  Ibid.

[4]  See www.savenmseeds.org.

[5]  Kevin Robinson-Avila, "Imports Scorch New Mexico Chile Producers," *New Mexico Business Weekly,* September 2009, www.bizjournals.com

/albuquerque/stories/2009/09/21/story2.html?page=all; Associated Press, "Despite Red-Letter Year, Domestic Chili Pepper Growers Worry about Foreign Imports," August 13, 2006, http://lubbockonline.com/stories/081306 /agr_081306001.shtml; Jerry Hawkes, James D. Libbin, and Brandon A. Jones, "Chile Production in New Mexico and Northern Mexico," *Journal of the ASFMRA* 84 (2008), http://portal.asfmra.org/userfiles/file/journal/291 _libbin_1.pdf.

6    NM Chile Task Force, Report 11 (2002); statement by Dino Cervantes at coexistence meeting conducted by NMDA, October 2012.

7    Press release, August 19, 2014, www.savenmseeds.org.

8    Theodore W. Sammis et al., "Improving the Chile Industry of New Mexico through Industry, Agriculture Experiment Station, and Cooperative Extension Service Collaboration: A Case Study," *Journal of Extension* 47, no. 1 (February 2009).

9    New Mexico State Legislature, Interim Economic and Rural Development Committee, September 2010.

10   Statement by Professor Steve Hanson, New Mexico State Legislature, Interim Economic and Rural Development Committee, Third Meeting, Barbara Hubbard Room, New Mexico State University, Las Cruces, NM, September 21, 2010; Suman Bagga, Jose Luis Ortega, Wathsala Rajapakse, and Champa Sengupta-Gopalan, "Development of Glyphosate Resistant Chile by Expressing a Mutated Chile EPSPS Gene," 2013 Graduate Research and Arts Symposium, http://web.nmsu.edu/~wwwgsc/gras/postabs_13.pdf.

11   Aguilar-Melendez et al., "Genetic Diversity and Structure in Semiwild and Domesticated Chiles (*Capsicum annuum;* Solanaceae) from Mexico."

12   http://www.nmda.nmsu.edu/wp-content/uploads/2013/10/NM-Chile -Advertising-Act-2013.pdf.

# Moms Across America: Shaking Up the System

Zen Honeycutt

Moms Across America is a national coalition of "unstoppable moms" committed to empowering millions to educate themselves about genetically modified organisms (GMOs) and related pesticides, getting GMOs labeled, and offering GMO-free and organic solutions.

Mothers all across America are aware of the long journey in their fight against those responsible for exposing their families to health hazards. Their struggle began when they found that their children were experiencing strange and unusual symptoms. The mothers were confused, scared, and angry when their babies broke out in unexplained full-body rashes or suffered chronic pain from intestinal diseases. Teens and young adults were having their rectums sewn shut and colostomy bags inserted. As early as at the age of twenty, some had permanent stomach nerve damage so severe that they were likely to be disabled for the rest of their lives. In addition to gut dysbiosis and a damaged gut–brain connection, vitamin deficiency, mutated DNA, infertility, and autoimmune issues that impact a myriad of diseases, including cancer—the number one killer of children today—food allergies, autism, and Crohn's disease were on the rise.

Not only were our children's gut bacteria, stomachs, colons, and immune systems being destroyed, the fabric of our society was being torn apart as well. We no longer trusted the government. We felt betrayed by our leaders, duped by our food manufacturers, and skeptical of doctors of Western medicine who continued to push vaccines and medicines made by the very companies who manufactured the toxic chemicals sprayed on our food. And so we decided to confront the issue, as well as those responsible, head-on.

When we launched Moms Across America in February 2013, our Facebook reach grew from 0 to 300,000 page views in just four months. That too, without paying a penny to "boost" it. Four months after our launch, 172 Moms Across America leaders and supporters in forty-four states across the nation rose up and marched in their Fourth of July Independence Day parades, where thousands of people lined the streets to see our message: "Moms Across America March to Label GMOs." For many, it was the first time they saw the words "GMOs" and "Moms" in the same sentence. And hopefully, when we handed them our GMO information flyers, they got access to a new pathway to health.

Mothers who had never been community leaders in their lives have now begun to reach out and gather groups of friends, neighbors, and families to march in hometown parades against the big seed giants. Mothers who have had trouble speaking about GMOs are getting motivated to overcome their fears and speak up anyway. Children who often felt "weird" being "the only ones" to eat organic food are becoming aware of the ills of genetically modified food and the benefits of organic eating. All across the nation communities have come together, and together we are part of a movement to strengthen our society through the issue of food, to ensure that the health of our people is not compromised.

We reach out to thousands of people locally and millions nationally in a single day, marching for health and freedom. We continue to march in numerous parades and create community events throughout the year. We now have more than four hundred leaders, who have created more than six hundred events, reaching millions of people. More than 270 media outlets, including CNN, C-SPAN, RT.com, the *Dr. Oz Show,* and Fox News, have picked up these stories. Moreover, we have combined our passionate, and anecdotal, experiences with sound science through testing of water, urine, and breast milk, and have found levels of glyphosate far above what has been shown to be harmful. As our movement has grown, Moms Across Africa and Moms Across

Ireland have sprouted up, and we are in dialogue with leaders in Argentina, Brazil, Australia, New Zealand, Russia, France, Germany, Jamaica, Japan, and China. "Moms Across the World" share this vision and are willing participants in the struggle against GMOs.

GMO promoters claim that we are "fearmongering moms" who are lying in order to take down the biotech industry and promote organic companies. The insinuation is as absurd as it is amusing. We have enough drama in our lives; we don't need to invent more. We simply want and share solutions, and are highly motivated to do just that. That is why our motto is: "Empowered Moms, Healthy Kids." In doing so, we believe we can strengthen our communities, our governments, and the world. What we must overcome is the resignation and doubt of the American people. Too many people think their voices do not matter or their phone calls would not count. But they do. Too many people don't speak up to their grocery store manager or preschool director about food choices, not because they don't want to, but because they do not believe what they have to say will make a difference. And it would.

If you read this and are inspired to do something, but do not know where to start, reflect on what matters to *you:* Is it pets? Children? The elderly? Hospital patients? Figure it out. Often people wonder why I founded Moms Across America and how it has grown as a movement in such a short period of time. They ask me what I did previously, suspecting I was an event planner or a lawyer. But my past has nothing to do with what I am doing today. Different things mattered to me then. The health of my family matters to me now. All I do is take actions based on what matters to me. I don't know how; I just do it. What could stop many of us from taking action is our perspective of ourselves. But what makes a difference is what you care about, what kind of future you want. Take actions based on what matters to you. Certainly, the future of our children depends on it, and we thank you. The inspiring commitment and courage of mothers all across America makes a difference in their hometowns and restores our faith in humanity across the world.

# Global South

# Seed Freedom and Seed Sovereignty: Bangladesh Today

Farida Akhter

In Bangladesh, rice is not just a crop; it is the life and livelihood of farmers throughout the country. The importance of rice may not be unique to Bangladesh, but it is only Bengalis who are known as "Bheto Bangalee," meaning "rice people." One can hardly separate a Bengali from the agroecology, lifestyle, culture, and daily livelihood struggle determined by rice cultivation.

Broadcast, transplanted, and deep-water wet-season plantings (*aman*) form the main rice crop in Bangladesh. Dry season or *boro*, the second-largest rice crop, is also grown all over the country, but mainly in Dhaka and Chittagong. Winter crops (or *rabi* crops) include wheat, potato, and a number of different vegetables; wheat and potatoes are grown in large quantities in the Rajshahi region; millet and sesame are also grown, but in smaller quantities. Most of the crops grown in Bangladesh, particularly those called "local varieties," are open pollinated and have been grown and selected for their desirable traits for millennia. They grow well because they have been selected under organic conditions; they have better flavor, are hardier, and are more flexible than hybrid varieties. Seeds are dynamic and adapt to local ecosystems, as opposed to hybrid varieties, which are static. However, with the introduction of the so-called "improved varieties," which are nothing but laboratory seeds found in packets and sold in the market, farmers' personal seed collections disappear. In the case of rice, the open-pollinated seeds started disappearing with the introduction of the Green Revolution. In the early 1960s, fertilizer application was

limited to tea gardens and government agricultural farms, and irrigation was practiced on only about 7 percent of land. The government
then set up the Bangladesh Water Development Board and Bangladesh
Agricultural Development Corporation (BADC) to procure modern
agricultural equipment, chemical fertilizers, and improved seeds, and
distributed them to farmers at highly subsidized prices throughout the
country.

Modern varieties (MVs) of rice seeds were made available to farmers in 1968, because they could supposedly withstand the dry (*boro*) season, while wet (*aman*) season tolerant crops were distributed mainly in
1970. By 1984–1985, the irrigated area where these seeds were grown
covered approximately 20 percent of cultivated land, which "facilitated the spread of modern-input-responsive MVs to cover one-fourth
of cropped land and one-third of the sown area under cereal crops."[1]
Ultimately, chemical-based and mechanized agriculture led to the un-
doing of people's sustainable livelihoods. Rural areas were turned into
semi-urban areas, and the monoculture of rice production led to the
loss of genetic diversity throughout the country. Of the fifteen thousand traditional local varieties of rice, presently thirty are promoted
as high yielding varieties (HYVs). In the Bangladesh Rice Research
Institute more than seven thousand varieties of rice are still extant.
Although seed collections in the national gene banks are impressive,
banks have absolutely no connection with farmers. Seeds and germplasm are kept in cold storage with no effort made to regenerate them.

## Seed Diversity and Traditional Farming

Farmers maintain the diversity of seeds for every crop they grow
through the practice of traditional and ecological farming. Small-scale
as well as middle-class and wealthy farmers maintain seed diversity
and treat it as their treasure. Small-scale farmers met their subsistence
needs and exchanged the surplus for diversity; wealthy farmers maintained diverse varieties so as to have special rice varieties for special

occasions, cultural and religious purposes, as well as safeguards against natural disasters. Seed varieties were also required for livestock, poultry, and horticulture. More than 300 wild indigenous species of plants have been identified as relatives of the cultivated crops grown in Bangladesh; the country has 12,000 rice accessions, 1,090 landraces of white jute (*Corchorus capsularis*) and 519 of *tossa* jute (*C. olitorius*), 700 tea accessions, and 300 accessions of sugarcane.[2]

## The Erosion of Seed Diversity

Currently, there are only fifty-seven HYVs and three hybrid rice varieties that have been released for commercial cultivation in the country; in addition, seventy-five rice hybrids have been introduced from China, India, and Thailand. There was a time when Bangladesh was a rich treasure chest of biological diversity. A survey in 1976 revealed that only six thousand of more than fifteen thousand varieties of rice are now available, together with a few local varieties in specific niches like *chamara* in Tangail and *kataribhog* in Dinajpur.

The situation for other crops is even worse. The traditional practice of mixed cropping and crop rotation has been replaced with monocultures of selected varieties and hybrids. The first remarkable case of erosion was that of the large watermelon, but other serious cases are evident among the vegetable varieties of Bangladesh—most local varieties of brinjal, cucurbits, amaranth, and spinach have been replaced with hybrids.

## Patents, Seed Laws, and GMO Contamination

The Bangladesh Agricultural Development Corporation was established in 1972 as an autonomous corporation of the government to deal with the issue of seeds. A Seed Ordinance was enacted in 1977, and has since been amended twice, once in 1997 and again in 2005. Seed supply for farmers has been increasingly controlled by seed companies, both national and international. Seed laws were modified, enforcing the compulsory registration of seeds and making it impossible for farmers to produce their own. As in other parts of the world, farmers were forced to rely on the market for their seeds.

In Bangladesh, government institutions have been involved in a number of biotechnological research projects. These include the University of Dhaka, Rajshahi University, Chittagong University, Bangladesh Agricultural University (Mymensingh), Bangladesh Forest Research Institute (BFRI), Bangladesh Institute of Nuclear Agriculture (BINA), Bangladesh Rice Research Institute (BRRI), Bangladesh Agricultural Research Institute (BARI), and Bangabandhu Sheikh Mujibur Rahman Agricultural University (BSMRAU). In addition, there are nongovernmental organizations and private enterprises like BRAC, Proshika, Grameen Krishi Foundation, Bangladesh Seed Foundation, CARE Bangladesh, PROVA, Syngenta, World Vision Bangladesh, Agriculture Marketing Company Ltd. (AMCL), and Alpha Agro Ltd. that are also involved with biotechnological research. The Department of Agricultural Extension, Rangpur Dinajpur Rural Service (RDRS), and Bangladesh Rural Development Board (BRDB) have implemented the extension of genetically modified crops.

Bangladesh ratified the Cartagena Protocol on Biosafety in May 2000. In late 2003, the International Rice Research Institute (IRRI) in collaboration with the Bangladesh Rice Research Institute organized the PETRRA (Poverty Elimination through Rice Research Assistance) fair in Dhaka, where details regarding the genetically engineered golden rice, carrying vitamin A related genes of the daffodil flower, were discussed. PETRRA informed the public that such genes have been introduced into BR-29, the widely cultivated rice variety of Bangladesh, so that vitamin A would be produced in its seeds.

The National Biosafety Framework (NBF) was developed following an extensive assessment of biotechnology and biosafety in Bangladesh. Surveys were conducted on the current use of modern biotechnology, existing relevant policies, laws and regulations, building activities, and expertise within the country. The framework provides the basis for the future regulation and management of GMOs in Bangladesh. The objective of the NBF is twofold: it provides an overview of the existing systems, and identifies future needs for effective and transparent legislation and administration.

The National Biotechnology Policy, 2006, is a prelude to creating a policy environment favorable to the promotion of commercial transgenic crops. This policy is not merely economic in nature, primarily for the benefit of US biotech companies, but is related to our security and survival. At least 70 percent of the 150 million people in Bangladesh belong to farming communities that are presently producing food for the country, and their success is due largely to their own ingenuity. The National Biotechnology Policy will benefit the small parasitic commercial class, eager to import transgenic crops and biotech products from the United States and other industrialized countries. A section of corporate-appointed scientists who are willing to turn our public education and research institutions over to the service of corporations will also benefit; but the majority of farmers will be severely affected, as they have been in countries like Argentina, Brazil, and Mexico. Such an uncritical biotech policy will permanently transform the agricultural sector of Bangladesh into an industrial food production system, bringing it under the logic and global control of food chains. Moreover, it will cripple the possibility of the agricultural sector entering the global market with ecological and organic products. It will also seriously compromise the country's ability to attain food sovereignty.[3]

## GM Maize

Maize is cultivated in many districts of Bangladesh. Farmers used to grow open-pollinated, high-yielding varieties of maize released from the Bangladesh Agricultural Research Institute, but during the 1990s the cultivation of hybrid maize increased dramatically. Extensions of maize hybrids were specially intensified among farmers by the Department of Agricultural Extension (DAE) after the heavy floods of 1998.

BRAC and the Grameen Krishi Foundation (a subsidiary of Grameen Bank), two microcredit NGOs, played a role in the introduction and extension of hybrid maize cultivation. They tied hybrid maize seeds to microcredit and compelled farmers to grow the maize hybrids as poultry feed. The DAE also distributed hybrid maize seeds free of cost. At present, there is a growing trend toward the expansion of the poultry industry in Bangladesh, as a result of which there is a market for maize as feed. Based on this demand, NGOs that deal with microcredit, along with a number of seed companies, have taken this opportunity to extend hybrid maize cultivation for commercial gain. The DAE organizes demonstration plots, field days, and other motivational programs for this purpose; at present, there are twenty-three hybrid varieties of maize under production in Bangladesh.

### Commercial Maize Varieties and Their Source

| No. | Variety | Source |
| --- | --- | --- |
| 1 | 900-M | Auto Equipment Co. Ltd. |
| 2 | N K-40 | Syngenta |
| 3 | Pacific-984 | BRAC Seed Marketing (Bangladesh, Thailand) |
| 4 | Pacific-11 | BRAC Seed Marketing (Bangladesh, Thailand) |
| 5 | Barnali | HYV (BARI, Bangladesh) |
| 6 | Shuvra | HYV (BARI, Bangladesh) |
| 7 | Meher | HYV (BARI, Bangladesh) |
| 8 | Khoi Bhutta | HYV (BARI, Bangladesh) |
| 9 | Swan-2 | Not known |
| 10 | PSC-3344 | Agri Business Corporation (India) |
| 11 | PSC-3322 | Agri Business Corporation (India) |
| 12 | PSC-105 | Agri Business Corporation (India) |
| 13 | PSC-HP-100 | Agri Business Corporation (India) |
| 14 | PSC-984 | Agri Business Corporation (Thailand) |
| 15 | Hybrid Mukta | India |
| 16 | Hybrid Madhu-1 | India |

| 17 | Hybrid Madhu-2 | India |
| 18 | Hybrid Madhu-3 | India |
| 19 | Hybrid Madhu-4 | India |
| 20 | Konok Bhutta | India |
| 21 | Hybrid Madhu-19 | India |
| 22 | Hybrid Madhu-21 | India |
| 23 | Hybrid Madhu-28 | India |

## Bt Cotton

Cotton has been grown in Bangladesh as a cash crop for generations. Experimental production of American cotton was initiated in the plain lands of the country during the 1970s, at which point cotton was grown on approximately 1,215 hectares. Following this, the Cotton Development Board (CDB) was constituted, which resulted in the intensification of cotton cultivation across the country; production was extended to thirty-four districts in ten zones following the constitution of the CDB, and subsequently four cotton research centers were established.

Earlier, two types of cotton were cultivated, one of which was *Gossypium hirsutum*, grown in the plains, and the other was Comilla, which was grown in the hilly region. Currently, twelve high yielding varieties have been released from the CDB; they include CB-1, CB-2, CB-3, CB-4, CB-5, CB-6, CB-7, CB-8, CB-9, CB-10, CB-11, and CB-12. There are two hybrid varieties in use, namely DM-1 and Rupali-1; in addition, there are two varieties of Comilla cotton, Pahari Tula-1 and Pahari Tula-2.

Many of the cotton seeds for cultivation in the plains are now imported from the United States, all of which are high yielding varieties. About 6–7 percent of the country's requirement of raw cotton is met by domestic production, while the rest is imported. Experimental production of eight cotton hybrids introduced from India was conducted in Jagdishpur Chowgacha, Jessore, in 1990–1991, but the seeds were rejected and cultivation discontinued due to the failed yield of these varieties.

*The Failure of Bt Brinjal*

More than 341,262 tons of brinjal are produced annually on fifty thousand hectares of land by small, medium, and large farmers.[4] As many as 248 varieties have been available in Bangladesh in different agroecological zones of the country for hundreds of years,[5] depending on their adaptation to agroecological, topographic, and local climatic conditions, consumers' choice, and market demand. Although many varieties have been lost, the regional diversity of brinjals is still present. These varieties display wide diversity in agroecological adaptability, and morphological (such as size, shape, and color) and quality characteristics. Farmers have been the real custodians of these brinjal varieties by preserving their own seeds; Nayakrishi farmers, for example, produce more than forty varieties in four areas.[6]

There was never a demand for developing Bt brinjal in Bangladesh; it was introduced in a very quiet, almost surreptitious way. Now there is growing resistance from environmental, social, and farmers' groups against the Bt brinjal program run by the Bangladesh Agricultural Research Institute that uses the technical program of Monsanto-Mahyco and is funded by the Agricultural Biotechnology Support Project II (ABSP-II) of USAID together with Cornell University. The Bangladesh government has given easy access to the biotech company to use Bangladeshi scientists as "researchers" and use land under the direction of its research stations for testing the genetically modified food cropping, so that it can go through the required process of approving its introduction.

Genetic engineering is done by inserting a crystal protein gene, Cry1Ac, from a soil bacterium, *Bacillus thuringiensis* (Bt), into the genome of brinjal cultivars. Its insertion, along with other genetic elements such as promoters, terminators, and an antibiotic-resistance marker gene into the brinjal plant, is accomplished by using an *Agrobacterium*-mediated gene transformation. The Bt crystal protein gene contains a toxin that endows pest resistance to lepidopteran pests, such as the brinjal fruit and shoot borer (FSB). It is lethally toxic and works via binding to protein receptors in the gut of FSB larvae as they feed on the Bt brinjal.

Insertion of the Bt gene into nine Bangladeshi local varieties (Uttara, Kajla, Nayantara, Shingnath, Chaga, Islampuri, Dohazari, Khatkatia, and ISD-006) was done in the laboratory of the Indian company Mahyco, which received the application rights of Bt Cry1Ac gene technology from Monsanto. The Bangladeshi varieties were backcrossed with transgenic brinjal containing Cry1Ac, leaving little or no scope for BARI scientists or other public institutions to acquire Mahyco's proprietary technology.

Bt brinjal research started in three countries—India, Bangladesh, and the Philippines—back in 2005. Monsanto-Mahyco failed to continue in India because of a moratorium granted in 2010, and in May 2013, Bt brinjal field trials were stopped by the Philippine courts, leaving Bangladesh as the only country to get approval for commercial release. Confined field trials were carried out from 2010 to 2013 on the farms of BARI's regional stations. BARI applied in June 2013 to the National Technical Committee for Crop Biotechnology (NTCCB) Ministry of Agriculture, requesting its recommendation to the National Committee on Biosafety (NCB) for the commercial release of four Bt brinjal varieties (Bt brinjal Kajla, Bt brinjal Uttara, Bt brinjal Nayantara, and Bt brinjal ISD-006). Bangladesh does not have a National Biosafety Act; it only developed Biosafety Rules in 2012. In order to get approval, BARI, rather than providing its own tests for toxicity and other relevant biosafety parameters, submitted Mahyco-Monsanto's self-assessed dossier on toxicity for evaluation. Nor did BARI follow the Cartagena Protocol on Biosafety adopted at the UN Convention on Biodiversity, to which Bangladesh is a signatory, that states no GM crop is allowed to be grown in any region that is the center of origin or diversity of that crop. According to the Russian botanist and geneticist Nikolai I. Vavilov, brinjal's center of origin lies within the Indo-Burma region, which includes Bangladesh.[7]

UBINIG, Nayakrishi farmers, and environmental activists protested against this application and demanded assurances regarding environmental and health safety before approval was given, and filed a writ petition in the high court in July 2013. The court ordered the petitioners to provide evidence that Bt brinjal is harmful, and BARI, that it is safe. BARI submitted no such evidence while the petitioners provided international research data on its harmful effects. However, the court dismissed the writ petition in September 2013 after petitioners withdrew the file so that they could use another court for future filing of the application. However, later that month another bench of the Bangladesh high court directed the government to not release Bt brinjal before assessing its health risks and asked BARI, the Secretary of Agriculture, and the Secretary of Health to submit a progress report within three months, after conducting independent research in line with GM food standards set by the Codex Alimentarius Commission. The report has not yet been submitted. BARI managed to get a stay on this order at the appellate division, and further hearings are pending. Lawyers and judges, both, are reluctant to take up this case.

Despite the protest rallies, appeals of international scientists and environmental activists, court orders, and the national food safety law,[8] the National Committee on Biosafety granted conditional "approval" for the limited field-level cultivation of four Bt brinjal varieties in October 2013, on condition that seven conditions be met. Agricultural minister Matia Chowdhury handed over the seedlings of Bt brinjal to twenty selected farmers in four districts—Pabna, Gazipur, Jamalpur, and Rangpur—for cultivation in their fields in January 2014. The time sequence of the approval and seedling distribution indicates that it was not research results but the "approval" that was necessary for promoters to go ahead with GM crop introduction.

BARI used mainstream media to claim the advantages of Bt brinjal varieties that would bring economic benefits to farmers and the country through (1) controlling the brinjal fruit and shoot borer, the main brinjal pest, which causes 50–70 percent of the damage to the brinjal fruit; (2) reducing the use of pesticides; and (3) reducing the cost of brinjal cultivation. The fruit and shoot borer is one of the main brinjal pests, but not the only one. There are a number of others, including insect pests, diseases, and nematodes, that inflict serious damage to brinjal crops, causing heavy yield losses. The four brinjal varieties that have been transformed into Bt brinjals—Uttara, Kajla, Nayantara, and ISD-006—are moderately resistant to the fruit and shoot borer and tolerant to bacterial wilt disease attack, and ISD-006 has multiple resistance to the fruit and shoot borer, jassid, bacterial wilt disease, and the root-knot nematode.[9]

No official report is available on the amount of pesticides used for vegetables only, nor any statistics available regarding the amount of pesticides used for brinjal crops. A calculation by a scientist in Bangladesh shows that since 24,583 tons of insecticide are used for all crops, occupying 14,943,000 hectares,[10] an estimated amount of insecticide required for 50,000 hectares of brinjal crops cannot be more than 82.3 tons. It makes no sense that such a huge investment for Bt brinjal is being made only to save 82 tons of pesticide. On the other hand, BARI scientists have developed a number of very effective nonpesticidal Integrated Pest Management (IPM) technologies for controlling the fruit and shoot borer and other insect pests and diseases, which are highly cost-effective and safe. The On-Farm Research Division (OFRD) in farmers' brinjal fields in 2009–2010 and 2010–2011 showed that as much as 61 percent of FSB was controlled by using IPM package technologies, compared to that controlled by pesticides.[11] Farmers have their own methods for controlling pests in brinjal—if pesticide reduction is the reason behind introducing Bt brinjal, why are IPM methods not applied?

The *Financial Express* (April 7, 2014) reported that in the Bt brinjal fields of two farmers in Shaitail village, Gazipur district, and one farmer in Khotkhotia village of Rangpur Sadar Upazila, they had already applied more pesticides than before to protect their Bt brinjal crops from attacks by different pests.

## Noncompliance of Approval Conditions

There are seven specific conditions for approval required by the National Committee on Biosafety, Ministry of Environment. There was a clear violation of condition 3, i.e., the formation of a field biosafety committee involving the officer of the Department of Agricultural Extension, concerned scientists of the BARI regional station, and district and divisional level officers of the Ministry of Environment monitoring biosafety; of condition 4, offering training to farmers regarding biosafety protocol and producing Bt brinjal in the proper environment; of condition 5, which requires the applicant institution and the concerned ministry to take appropriate steps on an emergency basis in case of an adverse impact on the environment or on public health; and of condition 6, which requires that the proponent institution will label Bt brinjal as such at the time of marketing.

In March 2005, a tripartite agreement was signed by BARI, Mahyco (the US seed giant Monsanto's Indian subsidiary), and Sathguru Management Consultants Pvt. Ltd. (India) for the development and release of cultivable Bt brinjal in Bangladesh.[12] Based on this agreement, Mahyco transformed nine local brinjal varieties of Bangladesh into Bt brinjal at Mahyco's biotechnology laboratory in India. The most striking aspect of the agreement is that BARI has granted indemnity to Monsanto-Mahyco and Sathguru for any kind of disaster concerning Bt brinjal research. By this agreement (signed without the knowledge of farmers and the general public), Mahyco and Monsanto now own the genetically engineered nine indigenous varieties of brinjal.

BARI claimed that:

> Bt brinjal was developed in the public sector by the government-operated Bangladesh Agricultural Research Institute for non-commercial purposes. It is not owned by any corporate entity. Seeds will be distributed to farmers in a non-commercial approach where small and medium-enterprise farmers will access seed through the state university system.... Monsanto has no ownership rights over Bt brinjal.[13]

Article 1.19 of the agreement, however, states clearly that "Monsanto/ MHSCL IP Rights shall mean all intellectual property rights that Monsanto or MHSCL owns or controls, which will be infringed by making, using or selling Licensed Domestic Eggplant Products containing MHSCL Technology or Monsanto Technology"; and according to Section 1.6 of the agreement, Bt brinjal seeds must be purchased from the seed company. Further, Article 2.5(b) states that the sublicensee shall not cross or backcross the Bt gene into any eggplant germplasm other than the varieties listed in Annexure 1. These varieties are: 1. Uttara (Accession # EC549409), 2. Kajla (Accession # EC549410), 3. Nayantara (Accession # EC549411), 4. Singhnath (B009) (Accession # EC549412), 5. Dohazari (Accession # EC549413), 6. Chaga (Accession # EC549414), 7. Khatkatia (BL117) (Accession # EC549415), 8. Islampuri (Accession # EC549416), and 9. Ishurdi local (ISD006) (Accession # EC549417).

Subsection (c) of Section 9.2 says that the agreement can be terminated by the sublicensor or Mahyco if the laws and regulations in Bangladesh do not provide assurance of protection for commercial and intellectual property rights. Subsection (e) of Section 9.2 says that BARI can cancel this agreement in case the fruit and shoot borer becomes resistant to Bt brinjal. In addition, Section 9.6 mentions that after cancellation of the agreement, BARI must cease distribution of Bt brinjal seeds and *destroy all seeds in the presence of the representative of the seed company,* and the representative shall submit a report in this respect to the seed company.

## The Threat to Public Breeding

The varietal improvement of crops is vital for farmers, especially in developing countries. Their efforts are aimed toward ensuring food sovereignty, raising farmers' incomes, and meeting the challenges of climate change. Yet many farmers were discouraged from continuing their breeding efforts due to pressure from the genetic "improvement" lobby. Farmers in less intensive cropping areas, like the salinity-prone coastal belt in the south and the drought-prone northwestern region, still continue their need-based breeding efforts for salinity-tolerant and drought-tolerant varieties of rice and other crops.

The toughest hurdles for farmers include government policy and rule; and coercion by national and multinational seed companies.

Multinational seed companies include Syngenta Bangladesh Ltd.; Bayer Crop Science Ltd.; A C I Limited; Global Agro Resources Incorporation; Macdonald Pvt. Ltd.; and Ganges Development Corporation. National seed companies are in collaboration with East West Seed Ltd.; Aftab Bahumukhee Farm Limited; Supreme Seed Co. Ltd.; Pasha Pashi Seed Company; Ispahani Agro Ltd.; National Agro-care Import and Export Ltd.; Lal Teer Seed Limited; Getco Agro-vision Ltd.; Ranks Agro Biotech Limited; Energypac Agro Ltd.; and Namdhari Malik Seeds (Pvt.) Limited, just to name a few.

There is no government policy that approves farmers' seeds; all policies and legal instruments are in favor of seed companies. The seed industry in Bangladesh comprises both public and private sector initiatives. The private sector has more than a hundred companies, with more than five thousand registered seed dealers operating across the country. The first decade of this century was marked by a transition from open-pollinated to hybrid seed varieties. As a country that depends on agriculture, seed is the key to the survival of the nation. In fiscal 2011–2012, there was a total requirement of 10,57,172 metric tons of seed in Bangladesh. Of this, 14 percent was supplied by the Bangladesh Agricultural Development Corporation; farmers themselves produced 40 percent, and the remaining 46 percent was supplied by seed companies. There are about 280 seed companies enlisted with the Bangladesh Seed Merchants Association (BSMA); and about thirty enterprises have reasonably organized seed businesses involving the production and marketing of seed. Thirteen are considered medium-sized, with annual sales of forty to one thousand metric tons of seeds, and the remaining seventeen companies have annual sales of less than forty metric tons. In addition to newly emerging companies, NGOs are also playing an important role in seed supply in Bangladesh; at present there are more than twenty NGOs involved in the production and marketing of seeds. Imported hybrid seeds are approximately ten times more expensive than locally produced ones. The price of one kilo of hybrid rice seed ranges from BDT 250 to 300, compared to BDT 20 to 30 for each kilo of rice inbreds. Small-scale farmers cannot afford to buy costly seeds every planting season. Moreover, the cost of production for modern varieties and hybrids is much higher because of high input costs.

## Corporate Influence on Research, Breeding, and Agricultural Policy

Agricultural research in Bangladesh has been coordinated by the Bangladesh Agricultural Research Council (BARC), which, however, has no control over the allocation of financial resources. According to Bangladesh Agricultural Research Council Bill 2012, twelve research institutions are affiliated with BARC, and include: Bangladesh Rice Research Institute (BRRI); Bangladesh Jute Research Institute (BJRI); Bangladesh Agricultural Research Institute (BARI); Bangladesh Institute of Nuclear Agriculture (BINA); Bangladesh Sugarcane Research Institute (BSRI); Bangladesh Livestock Research Institute (BLRI); Bangladesh Fisheries Research Institute (BFRI); Bangladesh Tea Research Institute (BTRI); Bangladesh Forest Research Institute (BFRI); Soil Resource Development Institute (SRDI); Bangladesh Sericulture Research and Training Institute (BSRTI); and Bangladesh Cotton Development Board (BCDB).

BARC and its twelve affiliated research institutes account for roughly three-quarters of the country's agricultural research expenditure, which has depended on donor financing, particularly World Bank loans, which facilitated considerable investment in infrastructure and equipment. The input of the private sector is minimal. Some NGOs are also involved, but their research activities, if any, are limited. The Bangladesh Rural Advancement Committee (BRAC), Rangpur Dinajpur Rural Service (RDRS), and Grameen Krishi Foundation (GKF), among others, have recently been conducting research on conventional agriculture, while research on ecological agriculture has been carried out by Proshika; Unnayan Bikalper Nitinirdharoni Gobeshona (UBINIG, Policy Research for Development Alternatives); Bangladesh Resource Centre for Indigenous Knowledge (BARCIK); Unnayan Onneshan; Action Aid; Caritas; and Christian Commission for Development in Bangladesh (CCDB).

## People's Initiatives for Seed Conservation

Some nongovernmental organizations, via the Nayakrishi movement, have been endeavoring to empower farmers and the farming community despite the onslaught by seed companies. The Nayakrishi Andolon (New Agricultural Movement), founded on biodiversity-based farming, is a movement for propagating ecological agriculture. It is based on simple practices, such as no chemical pesticides and fertilizers; soil management; and mixed cropping and crop rotation for pest management and risk reduction. Mixed cropping is crucial for increasing productivity through encouraging biodiversity rather than high yields of a single monoculture crop. The central approach of this initiative lies squarely in the conservation, management, and use of local seed and genetic resources, and adopting and improving production techniques appropriate for farmers' seeds. Hundreds of local varieties of rice, vegetables, fruit, and timber crops have been reintroduced within a short period of time. Farmers in Nayakrishi areas, for example, cultivate at least three thousand varieties of rice, and the number is increasing. The movement has been negotiating with the national gene bank to help them regenerate the collected germplasm and internalize the conservation of genetic resources as a built-in operation. At least three hundred thousand farmers in nineteen districts of Bangladesh practice

Nayakrishi. In all farming households, women have taken the lead as key players as they preserve seeds, and have formed the Nayakrishi Seed Network (NSN) in a systematic attempt to involve women at different levels. The NSN builds on the farming household, the focal point for *in situ* and *ex situ* conservation. Farmers maintain diversity in the field, and at the same time conserve seed in their homes to be replanted in the next season. The next step for the network is the formation of the Specialized Women Seed Network (SWSN), comprising women farmers who have specialized knowledge and skills regarding seed preservation and genetic resource conservation.

The activities of Nayakrishi Andolon are constituted as a system of relations between farming households. Individual plans and decisions are made collectively through meetings and the sharing of information. In the meetings, decisions are made to ensure that in every planting season all the available varieties in farmers' households are replanted and the seeds collected and conserved for the next season. From individual farmers' seed collection at the household level, Nayakrishi Seed Huts are established on the independent initiative of one or two households in the village who are part of the Nayakrishi Andolon, and are willing to take the responsibility for ensuring that all common species and varieties are replanted, regenerated, and conserved. These households are known as Nayakrishi Seed Huts (NSHs).

Community Seed Wealth (CSW) is the institutional setup in the village that articulates the relation between the village and the national gene bank. The CSW also maintains a well-developed nursery. The organization of CSWs is based on two principles: (1) the nurseries must be built from locally available materials; and (2) their maintenance should reflect household seed conservation practices. Any difficult scenarios the CSW encounters reflect the problems that farmers are facing in household conservation. Any member of the Nayakrishi Andolon can collect seed from CSW on condition that after the harvest they will deposit double the quantity they receive.

## Nayakrishi and Biodiversity

As an agricultural practice Nayakrishi is based on ten simple principles.[14] In addition to poison- and chemical-free agriculture, the production of biodiversity is built into their method of food production. As a fundamental principle, Nayakrishi farmers reject monoculture and base their practice on mixed cropping and crop rotation. With regard to productivity, output from Nayakrishi practices is either the same as or higher than that from conventional chemical agriculture. Apart from the ecological benefits, the main reason for acceptance of Nayakrishi is the economic return to farmers. The calculation of yield by Nayakrishi farmers is done first, not on a single crop yield based on a monoculture calculation; second, on the energy used as an input and the energy produced as an output, "sustainability" taken into account as the fundamental parameter assessing "productivity"; and third, on responding to the diverse needs of the community that cannot be satisfied by increasing the yield of a particular crop—biodiversity-based practice is clearly preferable. However, the addition of a new variety from the formal system to the existing genetic resource base of the farming community is seen as a contribution, and its integration into Nayakrishi farming practices is based on totally different parameters than those proposed by conventional agriculture.

## Endnotes

[1]   Mahabub Hossain, *Nature and Impact of the Green Revolution in Bangladesh,* Research Report 67, International Food Policy Research Institute and Bangladesh Institute of Development Studies, July 1988.
[2]   BARC, *The Second Report on Plant Genetic Resources for Food and Agriculture of Bangladesh: The State of Activities,* Bangladesh Agricultural Research Council, 2005, www.fao.org.
[3]   Farhad Mazhar, "Review Your Biotech Policy, Prime Minister," *New Age,* July 25, 2006.
[4]   Statistical Yearbook of Bangladesh, Bangladesh Bureau of Statistics (BBS 2010), Ministry of Planning, Government of Bangladesh.
[5]   M. A. Razzaque and G. Hossain, *Country Report on the State of Plant Genetic Resources for Food and Agriculture Organization;* Bangladesh Agricultural

Research Council, Ministry of Agriculture, Government of Bangladesh, *The Second Report on Plant Genetic Resources for Food and Agriculture of Bangladesh*, 2007, http://pgrfa.barcapps.gov.bd/reports/bangladesh2.pdf.

6  Nayakrishi is a biodiversity-based ecological farmers' movement, with involvement of more than three hundred thousand farming households.

7  N. I. Vavilov, "Phytographical Basis of Plant Breeding: The Origin, Variation, Immunity and Breeding of Cultivated Plants," *Chronica Botanica* 13 (1951): 1–366.

8  According to Clause 21(1) of the Bangladesh Food Safety Law (2013), the production, distribution, marketing, or import of any food derived from "genetically modified" crops or sources has been prohibited.

9  BARI, *Handbook of Agricultural Technology* (in Bengali), 1999: 331–333; BARI, *Improved Technology for Vegetable Production* (in Bengali), 2006: 11–20.

10  FAO Corporate Documentary Repository, Country Report, Bangladesh.

11  BARI Entomology Division, "On-Farm Validation of BARI Developed IPM Package against Brinjal Shoot and Fruit Borer," Annual Report for 2009–2010: 56; BARI Entomology Division, "On-Farm Validation of BARI Developed IPM Package against Brinjal Shoot and Fruit Borer," Annual Report for 2010–2011: 50–51.

12  Sublicense Agreement between Maharashtra Hybrid Seeds Company Limited (MHSCL), Sathguru Management Consultants Pvt. Ltd., and Bangladesh Agricultural Research Institute (BARI) signed on March 14, 2005.

13  http://btbrinjal.tumblr.com/myths; also please visit http://ubinig.org /index.php/home/showAerticle/50/english/Farida-Akhter/Mahyco-%E2 %80%980wns%E2%80%99-Bt-Brinjal-not-BARI-and-never-the-farmers!

14  *Principle 1:* The use of pesticides must be stopped immediately.
*Principle 2:* Seeds must be maintained in farmers' hands, on farms, in the field, and at home.
*Principle 3:* Cultivation must be done with organic manure, without the use of chemical fertilizers, slowly ensuring environment-friendly management practices.
*Principle 4:* Never promote the monoculture of any crop, always practice mixed crops and crop rotation, matching soil, season, crops, and other variables of crop production.
*Principle 5:* Ensure the management of cultivated and uncultivated spaces, and a method of crop production that allows many species of uncultivated plants to emerge, grow, and develop.
*Principle 6:* Maintain, manage, and utilize surface water for irrigation; underground water should be conserved.
*Principle 7:* Return from crop production is not calculated on the basis of a single crop. The total yield, return, conservation of biodiversity, manifestation of biodiversity, environmental and economic gains of household, village, and community are the priority.

*Principle 8:* Enriching the household through removing gaps in life, nature, and the productive base is the goal of Nayakrishi.

*Principle 9:* Creative use of water is vital in order to maintain aquatic biodiversity.

*Principle 10:* Increase the income opportunity of the community through enriching natural resources for improving livelihood options. Empowering every household in the Nayakrishi village and freeing them from the market is another objective.

# Monsanto and Biosafety in Nepal

Kusum Hachhethu

Nepal is an agrarian but food-deficit country. Around 70 percent of the population is involved in agriculture, which contributes 40 percent of the country's GDP, yet, according to the World Health Organization, 3.5 million of Nepal's 26.6 million people are food insecure. Until the 1980s, Nepal used to be a food exporter, but for more than a decade now it has been a food-deficit country.

Increasing agricultural productivity is vital to the overall growth of Nepal's economy and the reduction of hunger and poverty. In order to boost agricultural productivity, hybrid seeds were introduced in Nepal and vigorously promoted during the 1990s—today, these seeds are extensively used in many regions of the country, including remote areas. About 80 percent of vegetables grown in Nepal use hybrid seeds; these seeds, as well as biotechnology, are being sold as a solution to food insecurity and hunger by promising higher yields.

Maize is one of the staple crops of Nepal; its commercial cultivation became popular after the government initiated the "Maize Mission Program" that provides hybrid seeds and fertilizers to farmers, as an incentive to grow more maize as a crop but also as feed. Recently, however, there has been a recurring crop failure in various maize-growing regions that many have attributed to hybrid seeds. Some have even blamed Monsanto's genetically modified seed entering Nepal through an open border with India.

On September 13, 2011, USAID issued a press release stating that Monsanto had teamed up with the Ministry of Agriculture and

Cooperatives (MoAC) in Nepal to promote the use of hybrid maize and provide training to farmers, as part of a pilot project in Nepal. The announcement created an outcry among experts, farmers, and civil society members, who were critically aware of Monsanto's unethical history—as a result, the "STOP Monsanto in Nepal" campaign came into being. Although Monsanto had already marked its presence in Nepal more than a decade earlier, the announcement of its large-scale entry paved the way for a wider discourse on questions related to Nepal's agricultural future—including the use of hybrid and genetically modified seeds. A long-neglected topic was finally in the limelight.

This essay on the status of the seed focuses on recent maize failures in Nepal, and discusses various issues related to Nepal's agriculture sector, existing legal loopholes, and possible policy recommendations. It also discusses legislation regarding seeds and intellectual property rights under WTO. Finally, it presents alternatives to Monsanto and GMOs and provides evidence that Monsanto and GM seeds are not the only solution to food insecurity in Nepal—improved local varieties can also return a high yield. Rather than depending on multinationals and their seeds, the priority should be improving agricultural inputs via investment in irrigation, land management, and research.

## When Crops Fail

In late 2009 and early 2010, there was a massive crop failure in the maize-growing regions of Chitwan, Nawalparasi, Rautahat, Sarlahi, Bara, Parsa, and others. "The plant grew well, but none of the cobs had kernels," complained Krishna Prasad Kafle, a farmer from Gaidakot, Nawalparasi, who suffered a huge failure in 2009. Another commercial farmer, Thaneshwor Sapkota, faced a loss of 22,000 Nepali rupees (NRs) when his maize failed in 2010—after this fiasco he has completely stopped growing maize.

On June 7, 2012, maize farmers in Jhapa district organized a mass rally in Chandragadhi headquarters to protest losses incurred by them on nonyielding maize—similar problems were evident in Garamani, Jalthal, Prithivinagar, Balubadi, Rajgadh, Haldibari, and more than fifteen other Village Development Committees (VDCs) in the district.

While some blame climate change and unusual cold spells as the major culprits for the failure, others (farmers, civil society members, scientists, and agronomists) suspect "bad-quality foreign seeds" and local agrovets (seed distributors) who persuaded them to buy hybrids. "These agents from multinational seed companies approach farmers directly, sometimes even giving them loans to buy the seeds. When the crop fails, no one is accountable," said Basanta Ranabhat from Ecological Services Centre (ECOSCENTRE), an NGO dedicated to organic agriculture and indigenous knowledge. Unfortunately, we do not know what kinds of seeds are being sold to farmers. Could they be seeds that are not tested or registered? Could they be genetically modified seeds? We do not know. The weak regulatory mechanism in Nepal further exacerbates the situation.

When farmers demand compensation from the government for crop failure, officials tend to blame them.

> Farmers have a tendency of buying seeds from the market without consulting the authorities at the district agriculture office. They must use seeds that are tested by the National Seed Board and are recommended by the Nepal Agriculture Research Centre (NARC). We are not responsible for the failure of seeds that are randomly bought from the market, that are outside the list of our registered seeds.

So said Jaganath Tiwari, chief of the District Agriculture Development Office (DADO), Chitwan. But shouldn't the government be responsible for unregistered seeds flowing into every corner of the country? Turns out, even hybrid seeds that have been approved by the Nepal Seed Board (NSB) and tested at the Seed Quality Control Center (SQCC) are failing. Shouldn't government be accountable for this? The NSB is responsible for the publication of a list specifying the varieties of seed that can be legally distributed and sold in the country. In order to be included in the list, the seed variety must be officially approved and registered, as the objective of SQCC is to ensure the availability of quality seed to farmers by enforcing quality control.

## Failed Promises

In 2009, Laxmi Sapkota and her family planted maize seeds from two different companies on two different plots—one of them, Manisha 9497, failed, while the other yielded a normal output. If climate change and environmental factors had been responsible for the failure, plants from both plots should have failed, but this was not the case. The failed one, Manisha 9497, is a hybrid produced and marketed by Manisha Agri Biotech Pvt. Ltd., Hyderabad, India. "The local agrovet highly recommended it and persuaded us to buy the seed. But when the cob did not yield any kernels, they were in complete denial," complained Laxmi. "Only after we threatened to approach the national media did they provide us with minimal compensation," she added. While the Sapkota family managed to receive some compensation from the agrovet, many other innocent victims of maize failure do not have the means to fight back. These underrepresented farmers have no other option but to suffer the consequences of failure, and many have stopped growing maize.

> We heard that the government had allocated and distributed NRs 200 million to the victims of the 2009 maize failure, but we did not receive any compensation. None of my colleagues received a single rupee. In fact, I do not personally know of any other maize farmer who received a share of that money,

said Hari Kala Kafle, another victim from Gaidakot, Nawalparasi. Uneven allocation of the compensation is yet another case of corrupt political institutions in Nepal; even worse, some farmers received compensation in the form of subsidized chemical pesticides! Hari Kafle and many other victimized farmers have accused a hybrid seed variety, Rajkumar, from Bioseed Company, Hyderabad, India. "The local agrovet lured us into buying this particular seed, promising higher yield and better results," said Kafle. According to Ganeshwor Kadel, owner of Gaidakot Agro Concern (a local agrovet in Nawalparasi), Rajkumar is the most popular hybrid seed variety among farmers in the region. Kadel, who sells fourteen to fifteen varieties of imported hybrid corn (mostly from India), proudly declares that it is not worth selling local open-pollinated seed varieties. "I rarely sell local seed varieties; I highly recommend imported hybrid seeds to farmers—if these varieties are used along with suitable pesticides and fertilizers, these seeds can give extremely high yields," he boasts. And why would seed retailers like Kadel not promote costlier hybrid seeds? While local corn varieties are sold for NRs 40–70 per kilo, hybrid counterparts are sold for around NRs 200 per kilo (Rajkumar is being sold for NRs 190 per kilo at Gaidakot Agro Concern).

Similarly, in Nijgadh, the hybrid maize seed called X 92 (from Tex Company, India), spread over two hundred hectares, produced cornless cobs—similar consequences were seen in Dumbarwana, Ratnapuri, Manaharwa, and Fatterpur where X 92 was planted. According to Laxmi Prasad Subedi, professor of Genetics at Rampur University, the 2009–2010 maize failure was due to partially sterile seeds with faulty genetic makeup. Subedi, who is conducting independent research on the failure, updated his Facebook page to report that

> ... 9–10 genes from chromosome 1 segregated, including asynaptic which produced gametophytic form of sterility (even F1 hybrids segregate in their cobs for sterility). Tassel-less plants were also found segregating in F2, where size of the tassel is a quantitative trait (a 35 cm tassel x tassel-less, F1 will have an 18 cm long tassel, in short).

In simple language, tassel-less plants with faulty genetic makeup contributed to the failure.

Environmental journalist Pragati Shah quoted findings from a report of South Asia Watch on Trade, Economics and Environment that said,

> The use of hybrid corn seeds has escalated in Nepal from 2005 in the name of higher yield, but despite an increase in farm area allotted to maize production, yield is found to be declining.

If the large-scale entry of Monsanto in Nepal is allowed, it will experience the kind of destitution faced by farmers in India sooner or later. In fact, lack of economic capacity and unstable governance will make things much worse in Nepal; if the government allows Monsanto to promote hybrid corn in the country, it will inevitably be inviting an agrarian crisis.

## Grow More Maize ...

Nepal imports half the estimated 270,000 metric tons of maize it uses every year, from India, at a cost of NRs 200 million. "In order to enhance its production, the Maize Mission Program promotes the use of hybrid seeds, which are expected to give a higher yield, compared to OPVs," according to Santosh Raj Paudel, program officer at the District Agriculture Office in Narayangarh, Chitwan. Existing policies relating to agriculture such as the National Seed Policy (1998), Agricultural Policy (2005), and Science and Technology Policy (2004) have also emphasized minimizing food insecurity and poverty through the promotion and development of hybrid seeds. "In order to meet the demand, we must produce 5–6 tonnes of maize per hectare with 53,000 plant population per hectare—the current average is 2.2 tonnes of maize per hectare," says Chitra Kunwar, senior scientist at Nepal Maize Research Program, Rampur. "Hybrid seeds are able to meet this requirement." Although hybrid maize was present in Nepal as early as 1987, it became more widespread after the initiation of the Maize Mission Program. According to Mr. Kunwar, thirty varieties of hybrid maize seeds from twelve different foreign companies have already been approved and registered in Nepal. The registered companies include Bioseed, Zuari Seed, Kanchanjunga, Pioneer, Bisco Biosciences, Charoen, Aishwarya, and Monsanto.

Technically, Monsanto has already established itself in Nepal, with its products in the market since 2004. In 2010, 100 metric tons of Monsanto's seed were imported into the country. In 2009, four of Monsanto's hybrids—Allrounder, 900M, DKC 7074, and Pinnacle—were registered in Nepal, after the approval of the Seed Quality Control Center. Monsanto's GM seeds have also probably entered Nepal through a porous border with India; at a local agrovet around Chitwan in Nepal, several hybrid seeds (cabbage, carrots) from the Mon Son company were detected. An online investigation confirmed that Mon Son is, after all, the same Monsanto company of Saint Louis!

The fact that Monsanto is already in Nepal is not an excuse for allowing large-scale entry of its seeds into the country. The goal of Monsanto's official pilot project was to target twenty thousand farmers, who would also be trained in hybrid maize production practices. "In Nepal's context the target of twenty thousand farmers is certainly not a pilot project—pilot projects are supposed to be small-scale test projects," said Basanta Ranabhat of ECOSCENTRE. "Of course we have issues with Monsanto-introduced hybrid seeds; this company has never worked for the benefit of farmers," he added.

In April 2004, Nepal became a member of the World Trade Organization (WTO), but it has not yet made adequate preparations to implement the legislation and policies required by the Trade-Related Aspects of Intellectual Property Rights (TRIPS) Agreement. At present, IPR in seed and agriculture is not strictly followed in Nepal; however, a draft on its proper implementation has already been prepared and it is possible that it will be approved any time by the government. Often, multinationals like Monsanto engage in intellectual biopiracy by claiming a plant/seed as their invention, even when it has been cultivated by indigenous communities from ancient times. For example,

Monsanto's patent registered with the European Patent Office (EPO) claimed to have invented the traditional Indian/Nepali wheat plant (Nap Hal) for its soft milling trait—the patent was revoked after Navdanya filed a legal challenge against Monsanto in India.

Genetic contamination is another threat for Nepal, since GM seeds are widely cultivated in the neighboring countries of India and China. Transgenic seeds can contaminate nontransgenic traditional seeds through natural pollination and destroy Nepal's local crop varieties. We have already lost a significant number of our traditional seeds such as shobara, the indigenous red rice native to the hilly regions of Nepal.

## Biosafety Framework in Nepal

In March 2002, Nepal signed the Cartagena Protocol on Biosafety, an international agreement that aims to ensure the safe handling, transport, and use of living modified organisms (LMOs) resulting from modern biotechnology that may have an adverse effect on biological diversity, taking also into account risks to human health.[1]

Ten years after signing the Cartagena Protocol, the government has not yet designated a responsible institution for research, testing, and monitoring of GM seeds and GMOs. According to Chitra Kunwar, senior scientist at NARC,

> Although Nepal has regulatory acts on GM seeds, these seeds might already have been smuggled into Nepal. Unfortunately, at NARC, we do not have the necessary laboratory facilities to test the genotypic characteristics of seeds; if we did, we would be able to confirm that defective seeds are responsible for crop failure.

Agronomists and scientists have been requesting the government since 2002 to provide them with such facilities. Similarly, civil society members and environmentalists have been demanding a stronger regulatory act against GM seeds and hence, proper implementation of the Cartagena Protocol. Unfortunately, the government continues to neglect and postpone this imperative need. Moreover, NARC's agricultural Strategic Vision for Agricultural Research (2011–2030) seems to be in favor of biotechnology. NARC's "Meeting Nepal's Food and Nutrition Security Goals through Agricultural Science and Technology" report states:

> Biotechnology has the potential to address the problems not solved by conventional agricultural research. Owing to the development of biotechnology in global scenario and richness of diversity in plant and animal genetic resources in Nepal, there is a great potential to use biotechnology for increased food production. Biotechnology offers an incredible potential for those involved in agriculture. The scope for developing new biotechnology products that involve licensing, and hence royalties, should be explored.

As it has everywhere else, Monsanto played its game very well in Nepal. Before USAID made its announcement about Monsanto's official entry, it had already taken a few government officials on a field trip to India. Jaganath Tiwari from DADO said,

> We traveled from the north of India to the south, where we visited various farms using Monsanto's seed. They are doing really well. They seem satisfied with the seeds.
>     Nepali farmers also seem keen to try Monsanto's hybrid maize; if Monsanto is such a notorious company, why are farmers in the US using Monsanto's seed? When the rest of the world is using Monsanto's seed, why should Nepal lag behind?

What officials like him may not know is that various countries of the world are saying no to Monsanto. On April 25, 2012, the government of Gujarat (India) withdrew Monsanto's double-cross hybrid maize, Prabal, distributed to more than half a million tribal farmers in Gujarat via Project Sunshine in 2008. On June 4, 2012, Haitian peasant farmers burned several bags of hybrid maize seeds donated by Monsanto as a part of the postearthquake reconstruction program—the donated seeds had been treated with Maxim XO, a hazardous fungicide.

With a past full of unethical acts, Monsanto's history has long drawn criticism from farmers, environmentalists, health personnel, and civil society groups around the world. But Nepal's government remains ignorant of these protests. While USAID issued a press release that it would facilitate Monsanto's pilot project in Nepal, government officials from MoAC were in a state of denial. "No deal has been signed between Monsanto, USAID, and MoAC," said Hari Dahal, former spokesperson of MoAC. Subsequently, USAID also mentioned on its Facebook page that they had not come to a decision about the project: "We have discussed options with the government, but no decisions have been made yet." But deal or no deal, the deliberate obscurity of the project is yet another example of Monsanto's tactics and Nepal's weak governance.

## Misplaced Priorities

The current priority should be to regulate the uncontrolled import of seeds, and to ensure that only registered and properly tested non-GM seeds are allowed into Nepal. In addition, Nepal's government must provide NARC and the Seed Quality Control Center with the equipment required to study the genotypic characteristics of seed. Adequate funds should also be allocated for agriculture-related research—an "agriculture research fund" is another lag sector in Nepal. It is equally imperative to educate farmers on issues related to seed and agriculture, including the possible ramifications of hybrid and GM seeds. Vijay Raj Joshi, consultant at Practical Action Nepal (an INGO dedicated to sustainable development), says,

> Poor farmers do not know what is hybrid, what is GMO; they are simply looking for higher yield and short-term gain. In the process, they often get trapped into a vicious circle of debt and poverty.

Scientists at NARC are developing local improved seed varieties that are suited to Nepal's climate and topography, and can also assure relatively high yields. Rampur Composite (a locally developed improved variety of maize) can yield up to seven metric tons of maize per hectare. Promotion of such local seeds will not only prevent seed dictatorship by foreign multinational companies, it will also encourage local innovation.

If Monsanto's attempt to initiate a pilot project in Nepal did any good, it was to highlight a crucial issue ignored or obscured by our leaders. "We have used this Monsanto movement as a gateway to talk about MoAC's agricultural vision, its understanding of food security and sovereignty, and policy interventions required to address the issue," says Sabin Ninglekhu Limbu from STOP Monsanto in Nepal. In fact, in January 2012, there was a parliamentary hearing on Monsanto, hybrid imports, and agriculture vision, a big step toward prioritizing the agriculture sector of Nepal.

Farmers are also educating themselves and making informed choices. After the failure of the imported hybrid seed in 2009, the Sapkota family have learned their lesson—with support from ECOSCENTRE, they have switched back to organic farming with indigenous open-pollinated seeds.

Hari Sapkota says,

> Unlike the corn we get from hybrid seeds, our corn is not of consistent shape and size but we are glad we made the move—we are not just getting good results from the seed, we also don't have to feed any pesticides and fertilizers.

Food security and sovereignty cannot be achieved through higher production alone. Our real food security strategy has to be focused on promoting sustainable, ecologically sound farming practices. We must defend our seed sovereignty, which is the foundation of food sovereignty. The Interim Constitution of Nepal guarantees the right to liberty and to live a sovereign, dignified life. We must take the precaution of defending our food democracy from dictatorship by multinational corporations by protecting our seed sovereignty.

## Endnotes

[1]   Convention on Biological Diversity, *The Cartegena Protocol on Biosafety*, http://bch.cbd.int/protocol, accessed September 19, 2015.

# Sowing Seeds of Freedom

Vandana Shiva

Seeds are not just the source of life, they are the very foundation of our being. For millions of years seeds have evolved freely, to give us diversity and richness of life on the planet; and for thousands of years farmers, especially women, have bred seeds freely, in partnership with each other and with nature, to further increase the diversity of that which nature gave us and adapt it to the needs of different cultures. Biodiversity and cultural diversity have mutually shaped one another.

Seeds are the first link in the food chain and the repository of life's future evolution. As such, it is our inherent duty and responsibility to protect them in order to pass them on to future generations. The growing and free exchange of seeds among farmers has been the basis of maintaining biodiversity and our food security. Today, the freedom of nature and culture to evolve is under violent and direct threat, and the threat to seed freedom impacts the very fabric of human life and the life of the planet.

In 1987, I started Navdanya to protect seed diversity in India and safeguard farmers' right to save, breed, and exchange seed freely, in the context of emerging threats by the Trade-Related Aspects of Intellectual Property Rights (TRIPS) Agreement of the World Trade Organization (WTO), which opened the door to the introduction of GMOs in our country, and of patents on seed, and consequently to the collection of royalties. As a Monsanto representative later stated, "In drafting these agreements we were the patient, diagnostician, physician, all in one." Corporations defined the problem—farmers saving seeds—and they offered a solution. The solution was the introduction of patents and intellectual property rights on seeds, making it illegal for farmers to save them.

Patents on seed implied that any farmer saving seed is an "intellectual property thief." But there is more to this than meets the eye. A system in which seeds have become a corporate monopoly, a system in which a few companies control the world's seed supply, is, in effect, a system of slavery for farmers. Where seed freedom disappears, the freedom of farmers disappears along with it.

Navdanya means "nine seeds," symbolizing the richness of biodiversity. It also means "new gift," which for us is the gift of seed as a commons and as a source of life. Seeds reproduce and multiply organically. Farmers use seeds both as grain as well as for the next year's crop. They are free, both in the ecological sense, by reproducing themselves, as well as in the economic sense of reproducing farmers' livelihood. But this seed freedom is a major obstacle for seed corporations. If the market for seeds has to be created, then seeds have to be transformed *materially,* so that reproducibility is blocked; and their status has to be changed *legally,* so that instead of being the *common property* of farming communities, they become the patented *private property* of seed corporations.

Over the last twenty-five years Navdanya has both protected and conserved seeds and biodiversity as part of Bija Swaraj, or Seed Freedom. We have also resisted laws that threaten this seed freedom. We have set up more than one hundred community seed banks in seventeen states of India, many of which now run independently. From the first seed banks in the Garhwal Himalayas of Uttarakhand, the Deccan in Karnataka, and the Western Ghats, Navdanya has set up new seed banks in Ladakh, Jharkhand, Bihar, Madhya Pradesh, Maharashtra, Rajasthan, and Uttar Pradesh. Navdanya's partners in this work include the Beej Bachao Andolan in Uttarakhand; the Green Foundation, Navadarshanam, and the Centre for Tropical Ecosystems in Karnataka; Rishi Valley in Andhra Pradesh; the Centre for Indian Knowledge Systems in Tamil Nadu; Vrihi in West Bengal; Vidarbha

Organic Farming Association, Vidarbha; Prakruti Paramparika Bihana Sangarakhna Abhijan in Orissa; Kisan Samvardhan Kendra in Madhya Pradesh; Kisan Vigyan Kendra in Uttar Pradesh; Manvi, Indian National Trust for Art and Cultural Heritage, in Kerala; and Hazaribagh, in Jharkhand.

Navdanya has also established conservation and training centers at Ramgarh/Sheeshambara village in the Doon Valley, in Bulandshahr in western Uttar Pradesh, and in Balasore in Orissa. More than 3,800 rice varieties have been collected, saved, and conserved. Hundreds of varieties of crops such as millets, pseudocereals, and pulses, which had been pushed out by the Green Revolution and by growing monocultures, have been conserved and promoted.

## The Corporate Assault on Seed Freedom

What I have called "Monocultures of the Mind" cut across all generations of technology that strive to control the seed.

- While farmers breed for diversity, corporations breed for uniformity.
- While farmers breed for resilience, corporations breed vulnerability.
- While farmers breed for taste, quality, and nutrition, industry breeds for industrial processing and long-distance transport in a globalized food system.
- While farmers share their seeds, corporations define seed saving and sharing as an intellectual property crime.

Industrial junk food and monocultures of industrial crops reinforce each other, wasting the land, wasting food, and wasting our health. Whether it be breeders' rights imposed through UPOV 1991, or patents on seed, or seed laws that require compulsory registration and licensing, an arsenal of legal instruments is being invented and imposed undemocratically to criminalize farmers, seed breeding, seed saving, and seed sharing.

Every seed is an embodiment of millennia of nature's evolution and centuries of farmers' breeding; it is the distilled expression of the intelligence of the Earth and of farming communities. Just as the jurisprudence of *terra nullius* defined land as empty and allowed the takeover of territories by European colonialists, the jurisprudence of intellectual property rights related to life-forms is, in fact, a jurisprudence of *bio nullius*—life empty of intelligence. The Earth is defined as dead matter, so it cannot create.

## The TRIPS Agreement and Patent Monopolies

We are all members of the Earth Family, stewards in the web of life. Yet corporations, who now claim legal personhood, are also claiming the role of "creator." They have declared seed to be their "invention," hence their patented property. A patent is an exclusive right granted for an "invention," which allows the patent holder to exclude everyone else from making, selling, distributing, and using the patented product. With patents on seed, this implies that farmers' right to save and share seed is now defined as "theft," an intellectual property crime.

The door to patents on seed and patents on life was opened by genetic engineering—by adding one new gene to the cell of a plant, corporations claimed that they had "invented" and created the seed, that the plant *and all future seeds have now become their property*. In other words, GMO meant God Move Over. Article 27.3(b) of the TRIPS Agreement states:

> Parties may exclude from patentability plants and animals other than micro-organisms, and essentially biological processes for the production of plants or animals other than non-biological and micro-biological processes. However, parties shall provide for the protection of plant varieties either by patents or by an effective *sui generis* system or by any combination thereof.

This protection on plant varieties is precisely what prohibits the free exchange of seeds between farmers, threatening their subsistence.

The TRIPS clause on patents on life became due for mandatory review in 1999. India in its submission stated, "Clearly, there is a case for re-examining the need to grant patents on life forms anywhere in the world. Until such systems are in place, it may be advisable to: (a) exclude patents on all life forms ..." The African Group too stated:

> The African Group maintains its reservations about patenting any life forms as explained on previous occasions by the Group and several other delegations. In this regard, the Group proposes that Article 27.3(b) be revised to prohibit patents on plants, animals, micro-organisms, essentially biological processes for the production of plants or animals, and non-biological and micro-biological processes for the production of plants or animals. For plant varieties to be protected under the TRIPS Agreement, the protection must clearly, and not just implicitly or by way of exception, strike a good balance with the interests of the community as a whole, protect farmers' rights and traditional knowledge, and ensure the preservation of biological diversity.

This mandatory review has been subverted by corporations influencing some governments within the WTO.

## Defending Farmers' Rights in Law

Through our movements in India we have ensured that our laws recognize farmers' rights, as well as the fact that *biological processes are not inventions*. Because of our work with seeds, farmers' rights, and intellectual property rights, I was appointed to an expert group set up to draft The Protection of Plant Varieties and Farmers' Rights Act. The clause on Farmers' Rights states:

> 39.(1) Notwithstanding anything contained in this Act, (iv) a farmer shall be deemed to be entitled to save, use, sow, resow, exchange, share or sell his farm produce, including seed of a variety protected under this Act, in the same manner as he was entitled to before the coming into force of this Act ...

To counter the globalized IPR system to be implemented at the national level, Navdanya conceptualized the idea of Common Property Rights in Knowledge as early as 1993. The Research Foundation for Science, Technology and Ecology (RFSTE) and Navdanya drafted model laws that were then used and further developed by the Third World Network (Penang) and the Organization of African Unity for creating *sui generis* options based on community rights.

The 1970 Patents Act of India excluded patents in agriculture and product patents in medicine, but it had to be amended after India signed the WTO agreements, including TRIPS. However, because of strong local movements, clauses such as "What are not inventions" were strengthened; Article 3(d) now excludes as inventions "the mere discovery of any new property or new use for a known substance"; and Article 3(j) excludes from patentability

> plants and animals in whole or any part thereof other than micro-organisms but including seeds, varieties and species and essentially biological processes for production or propagation of plants and animals.

## Seed Satyagraha

In 2004, an attempt was made to introduce a seed law in India that would require the compulsory registration of farmers' seed varieties. Farmers' biodiverse, indigenous varieties are the basis of our ecological and food security. Coastal farmers have evolved salt-resistant seed varieties; Bihar and Bengal farmers have evolved flood-resistant varieties; farmers of Rajasthan and the semi-arid Deccan have evolved drought-resistant varieties; and Himalayan farmers have evolved frost-resistant varieties. Pulses, millets, oilseeds, rice, wheat, and vegetables are our guarantee for nutritional security. This is the very sector being targeted by the proposed Seed Act.

The Seed Act is designed to enclose the free economy of farmers and of seed varieties. Once farmers' seed supply is destroyed through compulsory registration and by making it illegal to plant unlicensed varieties, farmers are pushed into dependency on the corporate monopoly of patented seeds. The Seed Act is therefore the handmaiden of the Patent Amendment Acts, which have introduced patents on seed. The 2004 Seed Act has nothing positive to offer to farmers of India— but it promises a monopoly for private seed industries, which have already pushed thousands of our farmers to suicide through dependency and debt caused by unreliable, nonrenewable seeds.

From January to March 2005, Navdanya, together with its partners, undertook Bija Satyagraha campaigns to declare noncooperation with the new patent laws (which allow patents on life) and the proposed Seed Act, which would criminalize farmers. In the spirit of Gandhi's Salt Satyagraha, more than one hundred thousand people committed themselves to participate in the Seed Satyagraha if the Seed Act was brought into force. The declarations were handed over to the then prime minister; happily, the Seed Act has not yet been passed.

Resistance to unjust seed laws through the Seed Satyagraha is one aspect of seed freedom; saving and sharing seeds is another. That is why Navdanya has worked with local communities to reclaim seed diversity and seed as a commons by establishing its more than one hundred community seed banks. When we save seed, we also reclaim and rejuvenate knowledge—the knowledge of breeding and conservation, and of food and farming. Uniformity as a pseudoscientific measure has been used to establish unjust IPR monopolies on seed, and IPR monopolies reinforce monocultures. Once a company has a patent on seeds, it pushes its patented crops on farmers in order to collect vast royalties. Humanity has been eating thousands upon thousands (8,500) of plant species; today we are being condemned to eat GM corn and soy in various forms. Four primary crops—corn, soy, canola, and cotton—have all been grown at the expense of other crops because they generate a royalty for every acre of land planted. India once had 1,500 different kinds of cotton; now 95 percent of the cotton planted is GMO Bt cotton, for which Monsanto holds the patent. More than eleven million hectares of land are given over to cotton cultivation, of which 9.5 million hectares are used to grow Monsanto's genetically modified Bt variety. Corn is cultivated on more than seven million hectares of land, but of this area 2,850,000 hectares are used for a high yielding variety. Soy now covers an area of approximately 9.95 million hectares, and canola, approximately 6.36 million hectares. This mass shift toward their cultivation not only threatens the diversity of other crops, but endangers the health and well-being of natural resources— soil, groundwater—as this approach to farming drains the Earth of its nutrients.

To break out of this vicious cycle of monocultures and monopolies, we need to create virtuous cycles of diversity and reclaim our biological and intellectual commons. Participatory breeding of open source seeds and participatory framing of open source rights are innovations that deepen seed freedom, which has become an ecological, political, economic, and cultural imperative.

## Seeds of Hope

Climate-resilient traits in seeds will become increasingly important now that we are well into climate change. Along India's coastal areas, farmers have evolved flood-tolerant and salt-tolerant varieties of rice such as bhundi, kalambank, lunabakada, sankarchin, nalidhulia, ravana, seulapuni, and dhosarakhuda. Crops such as millets have been evolved for drought tolerance, and provide food security in water-scarce regions and during water-scarce years. Corporations like Monsanto have taken out 1,500 patents on climate-resilient crops. In an important initiative, Navdanya decided to save vanishing rice diversities of Orissa in its community seed banks. This came in handy while selecting seeds for empowering local communities to rehabilitate agriculture in disaster areas like Erasama in Orissa after the super cyclone in 2000; Nagapattinam (Tamil Nadu) after the tsunami in 2005; and Nandigram (Bengal) in 2007.

Navdanya has given hope to tsunami victims. Tsunami waves seriously affected the agricultural lands of farmers due to the intrusion of seawater and deposition of salt. More than 5,203.73 hectares of agricultural land in Nagapattinam were affected. The Navdanya team conducted a study in the affected villages in order to facilitate agricultural recovery; it distributed three saline-resistant varieties of paddy, which included bhundi, kalambank, and lunabakada, to farmers in the worst-affected areas. A total of one hundred quintals of saline-resistant kharif paddy seeds were collected from Navdanya farmers in Orissa for this purpose.

Navdanya Orissa now maintains four seed banks, three village-level and one central, where a diverse variety of seeds are conserved and renewed every year. Climate resilience is given importance in village-level seed banks while all available rice landraces are conserved in the central seed bank. Navdanya also encourages individual cultivators to save, exchange, and increase diversity in their own fields. Village-level seed banks are located in different and varied eco-climatic zones, like salt-prone, flood-prone, and drought-prone. The central seed bank has 700 rice varieties in its accession, of which 119 are climate-resilient. Thirty-three of these are salt- and flood-tolerant, including one aromatic variety; 47 are flood-tolerant; and 39 are drought-tolerant, including three aromatic and two therapeutic varieties. The remaining 581 varieties belong to the general category. There are 56 aromatic rice varieties, of which two have unique and diverse aromas, one smelling like fried green gram and the other, like cumin seed, and are not available anywhere else in the world. The therapeutic rices are used for old-age tissue rejuvenation.

Nearly three hundred thousand farmers in India have committed suicide since 1995, most of them in the cotton belt in Vidarbha. Monsanto now controls 95 percent of the cotton seed supply through its Bt cotton. While it does not have a patent on the GMO, it collects "technology fees" in lieu of royalty payments. The cost of cotton seed jumped 70,000 percent with the introduction of Bt cotton. During

2004, farmers had to pay Rs. 1,600 for a single 450 g packet of Bt cotton seeds, which included a technology fee component of Rs. 725.

Seeds of Hope in Vidarbha distributes non-GMO seeds to farmers and helps them make the transition to debt-free organic farming. Seed sovereignty is not a luxury; it is the very basis of life and freedom for everyone.

# The Loss of Crop Genetic Diversity in the Changing World

Tewolde Berhan Gebre Egziabher and
Sue Edwards

Needless to say, crop genetic diversity has not been evenly distributed throughout the cultivated parts of the world—it cannot exist in non-cultivated areas except in the trivial sense of it having been taken there to be consumed or stored. Owing to inherent environmental diversity in particular parts of the world, coupled with the history of agricultural development in relation to those areas, there have been hot spots of crop domestication and genetic diversification. These crop genetic diversity hot spots have come to be called Vavilov Centers, to honor the Russian scientist who first identified eight of them. Subsequent scientists have tended to think that, though such centers can indeed be identified, there are more than eight and that, more importantly, crop domestication and diversification have been more diffuse geographically than initially thought.[1] Many complex reasons are now causing a fast reduction in crop genetic diversity even in the Vavilov Centers.

The accelerating increase in communication is mixing ideas, technologies, cultures, and even people throughout the world, a process that seems to be taking us toward one homogeneous global culture. However complex this evolving global culture might turn out to be, it is inevitable that we will have lost much of the content of our erstwhile diversity in the process of achieving it. We have already witnessed a high level of attrition in our crop genetic diversity,[2] and yet, the very process of globalization is changing the world's environment, thereby increasing the need for such diversity to adapt agriculture to changing farm conditions. If human survival into the indefinite future is to be assured, therefore, globalizing humanity has to put all its efforts into increasing crop genetic diversity, rather than fatalistically accepting the accelerating decline.

Southern Europe constitutes a part of the Mediterranean Vavilov Center, that part of the industrialized world referred to as the Global North. The rest of the industrialized world is relatively unimportant as a source of crop genetic diversity. All the other important Vavilov Centers are in the developing world, referred to as the Global South. The problems of conserving crop genetic diversity are therefore geographically problems of the developing world, though, of course, its erosion concerns the whole of humanity. Because of these and related reasons, the difficulties in actions that are required to maintain crop genetic diversity remain intimately linked to problems of development that the South faces in this era of globalization. The fact that this globalization is led by the North while crop genetic diversity remains mostly in the South marginalizes the causes of failure to protect this diversity, and thus confounds the difficulty of taking action even when there is a global will to do so. Usually, in fact, there is insufficient national, let alone global, will to take all the action needed. And yet, the very process of globalization, which is exacerbating the erosion of crop genetic diversity, is also making that very diversity essential for the continuation of human well-being into the future. Though, like all futures, this particular one is uncertain, at least one facet is becoming clear—climate is changing,[3] and a commensurate increase in crop genetic diversity is necessary for adapting to that change.

In the second half of the twentieth century, many scientists and scientific institutions realized that the world's future food supply was endangered because of crop genetic erosion, and that something had to be done. The simplistic response was to store in gene banks that diversity that would otherwise have disappeared. There are now many gene banks globally that are trying to save as much crop genetic diversity as they can.[4] But their problems are many,[5] and their success has thus been limited.[6] The most recent and tantalizing quick-fix arose in

the form of genetic engineering that promised to synthesize any desired crop variety in the laboratory, but some of the newly synthesized
varieties emerged with unforeseen problems.[7] The evidence for the
complication of agricultural systems—because transgenes from crops
can get incorporated in the genomes of wild relatives through cross-
pollination and thus, for example, make some weeds pernicious—is
even more plentiful in scientific literature.[8] For these reasons genetically engineered crop varieties have now become highly controversial
in many parts of the world.

In Ethiopia, for example, there are vibrant farming communities
that are still increasing crop genetic diversity, both through breeding
new farmers' varieties of existing crops, and through domesticating
altogether new crop species.[9] However, when the whole trend is considered, the erosion of crop genetic diversity is far greater than its generation, even within the developing countries in Vavilov Centers, let
alone globally.

Most of the crop varieties currently under cultivation are protected by intellectual property rights and some, in fact, are patented.
This makes for a one-way track of availability of crop varieties from
the smallholder farmers of developing countries to companies mostly
based in industrialized countries. This one-way flow makes access to
crop genetic diversity from developing countries difficult, especially
for those very countries that gave rise to it in the first place. This is
especially true of patenting.[10]

Globalization has also induced a tendency toward uniformity in
eating habits. A report prepared for the United Nations Environment
Programme (UNEP) states that although about seven thousand species of plants have been used as human food in the past, urbanization
and marketing have drastically reduced this number—only 150 crops
are now commercially important, and rice, wheat, and maize alone
now account for 60 percent of the world's food supply. The genetic
diversity within each crop has also been eroding fast; for example,
only nine varieties account for 50 percent of the wheat produced in

the United States, and the number of varieties of rice in Sri Lanka has dropped from two thousand to less than a hundred.[11]

Partly as a reaction to the erosion of crop genetic diversity, but more because of a growing realization that industrial agriculture pollutes the environment and is, in the long run, unsustainable, the organic movement is now growing globally, which will help slow the erosion of crop genetic diversity. However, as far as limited current experience tells us, this movement is not making sufficient linkages with that local community farming that has not yet been swallowed up by the very process of globalization. And yet these two sectors have many commonalities and could well strengthen each other.

To be sure that agriculture can keep changing as quickly as it must, we need more crop genetic diversity than we ever had. If we stop atmospheric pollution immediately, the Earth's climate will still change, though it would probably stabilize after some time; even if we were able to stop polluting the atmosphere immediately, therefore, we would still need as big of a crop genetic diversity as we can muster. This means it is not only necessary for us to conserve all the crop genetic diversity that we have, but also to *regain in full* the capacity to generate the diversity that we have partly lost in the last hundred years. We must, therefore, sufficiently fund existing gene banks and build new ones as needed for *ex situ* crop genetic diversity conservation in order to (1) keep all existing unique collections, ensuring that they are all always viable and accessible for breeding; (2) regenerate all existing unique collections without genetic drift changing their unique identities; and (3) make new unique collections before they disappear for good.

We must foster organic movements in order to make their agricultural production systems crop genetic diverse so as to match the environmental diversity of the land that is under cultivation. We must also foster the establishment of mutually supportive linkages between the primarily subsistence farming communities in the South and the growing commercial organic farms in the North. This is necessary for developing agricultural systems suited to the diversity of environments, so as to maximize both production and crop genetic diversity. We should consciously foster, including through subsidies when required, the *in situ* conservation of crop genetic resources by organic farmers, both primarily subsistence and commercial, in the North and South; and help organic farmers, both commercial and subsistence, in research and development for maximizing both crop genetic diversity and yields in the diverse environmental conditions of the changing Earth. This is required because agrochemicals are becoming more expensive with time, owing to increases in petroleum prices; industrial agriculture may soon become unaffordable.

We need to condemn as immoral the patenting of crop varieties because the process sucks in crop genetic diversity from primarily subsistence farming communities, but restricts the resulting varieties into circulating only among the rich, especially when natural cross-pollination passes patented genes from genetically modified crop varieties to nonmodified varieties.

We must declare Article 27.3(b) of TRIPS immoral; make biopharming, using food crops, a criminal offense; reduce biopharming with noncrop plants to the minimum in order to protect the environment; and even then, use it under strictly contained conditions to ensure environmental safety.

## Endnotes

1    Kristina Plenderleith, "Traditional Agriculture and Soil Management," in *Cultural and Spiritual Values of Biodiversity*, ed. Darrell A. Posey (International Technology Publication, for, and on behalf of, UNEP, 2009), 317. Among many, Jack R. Harlan, J. M. J. De Wet, and Ann Stemler, "Plant Domestication and Indigenous African Agriculture," in *Origins of African Plant Domestication*, eds. Jack R. Harlan et al. (The Hague: Mouton, 1976), 3–19.

2    Board on Agriculture of the National Research Council, *Managing Global Genetic Resources* (Washington, DC: National Academy Press, 1993), 36, point out that this problem was already realized in the first half of the twentieth century.

3    G. A. Meehl et al., "Global Climate Projections," in *Climate Change 2007: The Physical Science Basis*, Contribution of Working Group I to the Fourth

Assessment Report of the Intergovernmental Panel on Climate Change, eds. S. Solomon et al. (Cambridge: Cambridge University Press, 2007), 747–845.

4   Ibid., 85–116.

5   Tewolde Berhan Gebre Egziabher, "Modernization, Science and Technology, and Perturbations of Traditional Conservation of Biological Diversity" (paper presented at the Biodiversity Convention Conference, Trondheim, Norway, May 24–28, 1993). Also Board on Agriculture of the National Research Council, *Managing Global Genetic Resources,* 27, 153–172, 322.

6   C. Fowler and P. Mooney, in their book, *Shattering: Food, Politics, and the Loss of Genetic Diversity* (Tucson: University of Arizona Press, 1990), have described in detail how much genetic erosion is occurring in gene banks.

7   For example, *New Scientist,* November 26, 2005, has an editorial and more detail under the title "Wheeze in a Pod," which reports on the work of Australian scientists who developed a transgenic pea with genes from beans at the Commonwealth Scientific and Industrial Research Organisation (CSIRO) over ten years, and abandoned it because the transgenic pea became highly allergenic to mice and would presumably also be allergenic to humans.

8   For example, reference may be made to: Anne Marie Chévre et al., "Gene Flow from Transgenic Crops," *Nature* 389 (1997): 924; and Thomas R. Mikkelsen, Bente Andersen, and Rikke Bagger Jørgensen, "The Risk of Crop Transgene Spread," *Nature* 380 (1996): 31.

9   For example, *Impatiens tinctoria,* a plant that used to be collected from the wild for cosmetic purposes, is now being planted as a crop under small-scale irrigation by many smallholder farmers on the mountain slopes of southern Tigray because of growing demand from urban women.

10   Board on Agriculture of the National Research Council, *Managing Global Genetic Resources,* 23–25.

11   Kristina Plenderleith, "Traditional Agriculture and Soil Management," 287–323.

# Seed Sovereignty and Ecological Integrity in Africa

Mariam Mayet

## Introduction

Following decades of neglect, the past few years have witnessed a growing external investment in African agriculture, including in seed systems. The context for this growth includes structurally higher food prices globally, driven by limited arable land and rising urban populations, as well as changing diets, both globally and in Africa. Maize prices are increasing as production in the United States (the historical generator of surpluses for food aid to Africa) is diverted to biofuel production. Greater surpluses are required, and where better to turn than a geographic area viewed as "underperforming" but with potential in the form of "underutilized" natural and human resources?

Africa is thus seen as the new frontier of accumulation.[1] Rising demand and constrained supply suggest profits can be made through investments in agricultural production. There is ongoing interest in using African land and resources for export of food commodities to other parts of the world, with China as the current driver. Biofuels, maize, rice, and cassava are key focus areas.

The dominant narrative is that Africa missed out on the first Green Revolution—the package of hybrid seed, synthetic agrochemicals, irrigation, and credit—that resulted in rising agricultural productivity in the rest of the world. Minot and colleagues talk about stagnating grain production per capita in Africa.[2] In the core capitalist countries of the United States and the European Union, Green Revolution technologies were developed and put into place early on; the Green Revolution adapted these technologies for use in Asia and Latin America, in particular.

Debate rages about why these technologies did not take root in Africa in the same way as they did in Asia. Whatever the reasons, the underlying premise is that the Green Revolution is desirable. Lessons over the decades from Asia and Latin America have shown that this technological package has contradictory results. It did result in increased yields, but, as Susan George and subsequently many others have documented, this was at the cost of concentration of land and production resources, the exclusion of many poorer producers, and serious social and ecological damage.[3]

The new Green Revolution for Africa pundits have adopted significant elements of agroecological practice—they appear to recognize the need to adapt technology to suit agroecology. Coupled with this is a recognition of the importance of soil health as a fundamental basis of sustainable agriculture, with acknowledgment of the centrality of increasing organic matter in the soil, the use of cover crops, intercropping, and crop rotation.[4] The World Bank belatedly recognizes the folly of a narrow focus on export markets, and is now arguing that "the most promising markets for Africa's farmers are domestic and regional for basic food crops and livestock products."[5]

When it comes to seed and agrochemical technologies, there is agreement in the mainstream that the ideal is to marry external technologies with indigenous or locally specific technologies and techniques. There are some divergences here. The Howard G. Buffett Foundation argues for a "Brown Revolution" rather than a Green Revolution, emphasizing soil health as the key focus.[6] According to the foundation, these practices already exist and only need to be supported, strengthened, and scaled up. On the other hand, the Alliance for a Green Revolution in Africa, sponsored by the Bill and Melinda Gates Foundation and others, argues that organic or agroecological techniques of production have proved to be inadequate in Africa and that external technologies and inputs, especially improved seed (whether hybrid or open-pollinated) and agrochemicals, are necessary for increased productivity.[7] The Buffett Foundation does not disagree with this in principle, arguing that a judicious blend of local and external technologies and techniques is required.

All investors share the principle that private enterprise is the ideal path to pursue, because the profit motivation generates economic activity. They do recognize that states can play a role, either in providing the basic infrastructure or more directly in public-private partnerships, especially around plant-breeding research and development. However, when it comes to propagating, multiplying, and distributing seeds for commercial use, these investors stand as one in the belief that this activity must be owned and managed privately for gain. The immediate emphasis is not on direct ownership by multinationals; rather, the short-term focus is on building markets. This means business and technical skills, institutional arrangements, and physical infrastructure (left to the public sector as far as possible, since few capitalists will be willing to invest in collective goods that their competitors will also benefit from). Alliance for a Green Revolution in Africa has this explicit goal, of building scientific expertise and private agro-dealer networks to distribute seed and other inputs. Successful seed companies may be acquired by multinationals at a later stage, and it is not necessary for multinationals to exert direct ownership over seed multiplication and distribution in the early stages.

What is of interest to them at this early stage is to set the legal framework for private ownership over germplasm, and this is the current front line of the battle for control over genetic resources. This may take the form of acquisition of companies that hold locally adapted germplasm (e.g., Pioneer Hi-Bred's recent acquisition of Pannar, South Africa's last major domestic seed company) or of securing intellectual property rights over imported varieties and techniques.

This explicit profit motivation for investment is given cover by the argument that Africans are victims of poor policies and interventions.

Food security and nutrition inside Africa are brought to the fore as reasons for investment in agricultural productivity. The recent G8 initiative, named the African Alliance for Food Security and Nutrition, is couched in these terms. It brings a humanitarian slant to profit-seeking investments in Africa, naturalizing the relationship between profit-making and humanitarian investments. Unsurprisingly, the major governments and agricultural input and food multinationals have coalesced into this alliance.

From both the "food security in Africa" and the capital investment angle, low productivity is a key focus. Sustained, increased productivity is a common goal across organizations and ideologies. Howard Buffett argues that "no one should be advocating for accepting current yield levels."[8] The key question is how yields can improve in ways that nurture social equality and ecological integrity. Yields can refer simply to the ton/hectare produced, but can also refer to improvements in storage capacity, drought and pest resistance, and volume produced with similar input, among other measures.

There are many in Africa who welcome these initiatives, whether farmers, states, or other agricultural entrepreneurs. The New Partnership for Africa's Development (NEPAD) lay the groundwork more than a decade ago for African states to intersect with this expansionist agenda. The Comprehensive Africa Agriculture Development Programme (CAADP) emphasizes regional markets, crop commercialization, investments in irrigation, conservation agriculture, entrepreneurship, local marketing infrastructure, and dissemination of new technologies. The orientation is toward foreign direct investment and public-private partnerships; some of these initiatives can potentially be of benefit to Africa's farmers, while at the same time laying the groundwork for a possibly unequal exchange of resources with external investors.

Seed sovereignty movements in Africa are confronted by these contradictory processes. Many members of smallholder farmer associations are attracted to the possibilities presented by these investments in infrastructure, capacity, and the development of markets. We should recognize that there is a process of class decompression and formation going on, and that seed and food sovereignty movements will need to consider how to engage with these contradictory processes being driven by capital, as well as more clearly defining their core constituencies among farmers.

## African Seed Systems

Apart from some enclaves or niches developed during the colonial era, African seed systems have generally existed outside global circuits of capitalist accumulation. The focus of these enclaves was on commercially viable crops, especially for export, as part of the colonial system of extraction.

The colonization of Africa produced two main types of economies: enclave and settler. In enclave economies, infrastructure was designed for the extraction of natural resources—the oil economies are most typical of this (e.g., Nigeria, Angola), with ports, roads, wells, and so on, but only as required for extraction. There was limited development of the local economy in this system. In settler economies, there was the setting up of a domestic market for the settler population linked to natural resource extraction (e.g., South Africa, Kenya, Zimbabwe).

This is significant in that African seed systems replicate the broader economic structure. Where domestic economies were developed for settlers, agriculture initially played an important role, and commercial seed systems were developed in line with this. Therefore, settler economies tend to have bigger commercial seed systems in the Western sense.

In the colonial period, scientific research was developed with a focus on what are now termed "traditional" exports: those crops nurtured for world markets under colonialism, e.g., cocoa, cotton, and palm oil in West Africa; and coffee, tea, and tobacco in East and southern Africa.[9] Local food crops were essentially ignored. Food aid played a major role in displacing local production; it started off as a subsidy to support industrialization and urbanization, but when supplies ran short African governments were forced to borrow money to pay for food. The roots of the debt crisis in Africa are to be found here.[10] Structural adjustment placed an even greater emphasis on export crops, including some "nontraditional" ones (e.g., fresh fruit and vegetables or cut flowers). Traditional crops are still of overwhelming importance in African agricultural exports, despite the recent growth of nontraditional exports.[11]

In the postcolonial period, the emphasis was on state interventions in agriculture, which translated into direct state participation along value chains, including monopoly ownership and marketing channels in some sectors. National agricultural research systems (NARS) were built up with multinational support through the institutes of the Consultative Group for International Agricultural Research (CGIAR). In Africa, the International Institute of Tropical Agriculture (IITA, based in Ibadan in Nigeria), WARDA (now known as AfricaRice, based in Cotonou in Benin), and the International Maize and Wheat Improvement Center (CIMMYT, based in Mexico but with offices in Ethiopia, Kenya, and Zimbabwe) were the most important of the international research institutes that focused on cereal crops.

From the 1970s until the early 2000s, African agriculture was neglected, as structural adjustment policies emphasized a narrow focus on export crops that could generate foreign exchange to pay off debts. At the same time, for the private sector, economies of scale are required to make profits, and most other crops are too localized to generate the necessary exports. This led to decades-long underinvestment in private sector R&D on other crops in Africa, often called "orphan" crops, even though they might be very significant local or regional food sources. Spending on R&D fell in about half the countries of sub-Saharan Africa in the 1990s.[12] During these lost decades, African agriculture fell behind in technology and innovation, and agro-food systems became prone to dependency on external assistance.

## Formal and Farmer-Controlled Seed Systems

What is the extent of the penetration of capital built on the commercial seed and agricultural infrastructure from the first wave of colonialism?

According to the International Center for Tropical Agriculture (CIAT), 80–90 percent of the world's seed stocks are provided through what they call the "informal" seed system, and Africa is no exception.[13] According to Smale and colleagues, more than 80 percent of all seed in Africa is still produced and disseminated informally;[14] consequently, Africa and the Middle East constituted just 2.7 percent of the global commercial seed market in 2007.[15] CIAT defines the informal as that which the formal is not. The formal system consists of government regulations on production and distribution of seed, and registered or otherwise officially recognized enterprises that must subscribe to centrally defined regulations and standards for recognition. A primary function of formal systems is to secure crop uniformity and quality for industrial processing, e.g., milling or machine selection. By contrast, informal seed systems—or what we may prefer to call farmer-controlled systems—are integrated and locally organized. They are based on the ways farmers themselves produce, disseminate, and procure seeds through on-farm saving and exchange with neighbors and others. This is connected to food supply and distribution systems, for example, through the use of a maize harvest for a combination of food, feed, and planting. According to CIAT, farmer-controlled seed systems for maize are disintegrating but are not being replaced uniformly by formal-sector products (hybrids).[16]

The formal seed system is thus a small component of Africa's seed systems, centered on maize and both traditional and nontraditional export crops. There has been some R&D infrastructure built around both under colonialism and in the postcolonial period.

Farmer-controlled systems do not always respond well to the need for new varieties to refresh biodiversity or for varieties with higher productivity, and seed selection practices and storage conditions and practices are not always optimal.[17] Expertise on these is available, but is mostly used to build the formal system targeting high external input agriculture. There is an important role for individual farmer experts as key seed distributors and even as local seed producers.

Louwaars and others talk about integrated seed systems that combine the formal (especially improved varieties, not necessarily hybrid) with the informal or farmer-controlled (especially in distribution) systems. There are many links between formal and farmer-controlled systems—e.g., new varieties of seed may be launched in the formal system but may quickly move into farmer-controlled systems and be recycled by farmers or disseminated through farmer networks.[18] Materials flow between the two systems, creating new fusions that are often more useful to farmers than those produced in the formal or farmer-controlled system alone. Farmers may draw seeds from both systems for different crops (e.g., maize through formal, beans or sorghum through farmer-controlled); they may also use different channels for the same crops.[19]

Almekinders and Louwaars show the pros and cons of different seed sources. Local and on-farm seed production and exchange are good as a source of seed, and do not rely on cash. Systems with links to outside technology tend to be good as sources of new varieties. Farmer-to-farmer exchange outside the immediate settlement is a good source of new varieties, and a commercial enterprise is not necessarily required. There are solid ecological reasons for on-farm seed saving and exchange, and one of the advantages of intersettlement seed exchange is that it does not necessarily involve cash. Drawing on work from around the globe, Sthapit and colleagues highlight "the importance of a large number of small farms adopting distinctly diverse varietal strategies as a major force that maintains crop genetic diversity on the farm."[20]

Because the majority of African farmers are resource poor and do not have access to credit, they cannot afford to purchase hybrid seeds, but rely on saved seed using open-pollinated varieties (OPVs). Hybrid seed is up to 20 percent more expensive than OPVs, and constitutes less than 30 percent of the southern African regional maize seed market (excluding South Africa). The formal seed system contributes about half of the maize seed requirements in southern Africa, but taking South Africa out of the picture indicates that other countries in the region generally rely on farmer-saved seed.[21] Although there does seem to be a speeding up of the process of commercializing some types of seed, Africa is also large and diverse, and it is not always as easy for capital to expand as it might wish.

AGRA has been established precisely to build the necessary infrastructure for the further entry of capital—scientists, laboratories, centers of knowledge, a physical, populated seed production and distribution system, and some initial capital in the form of investment funds. It is, on the face of it, a friendlier approach than colonialism: it is negotiated on a business basis rather than imposed by force, but the outcome is a second wave of extraction from Africa. It is similar to the first wave of colonialism in that it is based on the extraction of natural resources and building markets (social systems for the realization of exchange value under capitalism).

According to the World Bank, "The 'technological distance' between growing conditions prevailing in Africa and those prevailing in developed countries is unusually large, so technologies travel even less well to Africa than they do to other developing regions."[22] Thus there is a need to invest in the local adaptation of available technologies.

## Maize: The Thin Edge of the Wedge

The main exception to farmer-controlled seed systems in Africa is maize hybrids, which have been "the main growth engine for formal sector seed and for profitable commercial enterprise in Africa."[23] Maize is a staple food in large sections of Africa; in 2007 it accounted for 56 percent of total harvested area of annual food crops in sub-Saharan Africa (SSA), 43 percent of which is in southern Africa.[24] Because maize is so widely grown in the region, and African yields are so low when compared with other parts of the world, much attention has been paid to the improvement of maize varieties in Africa. Adoption rates of improved maize varieties (80 percent hybrid and 20 percent open-pollinated) are highest in South Africa, Zimbabwe (80 percent), Zambia (73 percent), and Kenya (72 percent); and low in Angola (5 percent), Mozambique (11 percent), Tanzania (18 percent), and Ethiopia (19 percent).[25] Rapid growth is being experienced in Zambia and Uganda, and to a lesser extent in Tanzania, Ethiopia, and Malawi.

Maize is thus an entry point for the expansion of commercial seed systems in Africa; AGRA's activities reinforce this perception. Almost two-thirds of AGRA's Seed Production for Africa (SEPA)'s program grants by value, from 2007 to 2012, were allocated to maize, followed far behind by cassava and groundnuts as other crops with commercial potential.[26] Markets and systems of production and distribution can be built and extended through commercialization of the maize sector. In this way it can be viewed as the thin edge of the wedge, introducing new systems that link to the expansion of a class of commercial farmers. Markets for both seed and imported synthetic agrochemicals are created. Where the colonialism of the past was largely about extracting natural resources as cheaply as possible, the new wave of capitalist investment in African agriculture is about building domestic markets, while also extracting surpluses in the form of debt repayments and dividends.

However, the basic infrastructure is not in place, and states do not appear able to create it. AGRA and others are doing the groundwork of building domestic scientific capacity (with multinational technical and financial backup), as well as basic production and distribution capacity and systems in and outside the state.

## Policy Battles

A key question is whether policy is a terrain on which we think any meaningful gains can be made. We can certainly see the long-term impact of policy decisions. For example, the NEPAD-inspired CAADP is a framework designed a decade ago, within which investment decisions are now being made. This is a long lead time and we sometimes lose the connections between neoliberal origins and material outcomes, which are only manifesting today. If we had engaged more directly with CAADP back then, we might have seen some slightly different outcomes. Therefore, we must look for current critical policy issues and see where they are going, with the possibility of making interventions that can have longer-term impacts in relation to building seed sovereignty in Africa.

The priority at this stage appears to be IPRs (also bound up in laws related to counterfeiting). Protection of imported technologies is of central importance in profit-making for multinational seed and biotechnology companies. Much effort is being expended on developing IPR frameworks that assist multinationals in extracting revenues from investments in Africa. The adoption of the 1991 version of the International Union for the Protection of New Varieties of Plants (UPOV) is an issue here. UPOV 1991 explicitly narrows farmers' rights to save, exchange, and sell seed. At present only Kenya, Morocco, South Africa, and Tunisia are signatories to UPOV 1991 in Africa;[27] a push for more countries to adopt the 1991 version can therefore be expected.

Property rights more generally may be an issue in some places, especially where land tenure is not explicitly codified or where the legal system cannot or does not respond to disregard for the law. Another area of policy contestation is around harmonizing policy across countries for regional trade. As indicated above, there is a strong focus on regional trade and establishing market connections across national boundaries. The focus of harmonization is on seed patent laws to ensure protection across the region for enhancing regional seed trade.

Regional seed trade also contains a strong phytosanitary element. This needs expertise and infrastructure for testing. Multinationals argue that if the seed has already been tested in the exporting country then there is no need to also test in the importing country. This requires trust in the integrity of the paperwork of another country. However, the United States and others would not accede to a similar process in reverse (i.e., entry of unchecked seed into domestic markets from Africa). The argument being put forward by the multinationals is that African capacity to monitor seed is weak and therefore should be left to the United States or other importing countries, which do have the expertise. In this model there is no transfer of skills or knowledge, and the argument is advanced merely to shorten the regulatory processes so as to increase the pace of circuits of accumulation. In this case seed sovereignty movements should argue that local capacity in scientific phytosanitary testing, inspection, and monitoring is a necessary part of the infrastructure; otherwise, consignments can be swapped and no one will be able to catch that. This can have damaging effects on biodiversity and ecological systems.

Although AGRA and others are not explicitly arguing in favor of technologies based on genetic modification (GM) in these early stages, the systems of production and distribution they are building are designed to spread hybrids. The same channels can be used for the spread of GM seed in the future. Across the board, investors consider that GM technologies have potential, but robust legal, production, and distribution systems, and greater access for farmers to agrochemicals and markets, are prerequisites for the eventual successful adoption of GM seed. Contestation around regulations for the entry and commercial distribution of GM seed therefore remains critical as the groundwork for a future planned expansion.

There is a global convergence around the importance of smallholder farmers. The corporate (profit-making) agenda focuses on integrating small-scale farmers into formal production systems, including the formal seed sector, essentially growing the market for technology owners, but also potentially for private corporations in other nodes of value chains. For example, TechnoServe is a private company that assists smallholder farmers to enter formal value chains. Monsanto is one of TechnoServe's sponsors, and Walmart[28] has recently contracted

TechnoServe to carry out a pilot project in South Africa. This indicates collaboration across nodes in agro-food value chains in realizing a particular vision for how African agriculture is integrated into global circuits of capital.

## South Africa's Green Revolution

We often hear that the Green Revolution passed Africa by. We can only take this to be true if we exclude South Africa from Africa. South Africa is a perfect example of the logic of the Green Revolution: high productivity, high input, high value outputs, but with a very concentrated economic structure and high levels of exclusion or "adverse incorporation,"[29] neglect of indigenous crops, and the decimation of an indigenous small-scale farming class. South Africa's Green Revolution was built on the back of apartheid, which is probably why it is not held up as a poster child. South Africa shows how Green Revolution technology is conducive to economies of (large) scale, and both relies on and facilitates mechanization and oil-based manufacturing processes.

As with commercial markets in Africa, maize is at the heart of a powerful livestock-feed-food complex in South Africa. It constitutes 56 percent of the country's formal seed market,[30] and South Africa's commercial seed sector is more than 2.5 times larger than the next biggest ones—Egypt and Morocco, followed by Nigeria in sub-Saharan Africa.[31]

Is South African agriculture a model to emulate? We can see and feel the effects of intense concentration in the commercial seed market as well as all along agro-food value chains. There is the growing dominance of multinationals in seed, primarily Monsanto and Pioneer Hi-Bred. Both have a long history of investment in production and R&D with local partners, whom they later acquired outright. Monsanto purchased Sensako and Carnia, two of South Africa's biggest grain seed companies, in the late 1990s. In 2012 Pioneer was granted authority from the Competition Appeal Court to proceed with their acquisition of Pannar, South Africa's largest seed company,[32] and the last of the major domestic seed companies in South Africa. Foreign multinationals now own more than 50 percent of all agricultural seed cultivars (horticultural, agronomic, and forage combined).[33] As with other multinational investments in South Africa, there is an eye on the African market. Pannar has an extensive African footprint and currently operates in twenty-five African countries.[34]

Although seed R&D in South Africa has extended to a wide range of commercial crops, including fruit, vegetables, and forage, much of this is in the private sector. The seed system is characterized by a neglect of indigenous crops. There are some very small efforts to recover indigenous varieties and make them available for reuse through the public sector agricultural research system, but the public R&D infrastructure is heavily reliant on paid contract work for the private sector on commercial crops. The result is a loss of biodiversity, as indigenous crops disappear. Some are still saved on farms, but not all.

Not a lot of work has been done on the ecological impact of commercial agriculture in South Africa. Irrigation is a big issue, with more than half of all water going to commercial agriculture, a lot of which is wasted through inefficient spraying methods. The commercial farming sector has a high reliance on synthetic agrochemicals, but little work has been done on the impact of this on soil health and water pollution.

South Africa has big GM markets in maize and soy and a smaller market in cotton, where GM dominates. This has increased yields to the extent of chronic oversupply and strenuous efforts to expand markets in Africa, both for consumption of GM crops as well as for sale of GM seed. The Southern African Confederation of Agricultural Unions (SACAU), driven by South Africa and Zimbabwe's (mainly white) commercial farmers' unions, emphasized this agenda in its 2011 annual general meeting where the topic was expansion of GM into the region.

## Questions on Technology and Profit

Technology constructs our societies as much as societies construct technology, and they are at play throughout the seed system on farms. At the base, farmers propagate seed, whether that goes into the formal patented system or not. Farmers may propagate and multiply seed on contract, but the technical expertise lies with them. Is it possible to detach that technical expertise from the credit-driven system of accumulation? This separation should in principle be possible because there is a material base to the technical knowledge that transcends its capitalist appropriation, i.e., it does produce use values in the form of food and fiber as well as newly created ecosystem values. Therefore, the immediate challenge is to develop practical working relationships with the formal scientific system to bring laboratory-based scientists closer to farmers and their production needs, based on diversity.

AGRA is busy building this scientific base, some of which will be of service to the agricultural system as a whole, such as new knowledge about local varieties. We can legitimately ask which varieties, and what "improvements," are being developed.

Where will the resources come from to sustain such an edifice? Research institutes need money to pay for staff, equipment, etc. The state used to pay this, with some global assistance in the form of the CGIAR institutes, but with deregulation this function has been partially privatized, through the contracting of public research institutions by private companies. Public infrastructure is now used for private benefit.

The state itself is reliant on corporate and individual taxes to generate income; otherwise, they are dependent on borrowing, as many African countries have come to regret. Borrowing may be a way out when the risk is low, which in the current structure means higher debt repayment—everyone wants safe debt and so it is pricier, if it even exists anymore. In fact, there is currently no guarantee of debt repayment, which is at the epicenter of the financial crisis now engulfing the European Union. The system is churning on, but creating bigger and bigger problems down the line. Even as money is created by the banks (the hallmark of neoliberalism—so-called "fiat money"), this money is given credence by the state system itself (bonds that can threaten the disruption of the entire state system if payment is no longer credible). How long that can last without collapsing is not known. We can logically conclude that a nondebt technological option is preferable to a debt-laden one in the context of a global debt crisis.

States therefore should be reticent about relying on borrowing to generate income. This leaves taxation, which relies heavily on the facilitation of circuits of capital accumulation. Although we can argue that the public sector should support the bringing together of codified scientific knowledge around seed and plant breeding and farmer-based knowledge, we may have to accept that states themselves are caught in a trap where they require capital (with the inevitable concentration of resources and exclusion of many from economic activity and fair reward for their labor) for their own continued functioning.

This means that when we look for alternative ways of producing and disseminating seed, we have to look beyond the state to our own collectives and activities for answers. With regard to seed and plant breeding, the starting point is to nurture connections between farmers to help them learn from and share with one another, and where possible draw scientific experts into the fold in noncommercial relationships.

External investments may come in the form of grants, loans, or equity. A grant basically just gives money for particular activities that align with the donor's agenda; to the extent that seed and food sovereignty movements share the agenda, this form of investment is welcome. A loan produces debt and repayment, and locks producers into a particular economic structure that includes hybrid and even GM seeds, synthetic agrochemicals, and often irrigation. Movements might best choose to argue against loans as a form of investment since it is a form of extraction for multinationals and investors in the early phase of market-building, when circuits of accumulation through commodity production are not yet fully operational. Farmers are bearing financial risks, as well as the inherent risks of weather, pests, and diseases.

## What Are the Alternatives?

First and foremost, farmers can save and exchange seed among themselves—they already produce the seed, and exchange is no more than a greeting. On-farm seed conservation is recognized in global treaties such as the International Treaty on Plant Genetic Resources for Food and Agriculture and the Convention on Biological Diversity. A number of challenges face international efforts to build *in situ* conservation systems, including current institutional arrangements and incentive mechanisms. Other challenges include locating crop populations for conservation and accessing material beyond the farm where it is being preserved.[35] This latter requires integration with formal systems or farmer-to-farmer sharing. *In situ* conservation can only work if local diversity and the associated technical knowledge both exist.[36]

A key question is where new materials will come from. If seed can be adapted for local use in a way that accords with the agroecological context, there is no reason why its productivity should decline, unless ecological conditions change. It can only exhaust the soil if the soil itself isn't properly nurtured, which means increasing organic content. There are many local solutions to this available, and most people agree that each of these systems works well. How to spread that knowledge and those practices across Africa is a positive agenda that all can subscribe to. This means farmer-to-farmer networks across the continent, on seed saving, food production, and whatever else concerns them as farmers. This is part of a broader organization that connects to nonfarming aspects of society. It is a transformation based on practice.

There is a focus among the seed and agrochemical giants—Monsanto, DuPont (Pioneer Hi-Bred), Syngenta, BASF, Bayer Crop-Science, Dow AgroSciences—on drought- and heat-tolerant genetic modifications. Drought-tolerant maize is projected to come out in Africa in 2017.[37] This is a technological answer for a particular form of agricultural production dominated by large-scale global agribusinesses. It has its upsides in yields, but many downsides, including loss of control over food and fiber production to private interests.

Seed saving and exchange thus have to integrate into agroecologically appropriate production practices. This means tailoring technologies to suit the agroecological zone, but also learning from the surrounding ecology. Agroecology is a term AGRA and Monsanto use with familiarity, since their business is partly the adaptation of technologies for new zones, including agroecological zones. This is why they need a local germplasm pool, found either in the big private seed companies on the continent, with some crops in the public sector agricultural research institutes, or on farms. This on-farm, *in situ* collection is a national treasure, nurtured through the practices of generations of diverse farmers. It is now available for sale to the highest bidder. Patenting of this resource base means parceling it out to those who can afford to use it profitably. What other mechanisms for the protection of input do we have at our disposal? Is there a collective form that can be developed that is built on sharing and cooperation? How do we go about building that in practice, or connecting up existing practices?

There is close collaboration among the international research institutes (CGIAR), national agricultural research systems (public and private), and multinational input companies. Agroecology is understood as zero-tillage, which GM is presented as supporting, since weeds are killed using synthetic chemical herbicides that the seed has been bred to withstand. Therefore, less need to hoe. Tilling the ground breaks up soil structure, but when soils are compact they may need to be tilled, especially to add organic matter.

To zero tillage, the Buffett Foundation in their "brown revolution" adds year-round organic matter soil cover and diversified crop rotations with the principle of increasing organic matter in the soil. These should be core elements of agroecological production for anyone.[38]

Resources are only sent in directions where there is "proof of concept," hard evidence in the form of income, that the activity is financially self-sustainable—hence the sponsoring of commercial seed enterprises that already exist to grow. The current investment gamble is that a comb through Africa will highlight many potential investment opportunities in the seed sector. Africa also has entrepreneurs; the question is how their activities align with the requirements of debt-constructed external capital.

The class dimension manifests strongly here. Commercial and debt-fueled interventions will accelerate differentiation among farmers. This has implications for a sovereignty movement's approach to "farmers" as an undifferentiated category. We should anticipate the emergence of divisions among farmers and be clear about who is the core constituency of a seed and food sovereignty network or movement.

Seed sovereignty may be defined as access to appropriate seed with production under farmers' direct control. For now, in Africa, it hardly matters which farmers, since there is high class compression. As a matter of principle, farmers should be able to have direct control over their seed if they so wish. This goes for large-scale commercial farmers as much as for resource-poor smallholder farmers and anyone in between.

Input supply must be brought back onto the farm, with sharing across farms. There will be specialization in seed and plant breeding, and in fertilizer and pesticide production, as part of agroecology. Not every single person will want to keep animals, for example, and animals are a key element of an organic fertilizer system. Therefore, some people may specialize in fertilizer production. The same goes for seeds, where not everyone will plant every kind of plant, resulting in some knowledge specialization about types of plants, especially within agroecological zones. Efforts can be made to try to connect these pools of knowledge.

The basis for that system exists in the present on farms and in farmer practices. However, these can be disrupted by the introduction of Green Revolution technologies. Ultimately, other systems have to be robust enough to confront that challenge and survive. It's for us to learn about them and share that knowledge with others.

We should work at bringing formally trained scientists closer to farmers in participatory networks. The state or research institutes would need to provide resources for this as a contribution to strengthening farmer-controlled seed systems. We need to put into practice, wherever we can, aspects of socially and ecologically sustainable agroecological production. The focus to begin with should be local production (household and neighborhood or settlement), moving outward as production expands. Again we come to the benefits of investment in capital goods: roads, storage and cold storage, processing facilities, information and communications technology. To what extent will these bring us into debt? What material basis does this debt stand on? The limits of growth can be considered in conjunction with this.

We have to think of systems that produce an alternative to surplus extraction as the driving force of economic activity. The emphasis for now can be on nurturing and building farmer-controlled systems of plant breeding; seed production, multiplication, exchange, and sale; or at least participatory plant breeding with formal institutions, integrating farmer selection and testing into R&D processes.[39] Building on-farm technologies (e.g., household and community seed banks) is another common agenda. The World Bank is now offering prizes for the most innovative on-farm storage technologies.[40]

Lessons from Cuba reveal the need for broader agroecological training of: (1) farmers, using farmer-to-farmer models of learning and sharing; (2) existing scientists and extension workers to reorient their focus; (3) schools and university courses, and specialized agricultural colleges. These in turn are built on the basis of improved education systems overall (numeracy and literacy).[41]

These strategies will not address everything, but they are in the right direction of trying to gain greater direct knowledge about food production than we currently have. This is a crucial defense mechanism in the current political-economic climate. From a trade point of view, states could assist by protecting local/domestic seed economies (through tariff barriers and technical support) to allow them to develop and grow.

## Conclusion

Seed systems in Africa are a focus for investment and capital accumulation at present. There is a basic formal infrastructure built around historical export crops, with some expansion into local crops in some parts of Africa. By formal we mean connected to the credit economy. The goal is now to expand that seed market deeper into Africa for the purposes of extraction of value. This will involve building food markets and assumes a population that has some financial wealth (a middle class or sizable working class) as a launching pad.

On the other hand, most seed on the continent is saved on farms and exchanged by farmers. This gives a very solid base for alternative seed systems that can exist and thrive outside the credit market.

It is necessary for seed and food sovereignty movements to build an independent alternative, an alternative that is not dependent on credit for its survival.

## Endnotes

[1]   Goldman Sachs, "Africa's Turn," *Equity Research, Fortnightly Thoughts*, no. 27 (March 1, 2012).

[2]   N. Minot et al., "Seed Development Programs in sub-Saharan Africa: A Review of Experiences," report submitted to the Rockefeller Foundation, Nairobi, Kenya, March 21, 2007.

[3]   S. George, *How the Other Half Dies: The Real Reasons for World Hunger* (Harmondsworth, UK: Penguin, 1976).

[4]   AGRA, "A Proposal for a Soil Health Program of the Alliance for a Green Revolution in Africa: Final, July 24," Nairobi, Kenya, 2007.

[5]   World Bank, "Awakening Africa's Sleeping Giant: Prospects for Commercial Agriculture in the Guinea Savannah Zone and Beyond," Agriculture and Rural Development Unit, Africa Regional Office, 2009.

[6]   Howard G. Buffett Foundation, "The Hungry Continent: African Agriculture and Food Security," 2011.

[7]   AGRA, "A Proposal for a Soil Health Program."

[8]   Howard G. Buffett Foundation, "The Hungry Continent."

[9]   Minot et al., "Seed Development Programs in sub-Saharan Africa."

[10]  H. Friedmann, "Distance and Durability: Shaky Foundations of the World Food Economy," in *The Global Restructuring of Agro-Food Systems*, ed. P. McMichael (Ithaca, NY: Cornell University Press, 1994).

11  D. Byerlee, "Producer and Industry Funding of R&D in Africa: An Under-utilized Opportunity to Boost Commercial Agriculture" (presentation to the ASTI-FARA conference on agricultural R&D: Investing in Africa's Future: Analyzing Trends, Challenges, and Opportunities, Accra, Ghana, December 5–7, 2011), www.slideshare.net/agscitech/byerlee.

12  M. Smale et al., "Maize Revolutions in sub-Saharan Africa," *Policy Research Working Paper 5659* (Washington, DC: World Bank, Development Research Group, 2011).

13  CIAT, "Understanding Seed Systems Used by Small Farmers in Africa: Focus on Markets," CIAT Practice Brief #6 (2010), www.ciat.cgiar.org.

14  Smale et al., "Maize Revolutions in sub-Saharan Africa."

15  Phillips MacDougall, "The Global Agrochemical and Seed Markets: Industry Prospects" (presentation to CPDA Annual Conference, 2008).

16  CIAT, "Understanding Seed Systems."

17  C. Almekinders and N. Louwaars, "The Importance of the Farmers' Seed Systems in a Functional National Seed Sector," *Journal of New Seeds* 4, nos. 1–2 (2002): 15–33.

18  I. Scoones and J. Thompson, "The Politics of Seed in Africa's Green Revolution: Alternative Narratives and Competing Pathways," *IDS Bulletin* 42, no. 4 (2011): 1–23.

19  L. Sperling and H. D. Cooper, "Understanding Seed Systems and Seed Security" (proceedings of a stakeholders' workshop, Rome, Food and Agriculture Organization, May 26–28, 2003).

20  B. Sthapit et al., "Community-Based Approach to On-Farm Conservation and Sustainable Use of Agricultural Biodiversity in Asia," *Indian Journal of Plant Genetic Resources* 25, no. 1 (2012): 97–110.

21  A. Langyintuo, "An Analysis of the Maize Seed Sector in Southern Africa" (presentation to a Rockefeller Foundation workshop on Biotechnology, Breeding and Seed Systems for African Crops, Nairobi, Kenya, 2005).

22  World Bank, "Awakening Africa's Sleeping Giant."

23  CIAT, "Understanding Seed Systems."

24  A. S. Langyintuo et al., "An Analysis of the Bottlenecks Affecting the Production and Deployment of Maize Seed in Eastern and Southern Africa" (Harare, Zimbabwe: CIMMYT, 2008).

25  Ibid.

26  African Centre for Biosafety, "AGRA and Seed Systems in Africa" (Johannesburg: ACB, forthcoming).

27  M. Bruins, "Seed Business Trends and Statistics in Africa and Globally," presentation to African Seed Trade Association Congress, March 8, 2012.

28  Walmart recently acquired South African wholesaler Massmart, which has a large African footprint and a strong distribution network. There is an explicit orientation to grow the share of the South African and African food market.

29  S. Hickey and A. du Toit, "Adverse Incorporation, Social Exclusion and Chronic Poverty," CPRC Working Paper 81, Institute for Development Policy and Management, University of Manchester, UK, 2007.

30  African Centre for Biosafety, "AGRA and Seed Systems in Africa."

31  Bruins, "Seed Business Trends and Statistics."

32  Indications at the time of writing are that the Competition Commission will appeal the decision, but it is unlikely that the acquisition will be prevented.

33  African Centre for Biosafety, "AGRA and Seed Systems in Africa."

34  Angola, Botswana, Burundi, Cameroon, Chad, Congo, DRC, Ghana, Kenya, Lesotho, Madagascar, Malawi, Morocco, Mozambique, Namibia, Rwanda, Senegal, South Africa, Sudan, Swaziland, Tanzania, Tunisia, Uganda, Zambia, and Zimbabwe. See www.pannarseed.co.za.

35  B. Sthapit et al., eds., "On-Farm Management of Agricultural Biodiversity in Nepal: Good Practices," IPGRI/Li-Bird, Pokhara, Nepal, 2006.

36  Sthapit et al., "Community-Based Approach to On-Farm Conservation and Sustainable Use."

37  Bruins, "Seed Business Trends and Statistics."

38  Howard G. Buffett Foundation, "The Hungry Continent."

39  B. Sthapit and D. Jarvis, "Participatory Plant Breeding for On-Farm Conservation," International Plant Genetic Resources Institute (IPGRI), Rome, 1999.

40  Ibid.

41  L. Garcia, "Agroecological Education and Training," in *Sustainable Agriculture and Resistance: Transforming Food Production in Cuba*, eds. F. Funes et al. (Oakland, California: Food First Books, 2002).

# Conserving the Diversity of Peasant Seeds

Ana de Ita

The diversity of open-pollination seed varieties has been rapidly eroded in today's world. Open pollination characterizes peasant seeds and enhances diversity, and is different from controlled pollination, in which the seeds of a crop originate from parents with known characteristics and are thus more likely to have homogeneous characteristics. Controlled-pollination varieties include hybrid seeds that are produced from two distant parent lines of the same species. The sowing of hybrid seeds yields the desired characteristics, but the resowing of the harvest from the hybrid seeds does not produce the characteristics of the parent and generally has a lower yield.

Globally, the progress of commercial agriculture is one of the main reasons for the loss of diversity of native and peasant seed breeds and varieties. According to the Food and Agriculture Organization (FAO), the erosion of biodiversity severely compromises world food security.[1] During the last century, at least three-quarters of the genetic diversity of agricultural crops has been lost; now only twelve crops are responsible for a major part of the world's food requirement, and among these wheat, rice, and maize contribute 50 percent.

Mexico is one of the seventeen mega-diverse countries in the world, which together account for 75 percent of all the species of known vascular plants and living land animals. In Mexico there are around 65,000 species of fauna, flora, and fungi; besides this, 10 percent of the higher plants of the world are also found in Mexico and more than 40 percent are endemic to it.[2] Mexico and the countries that form the cultural region of Mesoamerica are centers of origin for a large variety of cultivated plants, the result of a process of domestication and breeding of species carried out by farmers for around seven million years. The domestication of maize was the greatest achievement of the Mesoamerican civilization; and Mexico, besides being a center of origin, is also the center of diversification of the crop. Mexico is the center of origin of maize and there are a number of varieties depending on each producer, indigenous group, or climatic region.

Mesoamerican agriculture was based on diversity.

> It was not about producing a lot with only one species of graminae or legume ... but about producing a wide variety of crops and species in moderate quantities to take into account geographical, biotic diversity and annual climatic cycles, which were frequently erratic.
>
> The food system of the indigenous peoples is based on a thousand to thousand five hundred species with their variants, while the global food system is centred around 15 species.[3]

Currently in Mexico, commercial and peasant seeds selected by farmers from their own harvest are resown in the subsequent cycle; these seeds are informally shared on a constant basis and have been conserved through generations. A main reason for agrodiversity in Mesoamerica is *milpa*, a traditional form of cultivation that combines maize, beans, and squash, and thus constitutes a diversified sowing system. Historically *milpa* has adapted to different environmental conditions, resulting in sixty more breeds and hundreds of maize varieties, all of them open-pollination varieties. The *milpa* system also protects wild plants that are being promoted such as tomatillo, chives, and large varieties of greens (amaranth greens, purslane, chipil, quelite cenizo); aromatic plants such as the epazote or basil; as well as medicinal plants such as pericón (the Mexican marigold), ruda, or arnica, which are either grown along the edges of plots or interspersed. Magueys, nopales, coffee, and various fruit trees may also be present as plot fencing or integrated into the plot. At the end of the maize cycle, sweet potato, yucca, or vines such as chayote and passionflower are also grown. By continuing this form of cultivation, agrodiversity is maintained and the traditional practices and knowledge that sustain this agrodiversity, along with open-pollination varieties, are also conserved.[4]

The country report presented to the FAO in 2006 highlights that unfortunately native diversity is suffering severe erosion owing, among other reasons, to the process of adoption of improved varieties, substitution of *milpa* crops with more remunerative crops, or due to the migration of rural people to cities and to the United States. According to the INEGI (Instituto Nacional de Estadística y Geografía, 2002), in states with the largest production of maize, 70 percent of the surface is sown with improved variety seeds. In irrigated and rain-fed valleys with good annual precipitation conditions, native maize has been replaced by hybrid seeds. Given that hybrid seeds only maximize their yield in high-sowing densities, they impede the coexistence of other crops and militate against the diversity of the *milpa*. The increase in the use of herbicides has resulted in the disappearance of many local varieties and species of beans, squash, and quelites (green herbs).[5] Lack of labor for weeding and the commercial promotion of herbicides have increased the use of agrochemicals in rural agriculture. Permanent or temporary migration of peasants from rural areas to cities reduces the diversity of seeds, which when no longer sown, are slowly lost forever.[6]

The FAO warned about the erosion of varieties and stated that of the varieties of maize existing in Mexico in 1930, only 20 percent remain. In the last fifty years, many populations of the Celaya and Tuxpeño breeds, known for their high productivity, were lost; so were Tuxpeño-Norteño, Apachito, Nal-Tel, Tehua, Jala, and Tuxpeño and Chalqueño varieties, as well as maize for special use.[7] However, considering the overall population of farmers, the Census of 2007 recorded that 75.3 percent of all production units in the country sowed their own seeds, and in terms of the total agricultural land, 86 percent of it is sown with farmers' seeds. The report of the Agro-food and Fisheries Information Service in 2009 indicated that native maize was sown in 85 percent of the agricultural surface of the country, in 7.2 million hectares of rain-fed land, by farmers who own less than five hectares. The cultivation is done in a large variety of agroecological zones at altitudes ranging from 0 to 4,000 meters, from the equator to higher latitudes in the two hemispheres, and in regions with precipitation of less than 40 mm to 3,000 mm a year, in soils and climates that are very variable.[8]

In an analysis of native varieties of maize in Mexico, it was discovered that although there were new high yielding varieties available and supported by the government, farmers continued to maintain complex populations of native varieties in order to deal with environmental heterogeneity, combat the effects of plague and disease, comply with cultural and ritual necessities, and satisfy their dietary preferences. Hernández Xolocotzi and Ortega postulate that the higher the degree of cultural erosion and disorganization, the greater the level of erosion of open-pollination varieties.[9]

## Corporate and State Threats to Rural Agriculture

The decade of the 1940s marked the beginning of the Green Revolution, a project that was started under the auspices of the Rockefeller Foundation that emphasized increasing production in the private sector of Mexican agriculture. This would be based on research and promotion of a technology package that sought to adapt seeds used in the United States to local soils, as well as the utilization of a suitable mix of insecticides and fertilizers and the efficient use of water. In the beginning, the research was restricted to maize and wheat; later it included bean (1949), potato (1952), fruit and vegetables (1953), sorghum, barley, and fodder legumes (1954), and livestock (1956), which heightened the dichotomy between subsistence agriculture and commercial agriculture.[10]

The Green Revolution tended to concentrate the benefits in a small business sector that had good irrigated lands, at the cost of the majority of the nation's farmer population. Moreover, by focusing on a type of research designed for conditions different from those in Mexico, it cast aside research that was already being done for the improvement of the maize production in traditional Mexican regions.[11]

In the 1940s, two types of research programs clashed with each other. The first, with improved open-pollination varieties, had the advantage of permanence as the farmer could allocate a part of his harvest for sowing in the following year, as was done by traditional farmers; the other, which was imposed by the Office of Special Studies (OEE in Spanish) under the management and funding of the Rockefeller Foundation, aimed at greater yields through the introduction of hybrids of exceptional productivity, but only in the first sowing. In subsequent sowings the productivity could be even lower than the yield obtained with ordinary seeds. Besides, the high productivity of hybrid seed depended on its capacity to respond well to fertilizers, which in turn require a regular and abundant water supply, that is to say, irrigation. While the Institute of Agricultural Research (IIA in Spanish) worked to obtain improved maize seeds for areas of small traditional cultivation, OEE preferred to focus on the production of very high yield seeds, meant for irrigated regions and for producers with substantial resources. In 1948, approximately 80 percent of maize-cultivation land, sown with improved varieties, was of open-pollination varieties. Around 1956, the seed production program of the Secretary of Agriculture dedicated *96 percent* of its capacity to hybrids, that is, the commercial production of maize.

The Green Revolution found its principal promoter in the Mexican state. Hybrids would have had very little impact without the buildup of strong investment in irrigation, extension of credit, support for agricultural extension agents, guaranteed prices, and the creation of an infrastructure for the storage of grains, agriculture insurance, support for mechanization, etc. From the end of the 1950s onward, the state controlled public research through the National Institute of Agricultural Research (INIA in Spanish) and later through the National Institute of Forestry, Agricultural, and Livestock Research (INIFAP). A state company, the National Seed Producer (PRONASE), had exclusive rights over the development of public research centers, and was engaged in commercially reproducing and distributing the varieties of maize, bean, rice, and oil seeds developed by them.

In the 1960s there was a process of reorganization of the seed industry through the national system for Production, Certification and Marketing of Seeds, based on which all work associated with the research, qualification, production, benefit, and certification of seeds, as well as the distribution, sale, and utilization of certified seeds, was considered a public utility (although not a state monopoly). However, at the same time there was a significant expansion of the national private and foreign industry in the production of improved seeds.[12]

Until 1980, private companies were restricted to the production and marketing of seeds, with very little participation in improvements. The change in policy and in adjustment programs (1982) marked the beginning of the end of PRONASE, which was dismantled in 2007 once its production and market share had reduced drastically in the early years of the 2000s. The Seed Law of 1991 encouraged the participation of national and foreign private companies and ended the preferential access given to PRONASE to INIFAP varieties, which could now also go to private companies. The seeds produced by the private sector were meant for irrigated areas with good rainy seasons, whereas those produced by PRONASE were meant for other cultivated areas.[13]

The Mexican seed industry is formed by individual farmers, large transnational companies, private national companies, national institutes for research and production of seeds, such as INIFAP, and international research centers such as the International Maize and Wheat Improvement Center (CIMMYT). After the disappearance of PRONASE, transnational seed companies penetrated the Mexican market and also increased the import of seeds. According to Ayala and Schwentesius,[14] although there are around thirty major companies— Agroproductos Monsanto, Syngenta Seeds, Sakata Seed de México, Semillas Berentsen, Ahern Internacional de México, Bio Internacional

Genética de Semillas, Bonnita Seed, Red Gold Seeds, Mar Seed Company, Semillas Conlee Mexicana, Semillas del Río Colorado, Semillas Mejoradas de México, Semillas Western, and others—foreign companies predominate in the seed market by managing more than 90 percent of the capital.

## Market Value of Seeds

The Mexican Seed Association (AMSAC) reports that the value of the seed market in Mexico is around $1 billion. About twenty transnational and national companies control 80 percent of the market, with the remaining 20 percent accounted for by producer associations, which market seeds. Mexico imports its entire vegetable seed requirement, worth about $200 to $250 million, while between 60 and 70 percent of the sale of maize seeds is done by transnational companies.[15]

Improved seeds are a basic input in commercial production areas, with very high yields and in continuous growth. For example, in Sinaloa, in high-productivity, irrigated zones, almost all maize producers sow hybrid seeds supplied by four companies: Pioneer, Asgrow, DeKalb, and Monsanto. The only Mexican maize seed company, Ceres, ceased to be competitive in the northeastern region because of low yields when compared with transnational ones.[16] Producers say the cost of seed is very high and its useful life has been reduced to three years, due to market competition.

## Kilo por Kilo

Between 1996 and 2001, through the Kilo por Kilo program, the government sought to increase the use of certified maize seeds, from varieties produced by state research centers and intended for those areas with good production. However, the program also distributed seeds without certification, poorly suited to local conditions; instead of the expected increase in yield, they resulted in the disappearance of many criollo or native varieties.[17]

## PROMAF

Given the global food price crisis in 2007, the Mexican government set up a program for small producers from the central and southern states of the country, where the majority of small-scale farmers producing for their own consumption are located, and who still use the *milpa* and peasant seed sowing system. This program aims at increasing the yield of the maize and bean crop with the help of technology packages validated by INIFAP, with the use of improved seeds, population densities, and sowing and fertilization. Once again and in spite of this causing the erosion of varieties of basic crops and their importance in terms of food security, the Mexican government allocated its financial resources to replacing *milpa* and peasant, native, or criollo varieties with commercial hybrid varieties, produced by transnational companies, along with the inputs required for their production. The government is now focusing on opening new markets for the seed and inputs companies, instead of promoting an increase in yield based on improvement of peasant varieties, the enriching of soils, and the use of organic manure, which will reduce farmers' dependence on industrial inputs.

## Subsidies to Monsanto

Since 1996 the Mexican government has subsidized the acceptance of transgenic cotton seeds from Monsanto through the Alliance for the Countryside (Alianza para el Campo) program; the government paid for the license and part of the cost of seeds for those farmers who agreed to buy transgenic seeds.

A couple of years ago, through the Productive Reconversion Program, the Mexican government once again subsidized Monsanto by giving a subsidy to producers with low maize yield wishing to sow transgenic soy. The government has authorized the sowing of transgenic soy in 253,000 hectares in the Yucatán Peninsula, in Chiapas, and in the Potosina, Veracruz, and Tamaulipeca Huastecana regions. The majority of producers in Chiapas and the Yucatán Peninsula are small indigenous producers (Mayas, Tzeltales, Tzotziles) who cultivate in the *milpa* system for their own consumption, with few chemical inputs, in small parcels of land of less than four hectares, with their own seeds of native varieties. These farmers are also beekeepers. Subsidized transgenic soy is an attempt to expand cultivation to these areas, but it has been met with resistance by farmers and environmental organizations, who have filed various appeals against the authorization for sowing granted to Monsanto.

## Seed Laws of 2007

In 2007, the Federal Law on the Production, Certification and Marketing of Seeds was passed, replacing the 1991 Seed Law. After some effective lobbying, the seed industry was able to modify a legislative initiative that attempted to give the state a priority role. In its place, it promoted a seed law that outlaws the exchange and sale of farmers' seeds and reinforces the interest of the private seed industry to a greater degree than the law of 1991. The privatization of seeds is a global trend, and new laws promoted in different countries are oriented toward this. The Federal Law on the Production, Certification and Marketing of Seeds (2007) openly attacks peasant seeds and attempts to classify them as illegal and pirate. Although the new seed law does not go to the European extreme of charging farmers a percentage for resowing with seeds from their own harvest, it does prohibit the sale or exchange of peasant seeds.

The 2007 law is said to apply to all types of seeds, including varieties of common use defined as: "Those used by rural communities, whose origin is the result of their practices, uses and customs." It is part of a group of laws that were drafted by large federations of seed companies who came together under what is called the International Seed Federation (ISF). In Mexico, the ISF is represented by AMSAC, which is the Mexican Association of Seed Producers, AC, an association that has very little to do with the Mexican reality. It defines itself as follows:

>AMSAC is an association which brings together the entire seed sector in Mexico, which has power to influence government decisions, participate in laws and norms and is recognized for its services and infrastructure to resolve the issues of its members.

Monsanto, Syngenta, Dow, DuPont or Pioneer, Vilmorin Inc., and various other transnational companies are members of AMSAC.

The Mexican Seed Law faithfully complies with the objectives set by this transnational federation.[18] It lays down, by virtue of Article 34 and some others, that all seeds need to be either from the farmer's own production or purchased. There is no other alternative. Exchanging or gifting of seeds is now considered illegal and there is no exception to this. In Articles 33 and 34 it requires that any seed that is "marketed or placed into circulation," that is to say, exchanged, lent, gifted, purchased, or sold, "... should carry a label on the packaging with the details required by the Official Mexican Standard." The Seed Law of 1991, on the other hand, made an exception for peasant seeds. "The free marketing or circulation of seeds that are neither certified nor verified shall not be restricted."[19]

A second imposition is the concept that good-quality seeds should be uniform, that is, equal and invariable and also stable, that is, unchanged with time. This means that in a country like Mexico, native seeds are being forced to stop evolving in one way or another. Peasant seeds and seeds from Mexican indigenous peoples have survived only because they have been evolving. The strategic objective of the National System of Seeds of Mexico is that by the year 2025, 60 percent of seeds should be certified and all the certified seeds should be protected by patents.[20]

## Patents, Transgenic Contamination, and Laws

At present almost 80 percent of producers sow their own native or criollo seeds. Many farmers are used to sowing small quantities of hybrid seeds to promote the strength of their native varieties, and by crossing native and hybrid varieties they "creolize" them. This practice will be prohibited with progress in patent protection, as companies will claim payment for improved genetic material that may be in the criollo seeds, as in the case of Europe with its "compulsory voluntary contribution," although they have never had to pay for peasant seeds, which are the patrimony of the human race, and on which they made their improvements. In Mexico improved seeds have not progressed despite more than seventy years of the Green Revolution, given that there are no varieties for each of the ecological niches in which maize is sowed, and for which farmers have adapted seeds over seven thousand years of farming. Besides this, the dietary and ritual uses of maize in Mexico cannot be met by a reduced number of hybrid maize varieties; they require the cultivation of various varieties and species associated with them. Hybrid maize, in spite of the fact that it can increase the harvest on hillsides and rain-fed areas, with less use of fertilizers, is still not able to guarantee the food security of rural families as it cannot be stored for a large part of the year; in fact, within a few months, it is attacked by insects, unlike native or criollo maize that families in rural areas store from one year to the next and use slowly over time as food.

The transgenic contamination of native maize has become a reality in Mexico starting in 2001, caused by the import of seeds from the United States that contain a transgenic maize blend. The imported transgenic maize was distributed in rural communities by the Diconsa state stores, which led to the spread of contamination to various regions, many of them indigenous, which cultivate maize to eat, and which considered the invasion of transgenes as contamination of the seeds inherited from their ancestors. This contamination occurred in spite of the existence of a moratorium on the experimental or commercial sowing of transgenic maize, as Mexico is among the countries that form the cultural region of Mesoamerica, the center of origin and diversification of maize.

The Mexican state has systematically sought to make rural production disappear, promoting programs for productive reconversion to commercial crops; preventing sowing on hillsides or the traditional practices of slash-and-burn agriculture; and promoting the replacement of native seeds with commercial hybrids. It has also played a pivotal role by strengthening legislative mechanisms favoring patents and the interests of private corporations and transgenic crops. The Law on Biosafety of Genetically Modified Organisms was approved in 2005 and favors transnational corporations, as it only defines the steps to be followed in order that transgenic crops may be approved. It does not penalize corporations when they contaminate native varieties or distribute transgenic seeds illegally, and it paved the way for lifting the de facto moratorium, in effect since 1998, on the experimental or commercial sowing of transgenic maize. In 2012, Congress tried to approve a law on vegetable varieties that would favor transnational companies, but opposition by farmers' organizations, led by the National Union of Autonomous Regional Farmer Organizations (UNORCA), a member of Via Campesina, resulted in the initiative being rejected.

## Farmers' Resistance

In spite of the efforts of the government and seed production and agrochemical corporations to destroy the rural economy and the users of peasant, native, or criollo seed varieties, farmers have resisted, in order to continue with their way of life, sowing, and culture. Indigenous and rural communities have resisted by continuing to maintain the *milpa* system as the form of cultivation that ensures the family's food sovereignty. Many communities do not use the hybrid seeds distributed by the government; the more advanced have ensured that the government changes the industrial technology packages that it subsidizes into support for native and criollo seeds and organic inputs. Given the declaration of the transgenic contamination of native varieties of maize, organizations requested the help of the Center for Studies for Change in the Mexican Countryside (CECCAM) to carry out its own diagnoses on native maize varieties. They declared collectively, as the

Network in Defense of Maize, that they would not use seeds from outside the communities, not sow maize distributed by the Diconsa state stores, nor maize brought by immigrants. They would not buy hybrid seeds, and only exchange seeds with known persons, check their lands, and remove weeds or destroy maize plants that seemed unnatural or deformed. Later they learned to conduct a rural study to sample their lands and identify the presence of transgenics in them. The ejidos have sought to make progress by using the agreements of the assembly—a community institution that allows autonomous decision making on the land and its resources—to prohibit, via an agreement made between the ejido members and the co-proprietors, the sowing of transgenic crops or hybrid seeds in their territories.

These communities also continue to maintain an active interest in recovering scarce varieties. They conduct seed exchange fairs where farmers acquire different seed varieties suited to their region. The fairs combine the savoring of traditional dishes cooked with native varieties, with conferences and theoretical presentations on the seed situation the world over and in the country, and also have traditional music and dances.

Native seeds cannot be stored in isolation, without maintaining the way of life and culture that gives them meaning. The only way to maintain and protect the diversity of plants and varieties is to promote the indigenous rural economy.

## Endnotes

[1]   FAO, "Biodiversity to Curb World's Food Insecurity," Global Conference on Biological Diversity in Bonn, Germany, 2008.

[2]   CONABIO, SEMARNAT, *Estrategia Nacional sobre Biodiversidad de México* (Mexico: Comisión Nacional para el Conocimiento y Uso de la Biodiversidad, Secretaría de Medio Ambiente y Recursos Naturales, 2000), 14, www.conabio .gob.mx/conocimiento/estrategia_nacional/doctos/pdf/ENB.pdf.

[3]   J. Caballero, "Exploración de Recursos Genéticos Potenciales," in *Memorias del Seminario sobre Investigación Genética Básica en el Conocimiento y Evaluación de los Recursos Genéticos,* eds. H. Palomino and E. Pimienta (Mexico: Jardín Botánico de la UNAM, Somefi, 1985), 28–40, cited in Boege Eckart, *El*

*Patrimonio Biocultural de los Pueblos Indígenas de México. Hacia la Conservación in situ de la Biodiversidad y Agrodiversidad en los Territorios Indígenas* (Mexico: Instituto Nacional de Antropología e Historia, Comisión Nacional para el Desarrollo de los Pueblos Indígenas, 2010), 21.

4    Eckart, *El Patrimonio Biocultural de los Pueblos Indígenas de México*, 220.

5    T. A. Kato et al., *Origen y Diversificación del Maíz: Una Revisión Analítica* (Mexico City: Universidad Nacional Autónoma de México, Comisión Nacional para el Conocimiento y Uso de la Biodiversidad, 2009), 116.

6    Iván Hernández Baltazar, "La Milpa y la Agrodiversidad en la Economía Campesina" (Mexico, 2012).

7    E. Hernández Xolocotzi and R. Ortega, *Variación en Maíz y Cambios Socioeconómicos en Chiapas, México, 1946–1971* (Mexico: Avances en la Ensenaza y la Investigación, Colegio de Posgraduados, Universidad Autónoma de Chapingo, 1973), 11–12.

8    L. M. Mera and C. Mapes, "El Maíz, Aspectos Biológicos," in Kato et al., *Origen y Diversificación del Maíz*, 22.

9    Hernández Xolocotzi and Ortega, *Variación en Maíz y Cambios Socioeconómicos en Chiapas*, 12.

10    Cynthia Hewitt de Alcántara, *La Modernización de la Agricultura Mexicana, 1940–1970*, 7th ed. (Mexico: Siglo XXI Editores, 1999), 36.

11    Ana de Ita and Pilar López Sierra, "La Cultura Maicera Mexicana Frente al Libre Comercio," in *Maíz: Sustento y Culturas en América Latina. Los Impactos Destructivos de la Globalización* (Montevideo: REDES–AT Uruguay, Biodiversidad—Sustento y Culturas, 2004), 13.

12    Ibid., 15.

13    Ana de Ita, "Semillas Campesinas entre el Estado y las Transnacionales," in *Semillas del Hambre; Ilegalizar la Memoria Campesina* (Mexico: CECCAM, 2010), 38.

14    A. V. Ayala and R. Schwentesius, *Las Semillas Mejoradas* (Mexico: Centro de Investigaciones Económicas, Sociales y Tecnológicas de la Agroindustria y la Agricultura Mundial (CIESTAAM), de la Universidad Autónoma Chapingo, 2009), cited in "Producción y Comercio de Semillas en México," *2000Agro Revista Industrial del Campo*, www.2000agro.com.mx/agroindustria/produccion-y-comercio-de-semillas-en-mexico/.

15    Ernesto Perea, "Mercado de Semillas, Negocio que Germina y Crece," *Imagen Agropecuaria*, March 23, 2009.

16    Ana de Ita, "Semillas Campesinas entre el Estado y las Transnacionales," 43–44.

17    George A. Dyer et al., "Dispersal of Transgenes through Maize Seed Systems in Mexico," *PLoS ONE* Open Access 4, no. 5 (2009).

18    GRAIN, "La Nueva Ley de Semillas de México (2007)," in *La Semillas del Hambre: Ilegalizar la Memoria Campesina* (Mexico: CECCAM, 2010), 19.

19    Ana de Ita, "Semillas Campesinas entre el Estado y las Transnacionales," 31.

20    GRAIN, "La Nueva Ley de Semillas de México (2007)," 23.

# Seed Saving and Women in Peru

Patricia Flores

Peru, located on South America's central Pacific coast, is home to ancient cultures, having one of the oldest civilizations in the world. Its geographic regions extend from the arid plains of the coast to the peaks of the Andes mountains and the tropical forests of the Amazon basin. This geographic diversity gives rise to a diverse ecology, accounting for 84 zones of life of the existing 104 in the world, creating exceptional conditions for the cultivation of a wide range of important food crops.

Ancient cultures combine traditional and indigenous knowledge to make for an ancestral legacy. All this knowledge and wisdom, together with a rich natural environment, has been key in developing appropriate technologies for the wise use of genetic resources, providing a sound base for the staple food system of Peruvian society. Maize (purple maize, Urubamba maize), native tubers, roots, and grains, tropical and Andean fruits, chiles, and peppers are mostly grown by smallholder farmers in diversified production systems, providing food both for the local community and nationwide.

The National Association of Ecological Producers of Peru (ANPE Peru, in Spanish) is a grassroots organization working on agroecology advocacy and capacity building for best agroecological practices, local market access, leadership, and empowerment. Women's leadership has turned out to be an important initiative developed by ANPE, as women farmers are genetic resources conservationists, handle their agro-biodiversity, and are responsible for seeds at the family and community level. For ANPE's organic farmers, seeds are the master-pieces of *campesinos* and indigenous people.

Without seeds there is no agriculture. *In situ* conservation of the flagships of agro-biodiversity is a priority issue and for that local and national fairs are organized, Pachamama celebrations take place, and knowledge and wisdom are continuously exchanged and transferred from one generation to the next.

As in many other countries of the world, legal patents on seeds and other life-forms are jeopardizing the freedom of cultivating with eco-logical and culturally appropriate techniques. As a result of a national mobilization with opinion leaders against GMO liberalization, the Peruvian government declared a ten-year moratorium on GMO seeds.

In August 2012, as part of its strategy on the seed issue, ANPE established the Seed Safeguards Network, led by women farmers. Fifty women from sixteen different regions came together in a national workshop to hammer out a plan of action.

Who are these women farmers from ANPE? What do they think and what do they propose? I offer three profiles and testimonies.

## Marisol Medrano

Marisol, the president of ANPE, is from Abancay, Apurímac, a southern Andean region of Peru. She is married with four children. Her farm is two hectares and, together with the family farm, they can cultivate a total of seven hectares. The farm, as is usual in the Andean area, is split between two communities—Karkatera and Pacchajpata—and is located 3,000 meters above sea level. Here, Marisol and her family grow a diverse range of crops and raise animals in an integrated production system. All practices are organic with an agroecological approach.

> I grow a diversity of crops and raise livestock, but my strength is as a maize grower. I have around 120 ecotypes of colored maize on my farm. In my practice as a farmer I crossed my corn unintentionally.

Noticing that I had different types of corn as a result of cross-pollination, I began to segregate them systematically by appearance. I didn't know that I was applying breeding techniques. I handle my own maize seeds according to my crossbred varieties which are adapted to local environmental conditions.

Marisol sells her organic products at the local market fair of Abancay where she, as former president of the regional producers' organization, worked to establish a permanent space for organic producers to sell their products.

Marisol delivers her message strongly:

We farmers have to work on a diverse production system. Though it can be tough, it produces enormous benefits for the family: a diverse diet, a local pharmacy [she grows medicinal plants], a beautiful landscape [flowers], and a place where I can sit down to enjoy and reflect on life. I cannot do this if my freedom to use, exchange, sell, and conserve my seeds is taken away.

## Rosa Alvina Sifuentes Portocarrero

Rosa Alvina is married, and lives with her husband, her mother, and three children on a farm located in Duraznillo (Pisuquía in Luya province, Amazonas region) at 1,800 meters above sea level.

I have five hectares, of which two are for coffee and banana crops. In the rest of the area I grow cassava, fruit, sugarcane, peas, and fodder for my animals (hen, guinea pigs, ducks) and for family consumption. I also have cattle and horses for my transportation.

Rosa Alvina's farm is far from the next important city, Chachapoyas. She has to walk for three to four hours to the main market where she sells her coffee. At her farm, she produces beans, maize, and peas, and engages in conservation practices to preserve her maize and bean seeds.

The seeds are resilient to climate change effects. They are my heritage, and my family's food security relies on them. Banana is our staple food. I have seven banana varieties. Coffee is important as a cash crop and, thanks to ANPE, I started on coffee processing and now I can sell my coffee as special coffee. I also had the opportunity to showcase my experience at Mistura. [Mistura is a popular food festival that the gastronomy movement organizes every year in Lima. APEGA, the association that organizes Mistura, provides a strong political backup to ANPE's farmers.] Presently, I regard myself as a rural small entrepreneur. My family income has significantly increased, and that has been an important change in our lives.

Rosa Alvina is the leader of a farmers' organization in her region. It was tough in the beginning.

Male farmers do not trust females as leaders. But after they saw how hard I work for our organization, achieving results and being responsible, they understood my contribution as a mother and as a member of the organization. I will face the new challenges in the Amazonas Regional Association of Organic Producers. We are more than six hundred smallholders, and twelve native communities of the ethnic Awajún are members of our organization.

She ends with this message:

Organized women conserve seeds for our future. Food security and sovereignty to me means that we have to be capable of guaranteeing food for our families with healthy, safe, and local products. It means that we have the choice and freedom to grow our food with our own quality reference, which has to do with ecologically sound systems according to our culture and traditions. Hence, it is important that conservationist communities and smallholders get organized to preserve our seed heritage, to give our children what we once received from our ancestors.

## Gladis Dina Rurush Jorge

Gladis Dina was born in the rural community of Tauripampa (province of Carhuaz, region of Ancash). Her farm is 3,700 meters above sea level. She had a difficult life as a child and had to work as a grazier on mountaintops for her survival. She and her little brothers lived in despair and hunger. But with strong determination she completed her studies and graduated as a nurse. Her married life was difficult and she ended the relationship after the birth of her daughter. Her financial situation was so bad that her daughter had to depend on governmental food programs. But Gladis was determined to continue her fight and improve her living conditions.

Being a natural leader, she was elected the president of a local committee. She started learning about gender issues with the support of the NGO, Manuela Ramos.

> My family's tradition as farmers kept me close to my farm to produce the food of my choice. I have a diversified farm which fulfills all my food requirements. I only buy oil, sugar, and salt from the market. Despite all my problems, I managed to overcome my difficulties. Now I am proud of myself.

Gladis produces potatoes, mashua, oca, wheat, peas, broad beans, lentils, barley, quinoa, lupinus, and many other food crops. Adding up all the small pieces of land, she has three hectares in total. In the lower areas, she grows fruits and vegetables such as lima, avocado, Peruvian golden berries, tuna, maize, inga, peaches, and sweet corn. She also raises animals such as sheep, guinea pigs, pigs, and hens.

> Besides my own consumption, I sell my products with added value—70 percent of what I produce is for my own needs, 30 percent is for sale. With ANPE we now have better access to fairs and markets and have recently started a bakery initiative.

Gladis told us how she manages her production system:

> I start with the seed. I classify seeds and store them. Tubers are wrapped with *ichu* [a native grass] or *muña* [an aromatic native species], which will keep them free from pests and diseases. Cereals and legumes are kept in clay containers. I always keep seeds for the next sowing season. I rely on my own seeds.

Gladis is president of the Regional Association of Organic Farmers of Ancash. "I appreciate the confidence my peers have in me. As a promoter, they have huge trust in my dedication and ability, which gives me energy to continue on this path." Gladis also has another gift—she writes songs and sings. "As an extensionist, I use my artistic skills to write and sing songs related to the Pachamama and agroecology. I am soon releasing my third disc highlighting our agroecological messages."

# The Seeds of Liberation in Latin America

Sandra Baquedano Jer and Sara Larraín

In Latin America, the seed protection movement was born and is still led by peasants and indigenous communities, from Mexico to Chile. It is at the heart of the movement for food sovereignty, which has created a dialogue, through the Via Campesina (International Peasant's Movement) coalition, between the mestizo and indigenous peasants of Latin America, and the peasants of Asia, Africa, and Europe. This global coalition has been joined in recent years by local fishermen communities worldwide.

Food sovereignty in Latin America and the world does not just express a demand associated with nutrition and food production, as might be suggested by the concept of food security coined by national governments and the United Nations Food and Agriculture Organization (FAO). Rather, it embodies a serious cultural, social, and political dispute for access to the earth, water, seeds, and land and, in turn, to the forests, mountains, and water basins, which allow for the reproduction of life and the sustenance of all living beings, including humans. For this reason, food sovereignty and the movement for the protection of seeds as common goods, and as world heritage, includes the right of peoples to self-determination—to decide how to distribute and manage, from this day on, the water and the land that is sown and harvested and provides food—in other words, how to organize and maintain the food chain, which allows the subsistence of human beings, just as that of other species, but also the maintenance of knowledge, community, identity, and culture.

The environmental, cultural, economic, and political claims of both the peasant communities and indigenous peoples put, at the center of their demands, the protection and continuity of their relationship with their territories and with the biodiversity that supports their identity, knowledge, culture, and lives. This territorial claim was obviously neither understood nor respected by the conquerors and colonizers of America in the sixteenth century. Nor was it by nation-states, from the nineteenth century onward to today, following the declarations of independence from Spain. Neither is it a reality worth considering, nor a legitimate citizens' demand, for the majority of current Latin American governments, who have sold the sovereignty of their territories and the rights of their peoples to the national and multinational corporations who drive the overexploitation of the natural resources in Latin America, and dominate the global market's neo-colonization.

The worldview of the original peoples of Latin America—just like that of the peoples of India—envisioned the unity and interdependence of life, since in their practices and rituals, they thanked Mother Nature, the Pachamama. This great mother of the Andes mountain peoples also represents the preservation and reproduction of life. Thus, the original peoples would identify with their modern-day descendants as their children and counterparts, through the upholding of strong relationships of respect and reciprocity. The harmony of this relationship between human communities and Mother Nature was called "good life and living well," or *sumac causai*, in the Aymara language. Currently, the peoples of Latin America are repositioning themselves and culturally and politically championing this concept as an expression of rebellion against the neo-colonization of the corporate-driven global economy and in opposition to economic growth and material progress, the way of life and development that their nation-states offer them.

Protecting and taking care of seeds, land, water, and ecosystems under the demand of food sovereignty and living well, peoples' movements position themselves against so-called "progress." In particular, indigenous peoples and peasant communities in Latin America put food and territorial sovereignty at the center of their resistance to and self-determination demands of nation-states. They are disputing shared assets—land, water, biodiversity, knowledge, production, and consumer patterns—and lifestyles that are based in extractivism, productivism, and authoritarianism, which have demeaned the human condition, social coexistence and relations, and the reproduction of life.

The Green Revolution, along with export-oriented agro-industry and the promise to resolve the problems of Latin America's rural poor, arrived on the scene in the 1960s under the cover of the Alliance for Progress, driven by the United States. The alliance misappropriated the most fertile land in many countries of the region, also disregarding thousand-year-old species and crops that were the result of the knowledge of seed selection by peasants, and the fruit of a millenary reciprocal relationship between the rural peoples and Pachamama. Thousands of varieties of maize, potato, and quinoa, to name just some of the most important ones, were lost through genetic erosion or disuse, and part of the knowledge, the land, the culture, and the independence of the people was lost with them. Nevertheless, many varieties, just like certain cultures, were preserved in more isolated regions, or on land that the greed of the state-supported agribusinesses considered to be marginal or not productive enough.

During the 1990s, some varieties of genetically modified seeds arrived somewhat stealthily in several Latin American countries, such as Chile in 1992 and, more aggressively, in Argentina.[1] By 2008, Argentina was second only to the United States in land acreage dedicated to genetically modified crops; GM soybeans began spreading in Argentina in 1996 and maize hybrids were introduced at the beginning of the twenty-first century.[2] Currently, Argentina exports the majority of its genetically modified soybean crop and almost 70 percent of its maize produce to a market that is geared in equal measure toward the production of fodder for farmyard animals, and the bioenergy market for ethanol.

The introduction of crops aimed at reproducing seeds and mono-cultures, principally for animal feed, in addition to the genetic contamination of native varieties, has eroded the genetic heritage of countries like Mexico. Furthermore, it has had the effect of displacing crops used for both local and national consumption, generating new and intensive processes of concentrating land ownership in the hands of national and multinational agribusiness consortiums, and causing the forced displacement from the countryside to urban slums of not only families but also complete peasant communities. Thus it is that the mega, exporting agro-industry has colonized territories, greatly straining biodiversity and water resources, generating stagnant agriculture and the desertion of farmland. This phenomenon has separated both individuals and whole peoples from the Earth, disrupting their spiritual connection, knowledge, and culture, and consequently affecting the cultural identity, sense of belonging, and subsistence of millions of people.

Deforestation processes have been generated by industrial agriculture and extensive livestock farming in many countries, such as Brazil and Chile; but also by aggressive reforesting plans with commercial species, especially pine and eucalyptus, with the export of cellulose and wood in mind. In Chile, the establishment of a forestry industry supported by large state subsidies was the main cause for the loss of biodiversity and native forests between the 1970s and the 1990s.[3]

Subsequent studies show that, in 90 percent of the cases, this publicly financed destruction took place for the benefit of large companies, who first received subsidies to plant forest and then buy property rights to the land. This caused both land ownership concentration and the mass migration of peasant communities to urban centers—once a plantation is sown, there is no work for several years, it being necessary to simply wait for the trees to grow in order to then exploit them.[4] Thus it was that the incredible Chilean "forestry boom," paid for by its citizens through taxation, generated great profits for less than five or so companies and rich individuals, and simultaneously set in motion the irreversible damage to the ecosystems. Peasant communities, too, disappeared, converted into a mass of socially and economically vulnerable urban inhabitants and, therefore, a burden for the state's subsidiary obligations.

## Socioenvironmental Sensitivity versus Holistic Harm

In democratic societies, governments, as opposed to dictatorial regimes, need to obtain the majority vote of an electorate in order to be elected and form a government. The electorate votes every few years to choose between political continuity and a change in power. It is elementary that the people at least have a chance to pass judgment on their politicians and parliamentarians. Nonetheless, this is not enough on its own, since the brief periods that rulers spend in office prevent priority from being given to issues of great future importance, whose results may not be seen by those subjected to adverse measures and corresponding sacrifices. In practice, the majority of politicians are not prepared to risk taking nonpopulist measures in the interest of safeguarding future generations that do not yet exist and protecting interests that do not exclusively benefit the powerful economic haven that they defend. Doing so would require them to face up to the severity of a policy that would cost them votes and the rejection of those whom the measures affect.

An economy motivated by the pursuit of profit stands in contrast to a system characterized by greater rationality when measured against the Baconian program. Faced with this final legacy, nonconsumerist ways of life would morally be more equitable, fair, and superior in humane terms, to the extent that they meet collective needs better, and avoid unnecessary competition and the abuses of market production. If consumption were restricted, it would entail not just the saving of natural reserves, but also the assimilation of nature not as a means, but as an end in itself—as part of the *telos*, or meaning, of life.

An ascetic relinquishment of the market by the masses is something not only alien, but also contradictory to globalized, capitalist society. Although some features of asceticism are intrinsic to noncapitalist disciplines, the problem is that frugality has not necessarily been voluntary, but imposed. All the same, it is more equitable than a system that doesn't encourage us to reduce our energyvorous standard of living. Such a system is not some kind of Earth Democracy to be applied to and directed at all species; rather, it involves a tyranny of our species and the submission of the rest. Nowadays, the fact is that the accumulative force of disturbing and destroying the natural reproductive cycle—together with the urban and demographic explosion, until now uncontrolled—has, for mere survival, made it necessary to not only plunder the planet, in a more and more unnatural way, but to cause the human species to be treated as an object, with the planet unable to yield further.

Protecting and taking care of the natural environment requires value being given to personal sacrifices and greater altruistic relinquishment, these being sensitive to the *possibility* of holistic suffering, rather than being regulated and steered exclusively by public policies. The role of ethics and environmental education, as with all things, is fundamentally important in order to develop an adequate socioenvironmental sensitivity.

Global warming, the loss of biodiversity, deforestation, desertification, the demographic explosion, pollution, and other environmental problems put humanity within touching distance of self-destruction. Faced with the possibility of our species' suicide, the near future looks like the place for specific, sharper, and more radical harm than that which has already been done. The effects of this harm are possible socioenvironmental upheavals that threaten humanity, not only with regard to its permanence or survival, but with regard to its quality of life—that is, the way of life that future generations may be forced to suffer.

Generally speaking, the governments that have ruled in Chile and Latin America until now have no institutionalized rules that advocate the protection of biodiversity, even when faced with the threat of humanity's self-destruction. They foresee neither ecological disasters nor the risk of the environment's radical decline. Given the fact that we have already destroyed the planet, we must take responsibility for the harm done. The concept of responsibility involves the identification of a particular element for which one *has to* answer, bestowing upon us an active role, since, as responsible agents, we have a mission to protect the natural environment, judging it to be vulnerable and in a potentially forever worsening state. We have seen that, in the name of being responsible *for* a nation, war has been declared against another people, devastating it through pain and destruction. Or how, in the name of being responsible *for* the interests of a specific business, dams have been built, native forests have been destroyed and waters polluted, causing irreversible damage from a socioenvironmental viewpoint. Where there is a lack of sensitivity about the essence of human suffering, and the suffering of other species being a mystery, it is difficult to avoid it, even when there are more than enough reasons to try. Holistic sensitivity, unlike the concept of responsibility, allows no biased exclusion of the word "for," when it comes to being responsible *for* any detriment caused to others. Rather, it builds bridges with the word, to vindicate, socioenvironmentally, self-criticism.

## Economic Growth or Living Well?

In contradiction to the celebration of their bicentenary of independence from Spain, the majority of Latin American countries are suffering from accelerated processes of privatization and transnationalization of their territories and environmental heritage. Additionally, they have suffered from the dismantling of the state's authority to administer natural resources, social policies, and national territory, all of which has de facto meant entering a new colonial era. Such processes, initiated with structural adjustment programs and the privatization of public assets and services some decades ago, were subsequently consolidated through free trade and investment agreements, negotiated as much by social democratic national governments as by those on the right, and even by "progressive" ones.[5]

Chile, for example, managed to become the country with, globally, the second-highest number of free trade and investment agreements to its name. This entailed opening up its economy, regulations, and institutions to economic players from anywhere in the world, so that they might invest in, exploit, and export environmental heritage, under the slogan of successive "pro-growth" agendas. The intensification of such a strategy through free trade agreements, investments, commerce, and services in all Latin American countries has brought about the removal of regulatory frameworks that were favorable to the internal economy and to local development. It has also included "national treaty" criteria for transnational economic players, favoring the integration of local economies into the global economy as the only viable national development strategy.

Chile's integration into the global economy has meant an anti-democratic process of expropriating natural resources, state companies, and public services (with few exceptions), with detrimental consequences for Chileans, and the regions and territories where the natural heritage is located.[6] A clear example is the case of water, where the new Water Act has caused serious conflicts between human rights and market rules. The Water Act, unilaterally approved by the military government in 1981 (when there was no National Congress), with a strong pro-market bias, not only privatized water ownership, but also "separated the domain of water from that of land, allowing its free sale and purchase."[7] Such a mechanism appropriated the common property of water and favored the extreme concentration of water ownership under private control. In Chile currently, just three companies own 90 percent of water rights for hydroelectric energy generation,[8] and another three dominate water ownership for drinking water services.[9] Privatization meant the loss of public control over freshwater sources, as well as serious environmental and economic management problems that the national state has little power to resolve.

In all of the Latin American region, there are now dramatic conflicts about access to water, especially in Mexico, Peru, Chile, Ecuador, Colombia, and, more recently, Argentina. In all these countries,
citizens are now mobilized and articulated in their demand for water
access as a fundamental human right, over and above the rights of
businesses. In this context, mining development is the activity that
has most aggravated the destruction of biodiversity—water sources
for example, including glaciers in the Andes—and created serious air,
land, and water pollution in almost all the countries of the region. For
this reason, mining is today the activity most strongly resisted and
rejected by local communities and indigenous peoples who only experience its negative impact.

The wealth generated by mineral extraction and processing in
Latin America has primarily benefited transnational companies and
the countries they belong to. Chile is a sad example in this respect:
today it is the largest producer of copper globally (35 percent) and one
of the largest providers of minerals for the globalized economy. Over
70 percent of mining sector control is private (in 1972 it was just 15
percent) and in the specific case of copper is higher still, at 73 percent.[10]

As in Chile, the option chosen by the majority of Latin American
governments, for development centered on macroeconomic growth
through the extraction and exportation of environmental heritage,
has caused a growing depletion of their means of development, an
intensification of socioenvironmental conflicts, and serious problems
for democratic governance. This was the case, for example, with
then President Sebastián Piñera's right-wing government's repression
of the people of Aysén in Chile, who were opposed to the building
of five big dams on Patagonia rivers, and who asked for equal rights.
Or when progressive Bolivian President Evo Morales repressed the
TIPNIS indigenous march in defense of their land and against building an international highway for the regional and international market of raw materials, casting doubt on Morales's indigenous leadership
and his democratic integrity.

Development centered on exporting economic growth has at least three clear structural aspects that can be recognized in almost all the countries of the region, particularly in Chile, El Salvador, Peru, and Colombia. The first characteristic is that natural resources and territories are made available to the global economy; the second is that the expansion and intensification of markets, investments, and services (financial, environmental, cultural, or otherwise) occurs in accordance with the priorities of private economic players, principally transnational ones, and not for people's benefit; the third is that the negotiation conditions for economic development and public policy are determined by market priorities rather than for the common good or in the public interest. The national state thus becomes an institution that responds to the priorities of private interests and corporations. The consolidation of these conditions in Latin America has brought about a *policy of making decisions about national development using the logic of international competition,* a logic dominated by transnational economic players and small local elites. In this context, the peoples of Latin America have increasingly resisted and rejected the processes of economic liberalization and global integration based on free trade and investment agreements. As an outcome of their resistance, Latin American social movements have, in recent years, managed to prevent the Free Trade Area of the Americas (ALCA), driven by the United States, with the aim of tying regional economic integration to its own national economy. As an alternative to economic globalization and business integration, social movements and public interest citizen networks[11] have proposed a Hemispheric Peoples Integration, based on grassroots cooperation and people's alternatives, and on seven principles: (1) the promotion and defense of expanded social, environmental, economic, cultural, and political rights, and of collective human rights; (2) the protection and sustainable use of nature and ecosystems as common property for the reproduction of life (water, seeds, energy, land, and biodiversity), and the conservation of immaterial goods of the cultural and historic inheritance of communities and peoples; (3) the integrated management of natural resources and territories by human society, but under the recognition and respect of the complexity of living systems and the interdependence of species; (4) the sovereignty of communities and peoples over territory and common heritage, that is, the right to decide freely and independently how to live, and to the organization, production, and use of natural heritage without the availability of, or access to, said heritage, being affected for current or future generations; (5) the reciprocal and complementary nature of relationships and exchange of knowledge, goods, products, and services as an alternative to unequal competition, the ownership of resources, and the accumulation of capital; (6) the independence and self-determination of peoples, freely and from the perspective of their own land and culture, to decide on political orientations, rules, and regulations, and institutions for their coexistence and economy; as well as women's sovereignty over their own lives and bodies, and the right to live free of violence, oppression, or coercion; (7) living democracy and active participation as an alternative to democracy being restricted to electoral participation, economic administration, and the imposition of "state" priorities over and above people's rights.[12]

This concept of peoples integration has, in the past few years, generated huge mobilizations of people in various countries from the region, opening up great spaces for collective coordination and social articulation. One example is the World Social Forums, generally hosted in Porto Alegre, in the south of Brazil, where the articulation of social movements' agendas has been politically strengthened. This collective process has gone so far as to create a new ethical-political-social agenda in Latin America, based on the principles listed above. There are also some demands that have historically been promoted by diverse social movements: food sovereignty, energy sovereignty, free-flowing rivers, social and supportive economics, care for common property resources, cooperation between peoples, and respect and care for Mother Nature, among others. In turn, several governments, as in

Ecuador and Bolivia, have included both the human right to shared assets and nature's rights in their recent constitutions.

With a monumental effort and under this new model of ethical and social clauses, the citizens' movements and some governments organized the World Peoples' Summit on Climate Change and the Rights of Mother Earth, in 2010. This summit articulated an entirely different political agenda from the paradigm of development as economic growth, centered on the recognition of solidarity and cooperation among peoples and nations. Finally, as an even more radical alternative to the dominant economic paradigm, social movements have taken on the thousand-year-old principle of "living well" (*sumac causai*), a term coined by the Aymara peoples who lived, and still live, on the highlands and mountains of the Andes, from Bolivia to Chile.

The adoption of "living well" as a paradigm for the well-being (or good living) of human society, in harmony and reciprocity with Mother Earth (today and in the future), represents a direct and tremendous ethical, cultural, and political challenge to the visions and strategies of nation-states and global economic elites, driven by the expansion of investment, production, consumption, and markets. At the start of the twenty-first century, Latin American people called upon politicians and governments to adopt policies and actions for "living well" and for the abandonment of economic growth at any cost.

## Endnotes

[1]   M. I. Manzur et al., *Biodiversidad, Erosión y Contaminación Genética del Maíz Nativo en América Latina* (Red para una América Latina Libre de Transgénicos, 2011), 165.

[2]   Ibid., 166.

[3]   Chile Sustentable, "Desafíos para la Sustentabilidad de los Bosques y el Sector Forestal Chileno," in *Por un Chile Sustentable: Propuesta Ciudadana para el Cambio* (Santiago: Chile Sustentable, 1999), 138–157.

[4]   Ibid.

[5]   Such is the case with Ecuador, and Correa's current government.

[6]   Sara Larraín, "Naturaleza y Mercado," *Le Monde Diplomatique*, April 2012, 9.

[7]   Chile Sustentable, "Disponibilidad y Uso Sustentable del Agua en Chile," in

*Por un Chile Sustentable: Propuesta Ciudadana para el Cambio* (Santiago: Chile Sustentable, 1999), 218.

[8]   Ministry of Public Works, "January 2010—Proposal for Constitutional Reform, to Change the Articles Referring to Water Ownership" (law communiqué); Endesa Enel, Italy; AES Gener, United States; and Colbún, Grupo Matte, Chile.

[9]   Suez from France, the Ontario Teacher Pensions Plan from Canada, and Grupo Luksic from Chile.

[10]   Chilean Copper Commission, "Chilean and World Copper Mining Production, Percentages and Tonnages According to World Metal Statistics, 2009."

[11]   Red de Vigilancia Interamericana para la Defensa del Agua y de la Vida (Red VIDA), Red Latinoamericana contra las Represas y por los Ríos, las Comunidades y el Agua, Plataforma Energética Latinoamericana, Coordinadora Latinoamericana de Organizaciones del Campo (CLOC, Vía Campesina), Programa Cono Sur Sustentable, Alianza Social Continental, Jubileo Sur, Red Intercontinental de Promoción de la Economía Social y Solidaria, Promoción de la Economía Social y Solidaria, Marcha Mundial de las Mujeres, Coordinadora de Organizaciones Indígenas, among others.

[12]   Cono Sur Sustentable 2006, Santiago, Chile, 7–8.

# The Other Mothers and the Fight against GMOs in Argentina

Ana Broccoli

The US biotechnology industry has turned Argentina into the world's third-largest soybean producer, but the chemicals powering the boom are contaminating soy, corn, and cotton fields, as well as homes, classrooms, and drinking water. A growing chorus of doctors and scientists warns that their uncontrolled use could be responsible for the increasing number of health problems across the South American nation.[1] This essay seeks to reveal the history of how the genetically modified organism (GMO)–agrochemical business model became established and demonstrates the symbolic links between Argentine mothers' struggle for justice and the well-being of future generations.

Populated by little more than forty million inhabitants and occupying an area of nearly four million square kilometers, with a variety of climates and fertile soils, Argentina has been globally recognized as a food producer and exporter: a "world granary" and breeder of cattle, which graze on the vast Pampas. Agriculture allowed this nation to become one of the most prosperous on the continent, enjoying a powerful economy and comfortable lifestyles until it was beset by a series of economic crises, inflationary spirals, and capital flight in the mid-twentieth century. The deregulation that had been pursued by the corporations and facilitated by the state was retained and reinforced during the construction of the neoliberal model during the 1990s, with a particularly significant impact on Argentine agriculture. In the twenty-first century, the national agribusiness model resembles a corporate dictatorship: a dictatorship that is gestating more "bad memories" for the future.

In Argentina, workers' organizations and social movements are often portrayed in images of the Plaza de Mayo, traditionally the center of Argentine civic life, and perhaps best known for the fight for justice that was initiated in April 1977 by the "Mothers of the Plaza de Mayo." Over the years since their demonstrations began, drawing strength from each other, every week the mothers and grandmothers of thousands of young people who were "disappeared" during Argentina's military dictatorship marched together in public wearing their emblematic headscarves, demanding to know what had become of their loved ones. Despite, or perhaps because of, their weekly marches around the Pirámide de Mayo that occupies the center of the plaza, the military government tried to marginalize and trivialize their struggle, branding them "*las locas*" (the madwomen). Together with the number of kidnapped persons, the movement grew and gained international attention, seeking to put pressure on the Argentine dictatorship, particularly from other governments, by publicizing the many stories of the "disappeared," especially in 1978, when Argentina hosted the World Cup soccer tournament and the Mothers' demonstrations were covered by the international press corps.[2]

Today another group of mothers is seeking justice; this time they are fighting for the rights of their "contaminated children." They are the "Mothers of Ituzaingó" (a city in the province of Córdoba, to the west of Buenos Aires), who, more than ten years ago, first reported the impact on their children of excessive agrochemical use associated with GMO agriculture. Their struggle for justice is supported by popular gatherings, people's organizations against pesticide use, and peasants driven from their lands because of the violence of the industrial model of monoculture crop production.[3] They took their case to court in the famous "Fumigation Trial"[4] of 2012 and are leading national resistance against the GMO giant Monsanto's plans to build a seed processing plant at Malvinas Argentinas in the peri-urban area of Córdoba City.

Before relating the story of the Mothers of Ituzaingó's struggle, a few more details about the Argentinean context need to be explained in order to help us understand how this resistance movement was shaped. To borrow a euphemistic war metaphor, collateral damage among the country's human population became apparent as people were exposed to agricultural spray drift, although both combatant and civilian casualties were denied by the corporate dictatorship. As the world's second-largest adopter of GM technology, Argentina has become the premier ecotoxicological experiment, planting almost twenty-five million hectares of transgenic crops in 2013. Contrary to Argentine law, however, the precautionary principle was never applied.

## Glyphosate and GMOs as "Holy Water and Manna from Heaven"

The Argentine state has validated genetic engineering as a safe technology and does not consider that GM foods carry any risks to human health.[5] Biotechnology research is strongly supported and considered likely to foster a national transgenic industry and intellectual property that could one day challenge the dominance of global seed corporations. Meanwhile, the Argentinean public has no awareness of the possible dangers of consuming genetically modified foods. The national mass media supports the biotech industry and promotes a narrative of safety and freedom from any risk to consumers.

In 1996, the Argentine Secretariat of Agriculture, Livestock, Fishing and Food authorized GMO technology by means of two straightforward resolutions: N° 115 of March 14, 1996, established the protocol for seeking authorization for "experimentation or release of transgenic soybean seed"; while N° 167 of April 3, 1996, authorized production and commercialization of soybean products and subproducts that are "glyphosate resistant." This authorization, which radically changed Argentine agriculture, was granted in an administrative process spanning just three months. Argentina approved the cultivation of GM soybeans without undertaking any independent research, relying solely on studies carried out by Monsanto.

Thus, the Roundup Ready (RR) soybean gained rapid access in Argentina, and subsequently in neighboring countries that adopted GM technology without adequate legal frameworks for the regulation of transnational interests. RR soy is smuggled (as contraband seeds) into other countries, and was baptized in Brazil as "Maradona Soy." In 2004, reflecting the rapid spread and dominance of GM technology, Syngenta, one of the six global seed giants, created the advertising slogan "The United Republic of Soy," presenting a map of this imaginary territory that unified growing areas of Argentina, Uruguay, Paraguay, Bolivia, and Brazil. Indeed, corporations in the region encountered no barriers to the development of their transgenic empires: agribusiness production processes operated en bloc, with land tenure systems (sowing pools) and export companies completing the oligopolistic complex.[6]

The glyphosate + GMO "technological package" incorporates cultivation technologies that are advertised as promoting soil conservation and minimizing environmental impact while ensuring the reduction of pesticide use. Citing the view that the herbicide glyphosate displays low toxicity in the wider environment and therefore carries little risk of damage to human health, Dr. Lino Barañao, the current minister of science and technology, told the media that "people who had consumed a glass of the chemical to commit suicide had met with no success."[7] Despite claims to the contrary, the use of glyphosate has increased a hundredfold, while the application rate per hectare has increased from 2–3 to 8–12 liters. In the face of social movement claims about the harmful effects of glyphosate, in 2009, the government created the National Research Commission on Agrochemicals (NRCA) with a mandate to research, prevent, and treat the effects of agrochemicals on human and environmental health. Further, the National Scientific and Technical Research Council (CONICET) issued a report[8] on glyphosate that related any of its possible negative effects to poor application practices and, in the absence of sufficient research to establish otherwise, claimed low toxicity. Peers have criticized the CONICET report, claiming that it is biased toward research that regards glyphosate as safe, and that its conclusions lack independent corroboration.

In 2012, an audit of National Service of Agricultural Quality and Health (SENASA)—the agency responsible for registration, authorization, and control of agrochemicals—raised serious concerns regarding the agency's work and the health of the population exposed to glyphosate fumigation. In a report, it claimed that agrochemical pollution leads to "silent poisoning" because negative health effects result from long-term, repeat exposure, with chronic toxicity leading to enhanced morbidity and/or death.[9] Thus, glyphosate-related diseases are naturalized. By 2012, transgenic crops subject to systematic fumigation covered an area of twenty-two million hectares, inhabited by some twelve million people, excluding the population of large cities. The state has glossed over the highly critical SENASA audit, and no progress has been made regarding the need to proceed in accordance with the precautionary principle and for the agency to undertake its own scientific research independently of the agribusiness corporations.

Public acceptance of GMOs is also facilitated by the positive image presented by a coalition of government agencies, farmers, academics, and the media that projects a discourse of approval. The Argentina Society of Nutrition (SAN) contributes to the positive image of GMOs, employing the rhetoric of food security, which is often interpreted as food safety. In a 2008 report, SAN employed the principle of "substantial equivalence" and concluded that "studies to establish the safety of GMOs have shown, in all cases, that these foods are just as safe and nutritious as conventional crops."[10] The discourse of approval is also forwarded by those who claim that GMO agriculture has the ability to maintain a sustainable and healthy environment for future generations, supported by the myth of using fewer chemicals. All these narratives are propagated by university researchers and others involved in the production and industrial processing of foods, in health services, or in law. None of these areas of knowledge attempts to decode or deconstruct discourses that favor GMOs. The only exceptions are institutions such as the University Network for Environment and Health (REDUAS) and independent professors in transdisciplinary fields, such as Free Chairs of Food Sovereignty, Family Farming and Agroecology. It is only actors such as these who undertake field studies documenting the diseases that have accompanied the spread of the GMO-based agro-industrial model, and bring to light and denounce the tragedy that is unfolding in "The United Republic of Soy."

## The Mothers of Ituzaingó

The neighborhood of Ituzaingó is located in the southeast of the city of Córdoba. Established in the 1950s, it comprises an area of approximately thirty blocks, home to around five thousand people. The main source of employment is industrial manufacturing, but the neighborhood is surrounded by productive agricultural land.

In 1997, Sofia Gatica lost her newborn daughter, Nandy, due to a kidney malformation. Months later, when her son suffered paralysis of his legs, she began to realize that many people in the neighborhood too were suffering from similar afflictions. This gave birth to the Mothers of Ituzaingó.

The women of the neighborhood, alarmed by the increasingly frequent cases of cancer, especially leukemia, and birth defects, decided to meet at Sofia's home. They began to record all of the known cases systematically, undertaking a door-to-door survey to compile their own statistics, which they recorded on a map drawn by a neighbor, the only man who attended the initial meeting. Most of the people out of the two hundred cases they noted lived in the area bordering the fields sprayed with agrochemicals. The map was used as evidence presented to the courts and the authorities. They drew attention to the suspected link between the herbicide sprayed and health problems, and tested blood samples of local children as well as water, air, and soil samples.

Finally, in 2001, the Mothers of Ituzaingó association came into being and, thus, sixteen mothers set off on a long and painful road to spread word and seek recognition and redress from the authorities. The struggle that began in the streets continued in the offices of the public health authorities, with mothers demanding an investigation into the cause of unexplained illnesses. However, it was only when the mothers took their story to the media that the authorities finally agreed to investigate. With the help of the NGO Environment Defense Foundation (FUNAM),[11] three groups of contaminants to which the local population was being exposed were identified: arsenic, heavy metals, and pesticides. In combination with pesticides such as DDT and endosulfan, these contaminants acted as endocrine disruptors, with the continuous spraying of glyphosate and other toxic products on the fields surrounding the neighborhood completing the picture.

In 2006, analyses of thirty children revealed that twenty-three, including all three of Sofia's children, had higher than permitted levels of agrochemical residues in their bodies. A subsequent study commissioned by the government found that in the areas of Ituzaingó with the greatest exposure to glyphosate, 33 percent of residents had died of cancer, compared to less than 17 percent of the whole population. Rates of respiratory diseases, neurological problems, and infant mortality were also far higher than average.[12]

The repercussions of the mothers' struggle for recognition of their plight forced the national authorities to finance further tests. The presidency launched NRCA, which as mentioned above, concluded that the toxicity of glyphosate was low. Fortunately, other scientists such as Dr. Andrés Carrasco, a professor at the Molecular Embryology Laboratory of the University of Buenos Aires School of Medicine, who died recently, published results that demonstrated otherwise, that is, the damage caused by glyphosate in amphibian embryos. According to his study, published in the magazine *Chemical Research in Toxicology* in 2010, the herbicide was extremely toxic to amphibian embryos, even in doses much lower than those used in agricultural spraying.[13] Dr. Carrasco supported the mothers in their struggle until his final days.

Under pressure from the Mothers of Ituzaingó, who had mobilized themselves in defense of their rights to health care and environmental and sanitary safety, the province opened a public center, set up the Cancer Hospital of Córdoba, and in April 2010 created the Provincial Tumor Registry,[14] perhaps the most terrible object of registration measured in the absence of precautionary principles. During 2002–2003, three municipal ordinances were passed including the "sanitary and environmental emergency," which prohibited fumigation by hand within 500 meters of the neighborhood and aerial fumigation within 2,500 meters, creating a buffer zone around the community.[15] But it did not stop fumigation altogether.

Ten years after the association had been born, in 2011, the Mothers' painful and lonely journey started to show results. In February 2008, the health subsecretary of Córdoba City, Dr. Medardo Ávila Vázquez, denounced the use of aircraft to fumigate the Ituzaingó neighborhood. The aircraft owner and the two soy producers and businessmen on whose behalf the fumigation was carried out were booked as instigators of clandestine fumigation using highly dangerous products risking a helpless population. Several chambers rejected the conflictive cause until June 2011, when the 2008 lawsuit was finally brought to trial, "setting precedent for defending the right to health of vulnerable populations against the greed of soy businessmen who do not doubt in poisoning rural school, entire populations, original communities and, water wells in their race to increase the agrarian rent."[16] On September 4, 2012, the First Criminal Chamber of the city of Córdoba gave its ruling, sentencing the accused, an agrarian producer and a pesticide-spraying pilot, to a three-year conditional jail term for intentional environmental pollution, thus setting the precedent for future claims.

## Camping Mothers against Monsanto

A few days after the Fumigation Trial had begun, on June 15, 2012, President Cristina Fernández de Kirchner[17], speaking from New York, praised Monsanto for its investment, that is, the construction of a plant, in Malvinas Argentinas, a county near the capital of Córdoba province. On August 21, 2012, the day after the trial ended, the minister of agriculture, Norberto Yauhar, also announced official approval for Monsanto's "Intacta RR2 Pro," a soybean variety developed in the United States for non-US territories that uses stacked genes to resist insects and herbicides, and suggested the need for a "necessary change in the Seed Law" (N° 20.247/73), giving more control from the state to collect its right to intellectual property as well as controls that would avoid circulation of "outlaw" seeds damaging profitability.[18]

In Argentina, Monsanto started its activities of conditioning hybrid maize seeds in Pergamino, in the province of Buenos Aires, during 1978. Until 2014, it had five plants: two processing seeds (María Eugenia Plant in Rojas and Pergamino Plant); one producing herbicides (Zárate Plant); and two experimental stations (Camet and Fontezuela). Its project currently under construction in Malvinas Argentinas, in the province of Córdoba, includes another GM seed producing factory, supposedly the largest in the world, and two new experimental stations, one in Río Cuarto (Córdoba province) and the other in the province of Tucumán.[19]

Interestingly, Monsanto executives have been exhibiting the plant in Rojas, in the province of Buenos Aires, including visits organized for Malvinas's neighbors along with Monsanto-labeled gifts, in the belief that it adds credibility to the operation of their seed plants. This new plant would work on similar lines, processing the stacked genes variety "Intacta RR2 Pro" seed on a bigger scale. Environmental concerns regarding the transportation of the crop, around 216 grain elevators weighing 137 tons, and its agrochemical wastes, in addition to the subsequent processing of seeds that would be impregnated with highly toxic substances, forced the University Network for Environment and Health to publish a second report on the risks the population of Malvinas would be exposed to.

The environmental and health risks of the new plant to the population of Malvinas Argentinas were yet another challenge that Sofia and the Mothers of Ituzaingó began to deal with soon after the court trial ended. The announcement of the construction of this new plant triggered major protests throughout the province. Indeed, protesters, including mothers with their children, have been camping at the Monsanto construction site and maintaining roadblocks on all five entrances to the plant ever since. The campaign against the plant is led by Asamblea Malvinas Lucha por la Vida (Malvinas Assembly Fighting for Life), a resistance movement against the construction of the plant, comprising people from the neighborhood of Malvinas as well as other neighborhoods and communities in Córdoba. The Mothers of Ituzaingó have been an integral part of these protests too. These protesters claim that neither Monsanto nor the government has the social license required for such construction; moreover, they have not conducted any credible study on the environmental impact on the province either. On July 24, 2013, the movement celebrated a year of struggle with demonstrations, claims, and artistic interventions as a form of exposing the nexus between provincial and municipal officials and the seed giant. Moreover, the demonstrators revealed that many local residents were not taking part out of fear of losing their municipal jobs as well as the social assistance they receive from the government. Such declarations rupture the claims of the industry and government about the creation of jobs and employment levels that these plants are set to achieve.

The following are testimonies of two mothers who are camping at the construction site:

> Soledad Escobar has four children who attend a school located next to the lot where the plant is being built. She says: "I'm worried about the silos and the chemical products they use ... because of the changes in the climate, it's now windy year-round in Córdoba."
>
> Beba Figueroa, another mother, says: "What the TV and newspapers are saying, that there are political parties involved in this, isn't true ... most of us are mothers who are scared for our children." Referring to the environmental impact caused by this

construction, she mentions, "Strong north winds whip you in the face and legs because there are hardly any trees left in Córdoba."

The plant was to begin operating in March 2014. But construction work was brought to a halt in October 2013 due to protests and legal action by local residents, who have been blocking the entrance to the site permanently since September 18, 2013. On the morning of Saturday, November 30, 2013, troops escorted several trucks out of the construction site.[20] The trucks had forced their way past the roadblock on Thursday, November 28, 2013, when members of the construction union stormed into the camp set up by local residents, with the aim of breaking the blockade. More than twenty people were injured; the police suppressed the campers with batons, gas, and rubber bullets.

In the last few months, the police have cracked down on the protesters on several occasions. The demonstrators have received threats, too. When Soledad Barruti, a journalist and author of *Malcomidos: How the Argentine Food Industry Is Killing Us*, the best seller about the Argentine agro-food system, went to the Malvinas camp to express solidarity with the campers, she received an email from the head of government relations for Monsanto threatening her: "Soledad: I don't mean to offend you, but I don't think you are acting like a journalist, more like an activist. Take care." In the email, he even said it was a shame that she had a picture taken with Sofia Gatica.[21]

Sofia was attacked and brutally beaten just seventy-two hours after receiving a death threat. She later recalled: "They didn't speak. One jumped on top of me and they kicked and beat me. I screamed loudly and the neighbors came out to help me." On another occasion, she was threatened with a firearm on public transportation: "We will scatter your brains over Malvinas." They sometimes even threaten to harm family members by saying: "Your family members do not want to see you anymore in the camp or your children will suffer the consequences."[22]

Nevertheless, on September 19, 2014, the protesters celebrated "2nd Spring without Monsanto: First Year of Resistance." The fight against the seed giant has only grown stronger and reached Río Cuarto: "The mayor of Río Cuarto issued a decree ratifying the ban on a proposed Monsanto seed experimentation centre in the town, after the company also lodged an appeal asking the local government to reconsider the ban established in November 2013."[23]

Further, the Malvinas Assembly now wants a public consultation using the secret ballot. Such a ballot would comply with the environmental law and "guarantee citizens' full rights to decide on which model of local development and what kind of social and economic activities they want for their daily life, and what environmental risks they are prepared to take." In particular, an environmental impact assessment should include a public consultation so that citizens can provide the "social license" necessary for developing any social, economic, and productive activity that may affect their environment and health.

In March 2013, a group of academics from CONICET revealed that 57 percent of the Malvinas Argentinas community rejected Monsanto. And if there is a referendum, 57.02 percent of the community would vote against the installation of the plant, according to the CONICET data published in September 2014 as a result of the "Survey of public opinion and citizen behavior of Malvinas Argentinas," conducted at the request of the organization Avaaz. Besides, the report revealed that the survey participants consider health as the most important factor, then the environment, and, finally, employment or work.[24] With regard to the actions against the establishment, in particular those of the Assembly Malvinas Struggle for Life, 73 percent supported the resistance movement, with only 21 percent rejecting it. Also, the shareholders of Monsanto and government officials were considered the sole beneficiaries of the plant, with the entire community of Malvinas viewed as the main loser.

About this epic struggle, Sofia Gatica says:

This was born from a loss and no one prepares you for that. We happened as the Mothers of Plaza de Mayo … And we seek the same thing: that there is no impunity, that multinationals must not be allowed to commit genocide … What I learned is that we are fighting against injustice. And along the way I lost the fear and won the conviction that we will win. I do not know at what price, but we will win. Of that I'm sure.[25]

To conclude, I agree with the concept that Rita Arditti, the author of *Searching for Life: The Grandmothers of the Plaza de Mayo and the Disappeared Children of Argentina,* develops in her work about the activism of the courageous women who came together to fight for the identity of their "missing" grandchildren.[26] According to her, they did not seem to be

challenging the gender system and the sexual division of labor; the Mothers were committed to the preservation of life, and they demanded the right as "traditional" women to secure the survival of their families … creating a new form of political participation, outside the traditional role and based on the values of love and caring.… [They] transformed themselves from "traditional" women defined by their relationships with men (mothers, wives, daughters) into public protesters working on behalf of the whole society.

I see too in the struggles of the Mothers of Ituzaingó an expansion of the feminist movement to embrace the values of motherhood—the traditional role of a woman in the household as mother, nurturer, protector, and educator of the family and the children.

## Endnotes

[1] Michael Warren and Natacha Pisarenko, "Birth Defects, Cancer in Argentina Linked to Agrochemicals: AP Investigation," Associated Press, October 20, 2013, www.ctvnews.ca/health/birth-defects-cancer-in-argentina-linked-to-agrochemicals-ap-investigation-1.1505096#ixzz3CyUOLBz2.

[2]    Lester R. Kurtz, "The Mothers of the Disappeared: Challenging the Junta in Argentina (1977–1983)," summary of events related to the use or impact of civil resistance, International Center on Nonviolent Conflict, 2010.

[3]    Blog of the Mothers of Ituzaingó, http://madresdeituzaingoanexo.blog spot.com.ar/.

[4]    Blog of the court trial, Collective Stop Fumigating and Mothers B° Ituzaingó, www.juicioalafumigacion.com.ar/lacausa/.

[5]    Secretariat of Agriculture, Livestock, Fishing and Food, Strategic Plan 2005–2015 for the Development of Agricultural and Livestock Biotechnology, 2004.

[6]    A. Broccoli, "ArGENtina: Transgenic Homeland," B.O.G.S.A.T./The Responsibility, Bergen Assembly, an initiative for art and research, Bergen, Norway, 2013.

[7]    Interview of Minister Lino Barañao by Hebe de Bonafini, president of Mothers of Plaza de Mayo, in "Pariendo Sueños," La Voz de las Madres ("The Voice of Mothers of Plaza de Mayo"), Radio 530 AM, April 17, 2012, www.herbogeminis.com/IMG/pdf/lino-hebe_madres-2.pdf; http://tunein .com/radio/Pariendo-Sue%C3%B1os-p328134/.

[8]    "Evaluation of Scientific Information Related to Glyphosate in Its Impact on Human Health and the Environment," July 2009, National Research Commission on Agrochemicals Decree 21/2009, Interdisciplinary Scientific Council, CONICET, www.msal.gov.ar/agroquimicos/pdf/INFORME-GLIFOSATO -2009-CONICET.pdf.

[9]    www.agn.gov.ar/files/informes/2012_247info.pdf.

[10]   E. Ridner et al., "Alimentos Transgénicos: Mitos y Realidades" (GM Foods: Myths and Realities), Argentine Nutrition Foundation (FAN), Buenos Aires, 2007, www.sanutricion.org.ar/informacion-226- Alimentos+Transg%C3%A9 nicos.+Mitos+y+realidades.html.

[11]   www.funam.org.ar/.

[12]   1st National Meeting of Physicians in the Crop-Sprayed Towns, Córdoba, Argentina, August 2010.

[13]   Alejandra Paganelli, Victoria Gnazzo, Helena Acosta, Silvia L. López, and Andrés E. Carrasco, "Glyphosate-Based Herbicides Produce Teratogenic Effects on Vertebrates by Impairing Retinoic Acid Signaling," *Chemical Research in Toxicology* 23, no. 10 (2010): 1586–1595.

[14]   By Provincial Law N° 9769, dated April 7, 2010.

[15]   C. Carrizo and M. Berger, "Estado Incivil y Ciudadanos sin Estado: Paradojas del Ejercicio de Derechos en Cuestiones Ambientales" ("Uncivil State and Stateless Citizens: Paradox of the Exercise of Rights in Environmental Issues"), Instituto de Investigación y Formación en Administración Pública (IIFAP), Universidad Nacional de Córdoba, Proyecto Ciudadanía, 2012.

[16]   Blog of the court trial.

17  www.presidencia.gob.ar/discursos/25918-almuerzo-en-el-council-de-las
    -americas-palabras-de-la-presidenta-de-la-nacion.

18  Dario Aranda, "The Corporation," https://darioaranda.wordpress.
    com/2013/01/16/la-corporacion/.

19  Raúl Montenegro, "Monsanto Invades Malvinas Argentinas," text in memo-
    riam of Cristina Fuentes, a Mother of Ituzaingó, www.ecoportal.net/Temas
    _Especiales/Transgenicos/Monsanto_invade_Malvinas_Argentinas.

20  www.ipsnews.net/2014/01/argentine-activists-win-first-round-monsanto
    -plant/.

21  "El Periodismo según Monsanto" ("Journalism according to Monsanto"),
    interview with Soledad Barruti, Revista Anfibia, Universidad Nacional de San
    Martín, March 20, 2014, www.argentinaindependent.com/tag/monsanto/.

22  "Protester Sofia Gatica Attacked," November 23, 2013, http://revolution
    -news.com/monsanto-protester-sofia-gatica-attacked/.

23  "Monsanto Appeals Rejected," *Argentina Independent,* March 26, 2014,
    www.argentinaindependent.com/tag/monsanto/.

24  "Malvinas Argentinas Does Not Want Monsanto as a Neighbor,"
    https://secure.avaaz.org/act/media.php?press_id=593.

25  "A Woman: Sofía Gatica," *Mu,* Buenos Aires, 8, no. 79 (August 2014),
    www.lavaca.org/mu/mu-79-los-nuevos-consumadores/.

26  Rita Arditti, *Searching for Life: The Grandmothers of the Plaza de Mayo and the
    Disappeared Children of Argentina* (Berkeley: University of California Press,
    1999); Mary Kirk, "Searching for Life: The Grandmothers of the Plaza de
    Mayo and the Disappeared Children of Argentina (review)," *Feminist Teacher*
    18, no. 2 (2008): 160–163.

# Seeding Knowledge: Australia

## Susan Hawthorne

Each of us has a personal history embedded in a series of relationships with land and community. These links are very powerful, and areas where one has lived create understanding of climate, geography, wildlife, and plants. Some communities have connections going back many generations out of which the local culture has grown. Stories create knowledge of local conditions, and human activity takes place in that biophysical context. It affects every aspect of life.

I grew up on a farm in southern New South Wales (NSW), an area now being used to grow canola, where GM canola trials are being pursued (Wagga Wagga in NSW). The push in Australia is for GM crops to be introduced, but there is considerable resistance to their introduction among both urban and rural people, including farmers.[1] I hear the big seed companies say that they need to increase production, and I know that this is the wrong approach. The real problem is the destruction wrought by seed companies.

The advent of GM crops heralds a new form of intensification and disconnection in farming, and it will lead to more crises, not fewer. According to Andrew O'Hagan in *The End of British Farming:*

> GM crops are corrupting the relation of people to the land they live on. Farmers were once concerned with the protection of the broad biodiversity of their fields, but the new methods, especially GM, put land-use and food production into the hands of corporations who are absent from the scene and environmentally careless.[2]

This does not only apply to Britain. In many parts of Australia, monoculture farming has resulted in severe salinity of soils. The problem is especially severe in Western Australia, but South Australia, Victoria, New South Wales, and Queensland are also confronting salinity as a major threat to farming viability. Salinity is a challenge to the biotechnology industry, which simply wants to replace current crops with genetically modified salt-resistant crops. And so the biotechnologist then offers to solve the problem, making a profit as salinity offers a growth area. Not only is it a gap in the market, it is also a very good excuse to get GM crops into the farming industry through the back door. It won't be long before products of these GM salt-resistant crops will be found on the supermarket shelves.

In Tasmania, Australia, both Aventis and Monsanto have been accused of flouting protocols established to control trials of genetically modified organisms (GMOs).[3] Twenty-one canola crops were found to be resprouting out of a total of forty-nine former crop sites.[4] In South Australia, Aventis was found to have left harvested canola "in a roadside dumpster and on the local tip."[5] Monsanto has also admitted that genetically modified cotton seed has possibly entered the food chain in Australia through cattle feed.[6] In the United States, the corn industry is in dire straits due to a crisis in marketing, and consumer resistance to genetically modified foods, resulting in low exports to countries in the European Union, Australia, and New Zealand, where labeling and other restrictions apply.[7]

A new mantra is being recited by the megacorp seed and biotechnology companies. Every failure is a new business opportunity. Where I grew up, monoculture farming has been the norm for many decades, and it included the use of large amounts of fertilizer. The persistence of drought and bad soils means that every year fertilizer has to be used and returns are rarely better from year to year. GMO drought-resistant crops will be the answer, says the agribusiness marketer, and in nearby areas where irrigation has raised the salt table, salt-resistant crops are pushed. And if this fails, there is always another opening after the next failure. But this is not farming. Farming involves the production of food as its foremost aim. Agribusiness is about money, not food. In spite of the rhetoric about world hunger, the development of biotechnology has come about not for altruistic reasons, but because it has the potential to earn transnational companies money and to "sustain industrial agriculture."[8] Profit, not charity, is their goal. One has only to look at the daily stock market, or listen to the latest political statement on innovation, to see the value put on biotechnology stocks and the knowledge economy. New markets, new commodities, new ideas are the newest way of generating capital.

## Refining the World

The focus of megacorp agribusiness is perfection. They claim the moral high ground by maintaining that they are working to conquer global hunger, to create high-value seeds so that the poor and the hungry won't die. In fact, the interaction between new biotechnologies and marketing has a more sinister purpose. But before we embark on this analysis, let us go back to the origins of this way of thinking.

Colonization of the "New World" was undertaken only after certain experiments were carried on closer to home. The English, having cut down so many of their own trees, started to clear the Scottish Highlands. In need of wood to build ships, the outcome was "the clearances." The poorest were evicted, their lands enclosed by fences, and most of the landless took off for the newly acquired colonies: North America, India, South Africa, Australia, and New Zealand.

Unlike other areas of the colonized world, Australia and sub-Saharan Africa were subjected to the legal fiction of *terra nullius*, a concept that denies the prior existence and habitation of Indigenous peoples or the cultures of any peoples who lived on or visited the land prior to its colonization by Europeans. This legal construct denies long histories of relationship with the land and use of its resources for food, shelter, traditional medicines, and the development of spiritual and material cultures. I think it is no accident that Australia and sub-Saharan Africa, where *terra nullius* was used, were both regions where black people lived. That is, *terra nullius* is an artifact of racism.[9]

The concept of *terra nullius* meant that the colonizers considered the Indigenous peoples "uncivilized" and lacking in knowledge of the environment in which they lived. In fact, Indigenous Australians have lived on this continent for 60,000–100,000 years (possibly longer). Across the continent, they understand local conditions, climate, the uses of medicinal plants, food plants and where they grow and when. Some native plants need careful preparation before they are edible. All this knowledge and more was put under threat by the idea of *terra nullius* alongside racist laws and murderous behavior.

The colonizer has changed its strategy. These days, one hears the agribusiness companies talk about ecology, about learning from Aboriginal people. They use words like "work," "sustainability," "business," "education," and "royalties." What they really mean is well expressed by Ama Ata Aidoo.

> Post-graduate awards.
> Graduate awards.
> It doesn't matter
> What you call it.
>
> But did I hear you say
> Awards?
> Awards?
> Awards?
>
> What
>
> Dainty name to describe
>
> This
> Most merciless
> Most formalised

Open,

Thorough,
Spy system of all time:

For a few pennies now and a
Doctoral degree later,
Tell us about
Your people
Your history
Your mind.
Your mind.
Your mind.[10]

And if we are talking about plants, tell us about your knowledge of the properties of those plants. Agribusiness and Big Pharma will generate income that will be returned to the companies, not the people from whom they have gained their insights.

The recolonization of the poor is justified on the grounds that it will create new cures for diseases and feed the world's poor.

## Bioprospecting and Biopiracy

The term "prospectors" has some interesting resonances. According to the *Oxford English Dictionary*, prospecting is making a *claim*, and is associated with *drilling* and claiming parcels of land with prospects. A prospectus is an account showing the forthcoming likely profits of a venture *as a means of obtaining support*. As a noun, a prospect is a view of the *landscape* from any position; and when applied to time it is a view that looks toward the *future*.[11]

Bioprospecting is making a claim for the biological resources with a view to making a profit. In looking at this from a feminist perspective there are several ways to understand resources. Resources can be taken in a straightforward, unadorned way to mean simply the plants, animals, and products of the land. However, this does not adequately cover what is claimed by bioprospectors, since the claim is made as if we—all people—have equal and open access to all resources.

Bioprospecting is put forward as a beneficial event for Indigenous communities. Claims are made that it will generate money for social and other services in poverty-stricken communities. It is, however, a two-edged sword, because it involves making public an earned system of knowledge and entering into the contested knowledge systems of colonialist corporations whose main concern is to privatize knowledge as patents on life-forms. Although there are many who claim that benefits accrue to Indigenous communities in the form of royalties, I would argue that communities are much more likely to lose not only access to their traditional knowledge, but control over how that knowledge is used. Indeed, it was that loss that prompted Vandana Shiva and others to challenge W. R. Grace's patent on the neem tree, *Azadirachta indica.*[12]

The case against W. R. Grace's patent on the neem tree is one of the most important cases to be brought against biopirates. But the neem tree was backed by written Sanskrit sources. Most Indigenous communities, however, rely on oral not written histories.

This is the situation in Australia, as one of the megadiverse regions of the world, where the Western Australia smokebush (sp. *Conospermum*) grows. It has been used for medicinal purposes by Aboriginal people for millennia to treat rheumatism and lumbago. Its active ingredient, concurvane, is now being examined for use against HIV.[13] This may appear to be a benign, indeed very positive, endeavor. However, as Henrietta Fourmile from the Gimoy Clan of the Yidindyi Nation in Australia points out,[14] Indigenous people have not been consulted and are having their knowledge stolen. This appropriation of Indigenous knowledge through bioprospecting has been accompanied by a massive loss of biodiversity[15] through the process of colonization and the introduction of European methods of land management and farming, both of which are entirely unsuitable in the Australian context. Furthermore, the Convention on Biological Diversity (CBD) contains a loophole. It allows for the exploitation of any plants that have been previously collected. As Lesley Marmon Silko has described in her extraordinary novel, *Gardens in the Dunes,* the race for collection of biological samples in the nineteenth century was as great as it is now and so the Western Australia smokebush, among others, already exists in colonial and American collections.[16]

Africa faces similar challenges. The San people of the Kalahari challenged British and US drug companies who took out a patent on an appetite-suppressing ingredient of the hoodia plant. As a result of the court challenge, the San will now receive royalties in a "benefit-sharing agreement." A later paragraph in the news item suggests something more sinister: "The San are likely to be involved in farming and cultivating hoodia, and to be *offered scholarships to study so that their ancient botanical knowledge may lead to other products.*"[17] What better way in a knowledge economy to "mine" for information that can later be privatized and patented.

The concept of "value" is an interesting one in this debate. It resembles much of the debate that has centered on the "value" of women's work.[18] Michael Dove, in his study of rainforest management in Kalimantan, Indonesia, argues that whatever of "value" is found or developed by Indigenous forest peoples—particular tree species, mineral deposits, butterflies, medicines—will never earn for the forest people what it would earn in the open market. Instead, centralized power appropriates the resource, sometimes for allegedly public interest, and then pockets the profits.[19] A disjunction also occurs between what is known to be valued by Indigenous forest peoples and what is valued by government and corporate interest. Dove argues that UN-sponsored development projects define what they will "allow the forest peoples to keep ... butterfly farms, crocodile farms, fish farms, and medicinal plant collection."[20] This list, he suggests, is not for the peoples' empowerment "but for their *impoverishment.*"[21] For, if empowerment were the goal, the list would include trees for timber, hardwoods, gems, and the biodiverse resources that the rainforest holds, and the forest peoples would be in charge of forest management. His concern is not just for what has been taken away from forests, but what has been "taken away from forest peoples."[22]

The rainforests of Far North Queensland are being plundered in similar ways. These rainforests are the home of the endangered southern cassowary (*Casuarius casuarius johnsonii*). It is a large flightless bird (just under two meters in height) that inhabits lowland and highland rainforests along the northern Queensland coast. It is the most important distributor of seeds of native trees, especially fruiting trees. The local Indigenous people, the Djiru, say of the cassowary, *no wabu, no wuju, no gunduy:* no forest, no food, no cassowary. It is a virtuous circle because it's also true to say no cassowary, no seed, no forest. The cassowary plays a vital role in rainforest maintenance, as a number of rainforest seeds must pass through the cassowary's intestines in order for the seeds to sprout. When the cassowary comes under threat, it is not just about a single species but an ecosystem under threat. It is estimated that cassowaries eat at least 238 species of plants. Local rainforest and fruit trees include the wide range of *Syzygium* species, quandong, Davidson plum, and many others. Cassowaries swallow the whole fruit. They then digest the fleshy pulp and pass the seeds through their gentle digestive systems. The seed is then deposited in large piles of dung. A local bumper sticker has the words "My poo grows trees"; the dung is a natural fertilizer. Because the cassowary has a short intestine, it seems to be able to absorb potentially harmful toxins contained in some fruits. This allows other animals to eat the seeds in the dung and spread them further afield.[23]

The rainforest has recently become a site for bioprospecting. Under the rubric of the Australian Rainforest Foundation, which presents itself as an organization furthering ecology and is registered as a charity, bioprospecting is being undertaken. Among its directors, its Chief Scientific Advisor, Dr. Victoria Gordon, is a specialist in Queensland tropical rainforests. She is also "the co-founder and Managing Director of EcoBiotics Limited, a biodiscovery company specializing in tropical rainforests and based in Far North Queensland."[24]

The search for a new "product" is a key project of bioprospecting companies. Such claims tie in with the idea of perfection, put forward by other arms of the same companies or companies with similar aims. This is exemplified by the case of golden rice, which is touted as the latest "perfect food."[25] Golden rice is so called because it has been engineered to contain carotenoids, high levels of which are present in carrots. Carotenoids are also present in greens, mango, sweet potato, and melon, and support vitamin A production in the body. Vitamin A deficiency is associated with malnutrition, and golden rice is being marketed as a panacea for this condition. Indeed, it was represented as "the embodiment of the great promise of biotechnology."[26] But as Marie-Monique Robin goes on to tell, when it was "grown in real conditions, it produced such a pathetic amount of beta-carotene that it did absolutely no good."[27] Golden rice turns out to be more of a marketing campaign than a crop.

The major defense for spending huge resources on researching and growing GMOs is that of world hunger.[28] Richard Shear gives Monsanto's perspective:[29]

> In agriculture companies such as Monsanto, Ciba-Geigy, Plant Genetic Systems and others believe that crops could be "re-engineered" to provide technology for ensuring that the world could be fed as future population demands required.[30]

Aventis/AgrEvo has a similar view:

> Biotechnology holds great promise for increasing food production.... Seed is the vehicle by which this new technology will be delivered.[31]

Meanwhile, representatives of the World Bank talk about "poverty alleviation":

> A large number of poor households in developing countries derive their livelihood from resource-poor areas with difficult agroclimatic

conditions. Ensuring their access to technologies is therefore crucial for poverty alleviation.[32]

None of these quotations, or the articles in which they were embedded, mentions that the poverty of resources in areas inhabited by these households is in large part due to the impact of colonization, developments such as large dams and bridges, the Green Revolution, and more recent effects of globalization.

The purpose of transnational companies is not altruism. It is profit. In order to make profits, companies need to make sales of commodities, goods, services, or knowledge. The products developed in the different sectors of industry are those that are easiest to sell, or that are readily commercialized. A system, therefore, that takes account of complexity or of process, a system that considers ethically both means and ends, will not easily sit within the ambit of global corporatization. Biotechnology prefers the simple answer: one crop grown; one gene shifted; the one-size-fits-all approach to problems.

Uniformity holds a central place in the current ideologies of the owners of agribusinesses that represent the industrialized farming sector. Monoculture cropping was the first stage, followed by the Green Revolution rhetoric of high yielding seeds that displaced landraces and ecologically adapted local seed lines. Genetic engineering of crops— the gene revolution—is just the latest manifestation of uniformity, and it is likely "to be exacerbated by the availability of transgenic seed."[33] Timothy Swanson points to the reliance of industrial agriculture on biodiversity, in particular on the "wild stock"[34] that forms the basis of cultivated crops. He suggests that the wild stock will not be able to be sustained over long periods of time: "Plant breeding companies face biological forces that may render their products (cultivated crops) obsolescent within 5–7 years."[35] And although continuous research is carried out on related species, in order to maintain the vitality of the crop varieties used in agriculture, the cultivated crops must be "continually supplemented with infusions of new, more diverse germplasm."

However,

> [o]n average about 7–8 per cent of the stock of germplasm must be renewed each year at current rates of depreciation. This means that wild varieties and landraces are being accessed at a rate that potentially renews the stock of germplasm every 10–15 years.[36]

Biotechnology creates an endless spiral of opportunities for research and development, and capital gain. Our collective vulnerability to the ideological stance of perfection, immortality, and transcendence is a paradox in a highly technologized society with a utilitarian approach to problem solving.

## What Is at Stake?

In May 2007, the conservative Howard government, through the Minister for Indigenous Affairs, Mal Brough, withdrew its offer to the Tangentyere people of Alice Springs of $60 million to upgrade the housing and infrastructure in return for a change in land tenure, subleasing it to the Northern Territory Australian government for ninety-nine years. The Tangentyere refused because, as William Tilmouth of the Tangentyere Council said,

> I just hope that the Government learns that when you are dealing with Indigenous people, land is very important. Self determination and rights are very important, and people are very reluctant to relinquish those rights.[37]

These contests are about intellectual property as much as they are about property over land since land use and management would no longer be controlled by the Tangentyere. For Indigenous people, land and intellectual property are inseparable. For land is knowledge, and knowledge is located in land. This has not escaped the notice of large corporations, and governments are being schooled by them to get back the lands that lie outside their control. While the easiest target for this is Indigenous people, they themselves are acutely aware of the high stakes of this contest.

One hears governments and corporations claiming that intellectual property rights (IPRs) are the *sine qua non* for Indigenous people, as *the* way to prosperity. IPRs, as they are currently structured in the setting of the World Trade Organization (WTO), take no account of the issues raised by Linda Tuhiwai Smith in her book, *Decolonizing Methodologies.*[38] The WTO model of IPRs does not recognize that in Indigenous communities knowledge systems are nuanced in complex ways;[39] therefore, a universalized system of IPRs does not take account of the local system, nor does it recognize "undocumented traditional knowledge."[40] Documentation involves having the knowledge validated by scientists and written up in academic journals or other public forums. When access to knowledge is earned, as it is in many Indigenous communities, these communities are faced with a catch-22 when dealing with IPRs. If they maintain the system of earned knowledge, then it cannot be written up in scientific publications; therefore, it cannot be formally protected by the current global system of IPRs. If they agree to having the knowledge made public, then the community betrays an important element of their own system of protecting intellectual property: a system based not on money but on responsibility. Here one can see the tension between universality and a concern for the specific needs of a particular community, the eco-social system. These are concrete needs tied to a particular place and a particular culture.

I mention this because a bundle of rights is in competition, and as with native title, we need to be arguing for the intellectual property rights of all those whom the robber barons would like to erase with an intellectual clearance. We need to be arguing against the new intellectual property fences that are being raised, privatized, incorporated, and sold back to us in a distorted form. The cassowary will die out and be followed by cascading biodiversity loss; Indigenous peoples will be ripped off once again, their lands and property colonized; the food supply will be incrementally reduced, and fancy newly named products with far fewer nutrients will be sold to us followed by cascading unknown health problems; the megacorporations will have an endless series of new business opportunities at each technological failure; these new business opportunities will be launched with great fanfare and marketing, and those externalities will be added to the price, making it impossible for farmers to compete.

This battle over seeds, marketing, knowledge, and our food is connected to many other movements for social justice, among them reducing violence in the world, especially violence against women; building up genuine ecological action in which biodiversity, not money, becomes the inspiration; decolonizing across many areas, including the lands and knowledge of Indigenous peoples around the world; recognizing traditional knowledge held by farmers and women and those whose histories span multiple generations of encountering the wild.

We need a wild politics in which multiversity of knowledge, biodiversity in nature, and eco-social systems of justice are context sensitive and based on relationship not possession.

My hope is for a world filled with richness, texture, depth, and meaning. I long for a world in which the surprises and variety of culture and nature are retained. I crave a world in which relation is central to social interaction and reciprocity is encouraged. If this world could be sustained for at least forty thousand years, as Lilla Watson,[41] a Murri elder from Queensland, asks for, then I think we have some hope.

## Endnotes

[1]   A volunteer grassroots organization, MADGE (Mothers Are Demystifying Genetic Engineering), was formed in 2007 in protest at the Victorian government's lifting of the ban on the growing of GM canola. It comprises a group of self-funded volunteers, and was incorporated on November 11, 2009 (http://madge.org.au/). Also, Gene Ethics (www.geneethics.org) has been a thorn in the side of the GMO industry for more than twenty-five years by keeping the public informed about field trials, contamination, court cases, and changes in laws and regulations affecting the dispersal of GMOs. For more information on where field trials are taking place and on which crops, see www.ortr.gov./internetlogtr/publishing.nsf/content/map.

2   Andrew O'Hagan, *The End of British Farming* (London: Profile Books and the *London Review of Books*, 2001), 54.

3   Andrew Darby, "Crop Companies Flouted GM Controls, Says Minister," *Sydney Morning Herald*, Sydney, April 7, 2001, 11.

4   One year earlier it appeared likely to anti-GMO activists that Tasmania would go "permanently GE-free and perhaps organic." See Bob Phelps, "Gene Tech for Dinner—No Thanks!" *Habitat* 28, no. 3 (2000): 22.

5   Ibid., 23; Geoff Strong, "GM Crop Dumped at Tip," *Age*, Melbourne, March 25, 2000: 1.

6   This contradicts claims that Australian farming is clean and green. Eliminating intensive farming practices, including feeding of cattle, would prevent such problems from arising. See Mike Seccombe, "GM Seeds May Be in Food Chain: Monsanto," *Sydney Morning Herald*, Sydney, August 26, 2000: 3.

7   Phillip Toyne, "Ingredients GM Status: Certification Issues for Manufacturing Quality Assurance" (paper presented at Strategic Food Industry 2001, GeneEthics List, Sydney, June 5, 2001).

8   Sonja A. Schmitz, "Cloning Profits: The Revolution in Agricultural Biotechnology," in *Redesigning Life: The Worldwide Challenge to Genetic Engineering*, ed. Brian Tokar (Melbourne: Scribe Publications; London and New York: Zed Books; Montreal: McGill-Queen's University Press; Johannesburg: Witwatersrand University Press), 45.

9   There are of course many differences. Africa was colonized by many different cultures from Europe and had been engaged in trade with Asia for centuries prior to colonization, whereas Australia was primarily colonized by Britain, although both the French and the Dutch were also engaged in "exploration" and settlement. There is also evidence of trade between Aboriginal people and the people of China and Southeast Asia. Further, in both Australia and Africa, colonial regimes practiced extermination. In Australia, this was exemplified by the wholesale killing of Tasmanian aborigines and massacres of Aboriginal people across the continent.

10   Ama Ata Aidoo, *Sister Killjoy, or the Reflections of a Black-eyed Squint* (London: Virago, 1977), 86.

11   Susan Hawthorne, *Wild Politics: Feminism, Globalisation, Bio/diversity* (Melbourne: Spinifex Press, 2002), 266.

12   The neem tree, *Azadirachta indica*, grows in Asia and Africa. In India it has been used for millennia as an insect repellent, a spermicide, and a medicine for skin diseases, sores, and rheumatism. It is found as an ingredient in toothpastes and soaps and can be used to prevent fungal growth such as rust and mildew. Long called the "blessed tree" or the "free tree," it was not perceived as particularly important in the eyes of those from the West until the 1970s, when some of its traditional uses began to be taken seriously. US company W. R. Grace isolated the active ingredient and took out a patent on the neem claiming that patent on the basis of novelty. In 2001, this patent was revoked on the grounds that it constituted, as Indian anti-globalization activist Vandana

Shiva points out, "piracy of existing knowledge systems and lacked novelty and inventiveness." This is a positive move with regard to the recognition of traditional knowledge. But few cultures can trace written sources as far back as the people of India.

13 Jean Christie, "Enclosing the Biodiversity Commons: Bioprospecting or Biopiracy," in *Altered Genes II: The Future,* eds. Richard Hindmarsh and Geoffrey Lawrence (Melbourne: Scribe, 2001), 173–186.

14 Henrietta Fourmile, "Protecting Indigenous Property Rights in Biodiversity," *Current Affairs Bulletin* 1996: 36–41.

15 Marcia Langton, *Burning Questions: Emerging Environmental Issues for Indigenous Peoples in Northern Australia* (Darwin, NT: Centre for Indigenous Natural and Cultural Resource Management, Northern Territory University, 1998), p. 79.

16 Lesley Marmon Silko, *Gardens in the Dunes* (New York: Simon and Schuster, 1999).

17 Antony Barnett, "Bushmen Win Royalties on 'Miracle Pill,'" *Guardian Weekly,* London, April 4–10, 2002: 3 (my italics).

18 Marilyn Waring, *Counting for Nothing: What Men Value and What Women Are Worth* (Sydney: Allen and Unwin, 1988).

19 Michael R. Dove, "A Revisionist View of Tropical Deforestation and Development," *Environmental Conservation* 20, no. 1 (1993): 20.

20 Ibid., 21. The medicinal plant collection will remain in the hands of forest peoples only as long as no cure for cancer, or AIDS, or menopause is found in their region. On June 7, 2001, I visited the World Bank in Washington, DC. In the lobby was a huge display on "Biodiversity in the World Bank's Work." The World Bank is funding Indigenous peoples, such as those in Kalimantan, to preserve their heritage because it is worth billions of dollars. It is clear, however, that the forest peoples, the desert peoples, the fisher peoples are very unlikely to end up billions of dollars richer!

21 Ibid. (italics in original).

22 Ibid., 22. The example of the neem tree bears out Dove's argument as, until the 1970s, the neem tree was not perceived by the West as anything other than a "lowly tree." This is analogous to the ways in which women's knowledge is treated, that is, it is irrelevant until someone decides there's a profit to be made!

23 For more information about cassowaries, see Mission Beach Cassowaries, www.missionbeachcassowaries.com.

24 Australian Rainforest Foundation, www.arf.net.au/content. php?pageid=1262033574; accessed September 7, 2014.

25 Martha L. Crouch, "From Golden Rice to Terminator Technology: Agricultural Biotechnology Will Not Feed the World or Save the Environment," in *Redesigning Life,* ed. Brian Tokar, 34–35; Vandana Shiva, "Genetically Engineered 'Vitamin A Rice': A Blind Approach to Blindness Prevention," in *Redesigning Life,* ed. Brian Tokar, 40–43.

[26]  Marie-Monique Robin, *The World according to Monsanto: Pollution, Politics and Power* (Melbourne: Spinifex Press; Delhi: Tulika Books; New York: New Press, 2010), 326.

[27]  Ibid.

[28]  Gyorgy Scrinis, "Sowing the Demon Seed," *Age*, Melbourne, June 7, 1999: 13; Graeme O'Neill, "Ironing Out Fears," *Sunday Herald*, Melbourne, May 13, 2001: 52. Both sides of the argument have been aired in the popular press with Scrinis critical, while O'Neill published his with a photograph captioned: "Healthier Lifestyle: Genetically Modified Rice Will Help Correct a Severe Iron Deficiency for Millions of People." Also, see the arguments on golden rice in this essay.

[29]  For a critique of Monsanto's practices, see Crouch, "From Golden Rice to Terminator Technology," 27–29; on Aventis/AgrEvo, see Sonja A. Schmitz, "Cloning Profits: The Revolution in Agricultural Biotechnology," in *Redesigning Life*, ed. Brian Tokar, 47.

[30]  Richard H. Shear, "Perspectives from Industry: Monsanto," in *Intellectual Property Rights in Agriculture: The World Bank's Role in Assisting Borrower and Member Countries*, eds. Uma Lele et al. (Washington, DC: Rural Development: Environmentally and Socially Sustainable Development series, World Bank, 2000), 34.

[31]  David L. Richer and Elke Simon, "Perspectives from Industry: AgrEvo," in *Intellectual Property Rights in Agriculture*, eds. Lele et al., 41.

[32]  Uma Lele et al., eds., "Intellectual Property Rights, Agriculture, and the World Bank," in *Intellectual Property Rights in Agriculture*, eds. Lele et al., 1.

[33]  Mark Lappé and Britt Bailey, *Against the Grain: Biotechnology and the Corporate Takeover of Your Food* (Monroe, MN: Common Courage Press, 1998), 101.

[34]  Timothy Swanson, "The Reliance of Northern Economies on Southern Biodiversity: Biodiversity as Information," *Ecological Economics* 17, no. 1 (1996): 7.

[35]  Ibid.

[36]  Ibid.

[37]  William Tilmouth, in Murray McLaughlin, "Govt Pulls Pin on Town Camp Funding Grant," *The 7.30 Report*, Australian Broadcasting Corporation, 2007: 3, www.abc.net.au/7.30/content/2007/s1931466.htm: Broadcast: 23/05/2007; accessed September 25, 2007.

[38]  Linda Tuhiwai Smith, *Decolonizing Methodologies: Research and Indigenous Peoples* (London: Zed Books; Otago, New Zealand: University of Otago Press, 1999).

[39]  Diane Bell, *Ngarrindjeri Wurruwarrin: The World That Is, Was, and Will Be* (Melbourne: Spinifex Press, 2014), 361ff.

[40]  Graham Dutfield, *Intellectual Property Rights, Trade and Biodiversity* (London: Earthscan Publications, 2000), 64.

[41]  Lilla Watson, "Aboriginal Feminism," presented at 1984 Fourth Women and Labour Conference, Brisbane.

# Contributors

**Farida Akhter** is founder and executive director of UBINIG (Unnayan Bikalper Nitinirdharoni Gobeshona, or Policy Research for Development Alternative). A well-known health and women's rights activist in Bangladesh, she is the author of *Seeds of Movements* and several other books in Bangla and English.

**Isaura Andaluz**, a beekeeper and seed preservationist, serves on the board of the Organic Seed Growers and Trade Association, is a member of the Save New Mexico Seeds Coalition and of Slow Food, and is certified in permaculture. She is cofounder of Cuatro Puertas, an economic development corporation that established the Arid Crop Seed Cache—a living seed bank of native and drought-tolerant crops.

**Sandra Baquedano Jer**, D. Phil. Universität Leipzig, is a professor in the Philosophy Department, University of Chile. She has authored several books and papers on metaphysics and ecoethics in various journals of international renown. She is a researcher on Chile's National Fund for Scientific and Technological Development projects.

**Alexander Baranov** is a scientist associated with the Institute of Developmental Biology, Russian Academy of Sciences, Moscow.

**Debbie Barker** is the international program director, Center for Food Safety (CFS), a legal and public policy institute in Washington, DC.

She was formerly director of the International Forum on Globalization (IFG), a think tank that analyzes and critiques forms of economic globalization.

**Ana Broccoli** is associate professor of plant breeding at the School of Agricultural Sciences, National University of Lomas de Zamora, Argentina. A member of the Food Security and Sovereignty Group, Advisory Council of Civil Society, Argentina's Ministry of Foreign Affairs, she has authored various research papers on agroecology and the transgenic production model in Argentina.

**Tiphaine Burban** currently works at developing a local food policy for a city region council in France and is a member of the International Urban Food Network.

**Beth Burrows** is founder and retired director of the Edmonds Institute, an award-winning public-interest, nonprofit organization focused on the environment and technology; she also founded the Snohomish County Women in Black, a group that advocates for peace. She has served on the state-appointed Northwest Regional Citizen's Advisory Committee for the Washington State Model Toxics Control Act. She coedited *Genetically Engineered Organisms: Assessing Environmental and Human Health Effects* (2002) and edited *The Catch: Perspectives in Benefit Sharing* (2008). Her essay in this book was originally part of a talk given at Simon Fraser University.

**Sue Edwards** is a member of the National Steering Committee for the National Biogas Programme of Ethiopia, and director of the Institute for Sustainable Development, Addis Ababa, Ethiopia. She has authored more than seventy publications, and was awarded the twelfth Gothenburg Award for Sustainable Development for the Tigray Project in 2011.

**Tewolde Berhan Gebre Egziabher** is adviser to the Minister of Environment and Forests, Federal Democratic Republic of Ethiopia. He was general manager of Ethiopia's environmental watchdog, the Environmental Protection Authority, and led the African and Like-Minded Group in negotiations for the Cartagena Protocol on Biosafety. He was awarded the Right Livelihood Award in 2000.

**Irina Ermakova** is an international expert on ecological and food safety. She was awarded the Navdanya Navratna Gandhi Award in 2008 for outstanding scientific contributions to the ecological roots of disease.

**Patricia Flores** is Latin American coordinator, International Federation of Organic Agriculture Movements (IFOAM).

**Suzanne Foote** currently serves as executive director of the Manitou Foundation and Manitou Institute and Conservancy, Colorado. She founded Earth Origin Seeds, a program that has collected and grown endangered traditional seed species for more than two decades.

**Susanne Gura** is a policy analyst who writes extensively on agricultural biodiversity and rural development. She has contributed to publications of the Berne Declaration, EcoNexus, and others on climate, agriculture, and corporate concentration. Since 2009 she has chaired the largest German seed saving association, Verein zur Erhaltung der Nutzpflanzenvielfalt (VEN), and served on the board of a seed and breed conservation umbrella organization in German-speaking countries.

**Kusum Hachhethu** was an intern with Navdanya and worked on the seed issue in Nepal as part of her internship.

**Susan Hawthorne** is adjunct professor at James Cook University, Townsville, Australia. Her book *Wild Politics: Feminism, Globalisation, Bio/diversity* (2002) is used widely in courses on ecology, politics, and women's studies. She is coeditor of *September 11, 2001: Feminist Perspectives* (2002); her most recent nonfiction work is *Bibliodiversity: A Manifesto for Independent Publishing* (2014). She is a poet, novelist, and publisher. Some of her political writings can be found at www.susanspoliticalblog.blogspot.com.au/.

**Mae-Wan Ho** is director of the Institute of Science in Society. She was among the first to warn of the dangers of genetic modification, in her book *Genetic Engineering: Dream or Nightmare?* (1997). She participated in the UN negotiations that led to the Cartagena Protocol on Biosafety, and is on its roster of experts. A prodigious writer, she has published, apart from various books, more than 170 scientific papers and more than 670 popular articles across disciplines. She is also an artist and a poet. She was awarded the Prigogine Medal in 2014.

**Zen Honeycutt** founded the national coalition of volunteer mothers, Moms Across America, that empowers and amplifies the voices of mothers, locally and nationally, in the cause of safe food.

**Ana de Ita** is founding partner and executive director of the Center of Studies for Rural Change in Mexico, a think tank of the indigenous and peasant organizations.

**Florianne Koechlin** is a biologist and the author of *Plant Whispers: A Journey through New Realms of Science* (Basel: Lenos, 2015). She is managing director of the Blueridge Institute, Switzerland.

**Winona LaDuke** is an internationally renowned environmentalist and political activist working on issues of sustainable development, renewable energy, and food systems. She is cofounder and program director of Honor the Earth.

**Anna Lappé** is an internationally recognized expert on food systems and sustainable agriculture. Named one of *Time* magazine's "Eco" Who's Who, her most recent book is *Diet for a Hot Planet: The Climate Crisis at the End of Your Fork and What You Can Do about It*. She produced the first-ever international contest for short films on food and sustainability and currently directs the Real Food Media Project, which develops food system educational materials. She is an active board member of the Rainforest Action Network.

**Frances Moore Lappé** is cofounder of Food First: The Institute for Food and Development Policy, and a founding member of the Hamburg-based World Future Council. With Anna Lappé, she leads the Cambridge-based Small Planet Institute and Small Planet Fund. She has written more than eighteen books, including the best seller, *Diet for a Small Planet* (1971). *World Hunger: Ten Myths,* coauthored with Joseph Collins, is forthcoming (2015). She was awarded the Right Livelihood Award in 1987.

**Sara Larraín** is a board member of the International Forum on Globalization and the director of the Sustainable Chile Program. Cofounder of the National Ecological Action Network, she has coordinated the Greenpeace Latin America energy/atmosphere campaign and Sustainable South Cone Program with activities in Argentina, Brazil, Chile, and Uruguay. In 1999 she ran in the country's presidential elections, representing green organizations. Currently her main working area is establishing the human right to water and toward the protection of glaciers threatened by the mining exploitation in the Andes.

**Blanche Magarinos-Rey** is a lawyer, attorney for the association Kokopelli. She has chaired and participated in numerous public debates on health and environmental problems, and authored numerous legal and general publications. She advocates before European institutions on the protection of cultivated biodiversity and the necessity of improved sustainability in farming practices. Her book on European seed legislation is forthcoming.

**Maria Grazia Mammucini** is coordinator of the Scientific Committee of the Italian Foundation for Research in Organic and Biodynamic Agriculture, and vice president of Navdanya International in Florence. She was formerly director of Tuscany's Regional Agency for Development and Innovation in Agriculture and Forestry (ARSIA).

**Mariam Mayet** is founder and executive director of the African Centre for Biosafety (ACB), a nonprofit organization based in Johannesburg, South Africa. The ACB carries out research, analysis, advocacy, and information sharing with key organizations in their network to foster and promote informed engagement with policies and decision making that control the production and distribution of, and access to, food and resources.

**Marion Nestle** is Paulette Goddard professor, Department of Nutrition, Food Studies, and Public Health, and professor of sociology at New York University. She is the author of award-winning books, among them *Food Politics: How the Food Industry Influences Nutrition and Health; Safe Food: The Politics of Food Safety;* and *Why Calories Count: From Science to Politics.* Her most recent book is *Soda Politics: Taking on Big Soda (and Winning).* She blogs at www.food politics.com, and her Twitter handle is http://twitter.com/marion nestle.

**Stephanie Seneff** is senior research scientist at MIT's Computer Science and Artificial Intelligence Laboratory in Cambridge, Massachusetts. She has authored more than 150 peer-reviewed journal and conference proceedings papers. Until 2007, her research was mostly in natural language processing; since then, she has focused on researching the environment, nutrition, and health and has published more than a dozen papers on those topics in medical and biological journals.

# About the Editor

 **Vandana Shiva** is a physicist, a world-renowned environmental thinker and activist, and a tireless crusader for economic, food, and gender justice. She is the author and editor of many influential books, including *Making Peace with the Earth*, *Earth Democracy*, *Soil Not Oil*, *Staying Alive*, *Stolen Harvest*, *Water Wars*, and *Globalization's New Wars*. Dr. Shiva is the recipient of more than twenty international awards, among them the Right Livelihood Award (1993); the John Lennon-Yoko Ono Grant for Peace (2008); The Sydney Peace Prize (2010); and the Calgary Peace Prize (Canada, 2011). In addition, she is a board member of the World Future Council and one of the leaders and board members of the International Forum on Globalization. She travels frequently to speak at conferences around the world.